SECRETS OF THE ROCKSTAR

PROGRAMMERS:

RIDING THE IT CREST

About the Author

Ed Burns is currently a senior staff engineer at Sun Microsystems, Inc. At Sun, Ed leads a team of Web experts from across the industry in developing JavaServer Faces Technology through the Java Community Process and in open source. His areas of professional interests include Web application frameworks, AJAX, reducing complexity, test-driven development, requirements gathering, and computer-supported collaborative work. Before working on JavaServer Faces, Ed worked on a wide variety of client and server-side Web technologies since 1994, including NCSA Mosaic, Mozilla, the Sun Java Plug-in, Jakarta Tomcat, the Cosmo Create HTML authoring tool, and the Web transport layer in the Irix operating system from Silicon Graphics.

Ed has a Bachelor of Computer Science degree from the University of Illinois at Urbana-Champaign. While at UIUC, Ed took a minor in Germanic studies and worked for IBM in the co-op program, where he first acquired a fondness for computer history by working on System 370 Office Software.

Ed is a frequent speaker at international industry conferences, having presented many times at Sun's JavaOne conference, given keynote addresses at the W-JAX conference in Munich, Germany, and the Globalcode Developer's Conference in São Paulo, Brazil, and also has spoken at numerous Java User Group meetings. Further information and blogs may be found at http://purl.oclc.org/NET/edburns/.

SECRETS OF THE ROCKSTAR PROGRAMMERS:

RIDING THE IT CREST

ED BURNS

New York   Chicago   San Francisco   Lisbon
London   Madrid   Mexico City   Milan   New Delhi
San Juan   Seoul   Singapore   Sydney   Toronto

The *McGraw·Hill* Companies

Cataloging-in-Publication Data is on file with the Library of Congress

McGraw-Hill books are available at special quantity discounts to use as premiums and sales promotions, or for use in corporate training programs. To contact a special sales representative, please visit the Contact Us page at www.mhprofessional.com.

Secrets of the Rock Star Programmers: Riding the IT Crest

1 2 3 4 5 6 7 8 9 0   DOC DOC   0 1 9 8

ISBN   978-0-07-149083-2
MHID   0-07-149083-3

Sponsoring Editor
Wendy Rinaldi

Project Editor
Patty Mon

Acquisitions Coordinator
Mandy Canales

Copy Editor
Lisa McCoy

Proofreader
Paul Tyler

Indexer
Karin Arrigoni

Production Supervisor
Jean Bodeaux

Composition
International Typesetting
and Composition

Illustration
Dodie Shoemaker
International Typesetting
and Composition

Art Director, Cover
Jeff Weeks

To Amy, my best friend, partner, and wife.
Thank you for sticking by me and helping me
achieve my dreams.

Contents

Acknowledgments

Though the rock star programmers in this book are accustomed to getting accolades and acknowledgments, here is yet another: thank you. Obviously, without the dedication, persistence, candor, and tolerance (of my sometimes constant pestering) of these incredibly busy people, I would have no rock star programmer secrets to share.

Phillip G. Armour is a hero of mine, and having his insights on the Five Orders of Ignorance in this book is a real treat for me (and for the reader). Mr. Armour is a pleasure to work with and a real treasure to our profession.

I talked to several additional rock star programmers, but didn't have time or space to get their contributions into this book. I'd like to thank them for their support at this point: Luke Hohmann, Len Bass, Alistair Cockburn, Esther Derby, and Paul Graham.

In a world where more and more information is available only online, and much of that information is coming from self-published individuals, I want to say that the publishing system is still the best way to deliver high-quality, useful information in a portable and easily digestible way. A PDF file is no substitute for a dog-eared, marked-up, and well-worn book. After working with the publishing team at McGraw-Hill, I know why this is so. Acquisitions coordinator Mandy Canales did a great job keeping together all the disparate parts of the book and handling the consent and release forms for everyone interviewed. McGraw-Hill editorial director Wendy Rinaldi went through plenty of ups and downs on this project, but never lost confidence; I'm proud to deliver this book for her. Wendy went to bat many times for this book, and promoted it above and beyond anything I've seen before. Project editor Patty Mon is a total professional, with whom it was absolutely excellent to work. Patty went through chapter after chapter of incorps, copyedits, and page proofs. She never complained about my sometimes very trivial changes. Finally, thanks to copy editor Lisa McCoy. The readability of this book is absolutely vital, and copyediting is the process that makes it happen.

Special thanks to my longtime friend and high school crony, Joe McCabe. Joe's book, *Hanging Out with the Dream King: Interviews with Neil Gaiman and His Collaborators* (Fantagraphics, 2005), gave me the idea to do this one. It's also an excellent read and offers a great insight into the creative process of textual and visual artists. As such, I think Joe's book is a good complement to this one. Joe also leant his talents as an entertainment industry insider to this book by conducting the interview with the one real rock star in the book, Weird Al Yankovic. Of course, I have to think Mr. Yankovic himself for agreeing to participate.

The most important ingredient in continued success at being a rock star programmer is to have a supportive and loving spouse. Sixteen of the eighteen people interviewed in this book are married, and within that group, every one of them would agree with that statement. My wife Amy has been and continues to be a source of inspiration, support, and love. Thank you for your understanding and patience as I worked my way through this book. I could not have made it through without your help and commitment. Thanks also to my two wonderful sons, Owen and Logan. You two are the rock stars of the future!

I want to give a special mention to Kem Elbrader, who gave me a computer science undergraduate's view on what questions he'd like to ask the rock stars.

Thanks to Mom and Dad: Kathy and Edward M. Burns. Your solid support of my family has made it much easier for me to get this book done. Thanks also to my brother, Brendan Burns. Brendan, you know a thing or two about rock stars; I hope you like the book.

Thanks to the solid extended-support team of Lisa and Jon Lane, Diana Dean, Ryan Dean, Jeff and Tina Beckberger, Jimmy Marzo, Paul and Lisa Beckberger, and Steve and Lori Beckberger. I hope I didn't bore you too much by prattling on about this project.

Finally, I thank God for all the gifts bestowed into my life.

—Ed Burns
Altamonte Springs, Florida, U.S.A.

Introduction

With the rise of blogging, many of the world's most talented programmers have become celebrities in the field of IT. These "rock star programmers" are bellwether icons for their legions of readers: IT professionals trying to stay current. This book is a collection of incisive interviews, with A-list programmers centering on the themes of "spotting trends," "staying current," "how to avoid becoming obsolete," and "work/life balance."

Though the popular stereotype of a programmer may be that of an introverted, socially inept techno-monomaniac, the real-world practicing programmer, and especially the successful one, is very far from that stereotype. Alistair Cockburn summed it up best in his book *Agile Software Development: The Collaborative Game* (Addison-Wesley, 2006) by saying that software development was "a *cooperative* game of invention and communication" (emphasis mine). Books of interviews with players of other games (including performing artists) are an accepted genre of popular literature. Books of interviews with players of the software development game are less so. One stand-out exception is Susan Lammer's book, *Programmers at Work* (Microsoft Press, 1986). Susan's book is very much a forerunner of mine; it focused on the rock star programmers of its day. Though Ms. Lammer's book is not specifically focused on career enrichment, it is still a very good read and a valuable historical snapshot. Between our two books, one thing is crystal clear: People are the most important ingredient in software development.

Who Should Read This Book

To reuse and modify the slogan of *America* magazine, this book is for thinking programmers and those who care what programmers think. What is the first group (thinking programmers) thinking about when they come to this book? Since I am a member and representative of that group, the following sorts of topics come to mind:

- How in the world can I keep up with all this information coming at me every day?

- What can I do to ensure that I keep bringing value to my employer or client and to help ensure continued career success?

- What will the practice of software development look like in ten years' time?

- How do I know where to invest time and effort in stewarding my skillset?

The second group will find in this book a path to understanding more of what programmers are all about. If you're not a programmer yourself, you may be wondering:

- How in the world can a programmer spend so much time in front of the keyboard?

- What can possibly be so compelling that they can't put it aside, even when they're not at the keyboard?

- Is there a long-term career in being a computer programmer?

- Can I trust the software on which so much of our modern way of life depends? How do the people writing software ensure its quality?

The idea with this book is to find some of today's best programmers and gain access to their thoughts and insights on the above and many other topics. If you're a programmer, and you could have this lot as your co-workers, what sorts of things would you want to ask them? I'm sure there will be some questions you come up with where you find yourself saying, "How could he not have asked that one!?" Well, I tried to hit the high points, while allowing each interview to flow naturally.

How This Book Is Organized

The interviews in this book are grouped into four sections. Of course, several of the rock stars could be listed in more than one of the sections, but I found it helpful to organize them by the role for which they are most well known.

Software Technology Experts

In this section are interviews with world-recognized leaders in specific technologies or products. Naturally, in order to achieve such a status, one must also be a generalist, so even though the world knows James Gosling as the "Father of Java," he is also an expert in many other domains. For example, James is an expert in the real-world application of formal correctness techniques and in the art of introducing new ideas into the world and helping them take root.

Software Pedagogy Experts

In this section are interviews with world-recognized leaders in the discipline of teaching software development. I find that expert pedagogy is a separate skill, and a far less common one, than being an expert in software technology or the practice of software development. As such, the insights offered in this section serve to round out those in the other sections.

Software Development Experts

In this section are interviews with world-recognized leaders in the discipline of software development itself. Rather than being famous for a specific technology or product, or for teaching about the same, this last lot has made a career of rising above the fray and being generalists. Going back to Alistair Cockburn's *Agile Software Development*, he describes ways to break down software practitioners into three groups, taken from the lexicon of Japanese martial arts: Shu-Ha-Ri. The first level, Shu, applies to the group of practitioners who need to follow detailed steps or a script to solve a problem. The second level, Ha, is a group of practitioners who know all the scripts and know which one to choose to solve a problem. The last level, Ri, knows the problems and the solutions so well that they have internalized all the steps so that the mechanics of getting to the solution have disappeared. The rock stars in this section are famous for being at the Ri level in the practice of software development in general. I am *not* saying the rock stars in the rest of the book are not at the Ri level; it's just that their fame and rock star status derive more from a specific technology than from simply being at the Ri level.

Actual Rock Stars

This last lot has but one entry in this book, the programmer's rock star, and a personal favorite of mine, Weird Al Yankovic. As mentioned previously, software development is a collaborative game, and in that sense is similar to musical performance. Therefore, you'll find some commonalities between the content of this section and the other ones.

Within each chapter, there are four general sections, which give some organization to the topics therein. Not every interview has an equal coverage in each section, but nearly every chapter does contain at least one entry in each of the following four categories.

Soft Skills

In this section, you'll find topics that do not pertain to any specific software development practice, but are useful skills for any software development practitioner. Example question: Much of the work of enterprise software development involves being able to zoom in to a very fine level of detail and then zoom out to get the big picture—oftentimes, one right after the other. Do you think this requires a special proficiency in keeping things in perspective? Does this ability carry over to other aspects of your life?

Hard Skills

In this section, you'll find topics that pertain to specific software development skills. Example question. How do you attack hard-to-solve bugs?

Business

In this section, you'll find topics that pertain to the business of software, including knowing when to look for a new job and how to protect yourself from being outsourced. Example question: How important are business acumen and entrepreneurial instincts to being a career software developer?

Personal

In this section, you'll find topics that pertain to the personal history of each rock star, including topics such as education and work/life balance. Example question: How good are you at keeping your work and personal lives balanced?

Appendix A contains a by-question index of any question that was asked of two or more rock stars. With this appendix, you can quickly take the pulse of the software development industry, as represented by this collection of rock stars, on a wide variety of topics ranging from the psychological: "How important is it to be aware of your own ignorance?" to the concrete: "What is the relationship between developer success and tools mastery?"

Appendix B is a summary of a seminal article in the practice of software development, Phillip G. Armour's *The Five Orders of Ignorance*. I have found that the concepts in this article have been echoed in various ways by all of the rock stars interviewed in this book, and thus a summary of the article is appropriate to include.

PART 1

Software Technology Experts

CHAPTER 1

Rod Johnson

Fact Sheet

Name: Rod Johnson

Home Page: www.springsource.com

Rock Star Programmer Credentials: Inventor of the Spring Framework, which revolutionized Enterprise Java application development by popularizing "Inversion of Control"

Date of Birth: July 1971

City of Birth: Sydney, Australia

Birth Order: Only child

Marital Status: Married

Number of Kids: Two

Degree: PhD in 19th-century piano music

Number of generations in your ancestry (including yourself) that graduated from college: Two

Years as an IT Professional: 15

Role: CEO of SpringSource

Introduction

Rod Johnson has made his name and fortune challenging conventional wisdom. He has a successful combination of self-assurance, humility, and drive that has enabled him to build a successful consulting and technology company around a piece of software that originally started out as a running example for his first book, *Expert One-on-One J2EE Design and Development* (Wrox, 2002). This software eventually became the Spring Framework, and it has single-handedly become one of the most popular ways to build Enterprise Java applications.

Rod has had an interesting career path, starting out with a PhD in 19th-century piano music, and then segueing into C++ and, later, Java development. His ability to recognize a promising idea when he sees it and stick with it until it's good enough to solve real-world hard problems made me want to share his insights with you in this book.

Soft Skills

Ed: When you're doing your day-to-day work, maybe you are coding or designing or doing technology development, and you have the choice between doing the "right thing" or the "quick thing," how do you motivate yourself to do the right thing?

Rod: I am actually very biased in favor of doing the right course. One thing that I might do is make a deliberate decision as to what gives me the greatest velocity. So, for example, I might do it a quick and dirty way, verify that it works, and then come back and fix it immediately, because it's way easier to improve working code than to do something more complex when you don't have anything working. But, in general, I don't tend to take shortcuts, and one of the whole goals with Spring is to make the right thing easy to do. I mean, I think if you consistently find that the right thing is hard to do, there's something wrong. The right thing should be the right thing partly because it's easy and natural to do. If the right thing is unnatural, that is kind of an environment smell. It's beyond a code smell. It's telling you something.

Ed: In your current role as CEO of SpringSource, I know you spend much of your time outside of the software development role, but when you do take on that role, how do you stay current with what's going on in the technology world?

Rod: I tend to spend a fair amount of time looking at industry forums and the like—for example, things like Serverside, InfoQ *(both of which were created by Floyd Marinescu; see Chapter 10)*—I find that very, very valuable. Generally, I will try to choose the particular information sources that are not overtly spammed with mail. For example, if you look at some of the sites in Enterprise Java, the signal-to-noise ratio has gotten worse. I read a lot of online articles. I do read books; but generally, I get most of my information online. And I would try to do that daily. I would try to, when I get an opportunity, maybe even on my lunch break, start looking at some news sources and follow up on things that seemed interesting.

I have always gotten a lot of my information from downloading things and playing with them. I mean, I've always been a very practical person, in that if I hear about an interesting product that might help me be more effective as a developer, I actually want to kick the tires rather than just look at a Flash presentation.

Character Attribute

The need to see for himself firsthand, rather than trusting an article.

Ed: When you read an article, do you have any meta-cognitive process for understanding it, such as SQ3R (Survey, Question, Read, Recite, Review)?

Rod: I tend to read at different levels of abstraction. The first thing I will do with anything that I'm interested in is I will read it very, very fast. I'll skim through it. It's probably, I suppose, a bit like yours [SQ3R], but I don't have a name for it. It's just something that I've evolved for myself. So the first thing is I read it and very, very quickly decide whether it's interesting to me. Whether there are any ideas that really resonate. If that actually tends to be the case, then I will go back over the article and read it in more detail, try to understand it more deeply. I think that's pretty much my process with reading just about any piece of information. If I'm reading a novel, I will try to read every word and appreciate it. If I'm reading some kind of technical information, my first pass is going to be very, very quick. If it's something that I already know about, I'll see if I think there are any big red flags that just don't make sense. If I am intrigued at that point, then I will really start

SQ3R

SQ3R is a reading comprehension and memory technique introduced by Francis Pleasant Robinson in his 1946 book *Effective Study, Fourth Edition* (HarperCollins, 1970). Each letter stands for a step in the process: Survey, Question, Read, Recite, Review. The system works best on a self-contained unit of text, such as an article or a chapter. Briefly, the five steps are:

1. Survey: Skim through the text and get a general idea about it. Don't read in detail; just see if you can pick out a handful of major ideas being conveyed.

2. Question: Ask yourself some questions about the chapter. It helps to shape the questions around the major ideas you identified in step 1. You can write down the questions if you like.

3. Read: Now's the time when you sit and read the text straight through.

4. Recite: For each of the questions in step 2, say or write down the answer based on your understanding of the text from step 3.

5. Review: Test your recall and understanding of the text by asking yourself the questions and trying to answer them from memory.

to go over it in much more detail and try to understand the arguments that I may not have been able to follow at that fast pace.

Ed: Do you think this process that you've evolved is a success factor in getting you where you are today?

Rod: Oh, absolutely. One of the challenges I think we have in absolutely every walk of life today is that we're constantly presented with data. How do we decide what is the information in the data? There's a saying that, today, in one day, we receive more information than someone in the Middle Ages received in a lifetime. That's both good and bad. It's good if you have developed ways of finding the needle in the haystack—then it can be quite fun and challenging, but it's also, at times, quite demoralizing.

Ed: I've often wondered what it would be like for someone to travel forward in time from the Middle Ages. So this technique you've evolved is the way you deal with that?

Rod: Yes, it's something…I know that you often see advertisements for speed-reading courses…it's just been something that, I'm not sure where I picked it up, but I just evolved it and it seems to work for me.

Ed: You started your professional programming career in C++, but at the same time, you saw that Java was on the rise. What was it about Java that attracted you to it? How did you know to ride its coattails?

Rod: Two things. One, the first thing was that I ended up in a job where Java was the only option. This is back in the incredibly early days. It was Java 1.02, I think. No inner classes, no collections, none of that stuff. I was implementing a distance-learning program for the university where I was working, and we did it with applets. So I researched the best technology to do this, and we actually got it working quite decently. It was a success for applets back in 1996.

After that, it was a pretty calculated assessment. I was competitive as a Java developer. It wasn't until probably mid '97, even late '97 that I got a job in the UK as a Java developer. I still really wanted to do C++. In fact, I was trying to pick up more C++ work. I ended up doing a lot of C++ work in that job, and I was all in favor of that.

> **Character Attribute**
>
> Making calculated assessments of career options is part of Rod's core process.

Anyway, one of my colleagues, who was a bit of a mentor, actually persuaded me that Java was a real language…I'd been really skeptical. So I'd say I believed from September '99. I really believed that Java had what it took to succeed. Realistically, you looked at Java prior to 1.1 and compared to C++, it wasn't a real language.

Ed: It was a toy.

Rod: Yeah. But I was actually convinced by late '97 that this was real, it was better than C++. Pete actually convinced me, not only was Java not just the poor cousin of C++, that it was actually better.

Ed: But in what way? The absence of the linker, the simplified syntax… what was it?

Rod: I think the principal thing that he really turned me on to was the fact that by ripping things out, it had actually made the language better.

Ed: Okay. No multiple inheritance, no pointers, that sort of thing?

Rod: I'd previously been pretty skeptical about that, partly because it's natural to think that something, if it's difficult, it's gotta be good.

Ed: Not anymore it isn't. Thankfully, that meme is dead.

Rod: It is, yeah. So I kind of figured that C++ was what *real* developers coded in and Java was just too easy. The other thing that my colleague switched me on to was the fact that there was already an amazing bind to Java. There were a lot of libraries springing up, and it looked like it was going to provide a solution to the hideous problems that plagued C++ with its standard template library and all that kind of stuff.

Ed: How important was automatic garbage collection to you as a selling point?

Rod: It was part of the total package. I don't ever remember suffering unduly from garbage collection issues or memory management issues. And there is a category of problems that you're not aware of as a problem, but when they're suddenly taken away, you realize you can go so much faster, and I would class that in that space for me. *(This is exactly the "boiled frogs" problem Andy Hunt talks about on page 263.)*

On balance, I did see the rationale for getting rid of multiple inheritance, but I'm an old guy. The first version of C++ I learned was 1.0, so I was used to it anyway. And I really did miss things like operator overloading.

Ed: Okay. You mentioned an interesting problem. You don't know how hard it is to deal with a problem until the problem is taken away. The example we just came up with was memory management and automatic garbage collection. What are some steps you can do as a developer to be aware of those problems? And how important is that as a skill?

Rod: It depends on what you want to do. For example, a lot of the early work that shaped Spring came from a very deliberate analysis of a large code base that I was working on. For example, now it's fashionable to question checked exceptions in Java. In fact, I think recently was it Neal Gafter or one of the original guys who was questioning it.

Back in the days when I was still a heretic in 2001, I got hate mail, literally, hate mail, from people because I questioned checked exceptions, or at least, the way they were used. One guy—this is actually somewhere on ServerSide.com; I should print it out and frame it—argued that because I was a foreigner, I was advocating this to create buggy software that would bring down the U.S. economy.

Ed: Well, that's ServerSide.com for you.

Rod: Yeah. And the scary thing is, I think he believed it. But, for example, I'd never really thought of checked exceptions as a negative, and I read a fairly short comment by Bruce Eckel, which kind of made me think about

Character Attribute

Willingness to question the conventional wisdom.

it. Then I went and looked at this entire code base, looked pretty much everywhere, caught exceptions, and kind of had this realization, "This doesn't actually add much value." Then I started writing the precursor of the Spring JDBC Library, which didn't use checked exceptions. Then it was like, "Wow, the red block is gone."

So I think it's a matter of we all derive benefit from being methodical and aware of how we spend our time. I mean, one thing that I would say is that most developers have no awareness of how they spend their time whatsoever.

Ed: In this case, you mean people didn't have awareness of all the time they were spending declaring, trying, throwing, and catching exceptions?

Rod: I mean, I have very little [awareness of how I spend my time], but I still think that I have more than most, and even that little bit more has been beneficial.

Ed: Being aware of how you spend your time is one manifestation of the importance of awareness to being a software developer. Another aspect is ignorance. How important is it to be aware of your own ignorance?

Rod: It's among the most important things. Because you have to be prepared to know when to ask for help, either to look it up or to ask a coworker or ask in a forum or even a tech support call. You can't get away with bluffing in software.

There's definitely a category of smart people who know languages very well who are utterly useless as software developers, and most of those that I've seen have had ego issues that prevented them being aware of their limitations. The result was that they would do hideous things and basically never be willing to confront their ignorance.

Observation

Please see Appendix B, Phillip G. Armour's *The Five Orders of Ignorance*.

For a start, if you don't know your limitations, how could you possibly improve? I mean, you're not going to learn anything if you don't know what you don't know.

Ed: So a personal question for you then. What percentage would you say of your daily time do you spend in a meta-cognitive mode?

Rod: Define meta-cognitive.

Ed: Thinking about your thinking, analyzing how you're doing something, analyzing, "how am I performing, how am I feeling, what emotions am I feeling now, how is that affecting me in the task that I'm doing right now."

Rod: That's an interesting question. Now, more of the decisions that I make are related to management and business strategy than technical decisions, and I certainly regularly think about my motivations. For example, I find some of the hardest decisions to make are decisions where I'm in conflict with someone and, basically, I'm the boss. I can force my way, and that's really, really hard, because I have to unpick it and think, "Do I want to do this because we had a difference of opinion and I want to force my way, or do I want to do it because it's right?"

With respect to writing code, I guess thinking about your emotional state isn't that important. I think one thing that's very important is insight into your performance. I'm sure everyone has [had] the experience where there are days when you're on fire. I mean, you must have had this, Ed. When you have a list of ten things to do, you do them all.

Then you come up with a list of the next two things, and you do them, and they work. And then you start thinking of other things to do, and they all work. And I think when you feel that, you keep working as long as you can. On the other hand, you need to have the insight into when you're just not being efficient and just not working. There are times when, for whatever reason, you're just not—you're either tackling the wrong problem or your mental state is not helping you do the task.

It's hard to quantify how long I spend in a meta-cognitive state, but virtually, every time I do that it improves my performance, and I think it's very important. I mean, meta-cognition is an interesting thing. It's an interesting term for what I do best. I'm better at stepping back and wondering whether we're asking the right question than answering the question. I think that writing code is easy. Writing code—when you know what you want to do—writing code is not hard, and, I mean, basically anyone who can't write code reasonably efficiently isn't even at first base. That means it's not hard.

The thing that *is* hard or that I think is useful is making sure you're writing the right code, and I think that is something where I have been more successful.

Ed: What about your ability to leverage the success of others by building on top of existing code rather than rewriting it yourself? How important is it to avoid reinventing the wheel?

Rod: I care a lot about reinventing the wheel. There are two reasons why I care. One of them is the rational reason; one of them is the intuitive reason. The rational one is that if I'm reinventing the wheel, why am I doing it?

Why would I not be better standing on the shoulders of someone else and solving a new problem? The intuitive reason is that's just totally against me as a software engineer. I absolutely hate the idea of duplication. I believe that duplication is the enemy of any decent software architecture. As soon as you reinvent the wheel, you get a bunch of different, incompatible wheels. It's been a major driver for what I've done. I hate solving the same problem three times, because if you do that, clearly, you're wasting effort. You need to rethink about the problem and decide how you're going to solve it once and for all.

Ed: Over the years, the software industry has had many different attempts at having a true component reuse model, where people have some sort of registry where they can search for components that fit their needs and put them into their programs. Has that actually ever worked in practice?

Rod: It works in some areas, but not in others. I think it works in infrastructure. So I do think that infrastructural components absolutely can and should be shared and reused. For example, if you think about a Java EE application server, there's a bunch of components in there that do things like transaction management, deployment, etc. [These] have been implemented by the vendor, and you don't need to implement them again. I think that's clearly proven its value. With respect to business applications, I think there are far more issues. So when you get to business applications, one of the things that you tend to find is that components don't exist in isolation. So, for example, early on in Java EE, people were very excited about the potential for Enterprise JavaBeans (EJB) as the model for component reuse. Really, it didn't work out. Now, one of the reasons was, arguably, deficiencies in the EJB technology. And I think it's fair to say I wasn't a big fan. But another reason, the bigger reason, was that the goal was not attainable. The goal was not attainable, because if you look at real-world business applications, you can't really just take the code in Java or C# or whatever. You need to look very often at dependencies on sources of data, like relational databases, and very often, they depend on a particular product. The dependencies are typically so extensive that the notion of reuse is highly problematic. Frankly, I think software engineering is both an art and a science. The art side is knowing exactly where you can reuse and where you can't. That's the biggest thing to learn. That is the thing that every software engineer who really cares about their discipline should strive to get better and better at.

Ed: What are some concrete skills in terms of knowing how to do that?

Rod: I think that coming at it from a pragmatic perspective, I mentioned that as a software professional, I passionately hate reinventing the wheel. It's very important to be able to contain that passion, because there are some times when, frankly, trying to get to a more general solution is not worth the effort.

I think one of the things that is key is knowing when you see the general case. Because sometimes you can *think* you see the general case, and in fact you don't, because there's a more general case that you haven't seen yet. I also think you have to be very honest with yourself about whether or not there is enough similarity between cases to merit one codebase. A great example of this is that I've spent quite a lot of time working in the financial sector. I have seen a number of efforts to find the ultimate solution to derivatives modeling and the ultimate solution to an object model for derivatives trading to handle different kinds of products. And that has caused many, many problems, because these products are extremely complex. When you get to understand them more deeply, you get to understand that there are similarities, but there are also a lot of differences, and the effort involved in trying to come up [with] a solution that captures the similarities, yet respects the differences is so great that, frankly, no one has done it yet.

Ed: Well, knowing whether or not you really see the general case when analyzing a problem is certainly an essential skill, but it seems to be one that comes mainly from experience. What about just being a power-user? How important is it to be the kind of engineer who has a highly optimized work environment? I'm talking about shell scripts, keyboard shortcuts, macros, etc.

Rod: When I look at the majority of good programmers, like Adrian, they have far more customization than I do. I wouldn't rate myself as spending a good deal of time doing that. Yet, on the other hand, I've been on client sites, and it's like, "What do you mean you basically don't know how to do anything in your Integrated Development Environment (IDE) without going through seven levels of menu?"

I would say that I should make myself put more time into learning things. And every now and again, for example, I will Web search for "Eclipse cheat sheets and shortcuts", and make myself learn a couple more shortcuts. I don't spend a lot of time on it.

Basically, what I do to set up my machine—I don't care about my operating system that much for programming anymore, which is one of the good things about Java. The only reason I still use Windows is for Office. Apart from that I'd use Linux—I install Eclipse and a few plug-ins like the eXtensible Markup Language (XML) editor, Subversion plug-in, but not a huge number of plug-ins. I'd install Ant and Maven, probably CYGWIN if I'm running on Windows. That's about it with that and a Web container like Tomcat. At that point, I'm happy enough that I'm productive, and I'll gradually find more things that I want over time.

Ed: But I'm talking about the trait to continually want to make things better. So you've got making things better in your own work environment so you can get more things done, be less perturbed doing them. But then just working on code—you're trying to write clean code, you're trying to improve existing code. Is that a skill, is that a character trait that good developers possess and average developers do not?

Rod: You mean improving code?

Ed: Well, just this drive to improve the situation of things.

Rod: Yeah. I think it is. I mean, I would say coming back to the idea of meta-cognition and the fact that I would say the more I do of that the better my performance is. Realistically, I could probably benefit from spending a little bit more time optimizing my environment.

Regarding optimizing code, I think…there are two reasons, and a lot of developers don't do it. One is that they don't realize the problem. And another is that they don't care. I mean, basically, you want to fire the people who don't care. The people who don't realize the problem, you want to try to help to understand the problem.

One interesting point—I know this is probably off on a tangent… although I would rate myself as generally fairly compassionate, I have very little sympathy for underperformers in IT. Partly because I think as a profession we are paid so much compared to normal people that there really isn't scope for people who are lazy and not very good.

Most people in IT are just not aware of that. I mean, normal people don't earn what we earn, and we don't have a God-given right to that. *(See Chapter 6, Hani Suleiman, who mentions this.)*

Ed: Regarding the relationship between making money and developing software, SpringSource is in the business of making money. You have some products, like the Spring Framework, and you also do consulting and training. Do you think there is a different set of creative skills that one has to bring into play in a consulting mode versus the ones [you have] to bring into play in a product development mode?

Rod: That's a very interesting question, and actually the answer is that I don't. I think the answer is that you have to try to merge into one technical organization everything you learn, from interacting with customers doing consulting situations [to] developing products. I think there is a real difference in the ability to generate creativity between a software product company and a consultancy. Just in terms of the economic model—but I actually think that in an ideal world, you really want to look at everything you're doing in terms in technology and unleash the maximum creative power in that. Certainly, if I think about many of the most important things I've ever learned or discovered for myself in what I've done in software, they've been from immediate requirements. They have been from being in a consulting situation looking at an immediate requirement from the customer. So I think that it's certainly a mistake to think, "Hey, consulting is not creative; product development is creative." Unless your creativity is linked to some degree to what might actually be useful, you'll create things that are clever, but, so what? A great example of that is the Segway. The Segway is clever, but what does it actually solve?

Ed: How much of a role did luck play in getting you where you are professionally, being in the right place at the right time, with the right skills and knowing the right people?

Rod: It definitely played a part, but it is hard to distinguish, because I think that competent people tend to be lucky. Another way of looking at this is: What could have gone wrong?

I think about the difference "choice" has made for me and the difference "luck" made. So I made a choice early on that, although at the time I still found C++ more interesting, that I was going to struggle to find a decent job as a C++ programmer without very much commercial experience; whereas as a Java programmer with very little commercial experience, I was competing in a much more level playing field.

My decision ultimately proved to be the right decision: that Java was a good choice. That was a moment of luck. What if Java had failed? And the two other biggest pieces of luck in my career were that my book—I had no idea when I wrote a book about how much work…I'm sorry to have to tell you this…about how much work writing a book is and how profoundly stupid you need to be to write a book. So this was economically crazy [for me to do, it] resulted in me going through my savings, etc. Towards the end of the time I was writing my book, Wrox Press, my publisher, went bankrupt.

Ed: Wow. They're not bankrupt anymore.

Rod: Well, they approached bankruptcy. They scrapped 70 percent of their ongoing projects, and—I didn't know this until afterwards—my editor put up a messy fight for them preserving my book.

This was a great business call, because it was a best seller. So then they did go bankrupt afterwards, but at that point, my book had been on the market for a couple of months. It had done really strong sales, so Wiley bought the top 20 or 30 titles, including my book. So, obviously, Wiley is not going to go bankrupt. And they were great about paying my royalties and everything. They really honored all the contracts.

But, you know, that could have been a mess. I could have been left having gone through half my savings in 2001, just after September 11, when the industry was in dire shape, with a worthless book, no book contract, and no possibility of publishing it anywhere else.

The third piece of luck was that Floyd Marinescu read the first chapter of my book and liked it and invited me to speak at the ServerSide Java Symposium. *(See Chapter 10, Floyd Marinescu.)* But, then, this is where you come back to maybe it isn't all luck.

Luck gives you opportunities, and what you do with the opportunities is the bit that's beyond luck. So in the case of ServerSide, I had presentation skills that I developed when I was an academic. So I did a good job and got invited to other conferences.

In the case of the book, it actually proved to be, by most people's consideration, a pretty good book. So I think that if you look at anyone's career, if they've been successful, luck played a part. But there's also the ability to run with things when you get a break.

Hard Skills

Ed: Okay, let's run with that. Can you say more about some character attributes of successful developers?

Rod: Good general problem-solving skills…energy—I'm sure this is the same for success in any field. Highly successful people have abnormal amounts of energy and passion, and that's extremely important. To get outstanding results, you have to care more than average. You really have to care about doing the best that you can.

One thing that I've seen in the majority, not all, but the majority of outstanding developers, is a passionate desire to make it better. So, for example, I really can't live with code that's sloppy. It bugs me. I might appreciate, for example, a particular reason [why] it's just not justified to spend more time on refactoring it. This is good enough, but it does bother me. And I think that, by and large, good software developers have that characteristic. And intelligence. You look at outstanding software developers; they're pretty smart people. They may not be [well-] rounded people, but they're generally pretty smart.

Ed: How about ego?

Rod: Healthy ego. I've very seldom seen a highly successful software developer who didn't have a fairly big ego. I think it does seek to motivate. The question is whether or not there's the insight, the meta-cognition that it's getting in the way. And I think it's absolutely vital that people can cope with being wrong and admitting being wrong. But, on the other hand, the majority of very outstanding developers I've seen did have probably bigger-than-average egos.

Ed: But they kept them in check.

Rod: Yeah.

Ed: So you have to have it, but you have to keep it in check?

Rod: Yeah. Because, I mean, fundamentally achieving outstanding things very often does involve feeling that you know better and acting on it. And maybe this is only one way of motivating oneself, and this is just how it works for me. I'm quite aware that my ego is probably bigger that it should be, but it doesn't prevent me usually from making the right decision.

Ed: Who is the most productive programmer you've ever worked with? What was it about them that made them that way? Did they just crank out lots of code? Did they get things done faster than everyone else? What do you say about that?

Rod: Jürgen Höller. Undoubtedly.

Ed: And what is it about Jürgen?

Rod: It's basically all of the above, which is kind of demoralizing.

Maybe the difference isn't that big between Jürgen and other good people, but I've worked with some people that I would rate as better overall, but I've never worked with or encountered anyone who's better in every way. For example, if I look at the other people in the Spring team, some are faster [than others], but do higher-quality code. Others do higher-quality code, but are slower. Some of them, other than Jürgen, are probably better overall, but, nevertheless, you can break it down and see differences and weaknesses. Whereas, Jürgen, compared to anyone I've ever seen, is faster and his code is better. You asked how does he do it? I don't know. From what I've seen, it's not just my opinion. Jürgen's pretty legendary. What I've seen is that he works in a very different way from me or anyone else that I know.

For example, my way of working is very iterated. If it's a really complex problem, my first version would be embarrassing to look back on, my second version wouldn't be too bad, and the third version would be quite good. Jürgen would start with a problem like that, and this would take maybe a lapse time of ten hours' programming if it was a reasonably hard problem. Jürgen would start off by thinking deeply about it for three hours. Then he'd spend two hours writing code, and it'd probably be perfect. I can't work like that.

Ed: So much of the work of enterprise software development involves being able to zoom in to a very fine level of detail and then zoom out to get the big picture. Do you think this requires a special proficiency at keeping things in perspective?

Rod: Yup. Absolutely. Incredibly important skill. So, for example, about 90 percent of the work that I've seen where people are optimizing code in a business application is a complete waste of time, and they're simply making the application more bug prone. You need to have perspective. You need to reason about it. But, even more importantly, you need to back up your perspective by metrics. So, for example, one thing that I've done on teams that I've been running in developing business applications is have a strict rule: I'm sorry; you are not going to be optimizing anything. I don't care how simple you think the optimization is. You prove to me that it's a problem before you spend any time making it faster.

Now, with something like Spring or an app server, it's a bit different, because you can pretty much derive benefit from really any part of it being faster. But, nevertheless, you have to have a tradeoff. Optimization is one of the fundamental things that I come back to, because it is the chief culprit in lack of perspective that I see.

The other culprit that's pretty big in Java middleware is anything that deals with the database. I've literally seen coding guidelines that ban the declaring of exceptions on method signatures because it would be slow at the service level. Meanwhile, they had a woefully inefficient data-access layer. You can do the most inefficient thing you can do in the Java language two million times while you run an inefficient Structured Query Language (SQL) query.

Observation

Interestingly, Dave Thomas, on page 281 makes some strong statements about object databases that give some color to Rod's answer here.

One of the things in perspective is understanding what the definition of your application is. In the early days of Java, [the] developers were intensely arrogant. They knew that they were the guys who were going to inherit the earth. The database administrators (DBAs) were only there to keep things working until object databases came of age. And, therefore, you couldn't possibly learn anything from talking to them.

Their [the Java developer's] view of the interesting part of the application was the Java layer. If you define your problem as being in the Java layer, yeah, it kind of makes sense. Define your problem as being the Java layer down to the database, you instantly see that *this* cannot efficiently talk to *that*. It's impossible.

Ed: What are some strategies you employ in tracking down really hard-to-solve bugs?

Rod: Well, first, make sure that the tests for them are very rigorous. Try to strengthen the tests. Basically there are two things that I find are beneficial. One is to be utterly methodical. Try to do it in a calm, reasonable manner rather than an emotional manner, because the chances are you'll have a gut feeling of where the bug is and you'll be wrong. If it's a really hard bug, I'll write a checklist of things—like a decision tree—or things that get a kind of binary chop to narrow it down, and be patient work[ing] through that process. Because it may take longer than if you just fool around and go with your gut, but you are going to reach the solution.

Ed: So you would write the decision tree down before embarking on the path.

Rod: Yup. Probably before. If I saw a bug that really seemed like a surprising or profound bug, I would first write more tests, because I have seen situations where I've invested a lot of code and it turned out the test was buggy. So if it's something that's going to require a serious investment of thought and work, I'm going to be utterly sure that it really is what I think it is. I mean, that's happened to me a number of times, [where] it wasn't actually the problem that I thought it was, and I put a lot of effort into it and found something else that was masking it.

So it's first, utterly methodical and, second, if that really isn't working out, I mean, if you go through your process and you just can't think of anything else, step back. Chances are it's a design problem or something that's much higher level. *(Andy Hunt advocates the same approach in Chapter 11.)*

Another thing, depending on the time pressure, of course, is go and do something else. Go for a run or something and try to think about it fresh. I remember when I was at university, we were in third year, four of us, doing a software engineering project, which was actually writing an equivalent to artificial intelligence (AI) that accommodated multiple windows along cursors in C++. And we were about a day away from turning the thing in, and it just started crashing constantly, and we didn't know where it was.

I mean, we were pretty desperate, because the first process of the marking was automated, so we would have got zero for a semester's work for four of us. So we spent a lot of time looking for it, couldn't find it, and even myself and the other guy who was the second best at the group, we were pretty desperate.

So eventually I went to the bar and had a few beers, and Matthew was kind of thinking, "Oh my god, Rod's probably more likely to find it than everyone else, and it looks like he's going to get drunk," but it may have been just dumb luck. But I had a couple of beers, two or three beers, went back, and I found it within a half an hour. It was actually in Matthew's code, so it was quite funny to see him pissed off at me for drinking, and it was like, "You see, Matthew, where you didn't manage this string. You see, what's happened now is, as the codebase has gotten bigger, there's something overwriting it now."

Yeah. That was interesting. I don't know that alcohol's the way to do it, but I didn't think we were going to get a solution without changing something. And, for whatever reason, I was slightly drunk, I was thinking differently.

There are better ways to think differently, like go and have a workout, go and listen to some music. You may not have the luxury. You may be fixing a production problem that's costing your company money. You may not have that luxury. But if you do, try to step away from it. You can easily get into a mode where you're not productive.

Ed: What do you think of test-driven development (TDD)? When you're doing TDD, how do you deal with bugs in the test and the time it takes to debug those bugs in the tests? And what are some specific ways to reduce bugs being in the tests?

Rod: Well, like Winston Churchill said about democracy: "At least it's better than the alternatives," and TDD is like that. I can field intellectual objections.

One thing that does bother me from an intellectual point of view is that you look at tests with mocks, and they come so close with the implementation, that kind of bugs me. I don't generally have a big problem with bugs in test being a big drain of time. I just cannot write code anymore without writing a test first. I am rigorous about that. It doesn't even matter whether I'm just prototyping, whether I'm just kind of even half playing, I will write a test first. I actually think it's faster for me now.

Ed: How do you decide how much testing is appropriate during a development cycle?

Rod: Test coverage metrics, and also thinking about the test as a primary expression of the business requirements. Coverage metrics can't tell you everything. A coverage metric tells you how much of your code is tested. It doesn't tell you whether you've got the right tests. It may be that you need other code that you don't have tests for. So, certainly, I think you should be able to think of the business problem and try to trace your tests, or it may be [at a] lower level in the business problem. It may be, like, a particular component.

The first test I write will typically be: What happens if there's a null argument? What happens if there's an empty string? I write a lot of tests for fairly simple things, and I literally do write the code inside the method only. I'm not as extreme like some people have seen. It was interesting pair-programming with Eric Evans. Eric's the author of *Domain-Driven Design* (Addison-Wesley Professional, 2003).

Ed: Yeah. Adrian recommends that book *(see Chapter 2)*.

Rod: Eric's way of working was quite interesting. Adrian and I were kind of—what's the word for triple programming? We were kind of taking turns. Adrian and I work in a very similar way, actually. Interesting, I imagine that Adrian's non-technical answers are very different from mine, but I find it very easy to work with Adrian. I can pair program with Adrian more naturally than with anyone because we've even both got a fetish for 40-character-long variable names.

Ed: Me, too.

Rod: Really?

Ed: I love long variable names. It comes from my objective C days, but yeah.

Rod: Yeah. I'm quite fancy for it. So AbstractTransactionalDataSource-SpringContextTests.

Ed: Yes. I do them, too.

Rod: Yeah. There was one in the late-night coding sessions at the first Spring Experience where it was private—it was a variable inside a method, so no one was ever going to see it. But Adrian and I were having fun, and it was a good 50 characters.

Ed: If you've got an IDE that's going to do auto-completion, why not?

Rod: I don't get the people who don't like long variables. So, Adrian and I work in a very similar way, but it was interesting that we were both surprised by the fact that Eric—Eric literally writes tests before he's got a method. The test doesn't compile. He then uses the code fix [IDE feature] to implement the method, and I'd always considered that a bridge too far. But just observing it, I think Adrian and I were starting to think, "This seems to be going fairly quickly, so maybe this is worth trying." I haven't actually seriously tried it since. I don't know whether Adrian has.

Ed: Look into the future a bit for me. What are some attributes of the programming languages and programming environments people will be using in ten years' time?

Rod: That's an interesting question. I'm going to punt a bit on this. I think that domain-specific languages are very, very interesting, so it would not amaze me if there was a fragmentation of languages so that we weren't focused so much on general-purpose languages, but we moved towards more specialized languages. But, on the other hand, if that didn't happen, I'm sure we will be able to have this conversation, and with the benefit of hindsight, quite decisively explain why domain-specific languages were just destined to fail. I think the natural tendency in our discipline is for levels of abstraction to rise higher. I think that we will probably be not programming in a "language" in ten years' time; increasingly, it'll be on things like "the platform." So what, for example today, we might presently call an "application server" or what we might call an "ESB" (Enterprise Service Bus), I think that's become more important to how we program. There will be more assumptions about the environment in which the code runs.

With respect to language-level detail, I would hope that we've learned enough now to understand [that] certain constructs are important in languages and should be made more concise. But, frankly, I find it's better to be thinking at the level of changes in abstraction and business intent than language semantics.

Modeling tools help. I'm really not a believer in forward engineering in model-first development. However, I do believe that things like the Unified Modeling Language (UML) are a very valuable communication tool. And they can really help you work at a different level of abstraction.

Business

Ed: Speaking of the helpfulness of modeling, can you paint a model for the software industry? How would you break down or categorize the software industry today?

Rod: I would certainly see divisions in terms of language and divisions in terms of industry being served—business domain. And divisions in terms of layers as well. So I think one of the key divisions is definitely the language division. There are still loads of folks out there who work in C++. There are people who work in Common Business-Oriented Language (COBOL)—more than we would think.

In terms of layers, it's fairly obvious middleware and databases are distinct. Web stuff in middleware is less distinct. For example, in the typical Java team, you'll see folks having some degree of a responsibility for developing both Web and middleware. It'd be pretty rare to be purely one or the other.

I think the industry differentiation is very, very important. Because, for example, I spent a lot of time working with financial customers, and there certainly is a category of developer who, for example, has a pretty good knowledge of derivatives, and a Java developer with that background might have more in common with a C++ developer than they would with a Java developer who works for a dotcom.

Ed: We've established that knowledge of the business domain is important. How important are entrepreneurial instincts and business acumen to being a successful developer?

Rod: Some degree of entrepreneurial skill, I believe, is vital. Business acumen—I'm not so sure. It's useful, definitely useful. There's no such thing as a job for life. I mean, people need to have courage. If they want to get on in their career, if they want to do interesting work and be professionally and intellectually fulfilled, they need to have the courage to make the leap, and that's the same courage it takes to start a business, either courage or stupidity, depending on which way you do it. I strongly believe that someone who's going to have an intellectually fulfilling career as a software developer has to be prepared to take risks in the same way as someone who's starting a business is going to take risks. If they don't take risks, they're going to be in a rut. When Java is COBOL in 20 years' time, they'll be the guys coding Java.

With respect to business acumen, it is useful, and I think a lot of developers are more business savvy than they are given credit for. One of the things that I recommend to people if they want to make their job secure: understand the business that's paying for you. Some of the *least* effective developers I've ever seen were ineffective, not because they didn't have development skills, but because they fundamentally didn't care about the business. It doesn't matter how clever you are if you don't fundamentally care and understand where you fit in the picture of a business that's trying to achieve something.

I think that people who generally have achieved outstanding professional results are prepared to take risks, even if they're employees. Taking risks doesn't necessarily mean starting a business. It may well mean making the hard decision that you're not getting anything out of this job and you're going to take a pay cut, or you're going to move somewhere because you think you'll get into a different industry and take the risk of not getting a job. Ability to run a business—I think that's less important.

Ed: Can you say some more about how to know when it's time to change jobs?

Rod: When you're not learning anything. It's maybe not so easy to face that recognition that you're not learning anything, but to me, that's the sole criterion: if you're in a job and you're still learning something. If you go to work and you can learn from your coworkers, you can learn from what you're doing, you're still getting something out of the job. Maybe you could get more out of another job. But when you reach the point where you're not stretching yourself, you're not being challenged, you're not learning, you're not going anywhere.

I think as soon as people get into a situation where they're not learning, it is naturally inevitable to get intellectually fat and lazy. I mean, I used to play chess fairly seriously when I was a boy, and one of the things that is kind of an adage in chess—and that is probably true in any sport—if you spend time playing weaker players and obviously beating them easily, it is worse than not playing at all. It's the worst thing you can *possibly* do.

The best thing to do to develop your chess is to play someone who can beat you four out of five games. The fifth game you'll get a draw, you might even win, and you'll be really, really stretching yourself, and you will improve. And that's exactly the same in the workplace.

Obviously, if you're not able to do the job, you are not worth employing, so that isn't going to work out. But you need to be able to do the job well, but do the job well by running as fast as you can.

Ed: When I work at a job, I don't want to be the smartest one in the group. I want to have someone else who I can learn from. But when you get to certain levels, you *are* the smartest guy in the group. Is that when it's time to move to a new job?

Rod: When I first went into the IT industry full-time, probably ten, eleven years ago, I was the least experienced guy. It took me three, four years. I was the best guy in my job, partly because I was lucky in being in Java really early on. [At that point,] I wasn't really learning that much. And then, as my career has progressed, I've gotten to spend more and more time in the company of exceptionally good people, so I'm not the best person around anymore, and that's great. So, in a way, I've gotten back to where I started out.

Ed: So would it be appropriate, if you are the smartest one in your group, to maybe look outside the organization, start going to conferences, start getting involved outside of your organization? If you can't find a challenge in your group but you don't want to leave the job, for whatever reason, then what do you do?

Rod: That's an interesting question, and there's an answer to that question that didn't exist when I was in that place. The answer to that question is open source. So conferences—big conferences—like Microsoft TechEd, JavaOne, are not for people like that. They're more for corporate developers. Smaller conferences, like the ServerSide Java Symposium, the Spring Experience, that kind of thing, if you will, yeah. If it's a heavily technical conference of like 200 to 500 people, that could be very useful in meeting people you'll learn from. But the big industry conferences are predominantly for less advanced people. If you're a Java developer, there are plenty of ways to meet people outside the workplace.

And, obviously, you should try to challenge yourself. So another way you can challenge yourself—coming back to what I said about appreciating the business—is, let's suppose your…you live somewhere in a reasonably remote area. There aren't many employers. You love your lifestyle. You spend lots of time with your wife and kids, and you just don't want to move to another employer. Try to learn more about the company's business, and try to step back and think, "In terms of what we're doing in IT, my role, is there any way we could do better, perform faster, learn new technologies?"

It's possible to challenge yourself, but it's a lot [easier if you are challenged by your peers]. When Roger Bannister broke the four-minute mile, he did it using pacing runners. So *he* ran a mile, but there were people who ran with him for parts of the mile and then dropped off because, obviously, they couldn't keep up that rate. And, of course, it meant that he was constantly being pushed by someone who was fresh and could run faster than he could at that point.

Ed: It's often said that the average person in the workforce will have several different careers between the time they enter the workforce and the time they retire. Do you agree with that? Have you had to do that yourself? Do you have plans for doing that in the future?

Rod: I think that the world is a very competitive place. It is also a place that offers a lot of opportunity. And I've worked with and seen a fairly large number of people who were doing something that's totally different from what their highest degree was in. So, for me, my highest degree is in musicology. I happen to be an expert on piano music in Paris in the mid-19th century. That is not something that I directly use in my work every day, but I think the key thing is to try to work out, as you construct your career, how you can use the skills and attributes that you have. I think that we all invent our careers over time. There's not much difference between how a person evolves over time in their career and how a company evolves over time. I mean, you look at IBM. IBM has been around for many, many years. But is the IBM of today similar to the IBM of 1940?

Ed: So what is your non-IT plan B for earning a living?

Rod: That's actually a very difficult question for me, which is both a good and a bad thing. It's a bad thing in that I sometimes envy some of my friends who come from my music background, and, I mean, they know exactly what it is they want to do. For example, one of my best friends really wants to be a clarinetist specializing in playing late 18th-century clarinet music. That's pretty specialized. I can almost envy that in a way. I frankly don't know what I would do. I think at this point I would probably do a business role, because I quite enjoy that. So I'd probably try to start a company in whatever field that I found intellectually interesting. However, if you'd asked me that question, say, ten years ago, I imagine I probably would have gone back into being an academic.

I honestly believe that I could be happy in a variety of different occupations. The essential for me is [that] I really need to be intellectually challenged, and I really need to work with people that I can respect. If those conditions are satisfied, there's actually a pretty large range of things that I think I'd be quite happy doing.

Ed: In your role as CEO of SpringSource, how do you foster innovation inside your company?

Rod: One of the ways to foster innovation is to foster people who can innovate. We put a big emphasis on hiring creative people. It tends to be a bit easier when hiring people who come from the open-source community, because they offer loads of people who have innovated in the past. I think it is also very important to create a culture that supports creative people. Creative people don't like a strictly hierarchical organization. They like an organization where they can contribute on subjects that might strictly be considered to be out of their role, and they like to be listened to. So I think some of it comes down to management, some of it comes to producing the kind of culture that means that creative people think, "Hey, this is a fun place to come to work. This is not just about the paycheck. This is about somewhere where people really care about coming up with good solutions. It's somewhere where if I come up with a good solution, people will listen to me."

Ed: But having the latitude to do that and having longer-term software goals than just going from quarter to quarter, that is a challenge in a small-to-midsize company. I can see a big organization like Google and Sun and all the others that can afford to have very long product development cycles and that can afford to have people that are doing "dreaming" type things. But how do you do it in a company where you don't necessarily have those deep pockets?

Rod: I think this is actually one way of looking at the question of why we took SpringSource to raise money [from venture capital]. And certainly I don't have the power to go and do what Google is doing and try to hire everyone in Silicon Valley with an IQ of whatever their cutoff is. But, on the other hand, it really has been able to help to free up the creativity from that quarter-to-quarter tyranny, just having the cash behind us. I think we were very fortunate, because there was a lot of buzz about our software and we already had a core of good people. We were very fortunate in hiring absolutely fantastic people before we were funded. But one of the things we've been able to do post-funding is actually give those people more time to do things that aren't necessarily going to show up on the month or the quarter in terms of revenue. One thing that I've [said] is that it's very, very difficult to generate creative force in a consultancy model, compared to a product company model. Because the closer you are to that—"Hey, how billable was this guy?"—if you're asking that question every day, you're not asking the question of "How many great ideas did he come up with today?"

Personal

Ed: Do you keep a journal and how frequently do you update it?

Rod: I'm an inveterate note taker. With respect to every meeting that I attend, etc., I take copious written notes. For some reason, I find it much easier to handwrite them than to use a laptop. Also, I think it's partly a question of courtesy. It seems a bit impersonal and distracting to people if you're typing away. With respect to a journal, I often use exercise books to write about a particular project. So, for example, when I was writing many of my books, I would usually have an exercise book where I would write down my thoughts on particular topics and look back over it and see how it evolved. But I only do it with respect to particular projects. It's not something that I do in general.

Ed: What about a day planner. Do you use a day planner?

Rod: I didn't—not before I was doing mostly business stuff. Today, however, I tend to be totally calendar-driven, beyond where I can possibly make all of my commitments. I mean, I often have six to eight hours of meetings per day. I didn't use to do that. When I was in a purely technical role, when I was writing my book, I didn't use a day planner at all.

Ed: Did you use any kind of system, when you were in that role, to plan your own tasks and your own time?

Rod: I would make lists, basically. I used to tend to put Sticky Notes on my desktop or on my screen, with a list of tasks that I was trying to complete. I found that worked pretty well. I think it's partly the granularity of tasks.

So, very often with writing, I found that the granularity of tasks is not that fine. The granularity of tasks is something like, "Revise Chapter Three and make it make sense." Rather than my present day, which is more like, "Here are ten people that I need to talk to, this I what I need to talk to each of them about." One thing that I've also found incredibly useful in planning is making notes. I'm very prone to printing out anything that I've written and making incredibly detailed notes about how I need to revise it, etc. And often, particularly when I've been writing, I use that as a way of planning. Essentially, the notes that I make on a particular draft will actually drive how I next work with that particular piece of work. When I'm writing code, I'm a big fan of "TODO" comments. I will very often write the first version of something so I can get tests passing and actually put in "TODOs" about all the areas where it can be optimized or whatever. And I find that a very helpful technique.

Ed: What kind of student were you in college?

Rod: My academic record was extremely good in all subjects.

Ed: How much stock do you place in that as a predictor of developer success?

Rod: Not an enormous amount. I have seen plenty of very good software developers who had second-class degrees or, indeed, no degree. No, I wouldn't put an enormous amount of stock [in] it. On the other hand, we have two guys in SpringSource who have PhDs in physics, and they're exceptionally bright people and it shows.

I don't know how the grading system works here [in the United States], but in the UK, we have different classes of honors degrees. A second class honors is not too bad, first class honors is good, and third class honors is—by and large, it was probably good that you did this degree, but you don't have an academic career.

And I've actually asked candidates, "Okay, you seem to be a bright guy. You got a third. What was going on?" I mean, that's a pretty blunt question, but the guy actually gave me a very good and a very honest answer about things that were going on in his personal life, and I can't remember whether we hired him or not, but, by and large, I—that part of the interview I was quite satisfied with.

Ed: One of the things that can go on in college to give people lower grades is immense involvement in activities like marching band, computer club, sports, etc. It's possible to do so much of that that your grades suffer. How about you in activities in school? Were you involved in that kind of thing?

Rod: Yes. Not so much in first year. In second year, I certainly discovered going out and partying, and it didn't really affect my grades a whole lot, partly because I still made sure that I attended the vast majority of lectures; I always took notes. Even if I paid no attention to lectures, I got very good at mass lectures at writing everything down but paying no attention and talking to my girlfriend. Then I would study before the exams. I would not go out for an entire week before the exams, and I would just study from morning 'til night. I basically put very little effort into most of my subjects during term time, but I spent a week sweating for the exams, and that seemed to work.

Ed: What motivates you to succeed professionally, and is it different from what motivates you to succeed personally?

Rod: I think it is different. One famous writer, I think it might have been E. M. Forster, said when asked why he wrote, "To earn the respect of people that I respect." So, one thing that is important to me is I would really like other people to look at my career and respect it. I'd like them not necessarily to respect it because I was successful in a professional capacity, but to respect it because they thought I was ethical, they thought that I contributed, etc. That's quite important. It is very important for me to be economically secure. I think this is something that really relates to my background. I did not come from a very privileged background. My parents were educated, but they didn't have a lot of money. I came from a background that really valued education far more than money. That has left me with a strong desire to [do] something intellectually interesting. I felt a need to prove myself intellectually. But it also left a very, very strong desire to be economically secure. I don't so much have a passionate desire to be rich as I have a very, very strong desire to get to a point where my family and I don't need to worry about money. I mean, one of the big personal factors around this was that my father was 55 when I was born, and he actually remembers the Great Depression. And it left a profound impression on him, as it did on everyone in his generation. And I was quite close to him, so I guess it also left a profound impression on me.

With respect to my motivations personally, I would like to be a good father. And bring up my children without screwing them up [laughs]. So they won't be telling their psychotherapists in 30 years' time about their dreadful father and how he was responsible for all their problems. I would also like to have a strong marriage and give security, both emotionally and financially, [to] my family.

Ed: Several times throughout this interview, we arrived at the notion that the ability to keep things in perspective, to prioritize effectively, was a major contributor to success. If you have this ability in your professional life, would you say it carries over into your personal life?

Rod: No. Well, my wife would say it's because I put way too much intellectual and emotional level into work and far too little into everything else.

Ed: I've heard that elsewhere, too.

Rod: I would say that there is truth in that, but there's also another fundamental thing. Maybe I'm a bit cynical, but I think life defeats us all. You can't write a perfect piece of code, but you can write a piece of code that performs as expected that doesn't have bugs in production and you feel really happy with.

How are you going to have a perfect marriage? Maybe there are people who have perfect marriages, and good luck to them. I think living your life is a much harder problem than having a career. And also there are far more factors. I mean, intelligence and energy will get you a long way in your career, whereas I don't really think there's any evidence intelligent people are more happy. In fact, I suspect there's probably some evidence that they're less happy. So, some of the things that help you in your career don't necessarily help you [at home].

CHAPTER 2

Adrian Colyer

Fact Sheet

Name: Adrian Colyer

Rock Star Programmer Credentials: Pioneer of Aspect-oriented programming tools, project lead of AspectJ, one of the developers of the AspectJ Development Tools, CTO of SpringSource

Date of Birth: March 1971

City of Birth: London, United Kingdom

Birth Order: First of two

Marital Status: Married

Number of Kids: Two

Degree: Bachelor of Science in Computer Science, Southampton University, 1992

Number of generations in your ancestry (including yourself) that graduated from college: One

Years as an IT Professional: 15

Role: CTO of SpringSource, a Java enterprise consulting company that is the creator and steward of the Spring Framework.

Introduction

Adrian Colyer is one of those hard-core programmers you would like to have had as a classmate in your Computer Science program in college. He's passionate about software, methodical in his approach to building it, and a continual optimizer of the way he gets things done. A veteran of the legendary IBM Hursley Park Lab, in the U.K., Adrian cut his teeth on IBM CICS, the world's first commercial enterprise software stack. He was one of the first to bring Java and Web development into use at Hursley, eventually helping to integrate Enterprise JavaBeans (EJB) support into CICS. Adrian's approach to this task involved a design that used aspect-oriented techniques. Since then, Adrian has ridden the crest of aspect-oriented programming (AOP) to the point where he is an AOP community leader and recognized expert on this most popular post-object programming paradigm.

After exhausting the possibilities of Aspects at IBM, Adrian joined Rod Johnson's SpringSource (*see interview in Chapter 1*) to overhaul the implementation of AOP in the Spring Framework.

Adrian's skills as a programmer, in career stewardship, in trend-spotting, and in general technology crest-riding brought him to my attention when we met in a smoky bar (Café Mozart if you're curious) in Munich, Germany, during the 2005 W-JAX conference. To look at him, you'd think he's the quintessential British post-millennial computer science guy: well-dressed, casual attire; sensible, yet stylish glasses; and a lanky frame that indicates a fit lifestyle. Adrian speaks in a pleasant British accent that is as equally well suited to the keynote speaker's podium at an IT conference as to the local pub.

His current gig is the CTO of SpringSource, a global software consultancy most famous for the Spring Framework. He makes his home in the Green City of Southampton in Great Britain.

Soft Skills

Ed: In your current role as CTO of SpringSource, staying current is not just a career maintenance skill—it's actually a part of your job. What is your personal process for staying current?

Adrian: This is basically a huge problem because there is far too much going on for you to be aware of it all. So the first thing to realize is, either consciously or unconsciously, that you have to be selective, so you might as well do it consciously.

Ed: Right, okay.

Adrian: So I try and keep up to pace with things selectively. In areas that are close to the things I'm working in, I'll do it incrementally: follow the key blogs or the key sites, look at what's going on—adapt to the incremental changes that are happening. But in things that are a little bit further out from my core, I batch it. So I'm quite happy to leave to one side, something important, such as what's happening in the Ruby space. That's pretty important. It's very, very close to being something I'd want to incrementally keep up on. Right now, I'm not. I'm batching it. So I might not really pay too much attention to it for a few months. I'll just file away a few links and things, and then I'll spend time saying, "Okay, now I'm going to bulk-update myself on what happened in the last three months in that space."

Ed: Okay.

Adrian: And I might go read a book or two or read a few key articles. I keep day-to-day on top of the things close in, and I batch the stuff further out. One of the things that I think is really important, if you're able to do this, is to get outside of your immediate team and your immediate working environment. It's amazing. If you start to bump into different people, different perspectives, go to conferences, read the sites like InfoQ (*see interview in Chapter 10*) or ServerSide or whatever, just to make sure that you at least see the headlines flash by, you pick up a sense of what the topics are that people are talking about.

Ed: Right.

Adrian: Find out, "What's the conversation at the moment?" That's really useful. It's quite frightening when you come across a team that hasn't realized just how disconnected they've become from all those conversations and don't really know what's going on at all. It happens more than you'd like to think.

[With] many companies, you can't go to a conference unless you've got a paper submitted. That's hard, because if you never go to the conference, you don't know what the conversation is, so you can't put in a paper that's part of the conversation. How do you get into that? Do try and get out. One general-purpose conference or something at least. Meet people and talk about what's going on outside of the ten guys you sit next to.

Ed: Right. Okay. So you have a very definite intentional process for doing this. Do you schedule it in your week? Do you do it every day?

Character Attribute

Methodical and consistent approach to how he does work.

Adrian: It came across a bit like that, didn't it?

Ed: It seems like you are reading from a script.

Adrian: No, it's not quite as rigid as that. Reflecting on what it is I do— that's how it pans out. But it does come in bursts. It depends on what my weekly schedule is, what I've got on. I have a news reader, like everyone does. I skim blogs and the key news headlines fairly frequently, not in depth at all. I'll just skim it. I have this great little bucket on my hard disk called "Read and Review." If I see an interesting Web thing or something, I tend to print it to PDF and slam it in there. And if I'm on a train or a plane and I've got some dead time where I can't get connected, I hold those out and I read them then.

So in terms of a practical tip, that's one thing I do. I try to make use of those little bits of dead time. But no, I don't really schedule in, "Oh, on the 22nd of July, I'm due to look at Ruby again." It's more just in general, while I'm doing the quick scans. Something will go, "Oh, that's interesting. I haven't caught up in this space for a while," and I'll set aside a bit of time then, and I'll go look at it. Maybe a calendarized approach would be even more effective, but I'm not that organized, I have to confess.

Ed: When you're doing this non-calendarized, yet very effective-sounding process of keeping abreast of developments, how do you break down the software industry? How do you categorize it?

Adrian: The classic one I've lived with for a very long time is system software, middleware, and then applications. That's the broadest division I do. But there are a couple of other dimensions. Across that, you've got, commercial software or is it scientific?

And then, generally, you've got, is it server side or is it client side? If you take those kinds of three things, you get a three-dimensional space that pretty much carves up a lot of what's going on. No system of buckets is ever perfect, but that works pretty well.

> **Observation**
>
> James Gosling went further than Adrian here, completely eschewing the notion of categorizing the software industry for fear of unduly limiting one's perspective. See page 171.

Ed: So the initial three that you listed there, can you explain more about what system software is for you?

Adrian: Yeah, the operating system, your device drivers. Perhaps you put down there your compilers, interpreters, and virtual machines. And again, it blurs as you get to the top of that category: What's system software? What's middleware? Well, that changes a lot on your perspective and where you happen to be working in the stack. But certainly, it's operating systems and anything down at that level or close to it…probably a good range of virtual machines and stuff on top of them.

Ed: What about middleware?

Adrian: So middleware—well, the name gives it away. Right?

You can go back through academia and look at all the different definitions that have been given, but in general, "middleware" is support software that helps you to construct applications. Very often, people characterize that in the server-side application space. That is the sweet spot for middleware, helping you deal with all the concurrency and all the other issues you get in multi-user, real-time systems, or OLTP systems. They're not strict real-time. They do have middleware for that, too.

Ed: Okay, so message queues and that sort of thing.

Adrian: Oh, yeah. So, yeah, transaction processing, messaging, all of that good stuff is middleware.

Ed: Okay. Now, what about the breakdown of who is going to be using the software? A market-focused approach, developer-focused software or user focused software—does it make sense to split the data cube in that way?

Adrian: Yeah, that's a good point. Certainly, and you can think: Are you writing productivity tools that help people produce some other artifact, are you actually writing a business application, is it a reporting tool? Yeah, there are endless ways of cutting it there as you get into it.

I view some of those [sorts of applications] as in the application space. For example, Eclipse. It's an application whose domain happens to be writing programs. But it's an application still, so that's the bucket I would lump most of them in. But certainly, you may well care about whether you're writing an IDE (Integrated Development Environment) or whether you're writing a trade settlement system. Those are very different beasts.

Ed: Right. Okay. Well, why would you say it's important for a software developer to have a broad understanding of a categorization of the industry? How would that help you?

Adrian: One of the things about our industry—actually, one of the things that attracted me to it—is it's always changing. There is just an enormous amount of new stuff flying past you all the time. You have to have some way to systematize, tag, understand, file, and make sense of all that immense stream of data flying past you.

Ed: And it seems like you have a great system for that.

Adrian: And if you've got a way of, even at the first crude level, pigeon-holing what something is and putting it in a bucket, that's your very first crude understanding what on earth is going on. So that's one pretty important reason why you want to be able to categorize. Another one is, if you realize what layer and in which bucket something is working, as you come to understand what to expect of something with those characteristics, it's like having an abstract model. You should be able to both work out more quickly what it might do for you and also where you're likely to be stretching the boundaries, and you want to look to complement it

So the knowledge of the categories, once you put something in a bucket, if I know I'm writing an application and I find myself straying into something that I really feel is really middleware, I might start to ask, "Well, is there a piece of middleware that does this?" The death of the in-house framework—classic example there. [Adrian is referring to the oft-observed phenomenon of an IT shop writing its own Web application framework, as opposed to using an off-the-shelf solution like JavaServer Faces, ASP.NET, etc.]

Ed: Right, and then you can look at prior art. Speaking of which, how do you avoid reinventing the wheel in that case? Having worked with IBM CICS so much, you may have a different perspective than some of our readers who are newer to the industry. How do you feel about reinventing the wheel? Why must we continue to do it? Hasn't it all been done before?

Observation

In Appendix B, you can read about Phillip Armour's "Five Orders of Ignorance." In his book, *The Laws of Software Process* (Auerbach, 2003), Mr. Armour expands on the orders of ignorance and makes the assertion that software is not a product, but rather a byproduct of learning how to solve the problem. Adrian's answer here supports Mr. Armour's assertion.

Adrian: Yeah. It's interesting. It depends on why you're doing it. One good reason you might reinvent the wheel is to learn. So that's a strange one. But yet, actually trying to re-create something and look at its internals and think about how you have to design it, that's a great learning process. Not a very good business reason, but it's great for learning.

Another reason you see people reinventing the wheel, and there's often a lot of criticism for this, is to gain control. You could say, "I don't control that thing over there. I really feel I need control of it for some reason. I'm going to reinvent it, rewrite it." Now, technically, we all pour scorn on that, of course. But when you sit back, and if you look at it from a business perspective, maybe sometimes, that actually makes business sense. So perhaps you're going to reinvent the wheel for that sometime.

Sometimes, it's just a matter of there's a bunch of accumulated stuff that's grown up around it. It was originally written in a certain time that made certain assumptions and, perhaps, a critical mass of those have now become untrue, or it's carrying too much of its historical baggage, and you want to clean it up and move forward.

But in general, I would say reinventing the wheel just slows you down. Hopefully, you're trying to solve a problem that is at least in some way different from what this other thing did. So put an abstraction over it, adapt to it, graft it onto what you're trying to do, and get on with solving your problem. And if you really do need to come back later on and then replace that bit, if you put the barrier around it, you could.

Like many people, I strongly dislike reinventing the wheel. But I have a pragmatic enough streak to recognize that every now and then this happens, sometimes for technical reasons and sometimes even for non-technical reasons.

Ed: Okay. So what is some advice that you can give people to avoid reinventing the wheel, like the discovery of existing solutions? How do you recognize that what you're doing might already be done?

Adrian: Yeah. Well, one thing that always used to fascinate me—and I still think this is pretty endemic in a lot of our industry—if you are at university or you're in academia, whatever, you go into an area, the very first thing you're taught to do is a literature search. Basically, go out and find out the prior art in this space. And now build on that in terms of taking your research and doing something different.

We [in the software industry] actually do not have a culture at all of doing the literature search. We go very quickly from, "Oh, I need an X" to "How will I build an X?"

Ed: Right.

Adrian: It's instant. It just hasn't got engrained in the average software developer's mindset. There's no "do the literature search" phase.

The rise of open source has started to change that. People now do think, "Oh, maybe there's an open-source project that does blah." Something about open source has maybe put a little bit of that in people's mindsets, but the "do the literature search" equivalent is definitely the missing step. Once you're aware of the prior art, even if you decide not to use it, you're going to learn quite a lot from looking at the way they chose to solve the problem. You might see an approach you hadn't thought of that's interesting.

You might come across issues about or data about performance implications of a certain approach. Obviously the great literature search in the sky these days is called "Google." So it's actually much easier to do this than it used to be before as well. It used to be quite hard work, but now it's not. There really aren't that many excuses for not spending the time to realize that somebody else has probably been in this space, and let's have a look. See what they learned so I can build on it.

Ed: Earlier you established a classification scheme of the industry into three broad groups: system software, middleware, and applications. In what segment would you consider yourself working?

Adrian: Pretty much my entire career, I have been pigeonholed by middleware, commercial software, and server side. That's really the space that I've spent the vast majority of my time in.

Ed: And if you had to pick one language environment that the majority of the people in your segment are writing software today, what would that be?

Adrian: That segment is pretty dominantly Java at the moment.

Hard Skills

Ed: Okay. What are some attributes of the language that people will be writing in, in this category, ten years from now? What will it look like? Will it be Java? Will it be like Java with scripting? What are some attributes of the language?

Adrian: Yeah, that's a really interesting question. I have a fondness for language, having work[ed] with AOP, AspectJ, and things for so long. Ten years from now isn't actually that long in language time.

One of the first things I would say when I think about ten years from now is that language almost certainly exists right now.

Because things that people are widely using, if you look back at how long things take, maybe Java came a bit quicker, but in general the germs of those languages have been around quite a long time before they get to the widely adopted state. So it's fairly likely that the language is something that is there now. It's still going to be a C-family style of language, given how well entrenched that is.

I suspect it will be interpreted with a very smart interpreter. If you look at the way some of those virtual machines (VMs) and things are getting now, you always get more efficient than straight compiled machine code, which is a really disturbing fact when you first encounter it.

I hope it has a smarter distributed run time than we've got now. If you look at things like what underpins Erlang, you might not like the syntax on the surface, but you've got to admire that run-time system that they have. So that's really interesting, especially if you look forward ten years. I go down to the store now and I buy what for me is an £800 PC. It's already got two processors in it, and that's just my cheap, basic PC. Now, scroll that forward, we're going to have to starting thinking about concurrency and abstractions for it, smarter runtimes help with that.

I'd also like to think because of that, maybe we'll get back to more of a message-based way of thinking about what we're doing. You look at assembly, C, C++, Java, C#, go down that line—we really tend to think about invoking methods and calling functions, and that's the way that most of those programmers think about what's going on.

Ed: It's pretty much procedural, right?

Adrian: It's pretty much procedural. Now, there are a few people who—Smalltalkers prior to that—who bring across this whole message-passing way of understanding what is actually syntactically fairly similar on the surface.

I actually much prefer that message-based way of thinking about things, partially because aspects work much better when you think about things that way. But also, when you start getting into better dealing with concurrency, etc., that's a better foundation, and I hope we can make a shift to moving back to thinking about messages as a more primary paradigm.

Another thing is this whole notion of domain-specific languages and how they're going to fit in, their role. Two things you need to have for something to be a powerful language. You need both abstraction, the ability to hide details behind something and name it, and you need composition.

You need a way to then plot those abstractions back together again and say interesting things.

And again, actually, if you read—well, I wonder if I've got it. Hang on. I have it here somewhere. Here we are. [I'm] reading off the back jacket of a classic book, the old *Structure and Interpretation of Computer Programs* by Abelson and Sussman (MIT Press, 1996), or SICP. And there's a quote on there. Maybe even if you're trolling through the blog, you might have crossed me writing about this at one time. They just have this marvelous little thing that they say on the back. And it's the first paragraph: "This book presents a unique conceptual introduction to programming, and it intends to give readers command of the major techniques used to control the complexity of large software systems." And then it describes the three major techniques: 1) Building abstractions. Well, we do a lot of that. Right? 2) Establishing conventional interfaces. We know how to define interfaces. And 3) Establishing new descriptive languages. These are your three basic fundamental building blocks. And you think about how much more often in the mainstream now we are building abstractions and interfaces compared to how often we create a language to solve a problem.

Ed: Right.

Adrian: That's really interesting. When you look back at some of that old stuff and the power you get from the language side, you say, "Yeah, we are missing something there." What we've had to date with some of the domain-specific language (DSL) stuff that is creeping back into the public visibility again is we've got the abstraction piece. We know how to make a DSL, crudely, and to say some things in that DSL. What I think is really interesting—and maybe something will come through in this time; it will be very powerful if it does—is how do I, given a base language, a number of DSLs, and different parts of the problem domain all fitting around it, how do I solve the composition problem so that I can abstract into some domain-specific language, or several, and then put it all back together into one coherent program? And if I can get the composition half of it working, that's going to be really powerful. I hope something like that comes around.

Ed: It seems to me the plight of the developer in the next ten years, as we move towards that language for which we are describing the attributes, is actually going to become harder, because they're just going to have to understand more stuff, maybe more stuff with less depth, but you're still going to have to understand all of it and be able to reason about it. Right?

Adrian: And to an extent, I do feel sympathy with that position. I think back to when I first came to Java, for example, which was 0.8 or whatever it was, and *Java in a Nutshell* (O'Reilly, 1998). It was pretty thin. You could read it and know, "This is the language. This is the entire language. This is everything in the Java world," and you could learn it in a day and a half, and you were done.

Now, today, if you came to Java world, it would be totally daunting. There is so much of it. It's unbelievable. So to be a new person coming in now and hit that—I'm sure that's really not pleasant. And to some extent, as we grow, building more and more and more, that can happen. That's one of the reasons why new guys get a chance to come in and disrupt.

Because all the useful stuff and also the baggage just gets to be really, really intimidating and says here there must be a simpler way. And you start a new platform up, and it initially is simpler, and then you spend another ten years building all the stuff back on top, and then you can have another disruption.

Ed: Right. Now there's another dimension that we haven't talked about. You mentioned the three attributes from *Structure and Interpretation of Computer Programs* [1) Building abstractions. 2) Establishing conventional interfaces. 3) Establishing new descriptive languages.] The ability to do those three things is the purest definition of what makes a language powerful. There's also the business side of it, which is the number of programmers that know how to do it so you can hire them. And there is the vibrancy of the marketplace for tools.

Adrian: Yeah, all the surrounding stuff, yeah.

Ed: So how can you factor that into your ten-year picture here?

Adrian: Well, that's one of the reasons I said C family.

Ed: Aha, okay, I gathered that.

Adrian: Yeah, that's so entrenched now. Tools has been really interesting. That was a real lesson we learned on AspectJ. You really cannot get mainstream wide adoption of a new language now unless you very quickly jump to what's actually a pretty high bar in terms of IDE support. It's interesting to watch things like how Ruby comes along and the tool support for Ruby. There are some fundamental limitations in what you can and can't do in a language like that in the tooling world.

But even so, pretty quickly, you've got to get the plug-ins in Eclipse for it, and it's got to be supported. That's a necessity. You absolutely have to. If you're really going to try and be up there and invent this new language and open it up on the world and hope to get mass adoption, you've really got to think hard about a number of things. It's yes to language and its syntax. It's the run-time libraries and the class libraries or whatever you call it that comes with it. They are obviously hugely important.

It's how you bridge from this language to all the other stuff out there, because it's not going to live in its own little island—that's a trap that many people fall into. You just can't get widespread traction without being able to bridge. And it is the IDE and the tooling support and all of those things [that] have to come together. And if you're missing any one piece of the picture, it's going to be very hard for that language to take off. And then you need a chunk of good luck, and you need to be solving some particularly germane problem that your language does well. It's in the public eye at the moment and a whole bunch of other things that are much harder to control.

Ed: So it seems to me that when you have all of those conditions that need to be met—it's almost seems like success is an accident. You can't intentionally make your platform a success.

Adrian: You can do some things to make sure that you covered the bases. You haven't made an obvious mistake. You've got a good solid run-time. You've got the documentation. You've got all that stuff covered. You can make sure you're not shooting yourself in the foot. So you can stop yourself from being guaranteed to fail, but there's no way you can guarantee to succeed. You need, amongst a bunch of other things, timing and luck and all the rest of it.

Ed: Well, another part of the success of a platform is the availability and quality of books that document it. You mention SIPC as a classic foundational book. What are some other foundational books you find have influenced your practice of software development?

Adrian: What I tend to really like, and what I enjoy about software, is almost more than what the software actually does on the outside. I really like the crafting and expressing of the program itself, so that it's beautiful and elegant, and it just says it in a clean, nice way. That's the thing that has always really interested me, and these books reflect that. So early on in my career, two of the ones that really stood out to me were Steve McConnell's books *Code Complete* (Microsoft Press, 1993) and *Rapid Development* (Microsoft Press, 1996). They both have a lot of really pretty basic advice in them. And some of the things I learned from *Rapid Development* I'm still using now and still find a number of people who don't understand some of those things, so there's good advice in them.

Moving on, another one that I really like is called *Fundamentals of Object-Oriented Design in UML* (Addison-Wesley Professional, 1999), and it's by a guy called Meilir Page-Jones. Not at all for the UML part of the book, but I love the way he puts these so seemingly innocent little conundrums that [you] suddenly start to realize have these quiet little design issues underneath them. He has a very nice style of doing it, and I like the way he puts it—that's a good book.

Another one that had an impact on me at the time was *Refactoring* (Addison-Wesley Professional, 1999) by Martin Fowler for that different perspective on thinking about how code moves on once you've created it the first time round—that it's easy to miss out on that whole idea. Early on, I was really impressed with *Effective C++* (Addison-Wesley, 1991).

Ed: I like that one. Scott Meyers, yeah.

Adrian: That's right, yeah. That was an early one, wow, that's a really great book, and *Effective Java* (Prentice Hall PTR, 2001) would be the modern equivalent of that. It came to me later, so it didn't have the same impact on me as *Effective C++* did all those years ago.

Ed: Let's move from the core and foundational kinds of questions into some ones about the practice of software development. After doing some of these interviews, I've come to believe that mastery of tools is an important ingredient in being a rock star programmer. To me, there is a strong relationship between the need to customize a software tool and mastery of it. What correlation do you think there is between a developer's need to customize their environment in a way that is optimal for them and their success, including career success? Their ability to get things done? What do you think the correlation is?

Adrian: Customizing the environment certainly makes you a lot more efficient. When you see somebody who's really proficient in their environment moving around and doing stuff, it can be quite mind-blowing sometimes. However, I still think that the people who are really, really good programmers and software engineers, even if they had to use the exact same tools, with no customizations, as everybody else, they would still outperform, because the people aspects of software development are probably more important than the actual tool-based aspects. Even though they give you a big productivity boost, the most important thing is how you can think and reason about what you're doing. The tools can help or hinder that to varying degrees, but…

Ed: What about if your job involves a lot of bug fixing?

Adrian: Yeah.

Ed: Then someone who really knows the debugger and maybe IDE and all of the ways to get around there would be better than someone who just maybe doesn't have that skill, but is equal in terms of their problem-solving abilities?

Adrian: Oh, sure, say, you've got to be able to know how to use a standard tool. But you're asking me about a handful because you've got to customize the standard tools.

Ed: Right. Okay. That's true.

Adrian: Sure, you've got to know how to use the debugger.

Ed: Right.

Adrian: How important is it that you can make a certain key binding do something that came off the menu? Well, it'll give you an incremental boost, but not fundamentally. At that point, that human being becomes more important. What you want is the right person with the right environment, and then you've really got something special.

Ed: Okay. But then there're certain personality types who then have a propensity to want to get things customized. They cannot stand the annoyance of repetition.

Adrian: Yes.

Ed: Now what I'm talking about is, how does that personality type correlate to career success as a programmer?

Adrian: Interesting.

Ed: If one does not have that trait, is one less likely to be a great programmer?

Adrian: I'm just casting my mind back over good programmers and thinking, "Did they all have that trait?"

Ed: Mmm hmm.

Adrian: And…

Ed: Yeah, that's what I want to know.

Adrian: Quite a number of them do.

Ed: Yes.

Adrian: Yes. Yeah, it's that thing about trying to smooth out the ripples in their environment. They have a mindset that "I'm in control and the tool is here to serve me," rather than, "I will fit under what the tool wants to do." Yeah, I would say that not all, but quite a few of the clearly better-than-average programmers that I've worked with are also somewhat unique in the way they use their environment. Some of the ones I know are extremely fast typists, for example, compared to the average. And they are even typing their code fast. I do change some key bindings and things in Eclipse, for example.

Ed: Right.

Adrian: Run a unit test, for example. ALT, SHIFT, x t, that's just crazy for something that you're doing all the time. So I bind it to CTRL-R. It's just a world of difference. That tiny little thing. But you can't quite customize and control to the same degree.

Ed: Sure.

Adrian: It's more like somebody decided what check boxes you could have, and you can check or uncheck some of them, but in Emacs you've got complete control over what everything does.

Ed: So what steps do you undertake to customize a new computer when you need to make it ready for use for work?

Adrian: Well, when I was on Windows, the first thing that would go on would be GNU/Cygwin.

I use Z shell and Emacs. Those are the next two things I have to have.

Ed: Okay.

Adrian: After that, development-wise, on would go Eclipse and the various bits and pieces in Eclipse.

Ed: Various plug-ins.

Adrian: Yeah, the central set of plug-ins, which for me is probably: AJDT, Aspect J development tools…it would be Mylar (now Mylyn)…it would be Spring IDE.

Ed: How about the Web tools?

Adrian: Platform almost counts as part of Eclipse to me. That's probably the core ones that would go in for me. And then, in Emacs, I would see there's a bunch of things I'd want to suck in, certain modes I'm using. I'd pull in post mode and awk mode and in terms of e-mail, I don't use any of the built in e-mail tools anymore. I used an old terminal-based e-mail program called Mutt. I've got a little tool called Offline IMAP. And then I have a few basic key bindings, like the things I want to do commonly— they're all one keystroke. The other interesting thing I've done [is that] I integrate a tool called mairix, which gives you really fantastic file searching [of e-mail].

Ed: And you can just give it a maildir format?

Adrian: So, what you do is, yeah, you tell it "this is where my mail is," basically, and like in Mutt, for me, it's comma f, to start Find, and you type in your criteria, and what it does, it's really nice, is it actually creates a virtual maildir. So it creates a mail folder, and I probably call mine "Search" or something or "Search Results," in which all the mails are symbolic links to where the mail really is, so your mail user agent can look at it like it's a regular mail folder. And whatever processing you do on it gets done in the right place.

So, again, it's really quick and easy to integrate. So that searching capability and speed across all my e-mail is one of the things that blows people away.

Ed: That's great. It doesn't build an index?

Adrian: It does. One of the things [that is] really terrible in a GUI-based e-mail client is how you actually archive a message, which is basically drag and drop, which is the worst user interaction you can possibly do.

Ed: I know.

Adrian: Drag and drop is a disaster in terms of efficiency.

Ed: Right, right.

Adrian: You can drag this file, and then you navigate this tree, and it's just not good. My system, on the other hand, is really, really, really efficient. I want my mail to be so that I'm thinking it, and it happens.

Ed: We mentioned the importance of IDE mastery when it comes to debugging. I want to ask how do you attack a hard bug, a hard-to-find bug? What is your process when you're presented with a bug?

Adrian: Yeah, so my number one thing is try to reproduce it.

Ed: Okay.

Adrian: And almost, if I can't reproduce it, that's a terrible thing to me. I've gotta A), first reproduce it, if necessary, with your great big horrible system, and then B) try and narrow it down, narrow it down to the simplest thing that would make it fail. Normally have that as a test that would get checked in to our automated suite. Even at the institutional level. That's there, but locally, committed as a file. So we've got the failing reproducible test, and then I—it's a mixed process of instinct based on what you think might be going on and discovery to determine if your instincts are right.

> **Character Attribute**
>
> Automate as much as possible.

Ed: Okay. Application of a scientific method sometimes?

Adrian: I suppose it is. I'm not sure if it will truly pass a scientific test, but yet you're making a hypothesis, and then you're checking to see if that's correct. If I'm pretty sure it's gonna be in *this* part of the system, I might go to the boundary of that part, and say, "Well, when I entered this, did it look how I think it should look?" And that would give me some knowledge. Things that we used to do a lot in AspectJ, we have a special mode where if the compiler outputs any message, something like that. "Why am I getting this warning? Why am I getting this error?" We could turn on a special mode that we called Pinpoint that when the message came out, it would tell you exactly where in the code it had come from and trace the time, and so that is very useful. I do use a debugger; some people used to frown on that.

Ed: How could you frown on that?

Adrian: There's a school of thought where, "No, you should reason it out and only use the debugger as a last resort." I actually—one of the things you find with test-driven development and working with more bugs is…you're not really as smart as you like to think you are. It makes a lot of sense to go back and check on these things that you think are true; just watch it.

Ed: There's no other way.

Adrian: Yeah, so you learn a lot. So I use a debugger, I know some people who use it less, but I actually will fire it up, watch it walk through the code, check my hypothesis, and then, assuming you get close to, "Okay, this data is wrong in this place" and "What caused it to be wrong?" and, eventually, hopefully, you're going to start to work on a fix. And then, as you're doing the fix, you think, well, "What other consequences could there be here? Are there other bugs of this class around?" Maybe you write a few more tests now to flush out some of that boundary area.

Character Attribute

So well practiced at TDD that it's a part of the way he works.

Ed: Okay.

Adrian: And again, another, I've worked a lot on the compiler and weaver…pretty complicated, deep software where you really can sometimes have side effects that are obvious ones—you've seen it. But you might not remember to predict up front, so running the full test suite again, after each little part of the change, it gets complicated, [and it is] really valuable to make sure you're not tripping up.

Ed: Right.

Adrian: But essentially, then, you get your fix in, you run the whole suite, you check not only the test that captured it and reproduced it in the first place, but then the other ones you've added.

Character Attribute

Discipline.

That goes into the repository at the same time as the fix. Now, we've been very strict about that [at SpringSource]. You don't put it in without the change for the test going in at the same time. The idea being, of course, that you can never, ever fall over that exact bug again anymore. And that, over time, builds up a really, really valuable suite.

Actually, just last week at the Open Source Developer conference, this question came up: at this point in time, if you had to choose between keeping just the test suite for, say, AspectJ or keeping the actual code that implements all the compilation and weaving, which one would it be? And the more I come back to that horrible question—though I would hate to lose either—I would choose to keep the test suite.

Ed: Yeah, that is irreplaceable.

Adrian: Yes.

Ed: It's like a—you've heard the term "institutional memory"—but that's like an "executable institutional" memory.

Adrian: When I think back to how we were writing software not that long ago, relatively speaking, that would have been an unthinkable thing to say. When I first started in my professional programming world, developers wrote the code. That was the developer role, and there used to be a team called FV—functional verification—whose job was basically to do what we're now thinking of as writing unit tests or very low-level integration tests to see if a developer had done his job.

Ed: Right.

Adrian: And, as you can imagine, that process was not terribly effective and didn't work too well. But that was actually how it was done, and then there's another team that performed a system test to do the high-level tests. That model prevailed for a l-o-n-g time, and I just couldn't imagine writing software that way anymore. But the productivity boost [of test-driven development] and doing the test is not a burden. In those days, you never had that suite that was so valuable somehow.

Ed: Right.

Adrian: It would have been unthinkable to say, "Oh, yeah, throw away the code, just keep what FV produced." You just can't imagine anybody even entertaining the question.

Ed: What are some strategies you use to avoid introducing new bugs into the code?

Adrian: [There's] a great paper. By David Parnas. I have his book.

Ed: *The Collected Papers* (Addison-Wesley Professional, 2001)?

Adrian: Yes. There are some real treasures in there, aren't there? So you might have read it—there's a great one in there called "Software Aging."

Ed: I haven't read that one.

Adrian: It basically tells the story about a set of people who designed the system according to some principles, and then—it went into maintenance and the maintenance programmers took over. And during maintenance, problems arise, and they say, "Oh, there's the problem here," and they made some local fixes, etc., and they're doing it without really fully understanding the overall design impulse of the system, so they're making a series of local changes, but each seems to do the right thing. And this process goes on over time, and this is the aging process, and it is exactly what goes on in the real world. Then he has this devastating analysis. He says, "So, think about what's happening now."

He said, "The thing is, not any single person or [anybody] understands this software anymore. The people who are maintaining [it] never really understood the software, and the original designers once understood it, but now there are so many special exceptions and cases and extensions that they don't understand it either." And he moved up into this place where, through the degrading process, they send you the software, [it] has aged irretrievably, and you end up in the rewrite situation. And it is a beautiful, simple analysis of how you got there. It's exactly what happens. Anyway, you've got to understand that when you're trying to make a change or doing maintenance, there are two very important things, and you've got to have both pictures in your head. One is what's happening right here, right now, in this piece of the program. At this point in the execution, where are we and what's going on? But you've also got to actually understand the big picture of the software as well, and you need both. Therefore, the test-driven development approach, the gradually growing test suite, and the executable institutional memory can be pretty effective tools at combating the negative effects of software aging.

> **Observation**
>
> It takes more discipline than most software organizations have to avoid the pitfalls of software aging: losing understanding of the code, the code becoming brittle, etc.

Understanding just a local [context] without understanding the bigger context is actually a pretty dangerous thing. You really can't understand the big picture, but you have a clue what's going on here, and that's clearly bad. So the people tend to fall into the trap of having the local view but not the big view.

Ed: Right. But that's one of the things that object-oriented design is supposed to mitigate.

Adrian: Supposed to, yeah.

Ed: Yeah.

Adrian: To an extent, it does. Over our evolution of software engineering practices, we have better abstractions and better encapsulation. Some pretty rich interactions going on.

Ed: Yeah, coupling and cohesion.

Adrian: All the classics. You need to understand both, and having understood both, yeah, I'm heavily relying on the test suite to catch me when I slip up and on thinking about if there's a problem like this, what related problems might there be lurking, and let's test for those and put some things in to see if we can catch them.

Ed: So there's a related question there that I'd like to explore a little bit.

You're working on the bug, you are in a situation where, okay, you realize, "Oh, there might be some related things, that may also be bugs that haven't yet manifested themselves. I should see if there are and go fix them." But it's hard to do that. That's what I call the "right thing." Sometimes you're just too lazy.

Adrian: Or under pressure.

Ed: Or under time pressure. So what can you do to motivate yourself? Developers often find themselves in a situation where, "I really should do the right thing, but I don't want to, it's late, I'm tired. I gotta go. My wife's calling me. I'm late already." What do you do in that situation?

Adrian: Well, there's the "what do you really do" and "what should you do exactly." Sometimes you think, "I should do that," and you don't. And I'm sure we all have been in that situation.

Ed: And you just let it go?

Adrian: So, sometimes it gets let go, and that's human nature, right? For me, it's changed. As it's more and more open-source software, it's much, much better if I find a bug than if someone else finds it and reports it.

I'd much prefer that. And that should be true in closed-source software, too, but actually, somehow psychologically, in open-source software it is even more pressing. I'd much rather [fix it now] than have a JIRA or Bugzilla issue come in. You don't have to necessarily fix the other problems right now. You could just write a few tests that cover them. Sometimes, I will create tests that basically have no body, and they're just to-dos.

Sometimes, I've actually created an entry in the system to say we should write some tests to cover this area. I haven't written them yet, but here's where they should be. Spring OSGI actually has a lot of that.

And sometimes I've been under time pressure and I've like left a mental note and hope that one day I'll come back to it, but that's not the process you recommend, obviously.

Ed: Right, right.

Adrian: Pragmatism comes in and occasionally, yeah, that happens.

Ed: It seems you have been fairly introspective about your practice of software development. Can you share any general advice about continually improving your skills?

Adrian: Continue all introspection. Could I have done that better? What did I actually do? Could I have done better? What would be done? If there's somebody else who's doing that smarter than me, what are they doing that I'm not doing? And how do they make it more effective? You can learn to ask those kinds of questions a lot. It just seems to open your mind up to new possibilities that otherwise you might not ever see.

Ed: Is it possible to bring that level of continuous introspection out of the workplace and into your family life, into your interactions with other people?

Adrian: I don't think that's particularly tied to software. Your life is a general outlook of it, and to say, "How am I doing? What could I do better, etc.?" Somehow it spurs you on.

Ed: Right.

Adrian: Or at least it does for my personality, which is not actually insanely competitive, but there's a little bit of that in there. I know some people who are more extreme in that than I am, but...it's a gradual movement.

For example, a great salesman applies very similar techniques to learning how to interact with people, to put them at ease and build relationships, and actually, they're doing it for a professional reason because they're selling.

Ed: Moving outside of the workplace even further, how important is it to keep up on consumer technology? As a computer geek, having the latest cell phone, iPod, Tivo? I've observed, among programmers, that they tend to know a lot about that stuff, so I'm wondering what is the connection between an affinity for gear and being a great programmer.

Adrian: Ah, I've known people [on] both sides of that. Definitely there are those who amaze you with their knowledge of latest graphics boards and processors and numbers and—

Ed: Right.

Adrian: Also some esoteric numbers, not just basic CPU speeds and things like that...[they] are very much into various kinds of gadgets, etc., and I also know some people who are almost quite disinterested, and I actually fall probably somewhat in that category. I like using hardware, but for me, the fascination is in the art of writing software, rather than the actual chip sets and things themselves.

Ed: Right.

Adrian: At the time I need something new, I would go and investigate it and get the appropriate thing, but I don't follow it all the time, just for interest's sake. I have a good entourage of gadgets with me on this trip. So, maybe I've got my iPod and I've got my Webcam and I've got the headset for the Skype calls and I've got my little PDA with me, and having said that "I'm not interested," well, compared to the average person, I've got quite a set of things that end up being dragged around.

Business

Ed: How important is having an entrepreneurial bent or having business acumen in terms of career maintenance and professional programmer career maintenance?

Adrian: Pretty important, actually. It was always a great tension, and still is. I remember inside IBM—and you'd see it probably all over the place—"How far can you progress just being a really good programmer?"

Ed: Right.

Adrian: And that's always one of these classic questions. And for a few very exceptional individuals—but probably the percentage is an incredibly tiny one—simply being an outstanding programmer will get you an incredibly long way. But for most people, that's actually not true. Certainly for me, beyond just that individual being a great programmer, what really matters at the next level is can that person actually make a really great team, because an individual on their own is only so good which means that you can start thinking about things like their communication skills and all the rest of it. Actually [these] are very important as you progress through the ranks: "Well, you can't keep programming if you want to get to level X or Y."

In a sense, that is regrettable. I was probably unique at my level [at IBM] in the amount of programming I was still doing. But I really think if you—in any company of any size—understand and have an appreciation of the interplay between business and technology and how technology decisions impact your options in business, and vice versa, that's a really important space to have a grasp on. And in general, people who can understand that, I find, tend to progress faster and further than people who can't or who are just not interested.

I know many people who wish that weren't true, but actually in the cold light of day, in the real world, it is actually true.

Ed: You're in a CTO role now—that's pretty advanced stuff. But let's say, for some reason, you can't do IT anymore. Do you have a plan B? What is it?

Adrian: Great question. I don't have a serious [plan B]. Occasionally, I'll go, "I'm getting tired of this…I should do something like…" and the job that I've come back to is I should just be a forest ranger. I could like that. So [it's] outside and probably isn't confined to hours, but I always imagine it is, and like working in a different environment—I bet I could enjoy something like that. And if I had to retrain again, would I go for another high-powered professional career thing? I probably wouldn't at this point in time. I'd do something a bit more relaxed.

Ed: Your existing investment strategy would allow you to take that pay cut?

Adrian: It would be nice, wouldn't it?

Ed: Let's assume that you're not able to take the pay cut? So then what? What would you like to do?

Adrian: What would I do then?

Ed: Because, obviously, forest rangers don't make as much as high-powered computer programmers.

Adrian: There's a pretty significant difference in the income there. Yeah. I don't know what would be interesting. One of the things I've always hankered after…it would be a pay cut, but not so severely—would be to try and take up a research post in an academic institution. That's definitely something that appeals to me.

Not retire, that's not the right word, because it's damn hard work in academia, too, but change pace and get something that's a bit more reflective, etc., that would be interesting to me. The other thing I would probably do is start my own small company, just a local area company—that would be interesting, just to run a business.

Ed: Another reason some of us have to choose a non-IT plan B is outsourcing. Are you worried about outsourcing? A lot of people seem to be worried about it.

Adrian: Yeah, you see that, you see the concern around. And actually, I certainly witnessed an increase in it, as many of us have, and now I get to travel around, meet different clients and different countries and things. You can see that some sectors and segments it's affecting pretty aggressively. For example, when I was in the Netherlands, it was a real major, major topic, and not just that the system integrator type organizations were starting to do it, but their clients were *demanding* that they do it. It was really interesting to see. There's a shift there. I certainly don't buy this story; you see it less now, but we used to placate ourselves with this idea that, well, obviously, the offshore programmers are an inferior….

Ed: Oh, yeah, that's not true.

Adrian: Right. There are some really, really smart individuals. So, I don't believe that ["inferior" argument]. I do believe and have seen that they don't always have the process, maturity, and experience, but they're getting it. So, in that sense, off-shoring is changing things and there isn't much we can do about that. The roles whereby you need to be close to the client, of course, they are harder to off-shore.

If you can put yourselves in those roles that have client interaction, you're less likely to be vulnerable. And the other thing you've got [to realize] is [that] this is gonna change over time. It will shift, but where you've created the development lab for the critical mass of people, because moving something like that is a huge effort because it's not the physical facilities, it's the collective expertise that is that culture and set of people, and it's really hard to shift. But I would say I'm not worried about it. I don't lose sleep over it. I accept it. It's an inevitable thing that's happening in the industry, and good ideas are gonna come out, but if you've got innovative stuff and a good story and you're moving forward—in particular, the kind of things I'm doing—then you compete, essentially, globally anyway, and this is more competition. Well, great, bring it on.

Career Tip

Stay close to the customer.

Ed: Well, assuming IT is still a vibrant field when your kids are older, would you advise them to go into IT?

Adrian: I would say, yeah, I would be perfectly happy if my son ever wanted to go into IT, and [did] it because [he loved] the problem solving and the challenges. Don't do it because you think you're gonna make money. All the salaries are good in that sense. Maybe they won't be by then. I wouldn't say do it for that reason. And then [love] the intellectual challenge. And get prepared to cope with the backlash. Everything changes every few years, because it's different from other environments. Well, the whole society has changed in that way, but it's not as radical as it used to be.

Personal

Ed: It's a lot of work to juggle career, career maintenance, and family life. How do you deal with work-life balance?

Adrian: Goes in seasons. It's always been something that's actually fairly important to me, so I do manage to actually not work the majority of most weekends, which sounds— maybe that sounds a terrible thing to some people [that I don't work]—but to me, that sounds quite good.

Ed: That's what I'm going to tell my readers.

Adrian: And, if it goes into some evenings, especially with the time zones, it has to go into some evenings, but I do protect that time. I'm quite conscious of it.

One of the other things I do that really has worked for me—and this I can say over the years, I can really tell when I've been doing this and when I haven't, and I'm much more effective when I do—I try to stop in the middle of the day and get some exercise. For many years, it was running. At the moment, I'm cycling. I don't even really think it matters what it is, but it's a break in the middle of a working day. It actually works best for me when it is the middle of the working day, when I'm forced to get away from the computer, away from the keyboard, all I can do in the middle of running or whatever else I'm doing is think about those problems and what I'm going to do when I can get back to the desk. And that forced thinking time, sometimes it's conscious; I'm actually actively thinking about it. Sometimes, it's more subconscious. I find that really effective, not just to sit in front of the keyboard and the screen the whole time, but being forced to come away, to think about the right approach, to get a little bit more reflection on it, then come back and do whatever it is. And when I consistently get that time in the middle of the day, I think I'm much more effective. Now maybe that's because I'm fitter, too, but I also think I'm better, so that's also a part of the work/life balance. I'm doing something that matters to me, and I'm making time for it in the middle of the day.

Ed: Well, okay, but what I'm looking for is, when you're on weekends and you're home with your kids—you have kids, right?

Adrian: Yep. I do. Yep, two kids.

Ed: How do you avoid going to work in your head? You mentioned when you're running, you're thinking about these work problems. Personally, I have trouble with this. I have trouble putting the work stuff aside so that I can be fully present with my kids. Is that a problem for you, or do you…

Adrian: Sometimes, it is. Actually, I'll tell you when it's worse for me is when I'm coding. When I'm actually writing code, that's one thing that really consumes me, and I'm just, "Oh, I've got to do this now." And then I am probably most easily pulled back to it. But outside of that, when I'm working in my house, I'm quite strict about the parts of my house I work in, so only in the room that's earmarked as the office.

If I want to surf on the Internet on the weekend, I do not go to the office. We actually have a family computer that's somewhere else that I will use.

That door [to the office] gets shut at the weekend, and I try not to go in. I'm not perfect, but I do try.

Ed: It's really hard.

> ▶ **Observation** ◀
>
> Kohsuke Kawaguchi, on page 180, shares that he came up with the same solution to avoid going to work in one's head.

Adrian: And, once you're out doing an activity with the kids and things, it's okay. When you're in the home and in the evenings, you get tempted.

Ed: Yes. Okay. Well, another follow-up question: What is the relationship between success as a software developer and one's home life? If you have a miserable home life, are you going to be a miserable software developer?

Adrian: Huh, interesting one, [let me] try and think back over a few examples. Most of the people who stand out to me as really very, very good and effective at their jobs as software developers, which is more than, of course, just coding, have an acceptable, if not a good home life. Now, maybe I don't know that many people who have a terribly wrecked home life. I'm sure I could think of a few, but I actually think that you can only cope with a limited amount of stress and difficult-to-deal-with mental situations at that one point in time. And there's inevitably a drain on you and on your creative processes. If you're having to fight emotional and other battles in the house…I know it would make me less effective. Everyone's different, of course, but you don't want to be paying that tax to perform at your best. And given that there are enough programmers out there, if you want to rise to the top, you're probably going to have to be performing close to your best, so try and avoid that tax.

CHAPTER 3

The Java Posse

Fact Sheet

The Java Posse: Tor Norbye, Joe Nuxoll, Carl Quinn, and Dick Wall

Rock Star Programmer Credentials: "The Java Posse" is the most popular weekly Java technology podcast on the Internet. Each of the members is a rock star in his own right.

Name: Torbjorn Norbye
Country of Birth: Norway
Marital Status: Married
Degree: Master's of Computer Science, Stanford University 1995
Years as an IT Professional: 11
Role: Senior Staff Engineer at Sun Microsystems

Name: Joe Nuxoll
Date of Birth: June 1971
City of Birth: Seattle, WA
Birth Order: Sixth of nine
Marital Status: Single
Number of Kids: None
Degree: B.S. in Engineering Physics with emphasis on electronics, Santa Clara University, 1993.
Years as an IT Professional: 14
Role: Software architect and manager, Apple, Inc.

Name: Carl Quinn
Date of Birth: June 1963
City of Birth: San Rafael, CA
Birth Order: First of two
Marital Status: Married
Number of Kids: Two
Degree: B.S. in Computer Science, Santa Clara University, 1985
Number of generations in your ancestry (including yourself) that graduated from college: Two
Years as an IT Professional: 28
Role: Technical lead at Google

Name: Dick Wall
Country of Birth: United Kingdom
Marital Status: Married
Degree: B.S. in Computer Systems Engineering 1991, Masters in Computer Science 1992, University of Kent at Canterbury
Number of generations in your ancestry (including yourself) that graduated from college: Two
Years as an IT Professional: 15
Role: Software Engineer at Google

Introduction

Since their first podcast, "The Java Posse" has been among the most popular weekly Java technology podcasts, with per-episode listener numbers regularly in the mid-thousands. Throughout most of 2003, I had the good fortune to work closely in a software development capacity with all of the Java Posse members, before they were so named. They all came together to work on Sun's Java Studio Creator rapid Web application development tool. While Carl and Joe had worked together before at Borland, this was the first time all four had met. Dick came on to the project as a beta tester of Java Studio Creator for his then-employer Siemens. At the heart of Java Studio Creator (also referred to in this chapter as just "Creator") is JavaServer Faces technology, on which I had a development leadership role at the time.

From the outset, the Creator project was deliberately run by Sun as a skunk works endeavor. It had a fun code name ("Rave"), a team programming room ("The Rave Room"), and an uncommonly large hardware budget (for Sun) that allowed all the developers to get the best laptops on the market at that time. The project management team wanted to create an esprit de corps similar to the legendary Macintosh team. They succeeded, but the team stopped short of flying a pirate flag over their building, as the original Mac team had done in September 1983. Many of the developers did, however, use the aforementioned hardware budget to buy newly introduced Titanium Mac PowerBooks as their development machines.

I believe the management style for Project Rave definitely contributed to making the individuals who would later form the Java Posse into rock star programmers. After successfully shipping Creator, the team began to disperse, as often happens with skunk works–type projects, but the four members of the Java Posse remained in contact as they went their separate ways on their career paths. Around this time, podcasting began to take off, and there were already several technology-related podcasts on the Internet. Since the four of them would regularly get together and talk Java anyway, they thought, "Why not make a podcast out of it?" The popularity of the Java Posse began to grow, to the point where they had their own conference in Crested Butte, Colorado, in early 2007. I sat down with the Posse during JavaOne 2007.

> **Observation**
>
> This just goes to show the power of positive thought and visualization. If you think you are a rock star programmer (or if your management treats you like one) and you have the skills to go along with it, you will be.

> **Observation**
>
> Keeping in touch with co-workers whose skills you highly esteem is a good career move. It helps to continue to work together as a team, say on a podcast or open-source development effort.

Soft Skills, Part 1

Ed: Listeners come to "The Java Posse" to learn what's new and hot in Java technology. They want to know the trends and they want to stay current. How do *you* stay current so that you can feel confident you're giving your listeners what they're looking for?

Dick: You get to a certain point where you're tracking the news every week and you can start to see the ebb and flow of trends and that's a tremendous place to be. Obviously, there are easy things, if a story is repeated loads of different places, then it means two things: either it's a really interesting story or there's been this absolutely [huge] PR blitz. You can tell them apart pretty easily. But you can start to see related stories and…connections between things that really indicate where the interest is lying.

One of the predictions we made coming into [JavaOne 2007] was that phones and mobile devices would be a big thing this year, and I think that's because there's this groundswell of all sorts of stories that are happening around that area. It seemed to be where a bunch of things were heading. Some of that could be because there're leaks and stuff coming out. Another possibility, though, is that it's a consumer-driven thing and people are asking for it, so the smart companies are listening and saying, "Okay, this is where we need to go next."

Ed: Dick, I think the problem of "staying current" actually has something to do with the formation of the Java Posse itself, right?

Dick: I started to podcast because I was actually looking for a way to stay better informed by finding a podcast about Java. And I couldn't find one out there that suited what I needed. So I decided maybe it was a good thing for me to start one instead. And so that's when I started just gathering news items there. That's where it came from. And that process got refined over time.

Ed: Okay. So before that, how would you do it—before you were doing the podcast?

Dick: Before I was doing the podcast, it would be a lot of Internet surfing. I had favorite sites that I went to. Actually, to be honest, it was the same way that I do it for the podcast, just less exhaustive. There were a few sites that I followed, stuff that I'd read. I was getting sent the *Java Developer's Journal* in electronic form. And I'd keep an eye on that. And some of the Oracle magazines, things like that. Just reading up…on what was going on.

Ed: So was there ever a time—and this is probably a personality question— when it felt like a drag? Where you said to yourself, "Ugh. I'm tired of reading news. I really just want to get some work done." And you tuned out? Was there any period when you had tuned out for any length of time?

Dick: Not before I started doing the podcast, certainly. I only did it when I felt like finding out new stuff. And I guess I'm just a curious guy anyway. So it was easy. Quite often, I'd just sit down at home and grab a magazine or something and start leafing through it, looking at what was going on.

Ed: Right. Okay. Do you have a structure for how you approach things, how you do your searching now?

Dick: Oh, how I do them now? Yes, very much. It's a lot more structured now. And it's like a discipline. It's not a drag. But it is definitely more like a job than a quest at this point. I still enjoy doing it. But it's a much more structured thing. So really, it all evolves around a collection of Really Simple Syndication (RSS) feeds.

You get probably about 150 to 200 articles a day through the various feeds that I've got. And really, the trick is just whittling them down to a few interesting stories. That's the thing. There's a lot of information coming in, and you can skip past most of it very quickly. I pick up maybe four or five stories a day, on average.

Ed: What feed reader do you use?

Dick: I use Google Reader. I used to use Bloglines when it was better than Google Reader. And then Google started improving their reader like crazy. And I tried

Dick Wall's RSS Feeds

These are Dick Wall's RSS feeds for staying current. The most current copy of this list is at http://javaposse .googlegroups.com/web/google-reader-subscriptions.xml:

- www.cafeaulait.org/today.rss
- http://digg.com/rss/indexprogramming.xml
- http://digg.com/rss_search?search=java&area=all&type =both&age=all
- www.eclipse.org/eclipsenews.rss
- www.eclipse.org/home/eclipsenews.rss
- www.eclipsezone.com/forumRSS/18112.xml
- http://weblogs.java.net/blog/editors/index.rdf
- www.developer.com/icom_includes/feeds/special/ dev-java-5.xml
- http://developers.sun.com/rss/creator.xml
- http://today.java.net/pub/q/news_rss?x-ver=1.0
- http://weblogs.java.net/pub/q/weblogs_rss?x-ver=1.0
- http://radio.javaranch.com/rss.xml
- www.netbeans.org/rss-091.xml
- www.theserverside.com/rss/theserverside-1.0.rdf
- http://blogs.sun.com/theaquarium/feed/entries/rss
- http://blogs.sun.com/tor/feed/entries/rss
- www.frappr.com/?a=rss&gname=javaposse
- www.joelonsoftware.com/rss.xml
- http://new.linuxjournal.com/node/feed
- http://rss.slashdot.org/Newsforge/ newsforgeNewsforge
- http://rss.slashdot.org/slashdot/eqWf
- http://feeds.feedburner.com/javaposse
- http://groups.google.com/group/javaposse/feed/ atom_v1_0_msgs.xml?num=50

it various times. Then one day I tried it. And it was so much better. I stick with Google now.

Ed: You sit down and read through the day's news. So everything you get comes through RSS?

Dick: Not everything, there are all sorts of different sources. So I can find something just from browsing around the Internet, which is part of my job, day in and day out—doing research, finding new goals, and finding things on the Internet. And so if I bump into something there, I'll make a note of it. It can come from talking to other engineers a lot of times. [There are] all sorts of different sources. After a while, you get a second or a third eye, if you like, to these kinds of things. Every so often, somebody would say something. And as well as internalizing what they've said, you suddenly think, "You know that might make a pretty good discussion topic for the next podcast or something like that."

Ed: I observe that when you just read through regular, non-computer news, it doesn't matter what outlet you're at—you always can see the same few stories. No matter if it's NPR, BBC, Deutsche Welle, CNN, etc. All around, they're always showing the same stuff. Does technology news suffer from that problem as well?

Dick: It does. So actually, I think that the saving grace is that you see attempts by people to do that—to broadcast the story—in order to get press coverage and stuff like that. But when they do, it's pretty much always really obvious.

It's one of those things in which all the wording will be extremely similar or the same. And you can tell that someone's had a press release. And they're just taking it and altering the words a little bit and putting it straight back out there. And so the trends really stand out—because half of my feeds are not really big sites. There's a whole bunch of them that are smaller blogs and things that are not really directly related to Java even. One of my best sources for stories is actually a Digg (www.digg .com) search that I do on the word "Java." And that picks up anything that seems connected, even if it's only got a few Diggs. It's stuff that doesn't get noticed by the big guys a lot of the time.

Ed: Your process, then, is to look through the RSS feeds and then do your Digg search?

Dick: Yeah. The Digg search is one of the RSS feeds. It just shows up in there. And I really like the fact that all of my news…I've set it up so that all of the articles that I get from all the different sources get lumped into one big pot. Unless I look for it, I don't see which organization or feed they're coming from. I really like that. Because it stops me from prejudging a lot of the stories [based] on the source.

Ed: Right. It saves you from domain-ism.

Dick: Right. It's not that I ignore the source when it comes to looking at the actual story. If it's something that I think, "Well, is this really an interesting story?" *then* I look at the source and say, "Well, how credible is it?" But if the initial story doesn't catch my interest—I'm not saying, "Okay. This is from Slashdot, so I should really pay attention to it. And this is from some random guy's blog, and I probably don't need to pay as much attention to it." I try and treat all the stories as equal on the first pass through—to make the cut for [further investigation]. The feeds are only the start.

Ed: So is it fair to say that being proficient at using Web searching is a fundamental skill?

Dick: Binary search terms and groupings of words and things like that… when you're really trying to narrow down a particular site of items or to find out more information on a story—because a big story will get dug into quite a lot, usually in honing sessions. All of the stories that we do go to our "Main Stories" section on the podcast. They get a lot more research than just digging into the one story.

Ed: Okay. So you'll get a topic. And then you'll go into Google and then just use your subtleties of Google search manipulation?

Dick: Right. Exactly. And there are all sorts of things, from knowing the difference between a Google news search versus a Google Web search, through to things like eliminating words that are showing up that you don't want. So if BellSouth or Verizon or somebody has been in the news for something to do with Java, but they've also been in the news for something much bigger just recently, then you'll try and eliminate the stories by the other keywords from the ones that you're interested in. There are lots of tricks like that.

Ed: Those are some good search productivity tips. Staying with productivity, who was the most productive programmer you ever worked with? What was it about them that made them that way? Were they just cranking out lots of code? Did they get things done far faster than everyone else? How could you tell that they were genuinely more productive rather than just creating the illusion of productivity?

Tor: I want to start. It's actually Mr. Quinn.

Ed: Why?

Tor: I haven't seen someone before who was so relaxed, yet at the same time so productive. I felt like the code was really very clean. Plus, I liked his coding style.

Joe: I'm thinking [it's] somewhere between these two guys [Tor and Carl]…but also I recall another one [comparable] to you guys. You give him anything, and he turns around and hands it back to you the next day, "Here, is this what you meant?" You respond, "Yes, plus 10."

Ed: Why was he like that? What was it about him?

Joe: Well, he's the first guy I hired every time I went and did a startup. He was my right-hand man, just really clean communication between us. So we would talk about something, we'd whiteboard it. I would usually be doing the front-end part of it—he'd be doing the back end—but we would walk away and come back, and they would perfectly join. I think it was just because we had a very like mind and he's obsessive-compulsive.

> **Career Tip**
>
> I've seen several examples of this "bringing your crew with you to a new job" thing. If you can get into one of these crews or, better yet, become the leader of one, you'll be in a good place.

Tor: And on the Creator team, Joe and Carl and I worked extremely well together, but Joe wasn't doing more of the coding, more on the application programming interface (API) side. He would add one class [laughing], so that's why it doesn't apply to programming. But that collaboration, I think, was the best part of it.

Joe: It was fun. Sometimes I felt like I wasn't doing enough stuff, but I felt like these guys had it so well covered that I would just keep my head above the clouds and explain, "This is what it should feel like," and you guys would make it real.

Tor: That feeling of communicating—because you were just saying you communicated well with this guy Ryder—I felt that was one of those things where you could go to a meeting, you could talk, and everyone was on the same page, and it would just happen. I've had other times where I've just communicated…thought I was exceedingly clear…then you get something and you go, "Which meeting was this?"

I tried to figure out what it was I was so productive about, and I think one of the ingredients was the mixture of having a couple of in-office days and a lot of home time. A lot of the best times we worked were in the evenings. That's not so great for family life.

Carl: We were on IRC (Internet Relay Chat—an early, yet very effective, collaborative instant-messaging facility), talking all the time.

Tor: There was something about that. It was almost like social networking. You join that channel, and you're part of a community suddenly.

Dick: I don't think I've got any one answer, because I think I work with a lot of productive people who are productive in different areas. I just got to know what they were really good at and I just went to them when I needed something from a particular area. So I've never managed and I've never particularly wanted to manage people, so it would always be I'd end up doing a fair amount of work, and I'd just pull in people as I needed to help me there. I tended to find that the people I brought in, mostly I brought in because I found they had good instincts for a particular thing.

I'm thinking actually of my friend, Tim, at New Energy [a Siemens subsidiary]. He's probably the best instinctive problem-solving [role] model, if I had a word for it. He was extremely good. He wasn't a code monkey. He wasn't someone who could just bash out loads of code, but he could disassemble a problem and come up with an object model and extremely intricate design. You would get a sense of rightness about it before you even started coding. You would know that you weren't going to get in here and get screwed up halfway through by something he had forgotten. He was just extremely good at that. I think that would be my answer there. I think one of the reasons I answered the question like that is…productivity for me doesn't necessarily translate to loads of code.

Tor: I think maybe the key lesson I remember: Carl was really particular about spending time on choosing the right name [for code constructs such as classes and variables]. I think that actually is really a good attribute that I, hopefully, have picked up, that actually it is worthwhile to sit there and think about… "This is the wrong name for this." You put effort into what you want to name it and if you realize—if you come up with a better name later—even if the first one wasn't bad, you change it.

> **Career Tip**
>
> Take time to be aware of how much (or little) you are learning from your co-workers. Is it worth sticking around in that job if you're not picking up good things?

Joe: We were hyper-anal about naming [on Creator].

Tor: That's right. I think that actually is an attribute of good designers—that you really care about [naming]…it's not just a symbol…

Joe: It's how you think about it.

Tor: Because you are really tying it to the real world. You're modeling something, and that's important, and that goes all the way down to camelCase conventions, everything—it's all part of "The code must be pretty."

Ed: I think sustained productivity, as a habit, is aided by an understanding of the industry as a whole. How do you break down the computer software industry and the technology industry? Where are the segments?

Joe: Well, I can definitely take a swat at it. There are platform vendors. Those are your operating system folks, your—I think databases can count as a platform—so you have your Oracles, your Microsofts, your Suns, your community folks doing things like Linux. You've got Apple doing OS X, so there're platform vendors that try to build a base, the baseboard of the ship, in order to go build stuff on.

Dick: And then I think on top of that you start getting the framework providers, whether they're companies or whether they're for-profit or whether they're free.

I guess, depending on your definition of platform, I would class something like Ruby on Rails as a different kind of platform than Oracle. Oracle is there to serve as a database. Ruby on Rails is more of a solution. It's a more customized solution for a particular set of problems, and then beyond that you get into completely custom solutions…the IBMs and the [consultants] that swarm in and make things happen and come up with ideal solutions, and I think also what's interesting is that those lines are starting to blur a bit now, and people are talking about putting enterprise stacks on the hardware, ready to roll, so all of them are heading towards that now.

Tor: Another way to divide it, would be the people who do software engineering for fun and then there are the people who sell the software. Then there are other people who just basically sell services.

Dick: And even beyond that, people who do it just because they have a need for something. They're not even trying to think of selling something. They have a particular problem to solve. They may be completely focused on the problem domain, for instance.

Tor: Well, that would be the in-house. You're just building something for yourself. You're never gonna sell it. You have a salary, and you're spending those salary hours.

Joe: There's also a whole huge class of the ma-and-pa shops, just software shops that build things. I'm thinking on the Mac platform there's Unison and Coda [from Panic Inc.]—

Tor: That would be the independent software vendors (ISVs). That would be people who build software for profit. They sell it.

Joe: Yeah, and shrink-wrap things that either solve a particular problem or a suite of things. Yeah, there are the Adobe guys. They build a bunch of really cool pieces of software that solve specific problems. They don't own a platform. Well, they do actually now, so excuse that. They have a whole middleware flash and whatnot platform.

Tor: Yeah, I was basically not doing the "middleware, platform, graphical user interface (GUI)" thing. I was just basically saying some people do it for fun, and there are some people who do it to sell it, and there are people who basically just get paid to mess with it, such as the service consultants, and it seems like the business model's really changing a lot around those lines right now, whereas we're always gonna have user interface (UI), and we're always gonna have servers.

Ed: How important is it to let your analysis and understanding of the business of software inform where you invest your time stewarding your skill set, minding your career? How much does the business world impact the decisions you make in doing that?

Joe: So, for me, massively. You identify new tech that's coming out…go to JavaOne, see the latest stuff, envision "Where is that gonna go? What can come out of that?" Then you start sniffing companies that are gonna be leveraging that in interesting ways, and then you start planning meetings for potential moves.

Dick: My answer would be [that] a lot of the time I'm just messing around with this stuff on my own. Frankly, I don't care about the business side of it. In that case, it's whether it interests me or not. At some point, I may look at it and say to myself, "This might fit in with something I'm doing at work right now," and that's when that would start to take over, but I just like to learn a lot of stuff so I can come at it from a different angle. That's probably why I'm not holding my breath to become really, really rich or retire at 45, I guess, but you never know.

Carl: I guess a lot of times you see some kind of technology that's exciting, because it can do stuff and accomplish things and that other people are gonna like it and they're gonna get excited about it, and you can say, "Okay, that's gonna have a few uses for everybody." The people that work with it are gonna like it. What it does for people, everybody's gonna like, and it's gonna go somewhere, so you can jump on it and ride that.

Ed: Right. That's the subtitle of the book.

Dick: Sometimes it's just a happy accident. To apply this lesson to the Posse, I got really interested in the idea and the technology behind podcasting, and I did a bunch of stuff and experimented with it before even the Javacast got started. I was just messing around with the whole idea of audio that's delivered through episodes and through RSS, and I had no idea it was gonna end up here. I've always been interested in recording, and so I think that same attitude comes up a lot in my programming, so right

Character Attribute

Curiosity.

now I'm learning JRuby, partly because I'm interested in what Tor's been working on all this time. I have no real plans to use it on anything. I'm just interested to know it and want to be able to talk about it in some meaningful way. At some point, if I decide this would really, really fit here, then that's great, but otherwise I just do what interests me.

Ed: Right. Okay. So it seems that passion plays a large role in all of us here.

Tor: For me, it's completely that. Again, I don't look at the business at all, unless…if I think it's not gonna go anywhere, then, of course not. To me, it's whether or not it's cool that matters if I want to learn it, but I think I'm also less curious than, say, Dick. I think I stay a little bit closer to home in what I do in general.

Dick: I will also say that I recognize this as a major lack in my own skill set.

I have always said I will never run a business. I would be terrible at running a business. I'd go off and chase after every cool piece of technology, and the whole place would come crumbling down around me. I would get somebody else to run the damn business—who had a clue about it, and I think that's why, like I said, I think it's really good that we've got different skills here and we bring different things into the picture, because it just wouldn't work any other way.

Ed: As a software developer, how important is it to be aware of your own ignorance?

Dick: Oh, huge, really huge, and you've got to be honest about it, too.

Ed: Tell us more.

Joe: Depends on where you are.

Tor: Well, that's one of those things that they always say—that developers, if you ask any developer, they all think their skills are above average. Everyone thinks that *they* are really good developers.

Ed: Yes, but where are all the average developers?

Tor: Well, I think that the corollary is basically the whole thing about being aware of your own ignorance. You hear people say, "Hey, I *code* HTML. I *program* in HTML." I've heard people say that. I think that most developers probably aren't aware of their own ignorance.

Ed: Is that to their own detriment?

Tor: I think so, yeah.

Carl: Yes. It's important if you're building the team. In the event you're just part of a team and you're helping to bring new people on to the team, or if you're a manager or a tech lead, and if you understand your weakness, you can figure out whom to bring in to complement you. Like Dick said, "I need people around me who understand the business side."

Dick: Well, I see no shame in saying, "I don't know."

Joe: Well, there's no shame in that.

Dick: No, there is no shame at all in that. I think it's slightly better to say, "I don't know, but I think I can find out" and go digging. The best of all is, "I don't know, but I'm gonna make damn sure I know next time somebody asks me that question."

Joe: Yeah, I think it also depends, just back to the general question of do you need to know that you don't know stuff. It depends on the team.

If you have—I'm gonna pick on Google for a minute—if you have all these people, in many cases, a lot of them get dumped in to just go work on these things— "Go figure this little piece out." There are structures—engineering organizational structures—that work where you don't need to know a lot, and it's still efficient, and it still works, as long as there's *somebody* with their head up looking above the clouds, figuring out what different pieces need to be assembled.

Tor: Okay, "Those two groups are inventing the same thing. Let's connect those two groups."

Joe: Or those groups have been carefully told, "You build this piece, and you build this piece, and this is how they fit together," but they don't necessarily have to understand the big picture if it's well worded.

Tor: I was just agreeing with that. You have to have that person who knows what's happening everywhere, because in some companies, you have these two arms that are not talking, and they're both inventing overlapping things.

Joe: Yeah, and that can be done very well, and it can be done very poorly. I don't have any specific instances, but I bet it could totally happen where a group is working on something that's a complete duplicate of what another group is working on and not even know it, until some keynote [presentation where] you both show right next to each other and didn't even know. You know, that stuff happens.

Carl: It can also happen at some companies where two people are building the same thing and management's letting them because they want them to compete.

Joe: Yes, and that happens at Google.

Tor: That might be good. If you have the manpower to do it, you might get better results that way. Maybe it'd be better if they both worked together, but maybe by not polluting each other's minds, you get two creative ways of doing it. If you put them in the room together at the beginning, they might both zero in on the same solution. I think you might get more creativity.

Carl: [At Google,] people start stuff just from their own ideas, but once they reach the point where they're really starting to get traction and consume resources, then [management] usually will look at them and say, "Okay, let's bring them together" or cut one and move people around. The one I was thinking of is D-base at Borland way back, when Phillipe [Kahn] was having the two teams, three, I think, at one point, three teams working on the new D-base for Windows, and there was just a lot of angst, because people knew it. There was a good chance that their piece was gonna get killed, so they were working frantically, and it wasn't very positive.

Joe: No, it wasn't a big enough company to do that sort of thing.

Ed: I'd like to share with you an ignorance classification scheme I read in Phillip G. Armour's "Business of Software" column in the Communications of the ACM. He calls it the Five Orders of Ignorance. Briefly, zero order ignorance is a lack of ignorance. First order ignorance is lack of knowledge. For example, I don't know how to program in Haskell, but I could learn it if I wanted to. Second order ignorance is lack of awareness; you don't know that you don't know something. One example would be a specific piece of information within a domain whose existence [of which] you are completely unaware. However, once you become aware of the domain that contains that specific information, you are well on the way to reducing the second order ignorance into first order ignorance. Third order ignorance is lack of process; you have no effective process for reducing second order ignorance to first or zero order ignorance. Fourth order ignorance is meta-ignorance; ignorance of the five orders of ignorance.

Dick: I think that—and I would base this on knowing or having been lucky enough to talk to the real, ultimate leaders in particular fields—there should be a minus one on that scale. By the time you get to leading the field, you probably know that you don't know everything about it. You're cutting the leading edge on the thing. You ask a lot of these people for a yes/no answer, they won't give you a yes/no answer. They'll give you a set of conditions where something may work or something won't work. I think when you get to that stage, you've really made it. You know you're at some level above just knowing it. You know the limit—I don't know. It's hard to say, but it's like that's when you're a real expert on a subject: when you don't know. You've gone through knowing, and you've come out the other side to not knowing it necessarily, I guess, something like that.

Tor: Right. Well, that isn't always true, right? Or maybe I haven't reached that level, because I feel like there are some things I just really know.

Dick: There probably are.

Tor: And I feel completely confident in that there is nothing in that area [I don't know].

Dick: I think maybe you can do that for very specific things, when you start going—

Tor: That's what I'm saying, yes.

Dick: —when you start going into fields like quantum physics or quantum mechanics.

Tor: No, you can't know that. Let's make it something else.

Dick: That's it. That's what I'm saying.

Ed: All right, but Tor is talking about things like linker options or let's say the Java byte codes.

Tor: Okay, I've been there to know you could be the byte code expert, maybe because you own the byte code; if you remember it wrong, then you're gonna change it to be that way because you own the freaking byte code. I just want to add one thing on ignorance, too, because this is something I discovered very late in my education that it was actually cool to ask questions, that it didn't mean you were an idiot. So once I got to that confidence level that I wasn't an idiot and I could ask questions, I just learned so much more, and then I discovered that sitting up front [in a classroom setting] also helped me a lot.

Joe: Oh, man, totally.

Tor: I actually blogged about that, because there's this old survey that shows—

Joe: I always sat right up front.

Tor: —that basically it's not just front. It's also center.
     There's, yeah, there's basically this curve. If you have a large crowd, and you present them information, then you poll people from selected [regions], you can predict the percent of what they will retain, but I didn't know that. I just discovered that, hey, I'd better sit up front, because I can—some professors you couldn't really hear what they were saying. Plus in the back, it's tempting to pull out your notebook and—in college, I actually used to "code" on paper—

Joe: Big surprise.

Tor: —because I was really bored in linear algebra and I was doing some graphical cool stuff that I wanted to think about, so I was sitting there working out the math to rotate this object. That wasn't very good for learning linear algebra, so eventually I just started really sitting up front and asking questions.

> **Character Attribute**
>
> Tor seems to be always multitasking.

Personal, Part 1

Ed: Okay, well, I have some questions around college and education, so we'll run with it, and we'll go around. What kind of student were you in college? Did you do well on tests or traditional measures of academic success? Did you have a good GPA? How much stock did you place in your GPA when you were in school, that sort of thing?

Joe: I've got a stock answer to that. I absolutely aced tests. I got 100 percent on tests, but I never did homework—which murdered my grades, so I didn't do awesome in college, but I understood everything. I paid really good attention in class and took notes on everything, and I would study really well for tests, and I would nail tests, but I couldn't do the homework.

Carl: Yeah, I was pretty much in the same category, especially for a while. All through high school and through maybe the first year of college, I didn't even have to study at all. I could just go take the test and ace the test. Then things got a little harder, and I had to focus, but I found that I like to focus on just a couple of topics at one time, a couple of subjects in school. I remember there was one time I had a particular teacher for two classes, and they were both potentially very interesting classes, but I liked one more, and I spent all my time working on the projects for that class. I got an A in that class and a C+ in the other class, and at the end of the quarter, the teacher came in and said, "How come you did so much worse in this class?" I said, "Your other class sucked up all my time, and I had nothing left." I wouldn't do the homework, or just whatever was cool, I would work on that. I would just focus on the thing I liked to do.

Dick: I think in my case I didn't do well in primary school at all. So we have a different school system in England, primary, secondary, college, and university, and in primary school, I did very poorly, just didn't apply myself at all. In secondary school, I didn't start getting interested until I specialized. There's a period you go through in your third year of secondary school when you're about 13 or 14, called options, and you start choosing what you want to do, and I started doing better after that, and when I got to college, I started doing much better.

When I got to university, I was lazy. I didn't do homework. Fortunately, the testing in England is based mostly on results from exams, so I did well enough on the exams to get through it, and I think in my case I was just—I never applied myself to anything that I wasn't interested in, and it was as simple as that. I wasn't interested. I wasn't engaged at the early levels of school at all. It wasn't until I started actually choosing my subjects that I started to get really interested in what I was learning about, and that's when I started being able to learn better, and so that's just always been the way I am. This is why I only talk about things that interest me, because that's all I'm gonna go and learn about, so I have a pretty low tolerance for things that aren't interesting, I guess, is the outcome of that.

> **Character Attribute**
>
> Each of these guys is compelled by his very nature to be passionate about work that interests him and utterly indifferent to work that does not.

Tor: I was a bad student in primary school, and in eighth grade, I had a teacher like in [the film] *Dead Poets' Society*. The teacher didn't treat us like kids, and you didn't want to let him down, which was an opposite thing [from what I was used to], and I'm very conscientious and very driven, really, by not letting people down. It's almost a problem. So things went better from that point, and in college, I did really, really well. I worked extremely hard, but I was very different, I think, from you [Joe] because I did not pay attention in class, but the way I did it was to study the night before the exam because I would just read through the math chapter or whatever, do the problems, and I would ace the test.

Joe: Did you do homework, though?

Tor: Yeah, and I did that. I did the homework, the assignments and stuff. Computer science was really easy for me.

Carl: The hardware assignments are fun, right?

Tor: That was like dessert. The problem was—and I was so jealous of all my friends in Norway who went to the engineering school, because they do engineering [exclusively]—I had to say to them, "I'm taking, let's see, Asian-American literature. I'm taking biology. I'm taking all these GE [general education classes]," and I felt like I spent all my time on these things that I didn't care about. On the other hand, I'm glad we did it, because I'm glad people are broad. I don't want people to be completely one-track minded.

Dick: Some of that stuff, though, I didn't care about at the time and I care far more about now, so I hated all of the English language stuff that I did all the way through school 'til I got to university, and when I was doing my master's thesis, I had a great tutor on that one who wouldn't let me get away with anything, and since then, I got more and more interested in language, and now I actually enjoy writing. I never knew I would.

Joe: Yeah. I did a lot of psychology and philosophy and things like that as well, which I really enjoyed just because it was a different cut at things. Helps in business, too.

Hard Skills, Part 1

Ed: Returning to the concrete technical realm, when you get a new machine, what do you have to do to it before it's useful to you?

Tor: First I inspect that it has the Apple logo on it. It's critical. I live in my terminal, so the first thing I have to do is I have to get my shell. I don't like Bash. I want Z shell. I take my ~/.zshrc file and I go in there and I make it work. I used to do that on my ~/.emacs file. I have actually completely stopped using Emacs, so that's no longer necessary.

Carl: It's funny, because I used to sit and customize my machine. It would take *days* to get it set up. I've switched machines more and more frequently. I'll upgrade machines, and it would take me too long to get it set up again, or

I go to somebody else's machine and then try to sit down on their machine. It was too weird. I just became more and more used to pretty much a standard set of tools that I could find quickly. I've got a couple of tools I would put on there.

Tor: I have a perfect knowledge of that because I'm left-handed. The first couple of years I would always go and switch the mouse, the left-handed stuff. After using so many of these computers, I eventually stopped and now I'm much more comfortable using the right hand. I don't think I could use a left-handed mouse.

Dick: Literally the first thing I do on any computer I use is change the caps-lock key to a control key. That's the absolute first thing. Then beyond that, I'm actually a Bash fan, so I'm pretty happy. Everything seems to come with Bash these days, so I just dive straight into that. OpenOffice has to go on there pretty much immediately. I love OpenOffice at this point. One of the things that really I value above everything else is stability and reliability. I can put up with a lot, but if a thing crashes, especially after I've been doing a bunch of work—

Carl: It loses your day.

Dick: Yeah, if it loses a paycheck, that annoys the crap out of me. So I put on OpenOffice, because I know it really well now and it never crashes. I don't even care what it looks like. It's just damn reliable. So that goes on there, and then I customize that a bit, control keys and key bindings and that kind of stuff.

Joe: See, I'm all UI. OpenOffice just isn't pretty enough.

Dick: See, that's just totally different for me. The functionality and the reliability are the things that I have to have, and its familiarity as well.

Ed: How strongly correlated is proficiency with tools and effectiveness as a developer?

Joe: It's huge.

Carl: It also shows people's motivation, how much time they're willing to spend to learn the tools. When people sit down at a tool that they've been using for a couple of years, this is their tool and they just don't know how half of it works. [You can see the lack of motivation.]

Carl: [Ask yourself,] is there something that you can do that would have been a little faster than what you did before or another command you could have done?

Tor: I think a good sign of a developer is someone who's always trying to optimize. I discovered this about myself. In traffic, no one I know thinks the same way about well, okay, "The traffic light pattern is going to be so and so, so I'm going to go this way and I'm coming in this direction." I have my whole neighborhood mapped in my head, the best path. Or the thing about trying to slow down with it so you can make perfect flow through the lights, not too fast. Why should I care, really, about a minute here, a minute there? It's just a mindset, I think, of always thinking of the best solution. I don't want to take [the analogy] into [software] performance, because I'm not thinking, "Oh, this is going to be faster, just shift and multiply," I don't mean that, but it's in your mind. I'm just saying, "Hey, I'm a good developer (like all developers say). I do it that way." I see it in others, too. I think the kinds of people who are like that are the people who will learn, "How can I most effectively use the tool?" If people are of the mindset, "Okay, I'm just going to open whatever this thing is and I'm going to type something into it and I'm going to drag the mouse up and find the menu… I've done it a million times before, but I'm just going to do it again." The people who don't look, "Oh, CTRL-B would do that." I haven't seen great developers really stumble with their tools.

Carl: It's also like that in any other craft, I think. You watch the guy who's a wood carver. He's using his laser saw and he's cutting these perfect miters. You know he *knows* that tool. He knows how to use it every possible way that you can saw the wood.

Joe: That's a really good analogy. Any sort of woodworker or craftsman, you damn well better know your tools, or you suck.

Tor: One thing is just knowing the key map. For example, with a Unix guy, knowing how to massage text. I have this dataset, but it can be faster. I want to put this into my source file as a list of arrays. Okay, well, I can run it through awk, and then I can use an Emacs macro instead of going in and editing by hand, etc.

Soft Skills, Part 2

Ed: Popping back to soft skills for a moment. Let's say you're on a long-running project, how do you fight the waning interest syndrome? Dick, you mentioned you can't stay committed to something you're not interested in.

Dick: I'm terrible for that.

Ed: So some of the people I've talked to in this book stated that 80 percent of what you do in your job is uninteresting. Now what would you say about that?

Joe: Get a new job.

Dick: And I have. That's really the reason I left my previous job—and it took me a long time to do that. I was stupid, and I should have done it much sooner, but it had been such a great job, and I was holding onto the idea that [something good] was just around the corner. I was getting into a real rut of just not enjoying what I was doing anymore. Eventually it sunk in, and I did that (got a new job, at Google). Like everybody says, Google has the best possible perks you can think of, but if I'm not happy with what I'm actually doing in a job, that's far more important. The rest is icing. I do a crappy job when I'm not interested in something as well. I know that.

Ed: Oftentimes in software, you're on a long-running project, a couple-of-years'-long project. How do you keep up your interest in the project so the quality stays up, because, that last 5 percent kills? So what do you do?

Joe: Innovation and delegation. I'm in a job right now where I'm not just doing technology stuff. Right now, I'm doing pure customer-facing innovation things, so it stays very fresh, because we get to just invent new ways of doing stuff, all from the user interface perspective, but I also have a team, which is a wonderful thing. So I get to go build the prototype and do the high-level thinking of how we should do this and get it to work and show a proof concept. Then I get to hand it over to a team to go execute. It's awesome.

Tor: It sounds like you've got a really good gig where you don't have to do the unglamorous part.

Joe: I do.

Tor: My thing with Creator was I went through the entire [lifetime of the project], but what kept me going was, you really get attached to the project so I felt pride in Creator. I felt ownership, so to me, the fact that now we've got six months ahead of us where we've got no new features, we're only fixing bugs, it was still cool, because I really wanted this thing to be rock solid when we shipped. I wanted to be really proud of it. That was inspiration enough. Plus, I felt some responsibility. I put these bugs in there. I probably should iron them out.

Joe: I had a really hard time with Creator, because my role with these guys in the beginning was envisioning what we could do with it and how could we push JSF (JavaServer Faces) to do the stuff we needed to do from the bigger picture to make this a great tool, and I felt like we missed by *so far* [gestures to include a wide range]. I was insanely frustrated by the thing—there was so much more to it being "great"—so I had a hard time being really satisfied. There were parts that were really cool, but it was so far from what it could have been that it was difficult for me.

Tor: I see what you're saying. To me, I just take more local pride.

Dick: In your area.

Tor: Yeah. You say, "I'm gonna add some really cool features that no one else has"—you know what I mean? So it would be a gamble to put in just stuff that I thought was really cool. That to me was just so fun.

Dick: Before we go on from there, I want to take that one about the long project that's not interesting. I actually find most phases of the project are interesting as long as I believe in the project. Debugging is interesting. Documentation can be interesting. I discovered that I like writing. Docs are not always the best thing to do, but if you're really doing it right and you're explaining something that's very complicated to someone, there's a tremendous satisfaction that comes out of it.

Ed: Not just that, but documentation is almost as important as the software itself. You could arguably say it's more important than the software itself, because if you can't understand it, no one's gonna use it...

Joe: Especially if it's a toolkit. You damn well better document it.

Dick: Here's another way of dividing up programmers. There are programmers who want to be the expert on something. They want to gather everything in, hold it in close, and say, "This is my area. No one comes near here. I rule this area." Then you get the other side of things, which is people—and I'd like to consider myself one of these—who learn stuff and pass it on. They love to share the information. Doing that is a wonderful thing because it helps. It gets other people involved in the project. It helps you transition off of the project.

> **Career Tip**
>
> Managers love when you spread the information around. There is nothing that a manager fears more than the single-point-of-failure engineer.

It's a totally beneficial thing. People who horde the stuff, they're digging their own grave.

Carl: You staked yourself down to something. You're just gonna be stuck with it forever, right, if you're the only one who understands it.

Dick: Yeah, it's great to have ownership in something, but at some time, you're gonna want to move on, and when you do, you'd better make the transition easy.

Joe: Great piece of advice: Find and train your successor. In any job anywhere, make sure you're priming a successor.

Ed: You look like you want to say something, Tor.

Tor: Yeah, this... is... hard.

Joe: Something good coming.

Tor: It's hard in two directions, right? First of all, you're saying passing on. Well, you don't really want to pass stuff on to other people unless it's something you *want* passed on to you. What we're talking about here, really, is the kind of people who can always get a new job. That's something exciting. Not everyone has that option.

Ed: Absolutely not.

Tor: It's engineers who are good.

So hopefully that is your readership, right? These are good engineers.

Ed: I would think so.

Tor: Then they have options, and I suspect you're right, because they're the kind of people who would read this book, so I think the trick is to not take over someone else's turds, right?

Joe: Oh, yeah, yeah, yeah, unless they're not turds. What if they're gems?

Dick: What if they're great? What if I get hired to work on something that I'm extremely interested in?

Tor: No, that's perfect. That's a great situation.

Dick: The guy has done two or three years of his life: "I love doing this, but I'm ready to move on." I say, "Gimme, Gimme, Gimme. I want this."

Tor: So that gets me to the other part: what if your successor murders your baby?

Carl: Let it go, Tor. You've got to let it go.

Tor: The answer is to unsubscribe yourself—

Joe: This happened to Tor, just so you know.

Tor: from the commit alias. Stop reading the commits, and let it go.

Joe: Let it go.

Tor: It's very hard, because you put a lot of thought into something, and then you have someone who basically doesn't appreciate it, and basically he says, "Well, I think I know what this does. Rip. Rip. Rip. Put in something different," which breaks it in all these other ways. Let's say you've really thought about something, and you have a really clean performance idea of how this is gonna work, and let's say you've added assertions all over the code. This person says, "Well, I'm just gonna put logging in instead," which is just fundamentally different from assertions.

Ed: Absolutely.

Tor: It's a different thing, totally, and it's very hard to sit back and go, "Okay, go ahead."

Joe: Well, that's just bad software engineering.

Tor: That's the point I'm making.

Ed: If you don't understand the difference between assertions and logging—

Tor: No, but that's my point here about successors. This is your baby.

Joe: You have to find the right successor.

Tor: You have to find a successor that is not—

Carl: You have to find one that's either just really good and thinks like you and you'd be happy with or somebody who's open minded and will at least take the time to understand where you were going with stuff.

Tor: And having someone who takes the attitude of, "I know what this is all about," that's tricky, so…I've handed off other pieces of software, and it's been fine. This was particularly tricky for me, because I do read lots of CVS commits, not just for this, but in all kinds of areas. I just read CVS commits a lot. I like to know what's going on, and so I obviously read CVS commits to my old code. It's very hard to sit back and see stuff being done to it.

Joe: We've had to go walk him out of the building.

Dick: I've read this just recently. Somebody defined stress as basically having too much work and having too little control over how it's carried out. Those are the two things that lead to stress. It's okay to have a lot of work facing you, but if you have no control to change how it's doing, what that translates to in my mind is, if you are gonna leave a project behind, you've got to be prepared to leave it behind. You can't impose your will on the person coming in behind you. That's not fair. Choose someone you think is gonna do a good job, but you can't stand over them and say, "You're gonna have to use these tools and do it this way."

Carl: You can mentor them for a while—

Dick: Yeah, yeah.

Carl:—through the transition. It's recommended.

Tor: I think the ideal situation would be that person would have an appreciation for what's there, try to understand it, and when there's code they don't get, they talk to you or [ask] "Why was this done this way?" as opposed to somebody who basically never asks you anything and just break[s] it.

Ed: Coming back to the waning interest syndrome, have you ever had to fight it while producing the podcast? I'm curious about how you guys avoid that. You've been doing it for several years now. How do you keep it fresh? How do you stay committed to doing it all this time?

Dick: We seem to just come up with new stuff to try, I think.

Tor: For me, it's that I have a good time whenever we hang out.

Dick: That's a huge part of it.

Carl: If we get together and drank beers and talked about Java once a week, that's the stuff.

Dick: That's what it is.

Tor: It's our job is to talk about what we're interested in. That's our job. Well, if I don't care—but seriously, it's pretty much always fun to talk about the news.

Dick: It's never seemed like a grind.

Joe: Sometimes it is for me. These guys all know this about me. I'm less deeply involved in the low-level tech of Java now, so I'll be in a discussion— a lot of times we'll get into an esoteric thing, and I say, "Okay, I don't [care too much about this]"—then we'll get on to something I'm interested in, and I'll talk about that. It seems to work out.

Carl: We shake things up…"Oh, let's do a conference."

Dick: This year [2007] has been brilliant for that. We've tried all sorts of different things.

Tor: I think also—at least for me, the recognition is motivation. The fact that we have all these people responding and who like it, it's very exciting. Maybe we would do it if we had five listeners, because it is fun, but the fact is that it is between 5,000 and 10,000—and my impression is that the listeners we have are really quite amazing. The kind of people who want to regularly listen for an hour to "The Java Posse" usually are really into it. So we get amazing feedback, and that to me is inspiring. People enjoy it; I want to keep going.

Dick: Just to pull a couple of examples out, finding out that [core Java contributors] Neil Gafter and Mark Reinhold both listen to the show was just amazing.

Carl: Sometimes when you're sitting there, when we're getting ready to do a podcast and we're all busy and trying to get some news together, you want to say, "Let's just skip this week." It's really easy to do that, but when you start to think about it, the users are going to miss it; they're going to be sad.

Dick: Yeah, it's the responsibility aspect, definitely.

Carl: Then once we get going, it's great. It helps keep us motivated, like somebody having an exercise partner keeps you motivated to show up every day.

Joe: It's nice if you have four people, too. On occasion, somebody has to miss.

Dick: That's understood. I've been clear about this from the start. I don't want any of us to ever feel like it's something we've got to do. It's one of those things, the moment you start feeling that, you start feeling trapped and you resent it and you start hating it, and that's just bad stuff.

Hard Skills, Part 2

Ed: Let's get technical. Dick, I know you love going after a juicy bug. What is your process for attacking hard-to-find and hard-to-fix bugs?

Dick: I love that every time because it expands your mode of thinking to have to step back and look at it from a progressively higher place. You start right in at the bug and you can't see anything, so you step out to the next level. The really good ones get you stepping out to the point where you are [thinking], "This can't possibly happen. I can't understand how this can be the case," and you learn something from it. You're stepping out, stepping out, stepping out. It's something completely crazy in left field.

Joe: I've got one from a week ago that is unbelievable which I'll share with you in a minute.

Dick: I like it because—and it's the same reason I like reading Stephen King novels and things like that—it takes me to a place I haven't been before, thought-wise, and you can feel the boundaries in your mind being broken down by something like that, so you come further and further out. IT bugs, they're okay, but they don't expand your mind. The really hard ones, they're the ones that teach you something, and that's [the] goal.

Carl: I think my dad taught me how to debug when I was a kid. It was working on cars or working on other things around the house that were broken. You call it troubleshooting, and maybe that's a little bit different, but I think it's really good to learn how to troubleshoot. You're dividing and conquering.

Ed: So what's your process?

Carl: You just start to reduce the problem space until you can narrow it down, eliminating possibilities by substituting known good things, swapping out a part, putting it in—okay, that didn't fix it; the old part probably wasn't bad; put it back; dividing and conquering, to just narrow down what the problem might be. When you get close, then you can start to focus in on it.

Tor: The good part is when there're two broken parts, because that's when [things really get hairy].

Carl: You have to understand this logic and understand how the system works so that you can poke around at it.

Joe: Let me give a fun one on this. So this is just a couple of weeks ago. Firefox 1.5—Mac and PC—if you launch the app for the first time, so it's first time in memory, if you use the scroll wheel or the two-finger [Mac OS X laptop-specific way to scroll the page] first as your first scrolling interaction, JavaScript scroll events don't fire for the rest of the life of that session no matter how many windows, how many pages. It was really tricky to figure out what the heck was going on, but the way we solved it was, open your mind, think, you are the native code implementing this. You know it's a cross-platform browser, so there's some layer that's bootstrapping the native event system, the native toolkit.

If you started thinking, "Why would the scroll event stop being fired?" the thought came—maybe it's during initialization. The way it's bootstrapping itself is when first events come through; it sets up a code path. So sure enough, if you open up Firefox 1.5, and you click and the first thing you do is scroll by clicking and dragging the thing, it works perfect. So the bootstrap of that native event goes through a different code path than if it gets hit by something else. It was just a matter of, okay, stop, back up. What the hell could possibly be causing this, and we figured it out.

Carl: Divide and conquer is actually one of the most efficient ways of narrowing down the problem. If you sit there and try to microscope in, right from the very beginning, you'd be microscoping all over the entire system and you would waste lots of time. But if you can divide and conquer, replacing pieces and saying, "It only happens in this browser and not that one, only with this version but not that version, or this file but not that," as small as you can.

Tor: I haven't had hard bugs that you guys have had. If I can reproduce a problem, it always seems to be easy. Again, I'm not working on Solaris kernel. I imagine those kinds of things are really tricky, when you had an application running for six hours and something crashes—who knows?

It's probably [that] they got some weird patch on their system that is making Java freak out, something really horrible like that. We used to have a bug in Creator [in which] whenever you ran Creator, your floppy drive light would come on and it would make a humming sound. It was really strange. It was something weird. Actually, it would do something in Java file IO. It was actually like walking up the path, and it actually would touch the drive letter somehow on Windows. Those are the kinds of bugs…you don't have a Windows machine, you don't have the right locale, you're not running with a German keyboard or something, that's when it's really tricky. Those are the bugs that just sit [in the queue].

Joe: So here's another example, another category of bug. [Apple has some software that] is a vast system, thousands of computers and lots of different processes running different parts. We run into really weird things where you have a particular net-scaler [that] has a proxy cache set up, and requests from the pricing service are getting cached with an encrypted payload, and then somebody changes a configuration option on the net-scaler so they're no longer encrypted. One client from one of the applications that's getting price services knows how to detect that the header says it's an encrypted payload, and it's not, because the header was cached, but the body is not. So it realizes it's not; it reads it, no problem. Another process, somewhere way over there, doesn't know how to do that, and then it starts seeing that the price feeds are incorrect, so it calls back to just take it down, which kills the other system.

You have brownouts and things happening in really, really unpredictable strange ways. Some of the problems that happen in big server architecture are insane. It involves so many layers and pieces, and it's hardware knowledge, configuration knowledge, systems knowledge and on and on.

Dick: Those are the types of things I really enjoyed, though.

Joe: Oh, yeah, and we have some guys who are a lot like you [Dick], who go in and love those kinds of bugs.

Tor: That's why I haven't done that stuff, because distributed stuff is much harder. I just don't work on that.

Dick: That's where the challenge comes from. It is so hard that when you solve it, you say to yourself, "Damn, I pulled that off, I did that. I actually found that one."

Joe: It's such a different game, because you're thinking of a desktop app versus a system that can't go down. It can't go down, and so everything has to be designed to fail over intelligently, not brownout other systems and load shedding and automatically supporting another service to take load. There's all that stuff that just doesn't even enter your head.

Tor: I do have one memory that actually I was very proud of. When I joined Sun, there was this one bug that had been plaguing the product. It was a race condition. They had several top engineers look at it and put in some timing changes, I think. [That] was my impression: "Oh, fixed now." It kept coming back. One day I discovered by accident—I wasn't actually able to reproduce how this could happen—but I was looking at the code, and I discovered, "Hey, these guys aren't looking at the errno." You make a system call in Unix, and actually it could have been interrupted, and if it's interrupted, you got to restart. I then realized how this could, in fact, percolate. That was a good feeling back then, because I was just right out of college and I was trying to prove myself. That was really awesome to finally nail this bug for good.

Career Tip

It's very important to maintain and grow your reputation. It's almost like building your own personal brand.

Business

Ed: Let's talk about some business-related and career stewardship topics. Can you give me some insight into how you make your job choices based on how it'll impact your overall career?

Carl: It is just choosing the projects that you're working on. When I was at Borland, we were working on C++. That was great stuff, but when Java came out I said, "This is gonna be the future. This is gonna be really big. It is a cool technology. I like to work on cool, new stuff, but I think it's gonna be very important." So I wiggled my way over into that project—

Ed: That's what I'm looking for.

Carl: —and got on that, because I knew there was gonna be something big there, and after I left Borland, when I was looking around to figure out where to go, some of the main things that I was looking at were Java startups. And I ended up at something that wasn't a Java startup. There was promise of working on Java there, but that never panned out, really, but [I was] looking ahead: "Where do you think the market's gonna go? Where's the future gonna be for various technologies? What's gonna be big in the world," and "How can you ride those coattails?" Figure out where to be. Within your company, what projects are gonna be good?

Tor: Clearly, if I see a project I don't believe in, I don't want to work on it. I have to believe that this is gonna be cool. This is gonna be relevant. But I don't go nearly as far as these guys in actually thinking business. In fact, I'm quite the opposite. If the slides start including things like business, I'd probably tune out. I love technology. I love building stuff.

Joe: But you're working on tools, and you like to build stuff for a customer, right, for people that are consuming it—

Tor: No, I like to build stuff—

Observation

Nikhil Kothari, on page 113, also mentions being one's own customer as an important success factor.

Joe: —and it happens to be [for] other developers, but you really connect to them, right?

Tor: No, I love to build stuff for myself.

Joe: Okay.

Tor: And that's why I like tools. If I worked on the database or let's say I worked on TurboTax, I'd be building software for other people that they would use once a year. I love building tools that *I* use. To me, the really big return is just cool technology that's gonna go somewhere. Whether or not the market will like it, if I get paid to do it, and I think it's gonna be cool, then I'll take that chance.

Dick: Yeah, I'm with you on that one.

Tor: Back in the dotcom age, I had lots of friends who went to the same college, and they did their own startups, and they would say to me, "Hey, come join my startup." I was afraid that working for a small startup, even though I might get rich—well, that company does one thing, and I'd have to do that, and if I [didn't] like it, I'd have to find a new job. So I really like just staying in a large company where if I don't like it, I transfer, and I've been lucky.

Ed: Ah, see, I want to go way into that—are you risk-averse?

Tor: When it comes to some things, yes, I would say risk-averse. I really want to like my job, and when I like my job, I'm really afraid of taking another job where I might not like it.

Joe: In the companies that I've gone to and the positions I've taken it's been a lot of, "Is it interesting? Is it something I want to do?" When I'm going to a new company, it's also "Is this something that has a viable business model? Is it something that's gonna make money? Do they have the right connections with the right partnering companies in order to make it launch? Is it really viable?" I've been in a few that seemed totally viable, but there was some element missing. I've gone through enough startups and smaller companies to have learned that you can pretty easily sniff out if you're in a company with awesome technology but not necessarily the right connections in order to get funded or the right connections to get partnerships to launch your company. [In these cases,] the technology doesn't matter. I was at one particular one…it was one of the coolest pieces of tech I'd ever seen, and the CEO had no skills in meeting with the venture capitalists (VC) to raise money. The VC would ask questions, the CEO would answer some other question that was on their mind as opposed to the question asked by the venture capitalist. They never got funded, and it was really, really cool tech, a genius idea, but it didn't matter. So there's a big balance [between] doing cool stuff versus doing cool stuff somewhere where it's gonna pay off.

Tor: Well, I think the technology industry is full of that, right? Best technology doesn't win. You need to have good marketing. You need to have a little bit of luck and maybe a little bit of monopoly always helps.

Joe: Yeah. But it's hard for a startup to have a monopoly.

Ed: Dick, you recently joined Google. I would imagine you really feel the need to do especially well in your first assignment. Do you?

Dick: Not so terribly much. I'm with these guys—finding a job is not that hard. It would be great to do a good job, but I'm going to do a better job if I'm on something that I'm really enjoying. It's actually hard in a lot of ways to do a good job on this one, because it is set up. You spend so much time trying to make fairly minor changes, how, then, are you going to actually shine in this job?

Carl: Sometimes it's better off, when you get into a project that you're not going to like [that you] get out early. If you get entrenched, people depend on you finishing up; then it's a problem when you leave. If you realize you're not a fit for the project early on and you let people know, it's usually easier to get out…less of an impact on the project.

Joe: Then is it important to have some follow-through? You can't just work on a project, get bored, and move. It's a bad pattern to have.

Carl: You tend to burn bridges; that's not good.

Tor: Yeah, and my impression of job interviews—I've only been in one in my life.

Joe: So what's your impression of the job interview?

Tor: I've *interviewed* lots of people and asked them, "What have you done?" If someone just told me a bunch of projects they've never finished, that would be less impressive than someone who basically stuck with it; someone who has a completion rate that is more than zero.

Carl: But also, if you're talking about what they've worked on, and they stayed on this thing for a long time that they've hated and they complain about it while you're interviewing them, and they've done it years and years and years, that's also bad.

Ed: It's been said that the average person in the workforce will have several different careers between the time they enter the workforce and when they retire…different careers, completely different domains.

Tor: Not me, not me (confidently).

Ed: You don't think so?

Tor: I just feel so fortunate to work on something that I love because I've had other jobs in college and so forth, and there's actually nothing else I want to do, and that's sad.

Ed: Let's say the bottom falls out of the IT industry. Charles Simonyi's *Intentional Software* is perfectly successful, and we're all out of jobs. What is your non-IT plan B? What would you do?

Tor: I would work for change. I would be an activist. This morning [at JavaOne] when they talked about *Engineers Without Borders*, that somewhat inspired me. [Engineers Without Borders is a volunteer organization that provides opportunities for technology workers to apply their skills to help people who, for one reason or another, have not been sufficiently helped by the existing societal system in which they live.]

I'm an idealist. Basically if the computer industry crumbles and society fails, I think we've got to change something. I don't know. I wouldn't be happy, I don't think. There's nothing else I want to do, really.

Ed: How about you guys?

Joe: I'm all over the map. I'm in software by chance. I got into computers when I was in fifth grade or younger, somewhere around there. My degree is in engineering physics and electronics. I was going to be an astronaut. I love racing cars. I'd do that in a heartbeat if I could. Software for me is just—I like designing systems, I love user interface.

Ed: Joe, do you have a plan B, or are you independently wealthy so you don't need to work?

Joe: No, hell no. Not independently wealthy, but doing okay, though, in the industry. It's been a fun ride, so I'm going where it goes, but I'm not really worried at all about it falling out.

I think I'll probably slide more towards business. I've been a business development director, if you guys can believe that. I'll probably be a CEO at some point.

Carl: I could probably see me doing that, managing or building a company that did something that I was interested in, but I could also see just being an engineer at some other company. I like to build things. I got into software because you could build things really fast in software and make things happen quickly, but I could build anything mechanical. I like just crafting things. I don't know if I'm really qualified any more to do that. I could see going out in third world countries and helping them build houses.

Yeah, build towers so they have wireless connectivity out in the middle of the desert or something, I would like to do that. I don't know if it pays a lot, but if I became independently wealthy and I could just go and semi-retire and do that, I would like that.

Dick: Mine is almost funny to say, because it's almost something a kid would want.

Ed: That's fine. A lot of the answers I get to this question are.

Dick: I love solving problems and I love mysteries, and I would want to be a detective. I would totally want to be a detective and find out what happened. I think it's really funny to say that, but I think that would have been my other career choice if I'd have gone a different way.

Ed: So I want to talk about motivation because it's come up a number of different times. I've talked to people, and some of the people are motivated by pay; some people are motivated by approval. I want to explore the differences between the ways that one can be motivated and also the differences between one's motivation to succeed professionally versus one's motivation to succeed personally.

Joe: Work hard, make money, play with toys. I like to race cars. I'm motivated to be able to afford a damn car. I have a picture on my desktop right now, knowing that Apple's got to do well so that I can afford to get that car so I can go race.

Carl: In my career, I've had to balance things that I think would be cool to work on that would be just fun but they wouldn't make a lot of money with being able to make money to provide for my family. Sticking to something that's working out well, staying at a company where I'm making money but I don't really like what they're doing anymore, I may stay there for a few years until I can move on to something else that's fun *and* that makes money. That's the best, when you get both at the same time.

Joe: I was in the same situation, possibly same company. I ended up buying a house, but was not happy, wanted to move, and I needed to stay in it for a while so I could pay enough of that so that I could be able to move. So that happens, too.

Dick: I think in my case I'm motivated primarily by interest. That's a really big one for me. I like to know stuff, and I like to pass on stuff that I know. Both of those are things that I've discovered over the last four or five years that I really enjoy. The financial thing comes up every so often with "Posse." It's nice to have the idea of getting some money from it, but I think we get enough intangible, or even tangible, benefits.

Ed: I want to talk about that, too.

> **Career Tip**
>
> Secure your career by being famous.

Carl: A lot of it is intangible. The benefit to our careers is obvious. We're now known as The Java Posse. That makes it easier to get the next job if we walk into some place and they know who we are.

Dick: Yeah, that's an intangible. I like being taken seriously when we approach people to say, "We'd like to talk to you." That's something that was hard at first that has got a lot easier over time. Of course, that's a self-feeding thing.

Carl: Helps the job of Posse, but doesn't stick well, necessarily.

Dick: Oh, no, I think it does. I've used it occasionally—sparingly—to get some help with a particularly tough problem that I'm having. I'll pull a name—Gavin King, for example, on some question about Hibernate, and he's willing to answer it. So that saves me a bunch of time.

For something that makes absolutely no money, it's the most successful thing I've ever done.

Joe: We get tons of books, any Java book. We blog the notification for new publishings, and you just respond and say, "Yeah, I like that one."

Personal, Part 2

Ed: What's the relationship between having a good work life and a good personal life? How do you keep your work and personal lives balanced? How good are you at doing it?

Group: [Assorted mumbling. Not wanting to answer the question.]

Ed: Is anyone good at it? I'm not.

Dick: If I have a bad day at work, I'm thoroughly miserable. I go home. I don't sleep well that night. I'd like to pretend that it doesn't matter, but it obviously does, and sometimes you've just got to do it anyway. You've just got to do the unpleasant stuff. There's no other way around it.

I think that it's very tough. I think one of the things about separating work and career is making sure you've got lots of options for your career. You work your day-to-day job. You've got a lot more scope to take control of that if you know you've got a number of full bank positions. So the more you can do to keep [your] options open, I guess, the more outgoing and bold you'll be to do bigger things at work because you're not afraid of, "I'm going to lose my job, lose my house." It's good to have a lot of options so that you don't feel trapped. I think feeling trapped is the suckiest thing about being in a job that you're not enjoying.

Carl: There was one thing, though, one particular job I was working on, before Sun. I didn't like what I was working on, went to work, did the 9 to 5, came home, spent more time with my family. My wife liked that a lot. I wasn't very happy at work. I'd go to work, go through the motions. Occasionally I would get a project that was cool, I could get into it, but overall, I didn't believe in what the company was doing and it was just drudgery. On the other hand, when I get into something that I'm really passionate about, like when I was at Borland working on this [Java] stuff, I'd stay late, I'd be at work really late, bring work home.

Ed: How would that affect your family?

Carl: They didn't like that at all.

Ed: Not liking it is one thing, but I'm talking about "you're abandoning us!" Did it go there?

Carl: Yeah, yeah, yeah. It was very stressful. The kids were little at the time, and it wasn't good. I was trying to go through a startup environment where you're stuck at work and you're just putting in long hours. Sun was a nice balance. When I was at Sun…you're allowed to work at home a lot and get a lot done on your project and still spend time with your family. It's a nice blend.

Joe: I really liked working at home, too. That was nice.

Tor: So that's basically how I do it. I have a problem in that I'm very driven. I'm always at work in my head. It's a problem, and I have a hard time sleeping sometimes because I'm still doing stuff; I'm still thinking of things. All these tricks, have a notepad by your bed so you can write it down, they don't work for me. I write it down and keep working.

Carl: You need a notebook computer by your bed.

Tor: No, when I'm inspired, when I'm thinking of new stuff, it's very hard for me to let it go. My technique for going to sleep is to think about something peaceful. I'll place myself on a beach in Hawaii or something and hear the birds or whatever. That can work, but generally the trick for me is to listen to my iPod.

That is a problem, but since I work at home so much, I feel like I get to really maximize everything because I am around a lot. I pick up my kids from school, I do homework with them. On Friday nights, I do pizza and a movie. That's our routine. Half the time, it's a movie I don't care about and I've got my laptop on my lap and I'm doing a few things.

I know there's the whole thing about being there physically as opposed to, "you should *really* be involved." I feel like I have that, but also I always have my work at home. I don't waste my time driving, which from where I live would have been a huge amount of waste. Also, there are just lots of opportunities where there's an hour here, an hour there, and I'm right back into it.

So the problem is, I'm working out of my living room. I have my laptop in my living room, and so I don't have [a] very clean separation where I can go to work, come home, and—I don't really get that, and that's a little bit unfortunate. The fact that I love my job so much makes it work.

Ed: I'll share something about myself. I've found that it's doing a disservice to my kids when I can't put work aside. I'm trying to play with my kids, but end up thinking about this bug. That inspires guilt in me. What do you feel? Do you not have that, because I feel like I should be there 100 percent, not just there physically.

Tor: The thing is, when I'm doing homework with my son, I am there 100 percent. I can't actually sit there trying to explain concepts to him and also be thinking. It's more that when their activities are there, watching TV, at that point, I don't sit and have that shared experience. It's shared in the sense that I'm there, and usually my youngest wants to sit on my lap, which is a little bit hard on the keyboard. It's shared in the sense that I can check my e-mail with one hand or whatever. I still feel like I'm putting in the time.

Carl: You're involving your children in your work and they get to see what you do, and that's also good.

Tor: My daughter, her favorite thing is to come to Sun, which is [something] I've only done twice, but she keeps asking, "When is Father and Daughter Day?" She wants to keep coming back. What works for me also is my kids are a little bit older than yours, I think. They're in school from 8:00 to 5:30, basically, so because of that, I'm looking at a four-hour window at night: make dinner, clean, homework. Those hours are great, and the weekends I don't work.

Ed: You put it aside? You're able to shut down that background process?

Tor: Somewhat, somewhat.

Carl: It's a bit easier on the weekends, because you get enough of a day.

Tor: Exactly. So if we go to the city on the weekend or if we go to a movie or something, I'm not thinking about working in the movie theater, unless I'm under severe pressure, which I'm not most of the time. So it's more that it's just always there. I can easily grab the computer and do it, but it definitely is tricky to find that balance. It's the whole thing about risk for me. That's why I've never wanted to go to a startup, which is because I really want to have a job where I feel completely solid, that I will never get fired.

Joe: That would be really risky for you, just in terms of time. A startup is all-encompassing.

Tor: I know I can't do a startup. That was the choice I made. I chose working for a large company where I would not be expected to work [long] hours. Luckily for me, I'm fast. People think I work a lot, but I don't really. I pretty much work a normal day, but I get a lot done.

Dick: I think that was definitely true for me in my last job, and this is something else that I'm finding is a shame right now is [that] I have a lot of distractions day to day. When I get a sprint on, I'll do a bunch of work, but there are so many distractions that I probably am just about performing as expected. It's one of those things that working from home is brilliant for me for the same reasons. You could really just go on one of these intense burns and get a *ton* done.

Tor: That's how it started for me. I discovered that it was much faster at home. Sometimes they would ask me to do something unreasonable in terms of schedule, "Is there any way you can have this done in a month? We need it." I told them, "Yeah, but you won't see me for a month." Shake hands, and then I went and I did it.

Ed: One of the things I'm trying to discover with the book is the relationship between personality types and different strategies for career success. Going back to the notion of motivation, where do different personality types fit in with motivation? How does that work?

Joe: I don't know if you can break it down just by a personality type. I think there are also innovators, people who really want to do something new and in a different way—look at the way stuff is done and feel like it could be done way better. For some reason [they] are not encumbered to think they have to sit in those camps—so there are a lot of people that just [say],

Observation

Rod Johnson, on page 8, explores this character attribute using his experience with checked Java exceptions as an example.

"This is all wrong; let's do it this way," and then, luckily, people get in line and say, "Yeah, that's great" and start new things.

Tor: I'm not sure that I understood the question. I'm definitely approval-seeking; maybe [it's] my Norwegian upbringing or something, but I want to be well liked, basically. I don't like confronting people, and I get a huge kick out of recognition. So it's fun to see people talking about stuff you did. That's really exciting for me. Clearly, I want a good salary, but to me a good salary is also a way of recognition. I want that raise in recognition of my work.

Ed: Gain approval from the company and the market.

Joe: There is a difference between approval and recognition. Approval is more—it implies "in line," whereas recognition is "you've stepped outside of the box."

Dick: I seek approval until something kicks in that's more important. You don't go out of your way to piss people off, but you sometimes have to plant your feet and say no.

Carl: I think in the long run you may have to go against what people think is the right thing. In the end, you may make a better decision, and I would agree with you in the final outcome, but they may really think you're going the wrong way for a little while.

Dick: Career is important, but friendship and family are much more important. I'm pretty sure I'm going to retain the approval of my friends and family no matter what I do with my career. So that gives me a great cushion to say, "Well, maybe I'll have a really, really crappy few days where people are screaming at me and everything goes wrong," but I can always go home and I get unconditional support there.

Tor: I think I'm lucky I don't seem to have these controversies. To me, it's all about "go build something new and cool and impress people and then do it again." I love dreaming up features and implementing them, especially in tools. I've never really had to go and make some unpopular decision—that hasn't been my thing.

Joe: I always end up there. I'm less approval-seeking and more recognition-seeking, but almost always as a violator.

Tor: Explain your distinctions between approval and recognition, because I don't get it. To me they're all the same.

Ed: Joe, it seems you are equating approval with simple "consent."

Joe: I think you guys are all approval-seeking, and I feel like I'm not. We shoot for the same stuff. I feel like I'm shooting for recognition, and it's usually in my situations at the cost of approval.

Carl: Maybe it's the audience. As opposed to approval from some closed management group or somebody that's in the box—are you looking for recognition from a broader set of peers?

Joe: I guess I'm always looking "up" more. I'm never comfortable working for someone. That's always been my case. Even when I was at Sun working with you guys, I didn't feel like I was working for any of those people. I was working for the larger-scale platform—how do we get this fixed?—so I was in this battle against all the different factions and pieces to get it to where it ought to be.

Tor: One thing that helps me a lot at Sun is that there's this open culture, for example, of blogging, right. So approval doesn't have to be from your manager. When you get to be public about your work—I'm lucky I get to speak at JavaOne and do all this stuff, so I can get approval that way, even if my bosses hated me.

Joe: That's more recognition; when your boss hates you, that's not approval. That's the difference I'm trying to—

Tor: So say it again; I just don't get it.

Observation

This is one reason why Sun's CEO Jonathan Schwartz's embracing of blogging for all employees was a great move for the company. It's an end run around management performance reviews and provides another way (nearly cost-free to the company, I might add) to compensate their employees. As an employee who is a blogger, make sure your employer does not come to rely too heavily on this "fame compensation" as part of your total compensation package.

Joe: So recognition is industry-wide, it could be from your boss, whatever, but it's "you've done something good." For whatever reason it is, it's good. It's something innovative. You exercise good chi. Approval is not necessarily recognition; approval is just "you've done what you're supposed to do."

Tor: See, even if you've failed, you can improve. "Well, that was a good job," and that's in the bag. Is that what you're saying?

Joe: You don't fail, but you've done something that isn't groundbreaking. You've gained approval by the group, by the structure—

Carl: You met your deadlines.

Joe: You met your deadlines; you did the things you didn't like, but you got it done, whatever. You're getting approval. I feel like I don't give a crap about that because it's not something that's outside the box, pushing boundaries, and possibly pissing people off in the group I'm working in. What I want is the

Career Tip

This illustrates Joe's omnipresent focus on maximizing the true market value of what he does at work and explicitly claiming credit for that work.

bigger recognition. My boss saying, hey, I did a good job, that does nothing for me at all, because I don't feel like I'm working for them. That's my personality. It's more I want the industry to go, "Damn, that's a great thing."

Ed: As the parents among us know, approval is an important thing for kids. How do you motivate your kids to want to get into IT? I have a theory that because we grew up during the dawn of the home computer age and all that stuff was real popular with consumers, we gained a benefit that put us into the IT realm where we are now. Kids today don't have that, because it's all been done.

Tor: I totally agree. I'm sitting here thinking, "How can I get my kids into computers?" They're not, and the excitement of going into a store and typing `10 print 'so as an idiot'; 20 goto 10;` is not there. That was great. That whole thing, for example, "the computer can print." Now, even the DVR on the TV screen is doing alpha compositing.

Carl: What my son likes to do—there's GarrysMod.com a Half-Life 2 add-on, it's scriptable. So he uses the LUA programming language. He'll just find LUA script that's out there and mess around with it and play with it. It's part of the game, you can go in and create your own server and let people come up and start playing around on the server that's running in our house. He's got it all scripted to do stuff, such as set off bombs and have all these traps, make different weapons.

Ed: You found a way to get them into that.

Dick: I think there are different ways these days as well. I would say that one of [them that] right now is Second Life, and people are scripting up stuff in Second Life. People might say, "Well, that's not really programming." How can you say that? That might be the entire future of programming!

Joe: It is certainly the current tense of programming. It trips me out, though. I'm into graphics and whatnot, and the whole notion that you move the mouse and the mouse has a shadow. When you move the mouse past something, the thing is still there. I will spend time thinking about how complicated that is. Most users don't understand the layers going on here.

Also, in engineering physics, so down to electronics, I understand how the state is stored in the chip. There are so many layers to where we are today, it trips me out that all these children, as you're saying, they don't have any appreciation of that or any way of even having the time and the rest of the lifetime to understand all that. There's too much stuff built on top of it now. So you have to pick a place you want to play and go from there. I don't think anybody has time to go all the way down, which we had a whole life to do.

Carl: You can learn later, I think. You need to find some spot, and you can learn whatever.

Ed: You need to find an entry point.

Carl: Yeah, find an entry point, something that excites you, and you can actually get some—you can create something that's exciting to you.

CHAPTER 4

Chris Wilson

Fact Sheet

Name: Chris Wilson

Home Page: http://blogs.msdn.com/cwilso/about.aspx

Rock Star Programmer Credentials: Lead architect of Microsoft Internet Explorer

Year of Birth: 1970

City of Birth: Tulsa, Oklahoma, USA

Birth Order: Third of three

Marital Status: Married

Number of Kids: One

Degree: Bachelor of Science in Computer Science, University of Illinois at Urbana-Champaign, 1992

Number of generations in ancestry (including yourself) that graduated from college: More than three

Years as an IT Professional: 16

Role: Platform architect, program management

Introduction

Of all the programmers in this book, Chris Wilson and I go back the farthest. I met Chris during my undergraduate years at the University of Illinois in Urbana-Champaign (UIUC), through the student chapter of the Association for Computing Machinery (ACM). I credit my involvement with ACM@UIUC as the single most important career-influencing encounter of my education. Through it, I became involved with NCSA Mosaic, and through that was able to land a job as a new college hire for then-hot Silicon Valley employer Silicon Graphics. But it wasn't just the connection with NCSA that made ACM so important for me. ACM was my first real exposure to hacker culture and the accompanying notion that software hobby projects were fun and enriching pastimes.

Chris worked on the Microsoft Windows version of NCSA Mosaic during his undergraduate years and rode that crest to his career at Microsoft, where he has been leading the development of Internet Explorer for many years. In December of 1995, Chris and I attended the Fourth International World Wide Web Conference in Boston. Chris gave me a ride back to the airport after the conference. It being December, there was a blizzard, so this was no mean feat. We parted ways and stayed in touch with sporadic e-mails over the years until October of 2006, again in Boston, again at a Web conference. This time, it was the Ajax Experience, and Chris and I were panelists. We shared a laugh upon reflection that we were still doing the Web thing and what a fun ride it had been. Chris' career path exemplifies what I mean by riding the crest, and I think he has some valuable insights to share.

Soft Skills

Ed: In your time as a program manager, I'm sure you've been involved in a lot of hiring. What makes an interviewee stand out as someone you *really* want versus someone who's just good for consideration?

Chris: Program management is an interesting and difficult job for which to hire. The best attribute to have for a candidate as a program manager is the ability to sit back and listen and take in all of the problem space, and then synthesize what the real goals are, and being process-oriented about walking through the steps of solving the problem.

In general, at Microsoft, we don't hire necessarily for just technical knowledge. We hire for the ability to learn and explore and grow your knowledge, and be insightful about how you do that, because I think *that*, more than anything, gives you somebody who's going to grow and continue to get better and better at their job.

I like any program manager to be people-aware. How you interact with people really changes what you can get from them or what they will produce with you. Understanding how people fit together and how to motivate people in different ways for different people, of course, is a really key attribute.

Ed: Well, what about when hiring developers?

Chris: Developers are a little bit different. The people-awareness is a little bit less important, although I'd still like to see it. But I think when hiring developers, you want to get somebody who's really inquisitive and has the passion to dive into interesting areas and understand the problem end to end before trying to solve it and move on.

At the same time, you don't want to just say, "Okay, go solve every problem as deeply as it is possible to do before you can ever more on," because that makes it very difficult to get things done quickly when that's occasionally the goal.

Certainly, one of the attributes that I like to see in developers, too, is just being meticulous in what they do. If you paint everything with a broad brush, it will come back to bite you.

Ed: Okay. What about collaboration and the ability to listen and communicate?

Chris: Absolutely I think that's [one of] the [byproducts] of having good people-awareness: the ability to collaborate well.

Ed: As an individual developer, how important would you say it is to be aware of your own ignorance?

Chris: I think in any role—pretty much anything, in work, in life, whatever—being aware of the limits of your own knowledge and experience is absolutely critical.

Ed: How does that relate with having or not having an ego in the role of software development?

Chris: I think it's related in the sense that people who are frequently said to have large egos aren't very self-aware about the limits of their own intelligence. I look at it this way. I know that some of the time I'm the smartest person in the room. I also need to remember that I am *guaranteed* not to be the smartest person in the room all the time. In fact, a lot of the time, I'm [certainly] not the smartest person in the room, because everybody's smart for a particular area or particular thing, and everybody has great ideas that are brilliant in a particular context.

It's better if you can recognize that when it happens, recognize that somebody else is contributing, and then help seize on that and move it forward. The usual conception of what an ego means—not the Freudian definition per se [, but rather the one] that people talk about when they say, "Oh, so and so has a big ego"—that really is antithetical to work.

Ed: In the realm of being the smartest person, I have this theory that if you're the smartest person in your work group, then it might be time to consider changing jobs. Do you have anything to say about that?

Chris: A better way to put it is if I'm in a work group and I suddenly find that I have stopped learning anything new, then it's probably time for me to leave, in part, because I'm going to be bored. If I'm not learning something new or developing in some way, then I should move on. I should go find something different. I wouldn't ever characterize myself as the smartest person in a work group simply because, even if I am brilliant in that particular context, everybody else in that group is going to have occasional flashes of brilliance [and] I'm going to sit back and say, "Wow, that was a great idea. I wish I'd thought of that." That's what you learn from. That's what's exciting to me.

Ed: In your role as a developer, what percentage of the time, over the scope of a day, do you spend in a meta-cognitive mode, assessing your own state of mind and your own effectiveness on the job and the priorities of the tasks you're doing?

Chris: I think that deliberately assessing those things—not much, honestly. I try to think about improving effectiveness fairly continuously, but in a more integrated way than that. I'm sitting at my desk right now, and I'm not sitting here thinking, "Hey, maybe I could rearrange this and make it a little more effective," although I did that a couple of weeks ago because we moved into a new building.

I think that for me, also, I find that it's better to only do that periodically, because I need to have systems that I can be comfortable with for a while before I change them.

Ed: How do you improve your skill at seeing the forest for the trees? For example, having the realization to question the status quo, to realize "we've been doing [it] this way, but we don't really *have* to do it this way. We could do something else." To question the value of something that is generally accepted practice.

Chris: That's a great question. The best way I've found to open my mind is to learn to listen and not espouse an opinion first, and work with a bunch of people, preferably a bunch of very smart people. That way, you actually think about a bunch of different ideas. You don't just look at the one tree that's in front of you. You have other people saying, "Hey, look at this tree, look at this tree, and look at this tree." And so when you've looked at so many trees, you just magically see the forest, because you've looked at so many, not just the one that's in front of you.

Ed: Right. So it's almost like the way to get out of your own head is to collaborate with other people who, by definition, are not in your head.

Chris: Exactly.

Ed: How do you avoid being tunnel-visioned? When you're a software developer, a lot of times you get really focused on detailed things. At other times, you might have to zoom out to a higher level of detail to look at the whole architecture. Do you think this requires a special proficiency at keeping things in perspective, to be able to zoom so quickly like that?

Chris: The days when a single developer is responsible for doing that consistently, constantly, during the course of the day—most of those days are gone. Most projects are actually either bigger or require a lot of collaboration between people, or they're more targeted, and you're doing something that's smaller.

Ten, fifteen years ago, I think you were around, when some friends of mine and I wrote a dogfight game. John Mittelhauser and I, and I think one other guy, whose name escapes me at the moment. But basically, the three of us in our spare time wrote this neat little game. And it was fun to play. We had tons of people from around the college play it.

I look at what it takes to produce a game today, a game that would interest people enough to play. Unless you're doing a game in Flash or something, if you're doing a real honest-to-goodness *Everquest*-style game, that's a tremendous undertaking, and it involves dozens and dozens of people, and each one of those has a role.

Certainly there are people whose responsibility it is to look at the overview level and drive things forward. Look at what my job is [, for example]. My job is basically doing that for the Internet Explorer (IE) team. I do dive down into levels of detail, but I also have to learn to work with the experts in particular areas and learn how to get them to tell me what the important things are.

Ed: When you're working on a piece of code and it's late, you're in the time where you're having to put in long hours, but you come upon a situation where you have a choice between doing the "right thing" and the "quick thing," how do you motivate yourself to do the right thing in that case?

Chris: The first thing that I think of is that doing the quick thing is almost always the wrong answer. I've actually thought of it as, "I could throw in the cheap hack here, or I could go figure out what the right answer is and how it's going to work and everything."

Unless I'm prototyping something, and I know that it's a very limited sort of thing and I can mark it clearly as "this code has to go away or get replaced by the right thing later," it's probably going to be worth my while to do it right. This was hammered into me as a kid: Anything worth doing is worth doing well. So that helps.

I know I nearly always have other options. I can just stand up, go off, take a walk, get a cup of coffee. Go work on some other project for a little bit, if I'm having trouble focusing on that one part. So really just understanding that most of the time, the quick answer is probably going to come back and bite me later.

Ed: How do you keep current? Do you have a process for keeping up with the latest developments? How do you separate signal from noise when taking in technology information?

Chris: Fairly organically, honestly. I think that there are a number of tools to help you do that, but there's no silver bullet answer. Having a solid community of people, of actual people, is a really good thing to help with that. I have other friends who will forward me stuff all the time because they know that I may or may not have seen it before, and I do the same for them.

There are plenty of places you can go on the Net to find interesting ideas. You can go and read slashdot, and it's really high traffic. But there are always interesting concepts that come across there. And you know, you can go and dive into that and find tons of things that are critical for you that are also super-interesting, which is also a great thing to kill time.

Observation

Max and Libor, on page 300, relate a similar strategy for staying current.

Ed: Okay. Well, what about just coping with the huge quantity of information? Sure, it's easy to find stuff that's interesting, but how do you know where to invest your time in something that's actually going to benefit you?

Chris: I think choosing where you get your information from is one of those ways. I mentioned first the people who I work with or are friends with. They will give me the highest-quality information. And you know, there's the tradeoff: When others do this for me, I try to forward somebody a link and say, "Hey, this is interesting because," and give a two-sentence summary.

I think you can find places on the Net [that provide] that sort of summarization. You have to find ones that are good at it and provide additional value by helping summarize rather than just repeat.

Ed: Right. Do you want to name any names, put in any plugs?

Chris: Not really. I think there are a lot of them out there. I go to Technorati and see what the hot things are.

Ed: Can you tell me about some turning-point moments in your career?

Chris: I think there've been a lot of points in my career that have been significant in retrospect. Certainly I think my work at NCSA—there were a couple of points that were very significant. When I started leading the group—that was a big deal. Leading all the PC software development there. That was a big deal to me. Trying to organize multiple projects and more than just what I was doing.

There was a pivotal moment when we were developing the space game that I was talking about earlier. I remember the first time we got the networking working. We were sitting there, and we kept running it and trying it, and it wouldn't work. And we'd run it and we'd do something different, compile it, run it, try it. It wouldn't work. There was one time we compiled it, we copied it to both machines, we ran it on both machines, but we didn't see anything different. We just saw the regular screen. And [we were] sitting there feeling, "Ah, man, it didn't work again." And then for some reason I just reached out and pushed the thrust button. Whatever the thrust key was. And on the other screen, you see this ship zoom forward. We'd forgotten that we'd placed the ships right on top of each other by default. Just seeing that happen, seeing this networked connection live, working, that was really super-cool.

The first time I got the text layout engine in the first version of Mosaic working, that was also pretty cool, because I learned a ton about text layout from that. I've learned orders of magnitude more since, but I had to learn a lot just to get stuff on the screen and just to bold text and that sort of thing.

Since then, there've been a series of different turning points in there. There's certainly a lot [to be said about] working at Microsoft and being surrounded by people who are very effective and energized.

Hard Skills

Ed: Moving into some technology and hard-skill questions, what do you think are some attributes of the programming language and environment that people will be using ten years from now?

Chris: When I look overall [at] technology, I have to say, who knows? I look at what I needed ten years ago, and I think there are some [attributes] that are clearly wins, something that will continue to benefit me.

The principles of designing good data structures, those don't change, really. I still have the data structures book I got for my second computer science class. That would have been about 1990, and it's still valid. There are still a lot of good ideas. But I think that underlying principles, philosophies, won't change in the next ten years. I think languages and frameworks and platforms and that sort of thing, those certainly will.

Ed: What about strongly typed versus dynamically typed languages, or object-oriented versus functional languages? Do you have any predictions in that realm?

Chris: No, because I think those are largely like clothing fashion. They come in and out of fashion. A lot of that has to do with what is most productive for developers at the time. At one time, the most productive thing was assembly language, because it was how you got software that actually ran fast. Now that's no longer necessary, so assembly language is pretty much out of fashion, and maybe that'll really never come back, because you'll always have machines that are fast enough now. I think it will change based on what people are trying to get done.

Ed: Speaking of things that have come back into fashion, what do you have to say about the future of JavaScript?

Chris: I think JavaScript will continue to be the language that the Web platform is based on. I think it's easy to use, and that really is why it got popular. Right? I didn't learn JavaScript by going and reading a huge long book on it. I largely learned JavaScript by playing around with it, the same way I learned BASIC.

Ed: Right, but the fact that it's a functional language and highly dynamic, is that something that is a distinguishing feature of its success?

Chris: Over time, you do want to tune that and you want to make it better, and that does mean you need to start understanding what's happening under the hood. So I think that certainly has been one reason why it's been successful. Whether that's a plus or a minus in the future probably remains to be seen.

Ed: What are some conditions that have to exist when you're developing a software project when it is appropriate to start over from scratch?

Chris: I think there are a lot of reasons why you might get to the point of starting over from scratch. The point when you decide to start over from scratch is when the value that you have in that code is outweighed by the value that you would have by getting a clean slate. A clean slate is good and bad. It really does mean you're starting from ground zero for all the bad stuff, but you're also starting from ground zero for all the good stuff. And [with] most projects that have actually been in production for a while, [it's] probably a better idea to step back to ground zero and think about, "Okay, what do we want?" Then compare that to what you have today, and see if it's possible to evolve between those points.

Ed: In the history of IE, has there been a time when you've started over from scratch in any significant way?

Chris: Sure. When I look back at the IE 3 and IE 4 cycles, IE 3 was a process of really taking all of the components of this monolithic executable we had in IE 2 and saying, "We want to rebuild the concept of networked components into Windows, and then we'll build IE as a rendering engine on top of that and break out the rendering engine part, because that's a different codebase."

And then, with IE 4, literally, there was another team at Microsoft that was building a rendering engine, an interactive rendering engine, for Hypertext Markup Language (HTML) and Cascading Style Sheets (CSS).

And we switched teams completely. Practically the whole [existing IE] team went off to do something different, and the new one came in and started working, and we dropped it in.

There was a lot of work on getting the compatibility right. There'd been a lot of people working on that curve for a while already. I actually was the only one who moved from the old team to the new team and kept working on that component. I got an interesting insight into both of them.

Ed: There was a Microsoft HTML rendering group, and that's what you were in?

Chris: Yep.

Ed: How did Microsoft get into the situation where you had duplicate teams solving the rendering problem?

Chris: Well, there's a lot out there on the Net about this. The short version is we were looking around for a good [Web] forms package for some other reasons. And this team that was building a great forms-editing package looked and saw this idea of using HTML and CSS as the output system. So really, [there was] an interactive system and an editing system. And then one day, somebody woke up and said, "Hey, we should plug this in as the core engine for the browser, and then we can label all of this interesting interactivity and editing and everything else in the browser for regular old Web pages."

The rest is history, as they say. That's what happened, and that really catapulted the Web into being an interactive programmable platform, rather than being static Web pages, and maybe you could swap out an image or two, but that was about it.

Ed: In that regard, is there anything you want to say to set the record straight about Ajax?

Chris: If you look at what the first real Ajax application was, it was Outlook Web Access. And that isn't to say that other people haven't expanded that and taken Ajax much further than we might have envisioned back in 2000 or whatever, because that certainly has happened. Right? There are people out there [who] have done some really interesting things. But I think the story is pretty straight.

> **Observation**
>
> I'm referring here to the fact that Microsoft invented Ajax well before Ajax was even coined as a term. In 2000, Microsoft introduced the XmlHttpRequest object, which is literally the 'X' in Ajax.

Ed: What do you think of test-driven development?

Chris: It's a much more exacting method of development. We definitely use some components of it in our team today. It requires you [to] have a really, really great test team and that your testers [be] deeply knowledgeable as well. And that can be challenging to staff, frankly. I think testing is an underappreciated discipline. But other than that, I think you end up with very high quality. I think it also tends to take you a very long time to get there.

Ed: So do you have any suggestions for how to deal with bugs in the tests and the time it takes to debug them?

Chris: I think the short version is you really have to invest a lot in doing a great job. Yeah. You have to invest a lot in doing a great job at building the tests and debugging them up front.

Ed: How do you attack hard-to-find bugs? What are some steps you follow if you get a bug that's not always reproducible?

Chris: I think that when you learn an area, when you own an area, and you map out inside your head what that area of code and functionality look like, you develop an intuition about where bugs are. Certainly when I was still a day-to-day software developer, and even now occasionally, I'll run across a bug and I'll forward it along to a developer and say, "Oh, yeah, and I think it's around this function," because it feels that way.

Ed: So how do you hone that sense of smell?

Chris: Well, I think you try to build [a] picture inside your head of what that code area looks like.

Ed: Okay. So when you're making a change to code, perhaps you're doing some performance optimizations, what are some effective ways you can avoid introducing bugs to the code and also foster maintainability?

Chris: Well, for fostering maintainability, I think the best thing to do is when you write code, understand that you're not the last person who's going to look at that code. You're almost never the last person who's going to look at that code.

I think that in order to avoid bugs, there are a lot of processes that we've introduced over the last ten years, even since I was a programmer on the team, that have helped tremendously in that respect. But I think that a lot of it has to do with what we were talking about earlier. Being very careful and understanding that getting it right the first time is going to save you time in the long run.

Ed: Do you have anything to say about how important it is to keep up with consumer technology as a software developer? Is there any correlation between being a gadget freak and being a good software developer?

Chris: You know, that's a really interesting idea—a really interesting observation, and I've often wondered if that's just disposable income or the inquisitiveness of the gadget hound. For myself, I've got to say I'm actually a little bit of a Luddite. For example, my wife and I don't have a microwave.

This isn't some conspiracy theorist thing or anything. It's just a long time ago, we used to have one, and then we moved somewhere else and we didn't have one. And we found we didn't need it. So we heat things up on the stove just as easily, and it's not that big a deal. And I've had tons of people think we're crazy because we have a two-year-old, and we don't have a microwave.

I tend to be late adopter for a lot of things. I look at it, and if there's really significant value to be added to my life, then I will jump into it immediately. If I don't see a ton of value, I'll be slower to adopt it and I'll think about what the implications are. I do a lot of research into products that I'm interested in purchasing before I buy them, just so that I understand what it would be like.

A good example is I actually bought the first Windows smart phone very quickly after it came out. And this was because I was in a meeting with another guy, and he pulls out this brand-new smart phone, and he shows me this application that is the Seattle-area traffic map. A Microsoft research person wrote this application that pulls in the traffic map and displays it in this really nice, interesting way directly on the phone. And I do this commute that goes across a very traffic-prone bridge twice a day, and I immediately looked at that and I said, "Oh, my God, I need to have that now." I walked back to my office and ordered one immediately. And it had its problems as a phone—I think I'm about three smart phones past that one now. The value of that traffic map definitely was worth it to me.

Ed: Looking at the realm of productivity now, what do you think is the correlation between developer proficiency and mastery of software tools, such as interactive development environments (IDEs) and compiler options and Makefiles and that sort of thing?

Chris: Well again, I haven't really been a direct software developer for a number of years now. You need to understand how to use those tools very well. At the same time, that doesn't mean you need to know how to use every single tool perfectly.

I think about it like being a mechanic or working on your house. You need to have a tool that's the right one for the job. That doesn't necessarily mean you need the 500-piece socket wrench set in order to do something with your car. It just means that you need to have a wrench that's going to fit and work in that context. And if you do it a lot, then yeah, you probably do want that 500-piece socket set.

If you are really heavily into debugging, you need to absolutely understand how to use your debugging tools extremely deeply and broadly. On the other hand, if you're mostly around the build process, then you probably need to understand the compiler and the build process and the make files a lot better than a standard developer with a different job.

I think everybody needs to be proficient with the set of tools that they need to use on a consistent basis, but that doesn't mean everyone needs to be expert with every tool, either.

Ed: What about the relationship between developer success and the tendency to want to customize everything and have scripts and keyboard shortcuts and all these things to make everything really cozy?

Chris: If it works for you, great. I tend to customize a few things, but mostly I just learn what's there and what works. For example, I have one explicit custom macro set up in Office 2007, and that custom macro does a paste of unformatted text. I have to do this constantly. I want to grab data from one place, paste it into a document or whatever, and I don't want the formatting to come. I just want text.

Character Attribute

Pragmatic, not excessive, optimizer.

And this is a four-step process if you do it by hand every time, because you have to click the down arrow on Paste—if Paste is even available in the menu ribbon at the time. Otherwise, you have to click to find that category, that part of the ribbon. Click the down arrow of Paste. So that certainly is a big time-saver for me. I'm not going to go set up 500 of those, all the things I might possibly want to do, because remembering them is going to take up more work than I care to do.

Business

Ed: You seem to be passionate about Web standards. What is your take on the economic benefit of standards in the competitive software marketplace?

Chris: Well, really, the first thing to remember is that the browser is not the only user of standards. It's not like there's one piece of software that uses HTML and CSS and JavaScript and all that stuff. Even internally to Microsoft, multiple different software applications need to interact with HTML, support HTML, or author HTML. And when I say HTML, really, that's all of those Web standards I mentioned.

Having standards is really about interoperability. And there being so much software out there in the world, and certainly even there being so much software internal to Microsoft, we really do have to have that interoperability. And I think that's where a lot of the economic benefit of standards comes in.

Think of the standard as really just being a way to achieve interoperability across different pieces of software, across devices and different scenarios, and that sort of thing. And then it starts to become clear why it's a good thing. It's really a specification for interoperability.

Ed: Do you buy the whole "let's have the implementations compete on the basis of quality" argument for supporting standards?

Chris: Certainly, that's one point of competition. But I certainly don't think that's the only point of competition. One of the obvious places to compete for the browser is around the user experience, and that's not just what the menu bar looks like or whatever. It's what process the user goes through, how streamlined the overall process is for browsing for different things you might do on the Web—searching for subscriptions, for example—all of these sorts of things.

But even beyond that, certainly, in addition to implementing standards that are there, there's leading innovation. There's the fact that the standards are not a fixed target, and it's not like at some point we'll just implement all the standards there are and then we're done forever. There are always going to be new things that come up. There are new paradigms. There are new scenarios that we want to add to the Web standards.

Ed: How important is it to have business acumen and entrepreneurial insights as a software developer?

Chris: That depends on a couple of things. One's what scope you're working in. What sort of organization, and who else might be responsible for covering a bunch of that stuff. Certainly another thing, too, is what you mean by software developer. If somebody sits there and just writes code, business instinct is really not necessarily that important.

And entrepreneurship—there are some components of entrepreneurship, certainly, that are always of benefit. Inquisitiveness and out-of-box thinking and that sort of thing.

As a program manager, business acumen is a lot more important, because we do have to think about how we fit into the overall ecosystem of the product. That's really a lot of the program management [role]. How you fit into the system, how you work together with developers and satisfy their needs. Entrepreneurial instinct, I think, gets more important as you start leading teams, and you want to think of what the next project is and what the next product is.

Ed: How important is it to let your understanding of the business of software and the business of the company that you are working for inform where you invest in stewarding your skillset?

Chris: For me personally, I think understanding Microsoft's business has been one of the more important things for me to wrap my head around in the last few years. And some of the things that you might categorize as entrepreneurial instinct certainly are part of that as well. Just knowing that I have to go evangelize a product and understand how a product fits into the larger company is certainly important.

Ed: Are you worried about outsourcing at all?

Chris: Am I worried about outsourcing?

Ed: Yeah. For example, as an American new college hire, would you be—

> **Observation**
>
> Chris points out that outsourcing is for commodities. When you consider Phillip Armour's notion, in Appendix B, that software is not a product, but rather a byproduct of learning how to solve a problem, you realize that you do not want to be outsourcing the very heart of the knowledge of the problems your software is solving. These problems are often the core of your business!

Chris: I think outsourcing is an interesting fear, because it's a very nationalistic fear. Honestly, I think that outsourcing is not something to be afraid of, because outsourcing, as a term, is really for commodities. People have been finding this with software development. I think experience has started proving that it's not commodity. You can't just replace somebody who's been through a basic C++ course with another person who's been through a basic C++ course.

Particularly, when you think about building entire product teams, which is really an important thing to do, because I think about the product teams I've been on at Microsoft and elsewhere, and we do have to work together as a team, across development and testing and program management and management in general. Okay? And those develop over time. Right? You don't magically take a class and instantly you are a great manager or a great evangelist or a great project manager. Or magically, you take a class and you understand how to strategically think about a particular industry. There is no substitute for experience.

I think that developing that [experience] in other countries and in other cultures around the world, overall, I think that's a good thing. I think that there are more effects on the software development industry. I also think that it gives us a lot more flexibility, frankly. It gives us a lot of potential employees in places and cultures where we have customers, right? That helps us to build better software for those customers.

Ed: Do you have a non-IT plan B for earning a living? And if so, what is it?

Chris: There are a lot of things I could do if I wasn't working in software development. Certainly there are a bunch of different things I could do in software development and Web development in particular anyways.

I could be a contractor or something like that, and work on building houses or whatever. That'd be fine. I think what I really enjoy right now are two things in my free time. One of them is photography, and I spend a lot of time taking pictures and [that is often] combined with my other passion of scuba diving. I do a lot of underwater photography. I do a lot of diving in general. And I'm an assistant scuba instructor now. I actually could go somewhere and be a scuba instructor. I'd love to live somewhere very nice and warm with warm water to dive in, rather than the cold water here [in Seattle].

But at the same time, that's a very different life, and I wouldn't actually be affecting half a billion people every day like that. [Chris is talking about the number of people that use Internet Explorer.]

Ed: But this question is more like, "If you didn't have a choice…"

Chris: I think if I didn't have a choice, there would be a lot of different things that I could do.

Personal

Ed: Having had such a long experience at Microsoft, I'm sure there've been times when you are subject to crunch time and expected to work long hours. How do you feel that management handled that? Were they reasonable in their treatment of employees? What are some strategies for coping with the craziness and its impact on your personal life?

Chris: There have certainly been crunch times on nearly every product that I've worked on. I tend to be quite good about being firm and placing boundaries around my home time. I'm not the sort of person who is going to be happy or even productive if I'm working 16-hour days and coming in on the weekends, too.

I think, in general, I probably work maybe 45 to 50 hours a week. I try not to work longer than that. Unless there's an absolute emergency, I will not come in on weekends. That isn't saying I don't pay attention to e-mail at all or anything from home. But you know, my home time is really intended for me to decompress, and if I don't take that time, I really find that I'm not ready to come in at full force Monday morning and get going.

> **Character Attribute**
>
> Meta-cognition. By explicitly stating the purpose of home time, Chris is showing a fundamental level of meta-cognition that positively influences his professional and personal lives.

I think that management, in my experience at Microsoft, has been fairly understanding that you can run people pretty hard, and you can demand a lot from them and really get into a crunch, but it doesn't take too long to turn into a death march. And when crunch time turns into a death march, you're on the wrong track. You're not actually going to get to a good product at the end.

When I first joined Microsoft, there were a lot of horror stories about working long hours and all that other stuff. In my experience, it was overblown. Because, yeah, there were a lot of guys who had just left college and came in, and this was their personal life, too. And yeah, maybe they were playing ping pong in the building till 3:00 in the morning. That's not the same as being glued to your computer, cranking out code for that long. And I think that's generally true. You can't really push crunch time too much.

Ed: On a similar note, is there tolerance and acknowledgment that there are different types of folks? There are the types of folks who come in and they work, and that's their social life, too, so they are playing ping pong.

And then there are the nine-to-fivers who have a family life, and they come in and they kick ass during those hours. Is there any culture that would give one style of working precedence over the other that you've observed?

Chris: No, I don't think so. I think in some of the teams that I've been in, in the past, occasionally, it might have been true. But honestly, I've always been the nine-to-five-type person more than anything. I mean, my entire time at Microsoft, I've been married, and for the last three years, I've had a young daughter and I really want to be there for her, so I don't want to be hanging out at work till 9:00 P.M.

And I think it stays pretty even-handed. There are people on the team who are here every day at 6:00 A.M. because they wake up really early. And they get tons done in that early time before anybody else shows up. And I get here at 8:30 or so, and I get a ton done before anyone else shows up, too. And then there are people who get here at 11:00. And those are the ones who might be staying till 9:00 or 10:00, whatever.

Ed: So there is an acknowledgment in the organization that all of those different types are valuable contributors, and just because someone's there late, it doesn't mean they got there early as well?

Chris: Absolutely.

Ed: One last thing on this theme. What do you think of the statement "a properly managed project should not need crunch time for more than one week every quarter"?

Chris: I would actually replace crunch time with "quick response time." The project gets down to the wire, gets down to the point where you're trying to release, you're always going to get this time when the whole team needs to move in a concerted fashion a lot more tightly than they do during the rest of the project cycle.

That means everyone has to be ready to respond quickly and get their job done if their job is blocking a bunch of other people. You need to plan so you're not doing that constantly. Okay? Because eventually, you will burn people out like that.

Ed: So would you say instead of crunch time, it's synchronous collaboration time, where that's the main thing? Everyone's got to be there and present and available at the same time?

Chris: Sort of. It's not necessarily synchronous. It's more that everyone has to be on call in that time. Like the very end of the cycle, if you fixed all your bugs and you're basically done, you're probably off working on whatever follows after that release. But at the same time, while you're doing that, you have to be conscious of the fact that if some issue comes up on the release that is your responsibility, you need to dive in and just rock on it. You've got to get it done very quickly.

Ed: How do you go about making change inside your organization? For example, on your blog, you talked about this whole Web standards debate. I gather that you had to make a case for it to your management. How did you go about doing that?

Chris: The best way that I've found to do it is to define what the goals are, what the end results are *without* doing it, and paint the big picture for people. Paint the big picture of what's going to happen, what we should want to happen, and how we would go about doing that.

And I back into the organization goals in one way or another. If I'm trying to sell an idea to someone who's multiple levels up from me—somebody who's a vice president or something at Microsoft or higher—that really has to tie into Microsoft's business model. It has to show them how it's going to affect the bottom line.

Ed: All right. So basically, taking a sales approach to it?

Chris: Sort of. It's more targeting who you're speaking to and making sure that you're speaking to the right goals for them.

And speaking to Steve Balmer, yeah, effectively, I talk about how this affects our bottom line. If I'm talking to my manager, I will talk about the technology and how it fits in with our product plan and our project schedules.

> **Observation**
>
> The importance of customizing your message to the audience cannot be overstated.

Ed: You mentioned learning new things as a motivation for you. What are some other things that motivate you to succeed professionally and are they different from what motivates you to succeed personally?

Chris: Professionally, learning is certainly a big one. And honestly, that one carries through to my personal life quite a bit as well. Not learning so much in a traditional "read a textbook" way, but exploring new things and finding different things that I didn't ever think about existing, maybe, or finding out more detail about them.

> **Observation**
>
> Chris' "finding different things that I didn't ever think about existing" is a statement of reducing 2nd or 3rd order ignorance to 0th or 1st order ignorance (see Appendix B).

I think professionally, looking at my past history, the idea that I am making the lives of an unimaginably large number of people better in some way is really compelling to me. I've said before publicly that a large part of the reason why I work on IE is because we ship to over half a billion people.

Ed: That's pretty awesome.

Chris: *Half a billion people.* That's a significant percentage of all the humans on the planet. There are roles that do more than that, but I'm unlikely to become President of the United States or Bill Gates and his

Foundation sort of thing. And I think that's very compelling—just the idea that you can improve the access to technology for that number of people. And tied to that is enabling for people who aren't geeks, in effect. The idea that I'm trying to build software that my mom not only can use, but *enjoys* using, is a great and powerful thing to me.

Ed: How organized are you in your work life? What does your desk look like?

Chris: Maybe I should take a picture of it right now and post it on Flickr. It looks very messy. Inside my computer is where most of the interesting stuff is. But I have the priority piles. I have a very high-priority pile. Right now, my notes for our talk are sitting right on top of my keyboard. My low-priority pile is sitting right next to me and is mostly receipts that I need to file an expense report on. And other than that, everything is the low-priority pile that I never look at until the next time I move offices or it grows out of control.

Ed: And what about in your personal life? How organized are you there, with your health care records, home ownership documents, tax files, and stuff? Is it the same way, or are you neater in that regard?

Chris: Interestingly enough, there, I'm a lot more organized. Part of that is because I really do want to be organized, and there's just so much that happens at work that it's not worth enough of my time to keep up with an organizational system that I use.

My mortgage doesn't change that often. So keeping that up to date is pretty easy. The other reason, of course, is my wife is very organized, and that helps tremendously, because she helps make sure that we keep things organized. I keep the finances in shape, and she keeps everything else organized; we make a pretty good pair.

Ed: Do you keep a journal or any professional or personal notebook, and if so, what benefit does it provide you?

Chris: I don't, and I've thought sometimes that I really want to try and start that. I either feel like I'm talking to myself, which is a weird thing for me to do, or I'm being narcissistic, expecting that there are tons of people out there who want to know what I'm thinking day to day.

I do keep a blog, although I've fallen off of it for a little while recently. I think that certainly there's some introspection benefit to be gained there, but I also get a lot of that because I share pretty much everything that goes on with my wife, and we talk through a lot of things.

Ed: Okay. Do you use a day planner or anything like that?

Chris: Absolutely, my day planner is Outlook. I have a smart phone and a Blackjack and it synchronizes automatically to the Outlook calendar, and that's where I keep my day-to-day work schedule. It keeps stuff on the weekends even, so that I remember it.

Ed: What are some foundational texts or books that you have found useful in your career?

Chris: Honestly, no one or two really stand out. There are certainly a lot of good ones. Getting those ideas from more than one place is probably a good thing. I read a bunch of management books, even though I'm no longer a manager. I've read a bunch of technical books, and I've read a bunch of general productivity books and that sort of thing. And I think most of them have something good to say, and I think you can usually figure out a way to incorporate that into your overall understanding of how to attack a problem. I would say fundamentally, I think a lot of books around strategy and effectiveness in working with other people, a lot of them, frankly, they come out of Sun Tzu's *The Art of War*. There are a lot of things to be said for that book, not in the military strategy sense, but for the general themes in it. The themes apply to everything. They apply to personal relationships—not that personal relationships are wars, but because they're a give and take, and they're an interaction with another organic entity. There's a lot in *The Art of War* about how to deal with interactions with organic entities and how to deal with the unexpected. How to expect the unexpected.

Ed: What was your first computer, and how old were you when you got it?

Chris: The first desktop computer that I had was a TI994A.

Ed: That was my first also.

Chris: It was probably the early '80s when it came out, and we got one soon after that. It was released in '81. We had that for a while. Moved on to an Apple][, Apple][e for quite a while, actually. And then moved to PCs towards the end of the '80s, I guess.

Ed: Do you think that growing up at the dawn of the home computer age has influenced your career choice and your career success?

Chris: I think absolutely [it has]. There was so much unknown about computers at the time that it was a great place to go explore. It felt like there were limitless possibilities with computers. I think our generation is actually the one that's been responsible for enabling that. I have nieces and nephews who are in college today and are of school age, too, and I think about how they interact with computers. And it's really—it's totally just part of their life. They don't even think about it really as something separate.

I think my incoming class in college was the last class [at the University of Illinois] that didn't automatically get e-mail addresses assigned to them.

And I think about what it's going to be like for my daughter, who is in a pre-pre-preschool right now, and her teacher sends out lesson plans in e-mail!

Nikhil Kothari

Fact Sheet

Name: Nikhil Kothari

Home Page: http://nikhilk.net/

Rock Star Programmer Credentials: Architect of Microsoft ASP.NET and Silverlight

Date of Birth: March 1976

City of Birth: Jamshedpur, India

Birth Order: First of two

Marital Status: Married

Number of Kids: None

Degree: Bachelor's in Information and Computer Science, 1997, University of California, Irvine

Number of generations in your ancestry (including yourself) that went to college: Two

Years as an IT Professional: Ten

Professional Role: Software architect for .NET developer platforms

Introduction

Here is a story about there being only one way to skin a cat. In my role at Sun as development leader for JavaServer Faces (JSF), I had a little time to explore some side projects after our Java EE 5 release was completed. This was around December 2005, and AJAX was just starting to hit the red line on the hype-o-meter. The obvious synergy between JSF and AJAX was ripe for exploration. I had been collaborating with some people from the JSF team on an AJAX extension for JSF. One of the collaborators, Jacob Hookom, is well known for keeping up on industry-wide trends and approaches, and he had been a vocal admirer of Microsoft's Atlas project. Well, we kept on collaborating and refining and changing the design, and eventually we had something I could present at the JAOO Conference in Århus, Denmark, in October 2006. It just so happened that Nikhil Kothari was presenting Microsoft Atlas, now named ASP.NET AJAX, at the same conference. I went to his talk and he to mine, and the resemblance between our technologies was striking. Sure, if you dove into specific naming and syntax, there were big differences, but the concepts were pretty much one-for-one the same. This episode illustrates a rule of thumb in tool-making:

Observation

No animals were harmed in the production of this book.

The shape of the problem heavily influences the shape of the solution. ASP.NET and JSF are trying to solve the same problem. When these two technologies were made to solve the additional problem of AJAX, the same rule of thumb applied.

After Nikhil's presentation, I approached him to get to know him better. We had a good laugh about the similarities of our solutions, and after a few minutes, I learned that Nikhil's career path was another great example of riding the crest.

Background

Ed: Tell me about the role you played at Microsoft when we met in October of 2006 and what you've been doing since then.

Nikhil: When we met, I was the architect for ASP.NET and I had started working on AJAX stuff. It was an extension of the sort of things that the product was doing. It's interesting that I'm still the ASP.NET architect, but I'm also working on Silverlight as an architect. And I'm also working on things that are building on top of Silverlight as an architect. I haven't moved away from one thing to go to another thing, but the overall set of things I look at directly has increased. In some sense, it's just continued growth—that's what it comes down to. In general, my position is Web platform architect. As the Web platform grows, I get to look at more and more things.

I also help define the growth. A lot of the things that we're seeing in Silverlight were things that I prototyped.

Ed: It seems like you're in a pretty enviable role. How do you feel about being there?

Nikhil: It's exciting. It's right in the middle of all the stuff that's happening in the industry right now, and that's really nice. The other thing that's satisfying about this role is that I am often my own customer. I can personally relate to the things I want, the things I don't like, and the things I wish I had. It's a really cool thing if you can get that in your job. I'm always looking out for new challenges, so I try to engage in mini-projects, which sometimes turn bigger. Such projects can eventually get aligned with what I'm doing at work. It's a good place to be, but I'm also always looking for new challenges to re-vector that a little bit sometimes.

> **Character Attribute**
>
> Always on the lookout for new challenges. Nikhil's hobby project character attribute is also present in Kohsuke Kawaguchi (see Chapter 8).

Invariably, anything I start as a hobby project somehow, in the future, has some element of alignment in the day job. Even if I'm trying to do something that's completely not aligned, just for the sake of doing it, I somehow end up finding a way to align it. Not necessarily all of the project, but parts of it. In some sense, I've been lucky to have worked in the Web space for all ten years of my career at Microsoft, so I've gotten to ride the wave, a little bit, so to speak.

Ed: Well, that's the very title of our book. How did you get to where you are? How did you know to ride this wave? I'm in a similar position: I've been at Sun for ten years and I've been doing Web-related stuff the whole time. I was fortunate enough to work on Mosaic at National Center for Supercomputing Applications (NCSA), with your colleague at Microsoft, Chris Wilson (see Chapter 4), and that experience made me attractive as a new college hire for Silicon Graphics. Tell me how you rode your wave?

Nikhil: There has been a fair amount of luck that shaped some of the things. When I was in college, I started working on a search engine and a "shopping cart" facility for a small company just a few miles down the road from college. That was my first job. After that summer, I saw an internship at Microsoft. It was something on the authoring experience for the MSN network.

Ed: What year was this?

Nikhil: This was … late '95, early '96. I applied for the internship, but in the back of my mind I was thinking, "It would be great to interview with this group," which was called

> **Career Tip**
>
> When interviewing with a company, find out as much as you can about their active projects around the time you interview. Even if the project for which you are interviewing is not your favorite one, take it anyway. Sooner or later, you'll get to where you want to be.

Blackbird back then. Coincidently, and this is why I say it has to do with luck, I was placed in the interview loop that was interviewing with that team.

I don't know if I ever had a choice, but that's what they placed me in, so I interviewed with that team and joined [them], and that team turned out to be Visual InterDev, the authoring tool for creating websites back in '96, '97. I joined that group and started working on Web stuff. I actually worked on some things like remote scripting, back in the days before [it] was called AJAX. My first real choice, in terms of which direction my career would take, came about when the .NET Framework was just starting. I was divided between whether I would stay with the tools team or whether I would go to the platform team. The person who was going to lead the platform team talked to me and convinced me that it was the next big cool thing. So I decided—without a whole lot of intuition, without a whole lot of analysis— that's where I would be. And that turned out to be ASP.NET. From then on, the ASP.NET product team proved the definition of our Web platform group. It always remained exciting, so I just stayed there. That's how I rode the wave. It's not a lot of pre-determined analysis on my end.

Ed: Right, it's not like you're plotting...

Nikhil: ...to say, that's the big thing, let me go do that. I was placed in that role.

Ed: When you were making this choice between the platform group and the tools group, which weighed heavier: the meta-factors or the technology itself? By meta-factors I mean things such as the perceived quality of the team, how well managed the two teams were comparatively, etc.

Nikhil: I think it was the technology. The team I was going to join was brand new. It did not exist, of course, and there wasn't a lot of team comparison to make. The person who was going to lead it talked to me about where the technology would go. Also, the manager I worked with before I made the switch, I enjoyed having him as a manager, so it was certainly not a team thing. It was just the promise of what the technology would enable, what kinds of things it would grow into, and that vision is what ultimately made me decide. There's a preface: I was, literally, a year and a half or maybe two years, at most, into my career at Microsoft. I was "the young college hire." I probably didn't have a whole lot of intuition. I was fresh out of school, really, but I did hear some stuff about the platform being a key driver and shaper of where things would be. One strong complete point that was made: A lot of what's going on the platform is what shapes the tool or the direction of the tooling. You get to have stronger influence over the higher levels of the stack by working at the platform level. Certainly, there are deeper platform levels and higher platform levels. This was somewhere in between. I think that made some sense in my head at that time.

Ed: Can you talk about some other turning-point moments in your career? What about your book, *Developing Microsoft ASP.NET Server Controls and Components* (Microsoft Press, 2002)?

Nikhil: I worked on that right after ASP.NET version 1. Obviously, that was a great thing in terms of growing my career. It created a lot of credibility in the community, both internally as well as externally. Still, to this day, people ask questions about when I'm going to write another book, or that they found the book really useful, or that this book is always on their desk. It certainly helped establish myself as "the ASP.NET person." It was actually completely outside of work. It wasn't part of my job, to write that book. Writing a book forces you to think about how you talk about technology. If there's something wrong with the technology, it really highlights it, and you find it hard to explain.

> **Observation**
>
> If you work in a group where you have a separate team documenting your work output, pay attention to how much trouble they have explaining it. If they have a lot of trouble, consider redesigning to make it simpler.

[Writing the book] gave me that perspective. It's hard to pinpoint something that I would have done differently had I not written the book, but all these experiences—whether it's writing the book, or working on these little pet projects, or whatever—just help the mind grow and broaden the perspective a little bit. It gives you new ways to reason about things, new experiences that eventually contribute to your "gut feeling" about things. A lot of judgments are gut feelings. What might work, what doesn't work, that type of thing. It just shapes your subconscious in terms of how you think. And that just plays out in every day, in different ways, all along. You just can't pinpoint it at most times.

Ed: Would you call the book a turning point?

Nikhil: I guess I wouldn't call it a turning point. I think my career has been fairly sequential. There have been a series of things I've done: worked on ASP.NET v1, wrote the book. One of the pet projects I worked on, that wasn't so much of a turning point but just furthered me along the path, was WebMatrix, which I worked on for about a year. It was an ASP.NET editing environment fully written in managed code, outside of the Visual Studio shell. That helped me grow significantly in terms of my career. Both technically and it gave me my first opportunity to lead ... to get some people working on it and reporting to me. It also helped me show some ideas, and those ideas were incorporated into the bigger Microsoft tooling product. It gave me a chance to work with other teams and influence them. Then ASP.NET 2.0 came along, and I was the lead. I led a team of five people, and I had a role in the design of ASP.NET across the board. It was just growing in that path [on which I was already walking]. One—not so much of a turning point, but just a side trip—was working a year and a half on Internet Information Server (IIS). This bootstrapped a number of things that would be introduced in IIS 7. That helped establish some level of reputation and credibility within the division: "Here is this person who can go and start something from new, get it working, and then lead a team that can then take it up and go run with it." When IIS 7 was starting, I was asked to lead an effort to create some new tools and new experiences for how people would work with IIS 7. The reason why I was asked to do that was people said, "Hey, you started WebMatrix, and you have shown that you can go start something and make it work. We'd love for you to start something here and go make it work." When I succeeded at that, it further solidified the reputation. Then I came back from IIS to ASP.NET and started ASP .NET AJAX. That was a third go-around at starting something from scratch and getting it out there and being successful at that. That's been the constant cycle. [As for] ASP.NET AJAX, I worked on that for a year and a half. Then I worked on Silverlight and did something similar, where I prototyped some new ideas and made them a core part of a product.

> **Observation**
>
> Nikhil is aware of the importance of reputation to career growth and has consciously taken these steps to solidify his reputation.

Soft Skills

Ed: How do you keep current with what's happening in the Web world? How do you separate signal from noise with the enormous amount of information that's out there?

Nikhil: My first and foremost personal mechanism is: do it. Just do it for real, in a firsthand manner.

Ed: You mean rather than just reading, you get your hands on the technology and try to do something with it?

Nikhil: Yeah, I read very little [developer news] in the sense of true reading. I do subscribe to [some] blogs. My first filter is the subject line—whether it's e-mail or blogs or whatever. The subject line helps form the types of things that are happening. The equivalent thing is that I go look at a book. I actually request a lot of books from the library, and I don't read all of them, but I do flip through the chapters and read the headings and get a high-level mental model of what the book's saying or what's happening out there in the industry. Then I do some mental filtering [to determine if] this is what I'd like to read further or would actually like to go do, and then I dive in deeper. A lot of times it's about "here's this problem I'm having"—either it's on my website or someone told me about it—and you start to think up a solution, and then as you think of a solution, you have some missing holes that you need to fill that you either don't know about or don't exist.

So you start researching those, and you have some sense of what you're looking for, and you want to just see what's out there. That's the "search" approach, as opposed to the "browse" approach. And I just combine that with doing it firsthand. If there's some hole that needs to be filled, I'll try to go and do something [to fill it]. That's my first-order way of staying current.

> **Observation**
>
> The process Nikhil details is really a way to grow the size of his first- and second-order ignorance while shrinking his third-order ignorance. Please see Phillip Armour's *Five Orders of Ignorance* in Appendix B.

Ed: How important as a software developer is one's skill at seeing the forest for the trees? How important is it to be able to question accepted practice?

Nikhil: I put that in the bucket of being critical. You have to be able to question; your gut feeling tells you that "this isn't quite the right thing." I think that's what separates someone who programs to write code from someone who programs to actually create a solution. It's essential; you [must] have the ability to question and develop a broader sense of a mental roadmap of where things are or where things are going, and just take the status quo further than what's accepted. That's not to say that what is status quo is not right, but you have to have the ability to question things in your mind and get those answers, to be able to accept the things that are going on right now as the "right thing." It doesn't have to be out in the open, but internally, in your mind, you need to be able to have those questions and get those answers.

Ed: On the flip side, how important is to be aware of your own ignorance as a software developer?

Nikhil: Equally important, I think. Like I said, there are so many new things coming out every day. You have to accept that you don't know everything. And you oftentimes don't know what you don't know.

> **Observation**
>
> Many of the people I've interviewed in this book have mentioned this second-order ignorance in response to this question (see Appendix B).

That just goes back to questioning and back to learning. You can't ever afford to stop learning and questioning. This industry is basically all about thought and being creative about thought.

Ed: Cognition.

Nikhil: Yeah. It's a lot to do with how you think and what creative solutions you come up with, what interesting ideas you come up with, how do you connect those ideas. It's very much an intellect-heavy industry. Your mental skills are your prime asset, much more so than other industries, where, for example, physical skills are more important. All those things like learning and accepting that you don't know everything all go hand in hand.

Ed: What about one's ability to be meta-cognitive in the way they work, act, and live their lives? How important is it to be thinking about how you're thinking? How much of your time do you spend doing that sort of thing?

Nikhil: Reflecting on myself—I don't spend much time doing that. I don't know if it's a good thing or a bad thing. I personally think that that sort of mental awareness just has to be so deeply ingrained that you don't have to stop and think about it. It just plays out in interesting ways in everything you do. For example, there are certainly moments in time where you realize you're not making forward progress. You're stuck on a hard problem, and it's not working out. I've certainly found it useful to stop at that point and do something else, and bizarrely enough, some idea comes to your mind when you're not just looking at the screen working on that problem. For example, I had this problem at work. I had given up at some point late in the night and I'm driving home, and half an hour later, something just hits me: "Oh, I should go try that." And then it becomes a challenge: Do I stay up that night trying that or do I wait for it the next day? Or, for some bizarre reason, lots of great ideas come in the shower. The brain is still working at it, just behind the scenes. Sometimes, when I'm blocked, I just start writing on paper or on the whiteboard. Whether it's lists of things I need to do or lists of things that I've done or pseudo-code sometimes, whatever.

Hard Skills

Ed: How important is it to keep up with consumer technology as a software developer: the latest smart phone, DVR, high-def TV, and that sort of thing?

Nikhil: I think it's very important, much more so than we often realize. I'm not necessarily saying I do a good job of it. As a developer, I think, all these gadgets are an extension of where developers will want to be or already are. As part of a team that's offering a developer platform, you have to be able to make some sense of how people go for that [consumer technology] and what do you need to offer [in response]. I think those are all interesting things to be mindful of. There are the entertainment aspects of those devices, there's the social aspect, there're all sorts of different facets. But I think increasingly all of these things are becoming part of a larger fabric, as things all go digital. They are all becoming interconnected, and they're becoming an extension of all the things that developers are going to be interested in. In that sense, I think they are very relevant, once you keep track of them. If you're looking at it from the developer's perspective, you have to be able to piece it out from all the news and hype that are out there to see what's really interesting. What is the commonality so you can apply existing patterns and existing models for development to those things?

The iPhone is a great example. It doesn't have a development model for it other than a Web application. But a lot of times, you look at that and you put yourself in the shoes of a developer who wants to target that. Think about how that might play out. That's just as interesting in terms of growing the way you think about developer platforms. There are just different ways to draw connections, and in that sense, anything can be made interesting.

Ed: It's been said that "JavaScript is the assembly language of the Web." What sort of leaking abstraction problems do you see with treating JavaScript in this way?

Nikhil: I think it's actually a fairly leaky abstraction, given the state of the world. You have to be very conscious of what's possible in script. You have to be very conscious of the script engine in terms of its capabilities. You cannot forget the fact that you're writing to JavaScript, even if you're treating that as an output from a higher-level authoring model. I don't think we're at the level where you program in C# or C++ or whatever, and you don't really think about the assembly language. Sure, there are folks who do, folks working at the lower levels of the stack. But with script, I don't think we're there yet. There are still a lot of benefits to be gained from working at a higher level, most notably around productivity. While you can't forget that you're working at the scripting level, you can work at it more smartly, I think.

Ed: What about the future of JavaScript? Do you think it will continue to be an open standard?

Nikhil: I would guess yes for the following reasons: JavaScript is A) extremely ubiquitous. There are a lot of people who are relying on it, and they will naturally gravitate toward something that's open. If any one entity tries to take it in a direction that's closed or proprietary, they will not have the same following of the masses in order to be considered a replacement for JavaScript as it exists. I think there's a lot of that widespread following that will ensure it remains open. Then, B) there is a general acceptance of that among the [organizations], who are defining where it goes and directly taking it somewhere. So both sides of the story know it needs to remain open. There certainly will be people who want to extend it, who will want to have a better implementation, but there is some core substrate that's going to remain standard.

Ed: One of the things you have to do in software development is zoom in to a very fine level of detail and then zoom out to get the big picture. Do you think this requires any special proficiency at keeping things in perspective?

Nikhil: I think it requires a level of mental maturity. I look at different people at work, and sometimes I think that's something that distinguishes a software design engineer from an architect. Not that a software design engineer doesn't need to be able to do this. They certainly need to be able to work at different levels as well. But I think it's almost a prerequisite for someone having the architect role, because they need to be able to be hands-on when needed. They need to be able to very focused on a particular problem. But at the same time, they need to be focused on the other end of the spectrum. Whether I'm thinking three years down the road or I'm thinking about how these two things that different people are working on are related or could be related to be more successful, either individually or collectively, [it's about] drawing those connections when they don't even seem to exist. I view that, personally, as my job definition. I think that's a skill that any software developer who wants to grow in terms of the types of things they're working on needs to be able to do. There are people who just want to code because they want to make a living. They need to be told what to do, and they don't need this as much because someone else is doing the thinking. They need to be able to think at the level of code and the problem that they're working on right now. To grow, you need to be able to start thinking at a high level.

Ed: Do you think proficiency at this carries over to real life as well?

Nikhil: I would say yes it does. Your ability to do that translates to other things. How well you do it and how well you practice it depends on how much you like that other thing. If I have to do some chore that I just have to do because it has to be done, I'm probably gonna think of that as, "Let me just get this one thing done and I'll be done with it." I don't think at the meta-level when it comes to that. But if it's something that I'm going to enjoy, I'm not only going to do it, I'm also going to think of better ways of doing it; I'm going to think of what else is doable in that realm. I think the mind is funny, because even though it may have that ability, it's selective in terms of where it applies that ability. It's quite likely that everyone has that ability and they just apply it in different venues. I notice it when someone is applying it in the venues that I can apply it in. I don't notice it as much in something that doesn't resonate with me. Maybe it's the fact that everyone has it and you see what you yourself like to do.

> **Career Tip**
>
> Pay attention to which things in your life you find yourself optimizing and let those observations guide your career choices.

Ed: So this resonance thing that you just established, does the absence of this resonance in aspects of your personal life cause difficulties?

Nikhil: Yeah. If I were to [do] a 180° on where I don't like to spend time, or it feels like I'm draining my energy as opposed to building energy from doing it. It's being social, being outgoing. Any self-analysis tool would tell me that I'm a complete introvert, and I feel like I have to force myself to be more social, more inviting to people, being more talkative in a social sense. There are other people who are very good at that. It's really where it resonates with your mind and your personality. Everyone really has that capability of mind, and they just apply it in different ways.

Ed: Right. I think the challenge is not the act of applying it, rather, it's finding the venue—

Nikhil: —and once you find it, you feel like it's something you want to do.

Business

Ed: It's been said that Microsoft and Sun have taken very different business approaches relating to the separation of interface from implementation in software. With Microsoft, the interface definition and the implementation are all done in-house. For example, Microsoft does not license the interface definition of ASP.NET to third parties so they can provide their own implementation. In contrast, Sun, and in particular the Java EE organization at Sun, has made the licensing of their interface definitions to third parties a core part of their business strategy. In fairness, Microsoft has made great strides in terms of openness with its various shared-source efforts, but such efforts are short of demonstrating that licensing interface definitions are a core part of the platform business strategy. Can you say anything about the pros and cons of each approach?

Nikhil: First and foremost let me say that I don't have personal experience with the way the Java community works. Microsoft actually does both. In very general terms, [take] the example of the Web services stack Microsoft did. They were both a contributor to the spec process and provided the implementation. I haven't worked in that world. In my world, we do both [interface and implementation]. From my personal experiences, we've never worked in a mode where we said, "Here's the interface, let's now go implement it." We've never ever worked in that mode, maybe because we don't have to. We've continually designed something, done some whiteboarding, done some prototyping along the way to understand the space, and then, as we implement it, we iterate over.

Ed: I see, but I do need to point out that in the process of evolving something through the Java Community Process the expert group does prototype along the way. However, it's more of a breadth-first approach where we don't hand it off to be implemented by third parties until it's fully specified.

Nikhil: It might really be, then, that we're not doing anything different, except it's only one person [or organization] doing it. I'm not sure if there are pros and cons. There are more interests that you have to deal with and rationalize and reconcile when you're working collectively as a group of people.

There's just a lot more give and take. There is a lot of give and take even within [Microsoft], and so I can extrapolate that out and that might be even more painful at some times [externally]. There are probably some things that are more suited to that [open committee development] and some that are less suited to that. The things where you need industry-wide agreement and interop between different implementations, then I think it's a prerequisite that you have that collective working up front. Then, there are some things that don't need that as much. You optimize accordingly, as opposed to doing pros and cons.

Ed: Looking back on the "browser wars" of the late 1990s, it is now apparent to me that they were in fact "platform wars." Do you agree with that characterization?

Nikhil: I don't think that while the browser wars were being [fought] that we knew for sure that it was a platform war. I think at that time the Web as a platform hadn't emerged. In hindsight, it might have been—you could call it a platform war. Today, I've heard people say there's a plug-in war starting to happen.

Ed: What do you mean by that?

Nikhil: Well, all the interesting things are happening by virtue of adding plug-ins to the browser. Whether it's Flash or Google Gears or Silverlight, they're all plug-ins in some form or another. And those are the things that are increasingly getting attention as to how people will build the next generation of Web applications. I've read about people saying, "The browser wars are over and now we're going to have plug-in wars." The reason why there are such "wars," I guess, is that everyone is trying to establish a platform. In that sense, you're right. You could look at any of these things and characterize them as platform wars.

Ed: So what is a platform?

Nikhil: You are bringing a set of application programming interfaces (APIs), first and foremost. Then you're bringing a set of programming patterns and application models that determine how people will use those APIs. Then those patterns and app models determine the types of applications and the kinds of scenarios those applications are able to deliver. By virtue of getting critical mass in your particular set of APIs and application patterns, you hope to monetize parts of your platform; you hope to monetize the things that contribute to your platform, the things that go along with your platform. A platform is basically a way for someone to sell things that they produce. Whether it's associated products or services or whatever, that's what a platform is. It's a place to bring together the people selling the things and the people consuming those things. A particular one that works nice in terms of explaining the buyers and sellers is the platform vendors and developers.

Ed: Are you saying a platform is like a market?

Nikhil: No, a platform isn't a market itself; a platform creates the market.

Ed: It's more of a marketplace?

Nikhil: There's some platform that you need to give away in order to sell the other things that you care about selling. For example, .NET has APIs and application patterns and those kinds of things, and it helps sell the Windows platform.

> **Observation**
>
> On page 307 of Chapter 13, Max Levchin shares some valuable insights regarding the economics of platforms and developers.

Ed: But it's all a part of the platform, and it's helping to sell another part of the platform.

Nikhil: Yep.

Ed: At this point in time, what does a platform need to have in order to get in the game with the other existing players that are providing other platforms? Let's say someone wanted to make a brand-new platform. What would they need to have?

Nikhil: I think the big thing they'd need to figure out is having the vision necessary for the consumers of the platform to make money. To be able to derive some benefit out of it.

Ed: You mean monetization hooks?

Nikhil: Yep. A successful platform is one in which the developers have the room to grow and make money. That's what makes a platform successful. Obviously, it needs to be functional, but that's almost a given for you to even enter the market. What makes it successful is how much of a win-win [there is] between the platform vendor and those developers on top of the platform.

Ed: In your July 18, 2007, blog, you mentioned the emergence of the Facebook platform for developers. What do you think about that platform? Is it a revolutionary idea? What's your opinion on the growth of that market in the next five years?

Nikhil: I think it's still very early. Whether it will be successful or not still remains to be seen. In terms of a platform, the new thing to developers is the viral distribution of the application. It gives you this new model for reaching out to new users for your application. If you have the right product, you can induce users with the network effect. That's very hard to achieve through standard distribution mechanisms. That's a very big appeal to developers. There are certainly other aspects that the Web itself brings, not just Facebook, around advertising and subscriptions and other monetization models. Advertising, for example, hasn't been terribly successful at

Observation

In another strange coincidence, Microsoft bought a 1.6 percent share in Facebook four days after this interview was conducted.

Observation

This very practice of leveraging people's existing mental model when designing a platform was specifically applied in the design of Java, as James Gosling explains in Chapter 7.

Facebook just yet. But there are certainly some possibilities of some new ad models that allow specifically targeting the consumers in the right ways. That's an opportunity and potential in the future for this platform. But I think right now, we're seeing the first-wave applications. Some are successful; some are not very successful. Some are good; some are crap. I think this platform will continue to evolve. We'll see how it grows.

Simplicity is another key thing to any successful platform. So far, some of the basic things are simple to do in Facebook. It tries to do things that are good enough; it tries to do things that leverage people's existing mental model, how they think.

That's another key success factor. A third one would be [having] constant evolution and incorporating learning. The Facebook guys are obviously continually evolving their platform, whether it's offering new APIs tailored to new scenarios, filling in the holes, or fixing mistakes that they've done. And so the platform is continually evolving. That's why it will always be interesting to see what comes next.

Personal

Ed: Did you ever want to work for a startup?

Nikhil: Yes and no. The whole idea of working on something new appeals to almost any developer. I think it requires some level of risk tolerance that isn't necessarily in everyone. It requires you to have an idea, in the first place, that you think you can create a business on. While you have many ideas, you may not be able to transform those into a business. The idea of wanting to go have that experience has certainly been on my mind. At the same time, the idea of leaving and, in some sense, starting from zero, leaving everything that I've established here at Microsoft is also hard to think of. It's a hard decision. And obviously, I don't have a mental block against one thing or the other. But something really good obviously has to be there to make me want to take that step.

Ed: In a user's follow-up to your August 3, 2006, blog, a reader observed, "Microsoft's tremendous weapon was the understanding of developer needs over all the rest." How do you do it?

Nikhil: We are a platform company. This company's DNA is understanding developers and understanding their importance in the ecosystem as a whole.

We are very much conscious about how people work on top of our platform. I think that's the first thing. Just having it built into the way you think about everything you build. The next thing is to validate that what you are doing actually makes sense and is usable. We certainly do a lot of previews and dev-labs and get lots of people to come over and build stuff and tell us stuff. We engage in firsthand dialog. The ASP.NET team, and .NET in general, has been in the forefront in terms of being successful at it. A lot of it has to do with the people involved as well. It's not just the marketing guys and the evangelists, but also the actual [Microsoft employee] developers, the actual program managers who are working day in and day out on the product. Sometimes they have very direct relationships with the customers. Various folks in the management chain are very accessible to customers— sometimes, I think, too accessible, in terms of being tuned to every customer. The third thing is a lot of us have the ability to place ourselves in a customer's shoes, because we are customers of our own technology. Every team in the developer division is a customer of the lower levels that they build on. And so we're very much customers of our own product, in some form or another. We engage in app building, where we actually try to build apps using our stack. Even if I'm not a customer of feature X in my day-to-day work, I might be a customer of feature X in some app that I'm building. I think we have ways to validate firsthand what we are doing.

That's not to say we don't make mistakes. We certainly have our fair share of them, and we try to correct them in the next version. In between major versions, we've been successful at looking at what the market needs, where the industry is going, and catering to those things with "out of band" releases. Those have been pretty successful. Also, we've started some open-source projects. We've actually opened the sources out. We're always trying to incorporate feedback. I shouldn't leave out the fact that we have this Most Valuable Professional (MVP) program. It's the ambassadors of Microsoft in the community, so that even if you can't reach a particular person directly, there is an indirect way to reach [Microsoft's] developer population.

Ed: The MVP program is something where you find someone outside of Microsoft and nominate them and say, "You're an MVP now?"

Nikhil: Exactly. But the key reason why we're successful [at understanding developers] is that developers out there feel that they can be heard. I certainly get lots of e-mails directly from customers asking questions, telling me what worked well and what didn't. If you multiply that by all the folks working in the developer division of .NET, there is certainly a lot of chance to communicate.

Ed: Do you use a day planner?

Nikhil: No, I'm actually very disorganized. I make to-do lists multiple times, because I get so engrossed in a problem that I completely forget the list. That leads to some level of disorganization in general, when things just don't get done in time. Past attempts at using more formal things such as day planners have all failed. I still use to-do lists to remind myself, but that's not been my strong point, let me just say that.

Ed: Do you keep a journal?

Nikhil: Nope, not really.

Ed: Do you have a non-IT plan B for earning a living?

Nikhil: No, I guess all my eggs are in this basket. A lot of people tell me I should go do photography and work for *National Geographic* or something. Photography is a big passion of mine. Multiple people have suggested, "You could go earn a living doing photography." I'm not so sure if that's really the case. But if the software industry really did tank, that would be my next option.

Ed: How good are you at keeping your work and personal lives balanced?

Nikhil: Not very good at all. I suck at it [laughs].

Ed: What are the consequences? Are you trying to improve your proficiency at it?

Nikhil: It's certainly not a good thing. It's a source of some tension and stress, understandably, and I completely realize I need to improve on that, and yet I find it extremely hard. It's not so much that work is eating into personal life or personal time. It's just more that there is always something technology-related going on in my mind that occupies the foreground of activity at the cost of everything else.

Ed: Do you have kids?

Nikhil: Not yet.

Ed: I struggle with this, too. I'm not sure if it's obsessive-compulsive disorder or what, but it seems to be a problem: always having that programming-related background process running in one's mind. One of the things that started me writing this book was to investigate the connection between being afflicted with this problem and being a successful developer. So far from what I've seen, the answer is yes, there is a positive correlation. What do you think?

Nikhil: I don't know if one causes the other. I don't know if you are a successful programmer because of this. But I think if you were not successful at programming, your mind would not be inclined to spend time thinking about it, and hence, it would find time to do other things. It really boils down to what your priorities are in life.

CHAPTER 6

Hani Suleiman

Fact Sheet

Name: Hani Suleiman

Rock Star Programmer Credentials: Author of "The Bile Blog," well regarded among Java programmers as a source of honest, insightful critique of emerging technologies and their effectiveness on the job. Also Executive Committee member of the Java Community Process.

Date of Birth: August 1974

City of Birth: Baghdad

Birth Order: First of five

Marital Status: Married

Number of Kids: None

Degree: Master of Computer Science from University College London, 1998

Years as an IT Professional: 10

Role: Chief Technology Officer (CTO) of Formicary, a 50-person IT consulting firm based in New York and London

Introduction

Hani Suleiman came to prominence in the Java programming community through his incisive yet potty-mouthed "Bile Blog," which can be read at www.bileblog.org. Hani's insightful comments and take-no-prisoners style gained him so much notoriety, and so many influential readers, that when he applied to join the Executive Committee (EC) of the Java Community Process (JCP) in 2006, he was easily accepted by popular vote. It was the first time the JCP EC was open to public elections, and Hani was the first independent consultant not associated with a big firm to be on this influential body. This placed him at the same level as IBM, SAP, Oracle, Intel, and Sun in terms of influence over the future of the Java platform.

What's so special about Hani's blog? For Java programmers, the "Bile Blog" has become a trusted source of critical information for emerging technologies. Hani's readers count on him to search out the warts of the tools and technologies they use, to point out which technologies to steer clear of, and, finally, for a dose of humor that makes them feel special about their jobs. In my opinion, it's this "if you read this blog, you're on the *inside* of the Java community" feeling that is the critical ingredient of Hani's blogging success.

But blogging success is not what this interview, or this book, is about. This book is about being a successful software development professional, and Hani's success as a blogger could not have happened without him first succeeding as a software development professional. I met Hani on the Java conference circuit, first at the Server-Side Java Symposium in 2005, and thereafter at many other Java conferences. The interviews were conducted in a series of phone calls and interviews when our paths crossed at conferences in 2007. Hani is a quick talker and a quick wit. He frequently uses a communication style where he verbally puts his statements in quotes, as if assuming a character as he speaks. His English is flawless, and he's well versed in the contemporary American vernacular, though it's not his native tongue. He is Omani, but was born in Baghdad, Iraq, in 1974. Hani left Oman at age 17 for University College London, from which he obtained his master's degree in Computer Science. He currently serves as the CTO of a small IT consulting company that operates in New York and London.

Soft Skills

Ed: You started writing your blog in 2003, and the focus seems to be on quality, though from a contrarian's perspective. What are your core principles that help you asses the quality of a software technology?

Hani: I have a Computer Science degree. I would say that most of it is fairly instinct. I wasn't very good at attending my classes. But there was one class that left an impression on me, and it was certainly the longest lasting impression. That was a Human Computer Interaction class. And that approach is a very scientific approach to viewing how we interact with the world around us and the objects around us. Something about that stuck with me. So whenever I interact with software, anything in fact, there is a very cold, analytical part that says, "Okay, is this interaction optimal? Is it ideal? How am I feeling now? Am I happy, am I enjoying this, am I annoyed? Am I frustrated, am I confused?" And so, the "Bile Blog" is about that. It's basically me interacting with all this different software and just blanking myself and asking, "What are the emotions that are left?"

> **Character Attribute**
>
> Emotional self-awareness.

Ed: It is fair to say then that what comes up is fairly intuitive?

Hani: Yes. I don't think that what I say is a surprise to many people. I think that most people are pissed off when they think about what they do and how they interact with the world around them. I feel that a lot of people would feel the same way. I think that's why it resonates with a lot of people. It is feelings that they have, but, perhaps, weren't quite so explicit.

Ed: If you were to go through your entire blog and extract the wisdom of developing software from within that blog, you would have…

Hani: Be skeptical. Everyone is trying to sell you something. And it's your job to decide if you need that thing or not. There's too much eagerness: "let's follow this new approach," "let's do this new thing," and so on. And there is not enough, "let's evaluate," "let's think seriously," "what are the downsides?" Everyone looks at the upsides; no one looks at the downsides.

Ed: Are you giving a bit of an admonition to the buzzword chasers of the world? Those who try to pad their resume with the latest keyword technologies one finds on job-hunting Web sites?

Hani: Yeah, that's the thing. I don't think…I don't think the buzzword chasers do it. You're giving them too much credit by saying it's a career move. I think it's much more simple than that. I think it's just a childish delight in saying, "Oh look, it's a new toy." I know people like that. I have trouble thinking that these are calculated decisions they are making. It seems a lot more whimsical than that.

Ed: Well, this ties in to how several of your blogs point out people's inability to tell symptom from cause when writing new software to solve a problem. You say they're solving the wrong problem. So how do you tell the difference between symptom and cause? How do you solve the right problems?

Hani: You need to be able to step back, first of all. You're in a specific component; this is the behavior I'm seeing. This is the behavior I want instead. That's not really the right approach. The right approach is, "It's behaving this way, it's not what I want it to do, but let me step back and think *why* is it behaving this way." You have to keep stepping back until at some point you think, "Ah, I see the big picture now." The big picture presents itself in different layers. You might need to step back all the way and have a whole overview of everything that's involved. And the big picture might just be, "Let me step outside of three classes." But you can't just address local issues because that is not really…it's easier, certainly, it's much easier and it's a lot more gratifying, but your effort is misspent that way, because you are spending time on solutions that nobody asked for. It's much better to understand the problem before you come up with a solution.

Ed: So it's basically easier to fix the things that you can see, rather than to look at what's going on and really think about it?

Hani: Exactly. I feel like it's another rule of thumb, which implies the previous suggestion [be skeptical], which is, "be hesitant." Don't rush in. Ask "What's gonna happen when I rush in? Am I doing the right thing?" Think of your time as a very valuable resource. The cliché is time is money, but think of it exactly that way. Think, "I have $800 for today. What am I gonna spend this money on?" If people thought of it that way, they'd do their jobs very differently, if you thought of every minute as a dollar.

Ed: How do you deal with instances in your blog where you were wrong?

Hani: There have been cases where I have been wrong. I definitely never intentionally lie, so when I publish something, to the best of my knowledge, it is true. However, oftentimes, people will e-mail and say, "Oh, by the way, you said this, and you're actually wrong." In all cases that I know of, that I can think of, I have posted an update saying, "Oh, by the way, when I said that? In fact, so-and-so actually realized that I was wrong in saying so."

Ed: Well, I think this ties in with two things, really, humility and creativity, and I'm fascinated by the relationship between those two things. David Heinemeier Hansson, creator of Ruby on Rails, at one time or another had a big list of things about life on his home page. One of them was "I believe in ignorance (my own)." How important to what you do as a blogger and software developer is being aware of your own ignorance?

Hani: The thing is, it's very easy to pontificate about ignorance when you view yourself as having been blessed with a depth of knowledge. It's very easy to say, "We must combat ignorance" because…what that implies is that you're not actually saying, "We must combat ignorance." What you are saying is, "I'm a smart guy." It's just a more socially acceptable way of saying that. And so I'm always very wary when someone says that because, ultimately, I don't really think they are doing anything incredible or amazing. Because what we do is very similar to any other industry, to be honest. You have a bunch of people, the large majority of which are just hobbling along and it's just their job, a 9-to-5 job. There are a few people who are very enthusiastic and excited about it. But ultimately it boils down to human nature. So when you step back, it's hard to see there is anything revolutionary or grander, than what it is. Because people always want to make it seem grander, because it makes their life more exciting. [Affecting a grandiose voice] "It's an exciting time in my industry, incredible things are happening," and so on. But there can't be that many exciting times. But to get back to your question of ignorance, it takes a lot of courage to go to the world and say, "I'm really good at X, but I actually don't really know much about blah, so I'm not going to say much about it." Most people aren't gonna do that, and that's perfectly fine. But, the problem is that because many people are experts in field X, they always assume that gives them great insight into field Y…where that's not the case at all. Who is that guy… Paul Graham, I think?

Ed: Yes, Paul Graham, *Hackers and Painters*.

Hani: Right, yeah, that guy. I mean, he is good at a number of things, and he certainly has shown that he knows his Lisp, but he's said a number of things about Java, which is very odd to me, because he just doesn't know any better. And, unfortunately, because you have this aura around you, because you have succeeded at one thing, people assume that your opinions about something completely unrelated are worth listening to, when they are no better than any person's ignorant opinion. And with the Rails guys [Heinemeier among them], it's the same issue, where it's clear that he's attacking a very tiny subset of issues. And yet, because you can make big blanket statements, it sounds really dramatic, it gets people talking more, which is a part of the attraction. And it shouldn't really. If people were rational and objective and sensible, then none of this would happen.

Ed: How important, then, is maintaining a healthy level of ignorance and a healthy level of humility?

Hani: You can't maintain a healthy level of ignorance. Some people just have it and some people don't. There are very few people who I would say… it's certainly a minority who are humble. Because you don't notice when they are. Unfortunately, the way the world works, it's not really technical merit that gets you in the limelight—it's kicking up a fuss, and having opinions, and having a personality. But it is very important when you look inside yourself to say, "Well, I'm good at something particular," but you also need to know your limits. There's never a situation, or a technology, or any thoughts that I've had that I haven't met someone who is just better than me at it. And that's very, whether you like it or not, it's just very humbling. You very quickly realize that, "I might be reasonably good at A, B, and C, but for each of those things, there is a person who just beats me, across the board, in any given thing." And so very few people can claim to be "the best in the world at thing X." And so, just acknowledging that, yeah, there are people who are better than me; there are people who, when

Character Attribute

Humility.

confronted with the same problem, will solve it in half the time, in a much more elegant way. And just by exposing yourself to the Java ecosystem, you very quickly come to this realization: "You may be hot shit in your own company, but you're really very small fish in an ocean when it comes to the bigger picture."

Ed: This point ties into a theme you had in your August 1, 2003, blog, where you touch on one's inability to admit one's own mediocrity. How much of an impediment is it to being successful?

Hani: It basically is a barrier to learning new stuff. That's the problem. Because if you assume that everything is easy for you, nothing requires much work. So when you are confronted with issues that do, you immediately blame external factors. A good example in our industry that you see across the board, you will see people that blame the business or blame the requirements.

Ed: Blame the customer. Really?

Hani: Right. Few of us work in technology for technology's sake. All of us are subsidiaries of the bigger system, where someone somewhere has a specific business requirement. So saying, "I'm sorry, what you want is wrong," is very presumptuous, given that the role of technology is to enable these things. But that approach, of immediately casting about for other things to blame, is the manifestation of people's refusing to acknowledge that, "I wasn't able to make the situation work. I have my share of the blame for what happened." That's a hard realization to say, "This could have succeeded had I done these things differently." And this happens at every layer. Even if you're a developer with five layers of management above you, there is still an element of personal responsibility, and people are too eager to give that up in order to protect any preconceived notions they have about themselves, which is that, "Oh, I'm a great developer so, therefore, when my project fails, how could I possibly be to blame?" And if you talk to developers, you'll find this. It's rare to find a developer who will say they are mediocre. How can there be so many good developers? Everybody thinks they are a good developer. Where are these average developers that we are always complaining about?

Ed: Well, do you think that being hooked into a community of developers, being able to pull from their resources and pull from their smarts...is that a good solution to combating this "idiot programmer syndrome," as you called it in your blog?

Hani: Yes, but unfortunately, it's not something that can be regimented. It has to come from within. You have to do it "out of hours," to be honest. There has to be a basic drive, rather than rules and regulations, governing this. It is possible to encourage learners, but even then, I have found that you can tell developers that I'm gonna name five technologies that are interesting, that people should have a look at, and you could tell this to developers, all of whom are fairly smart—all of whom who view themselves as above average and are, in fact, above average, but all of whom are fairly busy during their day. You'll find that out of 20, maybe three will have a look. You can lead a horse to water, but you can't make it drink. It's that sort of thing.

Ed: Well, taking this issue of being able to admit you are mediocre and the importance of humility, how important do you think peer review is in developing software?

Hani: I'd say it's fairly important, because you need to be able to sell your ideas in your code to other people whom you would listen to. You should be willing to have your code discussed and analyzed by someone whose opinion you would take seriously. Whether that be a peer, whether even more junior developers can ask questions about it, so you have an open mind about it. The important thing is you have to be receptive to change. And so that's the key to improving quality overall. It's just going in thinking, "I would like to learn something new. I have written this code. It does what it is supposed to do, but what are the options out there? What is a better way to have done it?" And just by being bombarded by different ideas and approaches, you will absorb some of them.

Ed: Coming back to your blog, how do you maintain interest in the topics about which you are blogging? Don't you get tired of it? I have noticed that you are not immune to the "waning interest syndrome" with respect to the frequency with which you blog. How do you personally fight the waning interest syndrome?

Hani: The problem is that it does depend greatly on what else is going on in my life. So, for instance, during some of the very prolific phases I had, I was actually a consultant at a rather large bank and I had pretty much nothing to do all day. I was just literally paid to just sit there. And that was surprisingly draining, just sitting doing nothing—a lot more than if you were actually busy. It's not a happy environment. And I have all these unique ways of expressing myself. And, of course, I just put those channels into the blog. Other times, when I am much busier in work, there is a lot less to say. I'm only doing one specific thing. I'm not getting much various input. I'm not forming many different opinions. I could bitch about that one thing, but that's [a] one-day blog, and the project is two months. I'm right now in the process of writing a book. So a lot of my writing urges get put into that. If you think of it as a glass of creative liquid, it just depends where I pour it out. But then, on the other hand, there is also the fact that

Character Attribute

Productive use of downtime.

the field of Java is not that huge. Or, at least, the portion that I come into contact with. I'm just focused on the enterprise side of things. There are only so many framework libraries and so on. There's certainly not one new one a day. If there were, I wouldn't even have time to follow up, but at least they'd give me more fresh material. There are a lot of big names, but once you poke at them, it starts running dry after a while.

Ed: We haven't really nailed it down, in my opinion, satisfactorily. Let's say you're in a job, a software job, and you have to do it, and you need to maintain interest in something in order to keep the quality level up, but it's not so interesting. How do you address that?

Hani: We just have to embrace the fact that some times we have to do things that are just not interesting.

Ed: So you're saying that depth itself is not interesting.

> ◗ **Practical Tip** ◖
>
> In fact, most of the time, you are doing things that are not interesting. Success, in fact, is in embracing the boring. Anyone who just sticks to interesting things never focuses on anything.

Hani: There is a parallel story to this. There's a brilliant developer, really smart guy. But this developer's flaw is that he's absolutely awful at estimating how long things will take. When you ask him [about] a specific project and you think about the issues and all that is involved. And you say, "Okay, it's gonna take three days." Let's say it takes three weeks. When he makes his calculations, he only calculates the interesting things. He doesn't calculate the boring bits. And the boring bits of any project are the majority. And those are the things that always take the most time. So if all you think of is the interesting work and that's what you want to do, then, really, you won't even be able to hold a real job. I don't know of any job where all you get to do is work on interesting stuff all day. Because anything that's interesting, by the time you do it often enough, it's beaten out of you.

Ed: How do you think one's personal intelligence is related to one's susceptibility to this waning interest syndrome? Do you think there is a correlation? You mentioned a smart guy, but he seems to have it.

Hani: Yeah...it's tricky. It's tempting to make the assertion that, "smart guy...must need to be very stimulated mentally." But, that's not really a smart guy.

Ed: So even though this guy is really smart, the fact that he is subject to the waning interest thing indicates some level of where he could grow.

Hani: Yes, and you need to realize that most of life is boring. And you could, within that boring work, you could try to find little points where this could be more interesting, purely for the benefit of personal satisfaction. But then again, there comes a tradeoff, and you have to think: Am I doing this for the health of the project or am I doing it for my own benefit? You'll see that people will say, "We'll use [new technology X] for this application," and it's just a way of making it more interesting.

Ed: I do want to touch on that, as it relates to solving the symptom rather than solving the problem. The way of finding interesting stuff in the mundane stuff, which accounts for most of the time. Is it a fair thing to say that if you're able to do that you'll be more successful in your career? Right? If you spend 80 percent of your time doing mundane stuff, and you do *that* well, then you'll succeed?

Hani: Yep, exactly. First, you need to accept the fact that most of the work is not that interesting, so you're not constantly resentful because you are being underutilized, because in that sense everyone is underutilized. And, on the other hand, with that 80 percent that is boring work, see what you can do to say, "This is my life now. What am I going to do about it?"

Ed: So how does that relate to the concept of craftsmanship? Do you think that craftsmanship is just that: the ability to find interesting stuff in the mundane?

Hani: I'm torn about the issue of craftsmanship in software. As a developer, I like to think that there is an art to what I do. But as a scientist, I have trouble justifying that beyond just a gut feeling. Everybody likes to think that what they are doing is some form of art. There's an element of creativity, and you're not just following formulas and so on. But really, it's hard to justify that there is art in it, because it is; there are principles, you apply the principles, and it's like any form of engineering. You just apply the principles and see what you come out with. Often, [you] come out with fairly terrible things, but you have abstraction, it's object-oriented, and I have the right layers and all these principles that you are given. And yet you say it is art because you feel like you are being creative. And I don't know which side of the fence I fall on, to be honest. Sometimes, I like to think that there is an art to it. But the art often comes when you look at a complex problem that's broken down into really simple components, and you think, "I could have written that." And that's another issue—the complexity of code. People often feel proud of themselves when they have written really complicated code. And to me, that's a sign of failure. [The goal is…] they've boiled down this really complicated issue into steps that anyone can then maintain. A lot of this is in the eye of the beholder. What I think is art in code is likely to be very different from other people. I'm not one of those people who thinks terseness is art. I'm not one of those people who thinks, "Oh look, I can write a Web app in six lines" is art. It's a novelty, if anything.

Ed: I want to talk about originality. How concerned are you about it? How much do you care to avoid reinventing the wheel? If you do end up reinventing the wheel, is it intentional or accidental?

Hani: There are two issues here that could happen. A.) There's a perfectly good solution out there, in which case, it's just silly to do the "not invented here" approach and redo the whole thing. B.) However, there are many cases where you're inventing not the wheel, but there's a square wheel out there, and you think, "This wheel should really be round." So in that case, one could argue, "Yeah, you have a system that's grown accepted…it's standard, because it's what we all do now." But there is a better world. There is a place where all the noises that we now take for granted don't exist.

Ed: You have a new book coming out about software testing?

Hani: So the book is called *Next Generation Java Testing* [co-authored with Cédric Beust of Google and creator of TestNG]. There are two main themes. First of all, focus on TestNG…which is a testing framework. The idea there is to talk about testing new features and when you'd use a given a feature and the patterns that you should use…that sort of stuff. The other part of the book, and the overarching goal, is just testing in general and what should we test, when should we test it, what makes sense, what doesn't make sense. In contrast to a lot of testing books, it's a very pragmatic book. [Quickly.] But it's not pragmatic in the way that agile people would say they're pragmatic. It's pragmatic in the sense that, in the real world, we can't do what's best. For instance, neither of us [the authors of *Next Generation Java Testing*] works at a testing company. Neither of us has anything we need to gain. Testing, ultimately, is not even forced on us. Google doesn't force testing. My company doesn't. I decide if we're forcing testing or not. So…

Ed: Testing is forced on you more by reality.

Hani: Right. Exactly. It ends up being a personal choice in many ways.

Ed: But if you don't do it, it's a stupid choice.

Hani: Well, yes and no. Everyone always tells you that you should be ashamed of yourself if you're not testing, but in the real world, sometimes you have deadlines. [Starts to get agitated.] If you're not working in a technology company, which most people aren't, you have to realize that IT serves the business. The business has business goals; it doesn't have IT goals. And the business goals are "we must deliver X by X date." And testing is a luxury in these situations. And rightly so, because ultimately, the business doesn't care, "Here's my code. Oh, you can't use it. It works when you use it but, you can't actually use it, because I still don't have all the tests for it." So in that case, the book is all about how you integrate testing as part of your development process. How much of it to do. Because often, the answer is, "You don't need to test everything." And it's perfectly sensible to test after the fact. You don't have to start with testing first. And often, it's a bad approach. And things such as, how do you do code coverage, how does code coverage play into testing? Continuous integration: does it make sense?

When does it make sense, when doesn't it make sense? How would that play into testing? I'm generally a contrarian person anyway, so I like being told what doesn't work.

Ed: Anti-patterns.

Hani: I like being told what I shouldn't do instead of being told what I should do. And so the book is a lot about those practical sorts of things. In reality, it's actually not that comfortable or intuitive to do it this way, and so don't do it that way. Don't force yourself to work in ways that aren't comfortable and enjoyable for you.

> **Observation**
>
> Kohsuke Kawaguchi (page 187) and Dave Thomas (page 288) both had similar answers to this question.

Ed: We talked about discipline. This is a thing that requires discipline, but in a different way. You have a blog where you try to debunk extreme programming, and you take on the XP zealots. And you touch on an important peril in test-driven design: bugs in the tests and the time it takes to debug them. What are some specific ways to reduce this time?

Hani: It's surprising how much noise, what a big hue and cry there is over things such as TDD, XP, and all that stuff. In my experience, there are very, very few people who do all that stuff. They sound great, but in practice, it's, "Look, we have a deadline. We're not wasting time writing tests right now." They're a luxury, not a necessity. However, when it comes to writing tests, and how do you test, and so on, there are rules and guidelines that exist right now that are not practical enough, I find. They seem to assume that you're living in this magical nebulous world. Where you are able to spend all the time you want, and your time is worthless, and you can spend all this time getting it just right. In practice, though, it's not that easy. You have deadlines; there are issues that come up that are far higher priority than, "Oh no, look at this poor code. It has 20 percent coverage." So what I advocate is a very preventive approach. I see nothing wrong with going live with no tests. That's fine. But then what happens is, let's say you get a bug report. That is a very important test. Because it's not you who is deciding what to test, what you should cover. It's the user who is deciding what you should cover. The user said, "This thing doesn't work." You're gonna test something that potentially doesn't work. And so, once you have that test, it's very easy, because you have a verifiable bug. You have specific end conditions that you need to simulate. And so, in that sense, because up front it's very focused, and it's derived externally from your own opinions about your own code, it has a lot more value. And it becomes easier to debug and understand the results.

Ed: So you're saying, "Let the users write the tests and be agile and fix them as they come up." In that sense, you're advocating an XP practice of the continual release, or the perpetual beta. Delivering software where you can continually update it.

Hani: It depends on what you mean by continually updating it. Certainly, I don't think that one release every six months is good enough. But I don't think a release every week is practical either. Because, certainly, for all the projects I'm involved in, testing is far more involved than just a case of "let me run my unit tests…oh, they all pass…oh, you can ship now." And there are people whose job it is to test, and they do a great job of it, and they're needed, and you can't replace those people. How often are you releasing? And the whole thing requires three days of testing, then it makes things very tight. You have to be very pragmatic that way and take into consideration that certain things take a certain amount of time. When you're writing tests at all, there are different criteria for, "is this a showstopper… do you need a patch for this… or can it wait for the end of the month for a proper release?"

Ed: Now this dovetails with a question I have: when you're doing your day-to-day work, maybe coding, maybe designing, and you come upon a situation where one should "do the right thing," you don't *have* to do the right thing. You're presented with a choice. Do I "do the right thing" or do I just "do the quick thing?" What are some steps to make that choice?

Hani: Interestingly enough, doing the right thing is a lot more tempting. The thing that I find [is] that I always have to go through the mental process: "This might not be the *right time* to do the right thing."

Ed: So what do you do in that case?

Hani: I will force myself to do the wrong thing. Maybe it's because the nature of the work that I do, generally, is to serve business goals. I don't work for a company where the goal is having the perfect design and the perfect product. The goal is to make businesspeople happy. And so in that case, I often think, "This bit really sucks…" or at least, "Here's the perfect way of solving this specific business need. I could make it object-oriented—it'll be scalable, it'll handle these potential situations," and so on, but then the reality is that nobody *asked* for all those situations to be potentially handled. They asked for a very specific "just make this do that." Through screwing up many times and doing it the "right way," I've learned that my goal is to be efficient. And so then you say, "Okay, well, actually I will do it the '*wrong* way', because it actually is a net benefit doing it that way." And, in some cases, it's a judgment call, where you do need to say, "The business is actually doing the wrong thing, but [they are] just asking for this one small thing. This small thing is, in fact, symptomatic of a bigger problem somewhere else." In which case, you have to [raise a red flag]—and I think that just comes with trial—lots of errors, actually. Getting it wrong many times. Eventually, you learn to recognize the patterns.

Ed: So that's just something that comes from experience then?

Hani: I think so. I don't think you can have a good rule of thumb for that. The world is too chaotic and disorganized to be able to have rules for this kind of thing.

Ed: What do you need to do to motivate yourself to arrive at the decision that you ultimately choose in those situations?

Hani: I find fear is a good motivator. Having a tight deadline or having someone who's gonna be angry, for me anyway, works really well. I find developers are two kinds. There's the self-motivated kind who will relentlessly pursue a problem for the sake of the problem. And… there's another kind, which is all about the end result and how it's received. If I do work and it's not acknowledged or received, or if I see no reaction from the world of the work, then the work is not relevant. Whereas there are a lotta people who say, "The work is its own goal."

> **Observation**
>
> Dave Thomas (Chapter 12) is one of those people for whom the work of solving the problem is the motivation.

I need a reaction…to know what I'm doing. And so it's the promise or threat of a potential reaction that gets me, that allows me to then force myself to be that. And it's not that I'm scared and that I must do it this way. Fear is one option, but the other option is, in fact, I will make so-and-so happy. The business will be happy, I will get approval, I'll get gratitude. It is very narcissistic ultimately, and it does seem kind of weird to…

Ed: Do it for approval?

Hani: Yeah, exactly.

Ed: It's interesting you mention this. I've got kids, and I've done a little reading on parenting. There's this one author, Becky Bailey, who asserts that children are in either one of two states: calling for love or giving love. What you just said makes me think it's the same for adults.

Hani: I think adults are exactly the same. I think society has structured itself such that we've found many ways of disguising those basic things. There are lots of rituals involved to ensure that that's not basically what we're saying. But if you strip out all the social graces and what you can and can't say to people and how you couch your phrasing and so on, it just comes down to that.

Hard Skills

Ed: Could you characterize any process you might have for attacking hard-to-solve bugs?

Hani: [conclusively] Reproduce it. First thing. I won't even negotiate with whomever's reporting the bug until it can be reproduced in some way. I've been in too many situations where you're trying to debug just by someone describing something.

Ed: Oh yeah.

Hani: And it's just…it's an exercise in frustration. Because the problem is that there's bias in the person reporting the bug. They want to emphasize the point that they think is wrong. They won't actually give you a fair status of the system.

I'm actually always surprised with people's approaches to finding the cause of a bug. I find that there are some people who are very rigorous about it. And that seems intuitive to me. Because bug tracking is ultimately a process of elimination. Something's wrong, there are X things to look at, you just drive down the list until you arrive at the one thing. But I'm stunned by how many developers use a random algorithm for bug solving. It could be, "Well, I'll try this, then I'll try this, then I'll try this," and there's no real method to it. And I'm always shocked when it's a really smart developer who makes this mistake.

Ed: Because it wastes time?

Hani: The thought of being scientific about it versus going with gut feeling, I think that's the surprising thing. Most people go with gut feelings rather than thinking, "I have a bug, I have these components, and once you eliminate everything, whatever is left, however unlikely, is the cause."

Ed: So really, the application of the scientific method.

Hani: Yes…It's absolutely scientific method. Because there are so many [different] components involved.

Ed: With open source.

Hani: Yeah, exactly. We're used to bugs ultimately being in our application code, which is the first thing you always look for because you're always the weakest link in the system.

Ed: You assume…

Hani: Yeah, that should be your first assumption. That's actually an interesting point. So, when breaking down the problem, the first thing I'll do is I'll say, "I'm the problem." And I'll look at my stuff. And only when I really can absolutely eliminate myself, then I'll start trying to eliminate other things.

Ed: I call this "the back of the book is wrong syndrome." Whereas, in college, you're solving problems in a textbook, and the answers are in the back of the book. If you come up with a different answer than what the back of the book has, if you conclude that the back of the book is wrong, that's akin to the software you're depending on having a bug, rather than…

Hani: Yes, and I'm surprised by how many developers look to themselves last. They'll say, "It's a bug in Java." How many times have I heard that thing! Not even, "It's this specific bug report that I've researched and found out that happens to be my exact case."… nobody ever does that. It's always, "It's a bug in Java," or "The app server is broken." And it's really interesting how people are very reluctant to take responsibility. Because it makes far more sense. Which is the code that's been least used? It's yours, because you just wrote it. So far, it has likely one, two, three, ten users? Whereas there are thousands, millions of people using Solaris, Windows; there are millions of people using Java; there are millions of people using networking. All these things have had way more usage, so it's far less likely that they have bugs that are so obvious that you, as a standard application developer, are gonna run into.

> **Practical Tip**
>
> An essential precondition for a developer is to have access to, familiarity with, and skill at searching bug reports and forum postings for your immediate software stack.

Ed: Earlier, when talking about your new book on testing, you said you were pragmatic about testing, but not pragmatic in the sense that agile developers say they're pragmatic. In the name of pragmatism, you stated that it's not always desirable or possible to test. However, just now you admitted that the code that is least used, and therefore most likely to be broken, is the code you just wrote. This is the very premise of Test-Driven Development, the flagship of the Agile armada. Do I see a conflict here?

Hani: TDD is just as prone to bugs as any other code. There's nothing magical about code that happens to be tests versus production code. All you're doing is increasing the amount of code, and so increasing the likelihood of bugs. With testing code, the hope is that the benefit of the tests exercising other code outweighs the cost of the additional code of the tests themselves.

In fact, ask any developer who writes tests how much of their time is spent "fixing" tests. I'd be amazed if it's not significant. Tests break as often as real code does (in many cases, more often), and a broken test is just as likely to be bad code in the test as a genuine breakage in production code.

So I stand by my point earlier, the weakest link is always us. The end developer and the piece of code we're working on now. The same attitude can be applied to tests too; what's more likely, that JUnit/TestNG/your test framework is broken, or that your testcase is?

Ed: So do you have any tips for honing your sense of smell for where a bug might be? How do you start out?

Hani: I think you develop the sense once you follow the rules.

Ed: Can you enumerate the rules a little?

Hani: Reproduce the failure, first of all. Once you've reproduced it, however complicated the reproduction process is, it's fine. The first step is just reproduce it. It doesn't matter if you happen to need three databases and two machines and six people clicking. That's fine. Once you can reproduce it, then you strip away stuff. Then you notice, "Okay, well, clearly this is too cumbersome to actually debug. But I can reproduce it, so let me take off this little bit. Can I still reproduce it? And you keep stripping away stuff until, at some point, there's something that you do where you observe, the bug's not happening anymore. And you think to yourself, 'Okay, so it's in this bit.'" And, to be fair, that's an idealistic situation. Actually what I find more likely to happen is it's a side effect of what you did three steps ago that's finally manifesting itself for whatever reason. And so it's not: "eliminate, eliminate, eliminate." It's "eliminate, eliminate, put it back in, eliminate, eliminate, put it back in." You're zigzagging towards the answer. It can be frustrating, but you have to be rigorous about it. You have to always be willing to question what you just assumed.

Ed: And that's what I was getting at when I was talking earlier about "do the right thing."

Hani: Uh hum.

Ed: What about when you're just tired? You've been up late and for whatever reason you just don't wanna be methodical about it. You just want to be a monkey punching away at the keyboard. What do you do? Do you ever find yourself in that situation?

Hani: Sometimes, but I never expect any results out of it.

Ed: Oh.

Hani: I think, "Yeah, I'll piss around trying to figure this out." But in the back of my mind I realize, "Okay, well, tomorrow morning this is what I'm going to be doing for most of the day."

Ed: Ohhh, so you have a level of self-awareness that when you …

Hani: Yeah, I realize.

Ed: Make the wrong choice, or you're not able to be methodical for some reason....

Hani: It might not even be instant. It might not be beforehand: "Okay, I'm just gonna waste three hours poking randomly." It might happen in the middle of the thing: "I'm just stumbling about trying to figure out what's going on here, but something's going wrong, I can see it going wrong, but who knows…[optimistically] I'll try a few more things and…I'll do it properly later on." But there's always two separate phases where it's okay to stumble about. But really, it's a luxury. But if this works, it's like a present.

Ed: Ahhhhh.

Hani: More realistically…

Ed: It can happen.

Hani: Yes, it does happen, and if it does—great. But realistically, you're always prepared to say to yourself, "I'm gonna have to do this properly at some point." And it's nicer than when you're coding and you're putting in a hack, which we talked about earlier, because often, in the back of your mind, you're thinking, "I'll do this properly later," but there's no incentive to do so.

Ed: How do you motivate yourself to do it properly later?

Hani: When you're writing code?

Ed: Yes.

Hani: I think that it's a comforting thought.

Ed: It's an illusion?

Hani: A security blanket. If I cling on to that thought, I can allow myself to do this dirty thing I'm about to do.

Ed: It's a lie you tell yourself.

Hani: Yeah, you tell yourself a lie to make yourself feel better about what you're doing, and it's easier to think, "This is temporary; this isn't gonna be some poor schmuck's problem in two years from now when I'm long gone and doing something else, and they're gonna say, 'What was this guy thinking!'" [Instead], you're gonna think, "We're gonna get this out. We'll put the fix in next month when things have calmed down a little. I'll revisit this and I know what the right solution is and I'll do it then." That thought is very comforting. And with any luck, within a month, you'll have forgotten and you're fine [laughs].

Ed: Until the bug manifests itself and…

Hani: Until it actually comes to a head, which, depressingly, it often *doesn't*. Which is why there's so much bad software out there, because you *can* get away with it. There's no correlation between functionality and quality of code. Some of the most successful software out there is abysmally written. And that's fine. Software is to help people do stuff. To me anyway, it's not a goal in and of itself.

Ed: Well, that's the two kinds of people we talked about earlier.

Hani: Exactly, so it's very easy for me to live with, to accept the fact that software is badly written, that there are plenty of hacks that get in there that never make it out. That people will optimize on the wrong level. It's just human nature at play, and it's fine.

Ed: Given what we've just said, what are some concrete strategies you use, or advocate using, to avoid introducing bugs into a codebase?

Hani: I like incremental development. So when you're writing something, I will admit to being guilty of not writing enough tests. I just find that, in the real world, it's often hard to just continuously write tests. It's something we should strive for. I just want to. In practice, it's trickier to actually arrive at this answer or to actually turn the ideal into reality. It's something we all should be striving towards, because you test it once and you can keep testing it indefinitely after that. But failing that, what I'll do is I'll make a small change and I'll run the application, and check that this works. It's a very iterative process, so it's always small change, check, small change, check. The scariest time I have of it is when I'm writing big functionality. Anything that takes more than ten minutes is problematic, because then you think, "Oh my God—then there are lots of moving parts now. What happens here? How am I going to capture all the things I need to actually look out for? What if it goes wrong? Which bit do I actually start working with?" As a result of that, there are a number of fallouts from wanting this rapid iterative development process. Your tooling has to be really, really good. Startup time is everything. And so app servers that take a minute to start are not an option, basically. It's just, for development…you can't write 30 seconds of code and then have to wait a minute to see what it did.

Ed: There's a very interesting topic that I want to get into—the relationship between developer success and tools proficiency and the extent to which their work environment is customized. For example, I have noticed that people who are more effective as developers seem to be more adept at getting around in their operating system (OS) environment.

Hani: Yes.

Ed: They know all the keyboard shortcuts. They're good at the command prompt. How important is that sort of thing?

Hani: I think it's very important. But I think also it's something that you learn as a matter of necessity, in fact, because you realize: "Every day I find myself doing these four mouse clicks to do this one task. How do I fix this?"

Ed: So that comes from the toolmaker in each of us?

Hani: I think it's also something that, as you try different things…It's funny, I actually see the analogy to real life…when you're living in different countries [from your own]. People who have lived in different countries— I'm obviously biased as someone who has done so—I find there is a certain appreciation and depth because you know that there's no "one way." You know that there's no one true way of life. You know that there are people who could, in many ways, have completely opposing values to you in every sense of the word, yet are managing to live their lives and be happy and have children and love and laugh and cry and do all these things that are human. And it's the same, actually, in computers in many ways. If you just use [Microsoft] Windows all your life, you don't realize it's not the optimal way of doing things. And that was one thing, for instance, when I first switched to a Mac, I had trouble because I felt, "I can't install stuff. Because there's no installer! It's ridiculous." And then I realized, "I don't need it." It's a different way of doing your life. And once you've gone through a couple of these transitions, then you start questioning everything in your interactions. And you start asking questions such as, "Okay, is this the most optimal way? Am I comfortable with this, or am I doing it because I'm used to it?" I think that just through trying different things, you become more critical of your environment, because you've seen there are alternatives in almost every case.

Ed: So how important is it to be a continual optimizer of your work station or work environment?

Hani: There's a law of diminishing returns there. When I get a new machine, specifically Windows, the first thing I'll do is I'll do my certain things that I'm used to…

Ed: Which are what?

Hani: Basically just [Windows] Explorer, just tweaking Explorer, show system files, list view, show folders, status bar. I don't tend to install any extra tools either. Because once you've been on enough machines, you realize you don't have the luxury of installing your tools, so your brain automatically assumes they're not there. And funny enough, that's why I now use vi. I grew up on Linux. I never used vi. I used Pico or Emacs or any one of the easy editors where the arrow keys work. But professionally, I work with Solaris a lot, and arrow keys never work on Solaris. And there's nothing installed other than vi. So you use vi and you learn the vi keybindings. And then, because you've been on enough machines, you end up dropping to the lowest common denominator. And the customization with Windows is the same: "What's the bare minimum I can do to function in this environment?"

Ed: So you would say that being accustomed to an extremely customized environment is an impediment?

Hani: Yes. Definitely. In an ideal world, that's the only environment you'd work in, but in the real world, it doesn't work that way. You decide what things matter and what things don't. It has to be a conscious decision: "I will give up on these few luxuries that I have in return for these other things which I think are more crucial, because we're not at the point, technology-wise, where I can take my whole environment anywhere else." Integrated development environments (IDEs) for instance, are another one. See, for me, again, the first thing I'll do is I'll install [IntelliJ] Idea. I can't function otherwise.

Ed: Oh? Okay.

Hani: It's a bad thing. Because, again, I'm installing software somewhere. Actually, it's even worse than that, in that, not only will I, if a machine already has Idea on it, I won't use that version—I'll install my version. And I have my settings exported on a share I can get to from anywhere in the world. So the first thing I'll do is I'll install it, and I import my settings, and then I have my IntelliJ settings—cause my keybindings are customized.

Ed: Oh they are?

Hani: Yeah

Ed: Okay! And how did you arrive at those keybindings?

Hani: Some are actually hang-ups from previous IDEs. For example, I have some Emacs keybindings just because I used Emacs for ages and when I first used IntelliJ Idea, I felt there [was] no way I [could] change my brain. So basically trash that I've picked up along the way. But because it's *my* trash, it's...I've formed an association with it. Say you've lived in a house for ages, and you've accumulated all this stuff. It's worthless, really. You can't sell it; nobody wants it. And if you move to a smaller space, for example, you'll be very reluctant to get rid of it. Even though, objectively, it is worthless. It's stuff that's ten years old. It no longer serves any function, you've replaced it with other things, but you still have an attachment to it because it's yours and you bought it at whatever time, and you had fun with it, whatever. And it's the same thing in terms of our computer ticks. We develop them over the years and carry them with us.

Ed: How strongly correlated is proficiency with tools and effectiveness as a developer?

Hani: That's tricky. I've thought about this before and I've fluctuated between they're completely orthogonal and thinking that, "Well, if you can't figure out your tool, how could you be a good developer?" I'm always surprised. I see it often, someone who's a good developer...who doesn't know their tool that well. And there's sort of a cognitive dissonance there...

Ed: That seems surprising to me also.

Hani: You think, "What? That doesn't make sense. You're a really smart guy," like, "How come you don't know all the shortcuts? Why didn't you find out about all the shortcuts? Why have you never questioned your build process or your…whatever it is?" And so I've come to realize that it's not that there is a correlation, but it's not a rule of thumb. You can't say that everyone who's good at tooling is gonna be a good developer or vice versa. In fact, there are many more people who are really great at tooling that are terrible developers. Because again, it's like not seeing the forest for the trees. Where it's all about local optimizations versus the big picture.

Ed: Speaking about optimizations, how important is it for a computer professional to be up on consumer technology? You know, gadgets. Having the latest Blackberry, having the Tivo, the 1080p, whatever. How important is that?

Hani: [immediately] Completely irrelevant. I find that the two often go together, but I think it's just because of the way that we're wired that attracts us to that sort of thing. The kind of thing that attracts us to computers is the kind of thing that attracts us to gadgets. I don't think it's helpful or useful as computer professionals. I had an interesting realization of that. So everyone, I think all of us at some point, has built their own PC. And has taken great pride in the fact that they didn't buy a generic thing. I built my own PC. I made sure I got the best graphics card and the fastest hard drive, because in the Dell model, they go with a crappy graphics card. And we order the components and watch them trickle in through the mail. And finally it's all there now, and finally we hook it all up. And you stick it all together. And it doesn't boot up. And you get the three beeps that says that some wire's loose on the motherboard. You fiddle with the dip switches and the jumpers. And then you reduce the number of beeps and you feel smug and it's all working. So I used to do that. As many people did. And I remember at some point realizing that this is bullshit. I've wasted five hours of my life for something that really is…I have no measurable net benefit.

Ed: Hmm…

Hani: At the end of the day, I can feel smug about it. I have these skills already. I didn't really learn anything new in particular.

Business

Ed: So how would you break down the software industry? For example, categorize it. There's the middleware industry…

Hani: It's very difficult. There's academia. I'm not sure I can answer this question.

Ed: So in what segment of the breakdown do you consider yourself working?

Hani: Let me tell you my side of it and my immediate neighbors. Because I don't have a wide enough perspective to see what the industry as a whole is. Just my little chunk of it. So most of what I do is Java. So the people I'm interacting with are the database people. And the crazy enterprise people. The legacy enterprise people. The people who are running these big middleware systems.

Ed: Like SAP and such?

Hani: Older than that. MQSeries, CICS, they have tons of old databases and lots of FTPing files around.

Ed: Like AS/400 stuff?

Hani: Yes, that sort of thing. But their idea of integration is just shuttling files around. And the big new project to modernize everything is just to do it through Java Message Service (JMS) now or some kind of messaging application programming interface (API). But they are still just shuttling files around. So there is a lot of that. And a lot of the people I know deal with that. It is very boring, but that actually is a surprising percentage of the work that I deal with. So there are the people who are doing newer projects in those areas. And on the other hand there is the, I don't have a name for them, Web monkeys? These are people who often work in enterprise environments, but really just end up doing Web front-ends. Basically, it's just Internet apps. Web apps. You just have these six items, you want to be able to edit them, and add to them and that's it. And there's a lot of these people, I'd say the majority, in fact.

Ed: Majority of what?

Hani: Developers. And amongst those there are those who do it just for a job, and then there's the cutting-edge Web monkeys who are always in search of the new toolkit to play with. Just to keep things interesting. This is more prevalent in consultants. Because they are more able to easily take in, "Oh look, I just read about framework X. Let's use it for this project." Two, three months down the line, they're done, they're out of there and this poor business is now stuck with this unknown framework that came out last week to maintain.

Ed: You listed three segments there. Where would you consider yourself doing most of your day-to-day work? Is there one of those that stands out, or do you flip around?

Hani: I would say that I am closest to the middle-tier guys. The guys who are working with the application servers.

Ed: How closely do you follow the business of software? Does your job depend on where and how people are making money doing software?

Hani: Yes and no. I'm at a fairly high level in my company, so part of my job is to be on the lookout. But I wouldn't say that I'm an expert about it. I'm certainly always baffled by the relationship between software and money, because it certainly doesn't seem to be that good software makes money. And the measure of the market seems to follow a different metric of quality than code quality and good design and all those things.

Ed: Well, there are a lot of external factors that influence it that are not related at all to the quality of the software.

Hani: Exactly, and that's what I was talking about earlier about the relationship between the business and IT. The software is there to help the business. It's a small part of helping the business, and that relationship is born out of the relationship between money and software. It's unclear…it's not that good software sells, not necessarily—horrible software sells, too. So obviously, software is not that big of a factor.

Ed: So would you say that software is like fishing, where the software is the equipment you are using? And you might be able to catch a good fish with crappy equipment, but maybe you're more likely to catch a good fish if you have good equipment?

Hani: Yeah [skeptically], that makes a good argument. Although, again, it's hard assessing probability that way because I don't think we have enough of a body of area to make statistically meaningful conclusions from that. Because if you make an assertion that says, "If you use the right design patterns, then you're more likely to make money," I'm not sure you can [make such an assertion].

Ed: We talked about discipline. Would you agree, of all the methodologies out there, that XP requires the most discipline in the individual developer, the individual practitioner?

Hani: Um. Well…it's hard to answer this. I'm not so convinced there's much of a difference, to be honest. There are different approaches and they're all ultimately…whether any given approach works or fails depends greatly on the team itself. Good teams will work no matter what methodology you use. Provided you're not doing something just…plain silly. Bad teams will fail, regardless of what methodology you have. The XP folks are really good at making this point, or rather abusing this point, so that when an XP project fails, they'll say, "Oh, they didn't really follow XP." If an XP project succeeds, they say, "Oh, this only could have succeeded by using XP." Instead of saying, "These guys are smart. It doesn't really matter what approach they would have taken, chances are, they probably would have succeeded no matter what they did." Because the technology understood the business, they knew what to expect, they had decent use-cases, good focus, and that sort of stuff. That's what makes a project succeed.

Ed: Speaking about project success, I want to talk about something you view as an impediment to project success: The Senior Architect Syndrome. You describe someone so afflicted in your blog: "It's that older smug bastard who enjoys having his finger in every pie. The kind of guy who does nothing all day beyond maintain some production system in the name of work. The guy who believes in pictures and diagrams and believes that the way forward is by farting out endless white papers and 'visionary' ideas." Given that senior architects do exist in the world and they inexplicably have power, how do you deal with them?

Hani: It's very, very difficult. [laughs] The problem is, as you say, they do have power. But they're so far removed from the practicality of writing software, that all they have are nebulous high-level conceptual ideas. And those ideas are great; it's all stuff that everybody agrees on. But the problem is that in practice, they don't work so well. If projects were as trivial as those diagrams, then we'd all be out of jobs. But the reality of writing software is messy; it's complicated. It's like a jigsaw puzzle where eight pieces are missing and you're not sure why they're missing, and there's another ten pieces that just don't have the right edges. There's an organic element to it. The high-level senior architect view just does away with all this, with all these practicalities, and instead just comes up with these very pretty pictures, which don't map to reality very well. I'm not sure of the value offered by having that. It's akin to knowing, "Okay, roughly, we're going to use [some specific technology] for this project. Here's a language, some components, oh, that's fine." But to try and impose anything beyond that high-level view gets very tricky. So in terms of dealing with them, I'd say, just keep them isolated from the practicality of the work.

Ed: [laughs]

Hani: I'm serious! Say to them, "Look, we're following the guidelines, but we just don't care about how you feel about the implementation. Your job is not to worry about the implementation; it's the job of the technical lead to decide, okay, well, this is our contract with those external facing APIs; what we do inside is our own business." The technical lead should be running that, rather than the architect saying, "Oh, you must use this. All our APIs should have this method," and so on.

Ed: Would you say, then, it's appropriate for a senior architect to, say, advise where a company should invest its R&D dollars? "What sort of things should we chase? What sort of software should we go after?" Is that appropriate for a senior architect to do?

Hani: I don't think necessarily they have any better insight than anybody else, to be honest. But I guess *somebody* makes that decision. Yeah, sure, it could be a senior architect. I don't think they have a skill that enables them to make that decision any more wisely than anyone else.

Ed: So how does the information that you learn from following the business of software inform your career choices? How important is it to let the analysis of the business of software inform where *you* invest in stewarding your skill set?

Hani: I think it's important to actually have bigger factors than that—that is, how you personally feel and where you feel your strengths are. I think running after the money is a foolish approach. Because we're in a business that is doing fairly well compared to the average. And so I think focusing, being honest about your strengths and abilities, and then focusing on those is better than saying, "I think this area is going to make money. I know nothing about it. I'm going to jump in to it just because I think it's going to be profitable X years down the line." I guess I'm advocating a fairly conservative approach, in that I'm saying, "Stick to what you're good at."

Ed: Do you have a non-IT plan B to earn a living? If so, what is it?

Hani: No, I don't. In the same way that kids want to be spacemen and astronauts and firemen, I have that sort of thing, but it's not real; it's not reality-based, because I'm just not qualified. I'd like to do something that involves writing a lot.

Ed: Journalism?

Hani: Yeah, that sort of thing. But again, it's unrealistic, because really, who is paid to write about foreign policy? But that's what everybody wants to do. But yet, you have to, with journalism, if you want to do it, you really have to write stories about kittens for the first few years. How they need to be rescued every now and then. How an old lady lost her kitten and that sort of stuff. Just...even thinking about it makes me want to stab myself. But, yeah, it is completely unrealistic; it's never gonna happen. But I still feel I'm slightly more realistic than other people. Because I feel what I have is a fairly niche kind of voice. But, it's never gonna happen because IT is...even if it could happen, I think I would still choose to be, to be doing what I'm doing now. Um, I think for many of us, we're just amazed that, "Oh my God—someone's gonna pay me to do this stuff." So it's—and I've talked to so many friends in other industries—and we really don't realize how good we have it.

Ed: Right. Now, I *do* realize how good we have it, and that gives me some anxiety about *not* having it.

Hani: Yes, I know.

Ed: So you're saying you don't really have a concrete, fleshed-out, realistic plan B?

Hani: No, I might not have my current job, but that's okay, because it's a huge industry. I know I can find a job in the Java space.

Ed: But that's assuming the industry continues to be huge.

Hani: But I don't see why it wouldn't though. Again, I'm the worst person when it comes to being a visionary what-are-we-doing-ten-years-from-now thing. I always assume that things never really change that much. Sometimes, I've been right; often, I've been pretty wrong. But I just don't have the foresight to be able to confidently predict. It's easy to make a concrete prediction; it's another to genuinely believe it. I don't have that, and so for me, I think that given not just the momentum, in fact, given just the sheer volume of it, it's not going anywhere. What's the worst that could happen? Java doesn't do well and you have to learn another language? It's a bummer. It would be a bummer for me personally, but I don't think that it would be the end of what I do. I feel I would lose a lot and I would have to basically start at a lower level in many cases. But I feel there's enough variety and it's such a rich ecosystem, that there's any number of spaces where I feel I can fit in.

Ed: Well, what about outsourcing? Are you worried about that? Are you worried about the job you do being moved someplace cheaper?

Hani: (long pause) I'm not worried about my job specifically. I'm more worried about how it might impact our business. I'm in two minds about it. The practical, fair-minded altruistic person in me thinks, "Great. The more outsourcing, the better. Free market. They're providing the same service, or even providing an inferior service but at a much more competitive rate. Why shouldn't they get the business?" So I definitely don't feel that anything should be done to "stem the tide of outsourcing" or "we must protect our jobs." I don't believe in that.

Ed: Protectionism.

Hani: Yeah, in fact, I'm the direct result of being allowed to work somewhere where I'm not American. And yet, I can work here. And I think it's a good thing for every country to be able to attract foreign workers. I hate subsidies. I hate protectionism, but on the other hand, as someone who could be affected by this negatively, that sucks [for me]. For example, we're bidding for a contract but they go with a company that has a development team in India or Russia because their bid was a tenth of the cost.

Ed: Right—because the pressure would be on you to outsource.

Hani: Yes, exactly, and there have been times where there have been people who were saying, "Maybe we should look at this outsourcing thing; maybe it's not efficient to have 50 developers in the fancy London office." And maybe it isn't! And maybe it's foolish of us not to outsource. We don't do any outsourcing, and it's never been a serious suggestion. It's been like, "Ah well, I wonder if this is even a serious option." But there's more to it than just the bottom line in many cases.

Ed: Okay!

Hani: I'm lucky enough to work in a company where that does matter. We're not answerable to any shareholders. We don't have any VC [venture capital] money. So there's no external pressure to "cut costs [and] get more developers for cheaper." We're living in a fairy-tale atmosphere where we have the luxury of saying, "We like our guys, we don't want to get rid of anyone, we don't want to bring on a bunch of strangers, who aren't gonna be a part of the *family*." And that's easy when you don't have the problems of scale that bigger companies do.

Ed: So you're privately held.

Hani: Yeah, we're 50 guys, privately held…

Ed: Well, but the readership of our book is gonna be people who work for big, non-private companies, and they are worried about outsourcing.

Hani: I'd say, be good at what you do. I don't think you can do anything to affect it one way or the other. It's one of these economic forces such as interest rates—it just happens. And I think you need to accept that it will happen and will keep happening. I don't think there's a doomsday scenario that's fast looming, where suddenly all jobs will be outsourced, there'll be no IT in the U.S. or Europe or wherever you happen to be from where they pay you really well to do IT. But, you should expect that if your job is menial tasks that you're doing over and over again, and not really learning anything or bringing any value, then maybe you *should* be outsourced, maybe that is for the best. It's your responsibility then to figure out, "Okay, well, how do I make sure that I can sell myself in some way? How do I bring value in some way?" And it means that you can't get away with being lazy. Another option is just move to somewhere like Germany, where they have great labor laws and you can never be fired.

Ed: For the moment.

Hani: For the moment. But I don't see that changing, given how many people are taking full advantage of these labor laws.

Ed: Yeah, but the way the EU is going is to reform these laws.

Hani: They're trying, but they haven't gotten anywhere. You need to keep making sure you keep bringing value. You need to make sure that you know what's going on in the industry. You can't just sit there and wait for the axe to fall. Because it might. And it might not! But it might…why take the risk? And if you're the kind of person who wants to just sit there doing nothing, then find a job that's more suited to that.

Ed: So that's my next question then: How important is it to hone entrepreneurial instincts and business acumen in terms of career maintenance?

Hani: I think it's not important at all.

Ed: But what you just said would indicate it is.

Hani: No, there's a difference. You're a techie. Your domain is technology, in fact, most likely, a very small subset of the technology landscape. Within that domain, there's huge opportunity. You could figure out, "Well, I'm gonna learn this, and I'm gonna learn that, and I'm gonna focus on this, and I'm gonna make sure that I have domain knowledge of these specific businesses." Now that has nothing [to do] with being an entrepreneur or knowing how the business works or, rather, knowing the business world stuff. How the business works would be fine if you say, "I'm gonna make sure I know how the insurance industry works." That sort of domain knowledge is very valuable. Very marketable. I do lots of work with financials. IT guys who understand finance or how derivatives work or all these complex financial instruments do *really*, really well. Because they're very specialized and the market has a lot of money. So that's one way of doing it.

Ed: Hmmm, right, or go work at hedge funds.

Hani: Or you could just get a nice hedge fund job and then you're all set. [laughs] I don't believe in the "if you're an IT guy, you must understand… you must be an entrepreneur or have business acumen."…those are completely separate skills. They're great if you have them. But many people aren't wired to have them. And…okay, you're not wired to have them, so what? There are many businesspeople who aren't wired to be technology guys; we don't look down on them. Actually, we do [laughs]…but we shouldn't…they're making more money in many cases. Look at sales guys. They make the most money, but they don't know much about anything [technologically], but they're good at what they do. As developers, we can't do their sales job, actually…and yet it makes us feel better about ourselves to say, "Ah, this sales guy's got this dumb job…*I* could do this job." A lot of people have that approach. They don't take the sales force seriously. You always want to make yourself feel better by thinking, "I'm better than they are in some way." And that is…it's nonsense. Because, in fact, they have far more grounds for thinking that they're better than you. They may think, "Well, I make more money than that person…I'm able to interact with other people better…I'm more successful if you look at standard measures of success…why does this IT peon think that they're better than me?" Different people are good at different things. Find your own strengths and play to them. You're much better off that way in the long term. It's a big world; it's a huge market; you have to specialize. You can't just say, "Well, I'm gonna know a little bit of this, I'm gonna be a little bit of an entrepreneur, I'm going to do a little bit of development, I'm gonna do a little bit of sales." I believe that people should stick to what they're good at. It could be just picking things that you love because you put more effort and energy towards it. I don't think I have much business acumen at all… I'm okay with that, because I'll just make sure that there's someone around who has that business acumen, who can do that role, who enjoys it, who understands it, and will satisfy that end of the bargain.

> **Character Attribute**
>
> Self-acceptance.

Personal

Ed: Speaking about keeping up an end of the bargain, how good are you at keeping your work and personal lives balanced?

Hani: Very bad. Absolutely abysmal about it. My wife is constantly complaining. It's helped somewhat by the fact that my wife has a very stressful job. She's a lawyer, and she is often very busy, so it allows me to sneak in more work hours than I should be. But it is hard. We don't have any kids yet, and so I think for a lot of people that helps keep them honest in a way, because children do demand a certain amount of time. And, left to your own devices, it's very hard maintaining that balance, because you gravitate towards whichever happens to be more fun at any given time. Just because you have choice, and you're a normal human being, you don't think, "My work's boring now, so I'm gonna spend more time on the other stuff." Or it could be, "Oh, my work is fascinating now, so I'm gonna neglect my life for a bit." I think short-term blips are actually healthy, as long as over the long term it's fairly balanced.

Ed: What is your definition of a dysfunctional family?

Hani: Well, I'd say lack of communication. It is a very easy first step towards a dysfunctional family. It depends on what you mean. What aspect of the family? Because if it's interactions within a family, certainly communication is one that impacts everyone. But in terms of personal relations within a family, I think a very important concept is the idea of teams within the family. When confronting an issue, it's incredible how much of a difference it makes if you view the issue as a team and the family as the opposing team. And the goal is that *your* team should win. I find that what happens in many interactions between people who are on the same side is that, I'm on a team, and the other family member is the other team. And so it's interesting once you shift your mental viewpoint how much easier it is to resolve issues. We want our team to win. I don't want to beat you, but I want our team to win.

Ed: In an earlier interview, you once said that you had a very peaceful, easy childhood. So you felt that much of the rage that kids might express you didn't get to express at that time. This is in response to a question, "Why are you so angry?" Would you say it was pretty harmonious in your family of origin?

Hani: Yes. I am one of five. I'm the oldest of five. We always got along very well. We're all very close even though we all live in different countries right now. My parents are back home in Oman. I have a brother who lives in D.C. I have a sister in London. I have a sister somewhere else in England. And a brother somewhere else in England. So we're all over the place, but we are very close. I had a very easy, privileged childhood. I didn't realize it at the time, but I do now.

Ed: Would you say this abundance of harmony in your youth has impacted your ability to handle conflict in any way?

Hani: I would say actually it's the other way around—it hindered my ability to handle conflict. Because it all was so easy and just fell into place. It's hard to understand. I think the nature is that for most people in life, there is such a thing as conflict that you just can't resolve. It was only through living in other countries that I've come to realize, "You could have people who have very fundamental differences, and so there's conflict when trying to discuss any given topic if you have these fundamental differences." It's an interesting realization, but the idea is that there is no right answer, there's no absolute in many of these conflicts. It was that breakthrough that made it very easy going forward to have a more objective view of conflicts. It's travel that I give credit to, not upbringing.

> **Observation**
>
> On page 284 Dave Thomas made the same observation about the impact of observing very intelligent people with vastly opposing views effectively communicating.

Ed: So who did most of the parenting [from age birth to 12]? Was it a team effort?

Hani: I'd say it was a team effort. Growing up in Oman, it's a very different environment from the Western world because much greater emphasis is placed on family. So even though my parents were both doctors, they were both home after work, early. So I saw both parents every day for many hours.

There was no, "Oh, Dad's coming home late from work today." And so I think they were both very involved, and continue to be involved, much to my chagrin.

Ed: So I'll say this. I would say that the lack of that in the Western world is actually a crisis and would have a negative impact on how things are. How do you feel about that?

Hani: I resented the big extended family. I resented all the social obligations that came along with that. I hated the fact that everybody knew your business. For example, if you did well at school, there are random aunts and uncles who are congratulating you even though you haven't seen them in months. And there's a lot of "What are you doing tonight?" "Oh, we're going to visit Aunt so-and-so or your grandmother." And given that I'm a computer nerd, I'm actually a fairly introverted person, believe it or not. And so, it's a great hardship for me. But I live in New York now, and I can certainly see the argument that there is something fairly culturally enriching about having a very strong social network.

Ed: Getting into your teen years, what was the first job you had?

Hani: I actually did not have a single job until after school. Actually during school. Again, it's a cultural thing. In Oman, and in most of the Arab countries, basically, you're your parents' responsibility up until the point at which you can provide for yourself. If you're living at home, you're their problem. You don't leave home unless you're going to get married usually.

Ed: Tell me something stupid you did as a teenager. Do they have stupid teenagers like over here?

Hani: Yeah, well. Hmm, I'm trying to think of something particularly stupid…(long pause) Hmm. I used to sell software. And a friend of mine, this was back in the Commodore 64 days, he bought this hardware dongle that would allow him to copy protected disks. And I knew enough C64 Assembly to get past the software copy protection. And so what we did was we'd sell this, and it was fine, because in Oman there weren't any copyright laws then.

Ed: The number of people who actually had Commodore 64s in Oman was what, a few hundred, a few thousand?

Hani: So this was a good idea until someone figured out that they could get software off of us without paying [by breaking *our* copy protection]. And so that happened for a while until we realized that we what we could do, in fact, was just add in bugs, just to show, "here's your special copy." I managed to get away with it by saying—I sold out my friend—by saying, "Oh, it's all his fault." And so my friend got in trouble for that because then the other guys told on him: "This guy is just selling software at school, and he's not supposed to be doing it." So he got in trouble, and I pretended like, "I don't know what anybody is talking about." So I think it was slightly shameful that I sold him out that way.

Ed: So where is this guy now?

Hani: We lost touch for about 15 years, and through some bizarre accident, he bumped into my brother in D.C. a couple of years ago. We got back in touch and realized we'd both moved to the States and, oddly enough, got along just as well as when we were in high school. The interesting thing is that we still had the same rapport despite both of us growing a lot and all the time that had passed. Instead of discussing computer games, though, both of us happened to feel very strongly about politics and stood on the same side of the fence. Though he did it as a job, and I'm strictly an armchair pundit!

Ed: How has that episode shaped your conscience and world view?

Hani: I'm not sure it did. If anything, it taught me that the world isn't particularly fair and has no sense of justice. It's up to us to impose that on the world around us, as long as we always remember that "justice" and "fairness" are artificial constructs and have no real "mapping" to reality, sadly.

Ed: What would you say is the relationship between success as a software developer and one's personal life?

Hani: [laughing] Inversely proportional. I don't know. For me, personally, I think there is little to no overlap between the two. Because I find that, in fact, it's easy to pick up bad habits in the software world that then, hopefully, if you have a well-grounded, normal life, you realize are bad habits. So I think the software side is tempered by the real-life side. Certainly, you may have this perception that you're particularly good. And in reality, it knocks you back into shape. Because you're interacting with other people who aren't in your field, you realize, "It's a much bigger world out there then what my profession would make me think it is." And so, I think, personally, in that way, you could be successful professionally, but it's important, if you want to be well adjusted at the end of it, it would have to be tempered by your normal life.

Ed: Let's finish by talking a bit about pay and compensation.

Hani: We're all overpaid.

Ed: Right, we are.

Hani: Realistically. Unless you've just started this year, or maybe last year, chances are you're now overpaid. And if you just started this year or last year, don't worry—you'll be overpaid next year.

Ed: Yeah, but isn't that an anxiety-provoking situation…

Hani: Yes…

Ed: To be overpaid? Shouldn't we all be preparing to not be overpaid? Some day…

Hani: Yes and no, but on the other hand, you could argue that…why not enjoy it, instead. If it happens…

Ed: Well, CEOs are overpaid.

Hani: Yeah, we're all overpaid. So it's not just, an anomaly where this is one person in the company that's overpaid. If 20 percent of your workforce is IT guys, then 20 percent are making way more than they should be.

And it is a concern, [when I stop] to think about it; it *is* a problem, because what if someone realizes this one day and says, "These guys will actually do the same work if we paid them half what we paid them. 'Cause they enjoy this work. And we have a lot of people who aren't that interested anyway, which is the logical thing to do."

Ed: Well, that's a motivator for outsourcing, isn't it?

Hani: Yeah. Right, and it could happen, and it would suck for all of us, but I can't live my life that way. Unless I see the axe descending…but I'm not gonna live my life as if this is gonna last forever, either. You have to find a ground where you're not cowering in fear all the time from all the awful things that are about to happen. But you're not thinking, "This is the rest of my life now. I've arrived. I'm always going to be making this much money forever." And more and more and more. So, you have to be rational about it. You can't project ten years from now. Nobody can. Just look at your life ten years ago. There's no way you'd know that you'd be where you are now ten years ago. So why would that change for ten years in the future?

Ed: Right, okay. So, what's you're saying is that it's good to have—not good, it's essential—to have a plan B, but you don't have to know exactly what it is?

Hani: Yeah, you recognize that one day you might have to, on short notice, come up with a plan B. And not fall apart should that happen. Again, it ties into the thing I mentioned earlier: be skeptical. Because you don't know what's gonna happen. There is no one thing that you can guarantee in life. Nothing. So you accept it, you role with the punches. When you have a good thing, it's really important to enjoy it. That's one thing that I find that a lot of people don't do. Whatever situation they're in, they're always saying, "Oh well, this sucks and that sucks, and I'm working too hard, or I'm not; I'm bored at work; or I'm…" But nobody ever stops to think, "In terms of my entire life, this is actually the happiest I've been," but nobody thinks that. Nobody ever says, "I'm happy now." Everyone says, "Yeah, things are okay. I wish this was better, I wish that was better," and so on. And it's a tradeoff between always aspiring for something better, but also enjoying what you have. We're all very lucky. Most people in the world—95 percent of the human population—doesn't have what we have. They certainly deserve it, but we just happen to have lucked out.

Ed: I know!

Hani: It's great. It's so nice. It's so unfair, but so convenient for us.

CHAPTER 7

James Gosling

Fact Sheet

Name: James Gosling

Home Page: http://blogs.sun.com/jag

Rock Star Programmer Credentials: Father of Java

Date of Birth: May 1955

City of Birth: Calgary, Canada

Marital Status: Married

Number of Kids: Two

Degree: Bachelor of Science in Computer Science, 1977, University of Calgary; PhD in Computer Science, 1983, Carnegie Mellon University

Number of generations in ancestry (including yourself) that graduated from college: Two

Years as an IT Professional: 24

Role: Vice President and Fellow at Sun Microsystems

Introduction

In doing some research on the term "rock star programmer," I've found it fairly evenly split between negative and positive connotations. On the negative side, we have things such as a definition from www. urbandictionary.com: "A rock star programmer is a programmer who becomes popular, not because of technical achievement, but rather by the volume of fanboys who blindly consume his/her products." On the positive side are many individual "How to be a rock star programmer" blogs and articles featuring sound advice about improving one's skill as a software development practitioner. From this lot, we can infer a more positive definition of rock star programmer as someone who does all of the things recommended in those blogs so well that other people want to emulate them. Unquestionably, James Gosling is the latter.

I approached James during a technical leadership conference at Sun and shared the idea about this book. I asked whom he would recommend I interview. He gave me some leads, and I left it at that, not wanting to take up any more of his time than necessary. Unfortunately, space constraints don't allow me to include interviews with those he recommended. Only several weeks later did I realize I should have asked James for an interview himself! As a measure of his humility and quality in the highest sense of the term "rock star programmer," he took no offense at my omission and gracefully gave me all the time I needed to conduct the interview.

James has a plain old standard Sun office in each of their Silicon Valley, California, locations: Menlo Park and Santa Clara. His assistant, Cheryl Cline, explained this was to accommodate his crazy schedule, which I can certainly understand. I sat down with James in his Menlo Park office overlooking the salt marshes around the Dumbarton Bridge crossing the San Francisco Bay. I had sent James the questions in advance, since most of the people I've interviewed explicitly requested I do so. James, true to his rock star programmer core, didn't need them; he was comfortable just going off the cuff. He said, "Ask whatever you want. It's your book."

Background

Ed: It is widely known that the Network extensible Window System (NeWS), which you worked on in the mid-1980s, was ahead of its time. Where do you think NeWS would be today with respect to Ajax, Flash, and other rich-client technologies if you hadn't been forced to stop developing it due to Sun's decision to standardize on the X-Window System?

James: It's interesting to hear [Sun founder and former CEO] Scott [McNealy]'s description. Scott's one-liner was: "We got in the game of chicken; the other guy [the X-Window System] blinked the headlights, and we [Sun] drove off the road." I have no clue where we'd be if we'd kept going with NeWS. There were a lot of really good things about NeWS, and certainly the advanced imaging model [and] distributed computing stuff was really rather successful.

On the other hand, there were some issues that were problems with it. It's really hard to get PostScript to perform really well. And there wasn't much of a security model. If we had gone much farther with NeWS, those would have become big issues. In fact, I had been spending a lot of time trying to figure out how to make NeWS go fast. And in one of these weird twists, those issues with NeWS actually affected Java deeply.

Ed: Can you elaborate?

James: When I started doing Java, the whole idea was doing something script language-ish, but I had this series of experiences [with scripted environments] where it didn't take too long before the users were really pushing the performance envelope. I decided this time around that I really wanted to put together a system where I believed that I could get to "compiled code" performance, which is where we are today [with Java]. We're generally at or better than C and C++ [most of the time].

Ed: Can you say some more about the process by which you took the mistakes or the difficulties from NeWS and folded them into the process for developing Java?

James: All these things turn into requirements. The whole design space is this infinitely dimensioned thing. Requirements such as "must go fast" or "must be secure" partition the [requirements] space. You must have ways to say, "Well, what's my budget, in terms of instructions, for when I execute A = B + C?"

> **Observation**
>
> See Appendix D for the importance of requirements, the specificity thereof, to the process of knowledge acquisition. James points out how requirements constrain the shape of the solution. This is indicative of having 1st order ignorance about something.

You look at your typical scripting language—it's 100-ish [instructions]. In Java, it's one. And that's quite different. When you say "Yes, I want A = B + C to compile to one instruction," you're gonna have to think of things differently. If you believe that's a requirement, then various questions, such as dynamic typing, just answer themselves.

You just can't do dynamic-type determination for primitives. Similarly, consider requirements around reliability and security. There are all these lessons about security that showed that most security problems were, in fact, reliability problems. Well, the canonical example is in C: people not doing array subscript checking.

So you get the classic buffer overflow input problems. It's not like you can change one program and prevent buffer overflow problems, unless the one program that you're changing is the C compiler, and make it so that array subscripting is always checked and cannot be turned off. That's really the only way to make buffer overflow problems go away: Just mandate that they cannot happen. That became a principle in Java: that kind of error just could not happen. There was a fair amount of anguish over that. I spent a lot of time proving to myself that a sufficiently competent code generator could theorem prove the subscript checking away [most of the time].

Ed: Can you share your thoughts on what are some attributes of your ideal programming language and environment?

James: There's so much influence on context and the requirements. For the average stuff that I do, I really care about performance. And that's natural to me—that I really, really care about it. But lots of problems, [they're] not actually important. You don't actually have to be very fast to be "fast enough."

Ed: In some cases, expressiveness might be more important than performance.

James: Right, and generally, there are two parts to that. There's developing the software and then running the software. And, of course, if the software is gonna be run over and over and over again, then the cost of development time as a proportion [of the total cost] vanishes.

But nonetheless, it's really important to get that development cycle as tight as you can. It's often a difficult balance to get to know how much time to invest up front versus how much time you spend later on. Of course, a lot of the time [you spend] is about correctness. One of the attributes of a program language for me is not just "how easy is it to solve the problem?" but "how easy is it to come up with a correct solution?" And to know that it's correct.

Ed: Verifiably. Right.

James: And there are all kinds of levels of "correct." If you're writing a piece of software to put out a report as a webpage, if the formatting's screwed up now and then, you don't really care. If you're writing control software for an airplane, you really care about the most incredibly trivial things. So it's extremely context-dependent.

Ed: Okay. Is it true that your original vision for Java, as manifested in Oak, did not have a C++-like syntax?

James: No. It really started with a C++ syntax. In some sense, when we were originally talking about it as a group, we knew we needed something like this. We were talking about general scripting language-ish things, but I never implemented anything that had a syntax other than something like C++.

Ed: Okay. So it wasn't like you had to fit it to the C++ syntax to sell it inside of Sun or get the idea to be more palatable?

James: Well, actually, that *was* the goal. It wasn't that I was told to make it look like C++, but it was that I wanted to make it so that if I showed a page of code to somebody, they would understand it. And most people in the environment knew C and C++. So on the one hand, when you look at Java underneath, it's a lot more like Smalltalk or Lisp than it is like C++, and yet, you show a Java program to a serious C++ programmer, they can basically figure out what's going on.

That was a very conscious piece of subversion. I really wanted to try to get people to think of Java as something familiar, even though in its heart of hearts, it wasn't. And in many ways, I think one of the biggest accomplishments of Java is getting bankers to use garbage collection.

Ed: Sure. That's a big class of bugs that have been defined out of existence.

James: Right. If I had said, "Well, okay, but first you've gotta learn this whole weird syntax that involves an incredible number of parentheses." Pft. People wouldn't have even listened beyond the first five minutes.

> **Character Attribute**
>
> Explicitly addresses the problem of overcoming people's reluctance to change.

The syntax, the language, is, at some level, window dressing, but at some level, it's also the boundary between the human and the machine.

Soft Skills

Ed: As a software developer, how important do you think it is to be aware of your own ignorance?

James: Being aware of your own ignorance is crucial to everyone. And that's not particular to software development. I don't care whether you're a writer or you're flipping burgers in a McDonald's. You've gotta be aware of your own ignorance. And not be ashamed by it. It's not like everybody knows everything.

Ed: Right. So how about being meta-cognitive; being aware of your own ignorance is one type of this meta-cognition. How much of the time in your day-to-day job do you spend thinking about how you're doing, thinking about your thinking process?

James: Almost none.

Ed: So you're mostly in the mode, in the flow state.

James: Absolutely.

Ed: Would you say that's been a successful trait for you?

James: Yeah. I sorta bumble on. I often realize later in the game weird things about my thought patterns, but—

Ed: So it's not that you're in your head, optimizing, [saying things like] "How am I feeling today? I'm not really being very productive in this task. Maybe I should put it aside." How often do you check in on that level?

Observation

Andy Hunt, on page 258, relates the same advice when he says, "step away from the keyboard."

James: I check in not very explicitly. I certainly get to points in problems where I know that slamming my head against the table isn't gonna—it's time to just switch topics. And somehow or other, magically, when I come back ten minutes later, an hour later, things have settled. It can be almost anything. Go and cook dinner or play a game of solitaire. Whatever. All kinds of things help.

Ed: So a lot of the folks I talk to in this book have been in the industry for a long time. Some, like me, I'm only 35. I've only been in the industry for only 12, 15 years. Others have been around longer. But one theme that has emerged among all of the people is that they derived benefit from entering the computer industry at a point in time when some seminal moment was happening. Do you think that the historical accident of you being born in '55 has had an impact on how your career turned out?

James: Oh, yeah. There are lots of accidents along the way. My parents had a house two miles from the university. I could go over there all through high school and a good chunk of junior high school. Getting a job with the physics department when I was still in high school—that was quite a big deal. Going to Carnegie Mellon, where they were doing multiprocessors when most people thought that was a crazy thing to do. Being right there when the Advanced Research Projects Agency Network (ARPANET) was happening, writing all kinds of networking protocols. I wrote my first network protocol stack almost 30 years ago.

Ed: Was it a Transmission Control Protocol (TCP)–type thing?

Character Attribute

Deep understanding of the whole software stack, including network protocols.

James: It was a precursor to TCP. I actually did quite a few. One of the ones that I did was maybe the only independent implementation of the PUP VSP [PARC Universal Packet Vendor Specific Protocol] protocols. If you look at PUP VSP, they're almost identical to what Transmission Control Protocol/Internet Protocol (TCP/IP) turned into. In fact, a lot of the learning from the VSP experiments really affected the TCP/IP design. So I knew what was going on at an ultra-low level in the very, very early days.

Ed: Right. Okay. So having that low-level understanding to build on has been very important.

James: Right.

Ed: Well, do you have any advice for people who may be entering the industry now, late in the game, from the perspective of you and me? Maybe they're coming out of college now? They didn't have that experience of growing up with an 8-bit computer at home. Their first computer was already a Pentium or something. How do they account for not having that historical background?

James: Reading helps a lot. Playing helps even more. Play with networking protocols. Implement your own just for fun, then throw it away.

Ed: So that comes to the question of what are some character attributes of successful developers. As you just stated, curiosity is one of them. Can you talk about some other attributes of a successful developer?

James: You need persistence. It takes an unbelievable amount of dogged determination when something is just not working, to just go bang at it and try to figure out what the hell is going on. Lots of people give up easily. [On the other hand,] a lot of people get really tied to the stuff that they do. The only way that you can ever move forward is to throw stuff away. I'm a big believer in throwing stuff away, and for anything that I think is important, I usually believe that you have to build it at least three times. The more important something is, the more times you have to throw it away. One of the flip sides for that is that lots of people sit down, and they'll analyze the hell out of something before they start writing. And I just assume I'm gonna throw it away, so I do very little up-front analysis.

I'll think hard in the shower or wherever, but the "it's time to start coding" threshold is low. I start coding, get into it—lots of people get all cranked up on this notion that anywhere I got lines on the page, I gotta make it work. No. If this shirt chafes, take it off and try another. I'm a big believer in trying the experiment. You learn what you learn.

Ed: What about collaboration skills?

James: They're certainly important. Collaboration's a funny thing, because most people do a particular piece of code or particular algorithm when they're really deep-wound into something. I find there are a couple different levels of collaboration, at least. One is, "I do my piece, you do your piece, we'll fit them together." Another is two people staring at the same algorithm and trying to work things out.

Ed: Pair programming.

James: Pair programming or working in a pair on a whiteboard trying to come up with data structures and algorithms. I've actually been rather successful with the second one, with pair programming, except that it requires—at least for me—I can't do it with just anybody.

Ed: It requires a fit.

James: It requires a fit, and I've found that fit's fairly rare. It gets rarer as I get crankier with age. But there have been people [who] I've been able to program with that have just been wonderful. It's great if you can make it work. But if you can't…eh. But the group dynamic, where each person has a part and you fit it together, that's really crucial, because almost all the projects that have been good, more people have to work on them.

Ed: The thing that puzzles me, talking to people and doing this book, it quickly emerges that there haven't been really any new ideas in a long time. The things that are truly new, a lot of it was already done in the 1970s. NeWS, you said, was done in '84. If that's the case, then what are we doing today? If it's all already been done, why is there still so much churn? Everyone's trying to tune these knobs on this machine to get the optimal setting, but no one has quite figured out what that is yet.

James: Well, the whole concept of a new idea, innovation, is really kinda weird, because if you wind the clock back 20 or 30 years ago and you pick some area such as multiprocessing, people did a lot of invention around multiprocessing. I was in the middle of a bunch of it. We did a lot of it at Carnegie Mellon when I was a grad student. Lots of people wrote lots of papers, but it was completely useless because there was just no way that any of it was practical.

Ed: Its time had not yet come?

James: Yeah. And most really breakaway ideas, their time has not come. So then they just sit on the shelf there for 20 or 30 years, and lots of things around them have evolved. Microprocessors have really caught up. Yada, yada, yada. All of a sudden, those ideas actually fit. They actually work. People are working on a lot of ideas today that really are retreads of ideas that people had 30 years ago. But 30 years ago, the ideas were silly because they were completely impractical.

Ideas just naturally go through this long gestation period from popping out of somebody's head, being completely impractical, to the point where they're actually working. And at what point do you call that innovation? Right?

On the one hand, people say Arthur C. Clarke invented the [geostationary communications] satellite.

[Clarke's 1945 *Wireless World* article titled "Extra-Terrestrial Relays" was the first published work on the subject.]

Well, yeah, he wrote a book that did that, and the whole idea of something like a moon-like thing being out there was, yeah, really obvious. But how the hell do you actually make it work?

So it's not like Arthur C. Clarke invented the satellite and then nobody after that ever contributed anything. Because actually realizing that sort of insight in itself requires a lot of insights. So if you wander around today, you'll find lots of people with crazy ideas that are completely impractical. But you wait 30 or 40 years, and a lot of them will look like, well, that's dumb. Somebody thought of that 20 or 30 years ago.

Ed: Here's one along the lines of making one's crazy ideas work. When you are working on a software project and you're faced with a choice at the implementation level of "do the right thing" or "do the quick thing," what are some things you do to motivate yourself to do the right thing?

James: Well, I always ask myself about the context. If I'm doing a quick hack for a demo to show somebody something, whatever works. If I'm working on some piece of platform thing that I know is gonna land or even has a chance of landing in a billion cell phones or something like that, I sweat over getting it right 'cause there are all kinds of mistakes that have lived on way longer than they ought to.

I've committed more than my share of sins in that regard. I try to avoid it. I find that one of the strongest forcing functions to get myself to do the right thing is having not done the right thing often enough. I got enough scars on my body to be motivated.

Ed: How do you keep current? Do you have a process for keeping up with the latest developments? How do you separate signal from noise with all the information that's out there?

James: Signal from noise is a really hard problem. In general, I don't read blogs, just because the signal-to-noise ratio is so bad.

Ed: Do you find that you rely on your team to be doing that and filtering it?

James: I don't have a team. But I have friends.

Ed: Yeah. That's what I mean.

James: Yeah. And I get e-mail from friends saying, "Oh, check this out. This is really cool." That's probably the highest signal quality channel I know of.

> **Character Attribute**
>
> Part of a group of friends that shares "cool stuff" stories.

Ed: Absolutely.

James: But I do the usual website trolling. There are a few that I pop to fairly regularly. I just do a lot of reading.

Ed: So if you are reading an article, an announcement, or something, or there's a new software technology out there, how do you assess the quality of it?

James: Usually the quality of the idea is clear. Is it solving an interesting problem? Is it a reasonably efficient solution? Is it an elegant solution? Is it a simple solution?

Hard Skills

Ed: Earlier, you mentioned you had to prove to yourself that Java solved the buffer overflow problem. Did you do a formal correctness proof?

James: Well, there's formal correctness and then there's formal correctness. I never did formal correctness in the sense of full proofs. The problem with formal correctness is that as soon as your problems get even slightly complicated, the proofs just go out the window in terms of complexity. But nonetheless, the formal proof techniques, while they may not be terribly useful as proof techniques directly, I find them really good as ways to think about how you construct programs that are correct, to think about preconditions and postconditions, what needs to be true here. What are the invariants that this particular data structure is trying to maintain? I think about that basically every instant.

Ed: Ah. Okay. So that's a meta-cognitive process that you are putting into play if you're always thinking of pre, post, and variant.

James: Oh, yeah. Those are always there. And in my type of programming process, all those things are just the way that I think about it.

Ed: Is that something you evolved as you learned to program? Not everyone has that "design-by-contract" way of programming. How did you get to that?

James: I think I was bumbling towards it, but then, in grad school, I took some really great courses by a couple of really great Analysis of Algorithms professors. Two guys named Michael Shamos and Jon Louis Bentley. I took any course they ever taught while I was a grad student at Carnegie Mellon University. And they very much thought of everything in terms of the proof. And, wow, they were actually good mathematicians, and I'm a piss-poor mathematician. At least as a formal structure for thinking, [Analysis of Algorithms and Formal Correctness] works well.

Business

Ed: How important is it, as a career software developer, to have business acumen and entrepreneurial instincts?

James: It depends on what you're working on. If you're just doing what you're told, cranking out code, you don't need much. But the more that you have to be involved in the design of the systems and the systems tend to need to fit into somebody's business, the better you need to understand the context. And that might be business acumen, if what you're doing is generating something that drives somebody's website. It also might be needing to know more organic chemistry if you're working in controlled software for a chemical plant. Your software always fits into the context. And knowing the context is always a big deal.

> **Observation**
>
> This is the same as Hani's "IT serves the business" answer on page 136.

Ed: Do you have any thoughts that you want to share about the impact that Google's hiring prowess has had on the state of available software talent today?

James: Well, they certainly are sucking up everybody. They do make life difficult for everybody else. Various companies have done this sort of stuff. Microsoft certainly went through a phase when they were hiring anybody with a pulse. IBM certainly did that. And Sun has gone through phases of doing that. If you look at a physical organism, like part of your body started growing that fast, you wouldn't call it growth, you'd call it cancer.

Most organizations that go through that kind of growth discover that, eh, it's not a real great idea and it becomes self-limiting. They can't double the number of engineers every year forever.

Ed: Do you have anything to say about the ontology of the software industry? Is there any way you could categorize the software industry? Do you have any breakdown that you use to put things into buckets?

James: No. There's this goofy quote that shows up in *Wayne's World*. Something like "if you label me, you nullify me" or something?

[The quote is: "Was it Kierkegaard or Dick Van Patten who said, 'If you label me, you negate me?'" It was Kierkegaard, and the quote is "Once you label me, you negate me."]

> **Character Attribute**
>
> Well-versed in pop culture.

I'm not into labeling things, if only because the labels become the thing that defines the universe, and for me, the really interesting stuff is the stuff that doesn't fit. There's a big piece of the programming culture these days where their entire universe is the stuff that generates HTML pages and the stuff that goes onto those HTML pages, the JavaScript, and that kind of stuff.

And [I want to say,] "Guys, don't you realize you're in this tiny little corner of things? There is so much more cool software out there—everywhere—from people doing large weather simulations to people doing sensor nets." A lot of the ontologies I see people come up with, they always leave great, huge tracts of land completely unlabeled and, therefore, nonexistent.

Ed: If you're gonna use ontology, use it with a grain of salt.

James: A grain of salt. A huge grain of salt.

Ed: What do you think drives innovation in the software industry? And is it any different now than it was ten years ago?

James: For my money, there are two major forces that drive innovation. One is there's just this thing in people to build new stuff. It's like the drive to give birth and—

Ed: The creative force.

James: This creative force. And the other is: just wanna make money. And they often get commingled. One of the things that often happens is somebody will come up with a really bright idea that really gets them excited, but they're probably the only person in the universe that would actually find it interesting, and there's no way that it would actually make any commercial sense. They go around being really puzzled by why it is that nobody wants this completely wonderful thing. I have certainly been there. And the interplay between the pure, deep technology side and the business, financial side is important and hard for most people to get to.

Ed: How satisfied are you with how the world has changed as a result of OpenJDK? Has it come as far as you would have liked?

James: As far as we can tell, yeah. It's still early in the OpenJDK thing. We've been running it as an open process for 12 years now.

Ed: That's true, and the Java Community Process has been fairly open as well.

James: Yeah. In that sense, I'm really happy with it. But given that we don't really have live [source code] repositories out there yet, it is still early in the lifecycle.

Personal

Ed: Can you tell me about some turning-point moments in your career, where you made a choice that propelled you forward or did not?

James: Or not. Some of the more spectacular ones in my life are ones that did not. When Sun was founded, I actually had lunch with Andy Bechtolsheim the day that he signed the papers with Scott McNealy [to create the company]. I and a friend of mine had lunch with Andy, and Andy was going, "You gotta join us." I said, "Andy, you nut case."

Ed: And you chose not to?

James: And I chose not to. And then he and Bill Joy spent the next year and a half beating me up to come and join Sun, and I eventually came and joined Sun, and [said], "Damn. Why didn't I do this a year and a half before?" But a year and a half before, I looked at what IBM was building and [what] other folks were building, and I figured "Andy doesn't have a chance." But everybody else managed to be colossally stupid. And it worked out.

Ed: Have you ever had a career mentor? Maybe in college, were Bentley or any other professors there influential?

James: There were a bunch of them that were influential. Bentley and Shamos certainly were. I got to know Bentley moderately well. I had two thesis advisors who were just wonderful: Bob Sproul and Raj Reddy. Bob was my advisor, and he was just wonderful. And Ivan Sutherland was also on my thesis committee, and he was really, really great. They weren't exactly mentors in the usual way people think of the word "mentor." All in one fashion or another were real role models. Even now, they're real role models. I get to see Ivan every now and then. In fact, I'm going to be spending the rest of this afternoon with Ivan. Ivan's really high on my list of the world's really, really cool people.

Ed: How organized are you in your work life and your personal life? Would you consider yourself a neat person? I look around your desk; it looks clean.

James: I wouldn't call it terribly clean. I think I'm middle of the road. My wife thinks I'm messy. Compared to my dad or my grandfather, I'm tidy.

Ed: Do you keep a journal?

James: No.

Ed: Okay. What about a day planner? Anything like that?

James: If I could get away without it, I would. I would not do it. I use a calendar. I don't use a paper daytimer, but my life requires a certain amount of scheduling. I have an admin; she's wonderful. I hate the fact that I *need* an admin.

Ed: Was there ever a point in time where management at Sun said to you, "James, we're going to build a brand around you, specifically, as 'the father of Java'." If so, how did that sit with you?

James: Well, various people have tried to do that, and any time I've been asked, I've said no! But it subversively happens.

Ed: So how do you feel about being that way now?

James: It's a mixed bag. I'm more uncomfortable with it than anything else. It still feels weird when people recognize me in the street in the damnedest places and I have no clue who they are. When you meet somebody in the street, it's like, "Oh, hi." You kinda know each other. But when they know you and you have no idea who they are, I always think to myself, "Jeeze. Is this some old friend from high school that I ought to remember or is this just some completely random person?" It's often hard to tell. But my kids find it cool that we can be standing in line for an ice cream cone at some arbitrarily weird place and people in line know who I am. It's either odd or cool.

Ed: What were some of your favorite courses in college and why?

James: The way that the courses at CMU worked when I was there doing computer science was that there was no course requirement for anything. There were these seven qualifying exams, and to get your PhD, you had to pass the seven exams, have one paper accepted by some journal somewhere, and you had to write a PhD thesis. And in general, it was the seven qualifying exams that were the hard part. Various professors had these semi-formal semi-series to help people learn what they needed to get through the qualifying exams, but they were much less structured than a normal course would be.

Those were really good. When I was an undergraduate, I took all the usual survey courses, but there was one course that was called "Surveys in

Computer Science," which was kind of a roll-your-own course. You had to go up to a professor and say, "Hi, I'd like to spend this semester studying this." And they'd say, "Okay." And then you'd spend a semester doing that. You'd usually write up a paper or something. And you'd get to do something weird.

Ed: What did you pick?

James: I actually took the course three times.

Ed: Sure. Why not?

James: Right. It was an odd deal. You could take that one course multiple times and get independent credit for it.

Ed: Right.

James: One that I did, it was an image-understanding task. There were some folks who had a scanning photo multiplier, which is like a TV camera, where you could steer the beam, and they wanted to be able to find clouds and find edges.

Ed: Edge detection. Right.

James: But it was a strange edge-detection problem, because you didn't have a full image, particularly then. You couldn't put a megapixel image into memory because none of these computers had anywhere near that much memory. And the scanner was very high-resolution, so what you had to do was [conduct] a course-grid sample, and then I came up with all these techniques for essentially binary searching to find the edges—find the cloud layers and such. That was fun. I did that for credit.

There was a book by Bill Wulf called *The Design of an Optimizing Compiler* (Elsevier, 1980). And my course was basically, "read that, talk about it a lot." And that was cool.

Ed: So what other texts have you found useful in your career? A lot of people refer to *Structure and Interpretation of Computer Programs* (SICP) by Harold Abelson and Gerald Jay Sussman (The MIT Press, 1996) as the gold standard for computer science texts.

James: No. The big one for me was *The Design of an Optimizing Compiler* by William Allan Wulf (Elsevier, 1980). That one was way up there. Brian Kernighan and Dennis Ritchie's *The C Programming Language* (Prentice Hall, 1988) was a big one. The Simula 67 manual was a big deal for me. Knuth's series.

Ed: *The Art of Computer Programming?*

James: *The Art of Computer Programming* by Donald Knuth (Addison-Wesley Professional, 1998) was a really big deal. I got an awful lot just from the architecture manuals for the machines like the PP8 and the CDC6000 series. I read all of those about 100 times.

CHAPTER 8

Kohsuke Kawaguchi

Fact Sheet

Name: Kohsuke Kawaguchi

Home Page: www.kohsuke.org

Rock Star Programmer Credentials: Creator of the Hudson continuous integration tool

Date of Birth: July 1977

City of Birth: Washington, D.C.

Birth Order: First of two

Marital Status: Married

Number of Kids: One

Degree: Bachelor of Science, University of Tokyo, 2001; Master of Engineering, Cornell University, 2003

Number of generations in ancestry (including yourself) that graduated from college: Two

Years as an IT Professional: 12

Role: Senior Staff Engineer at Sun Microsystems, Inc.

Introduction

I've asked most of the programmers in this book who they think is the most productive programmer they've ever worked with. For me, the answer to that question is Kohsuke Kawaguchi. I first encountered Kohsuke's work when it came time to publish the binary deliverables for JavaServer Faces to a public code repository known as "Maven." Kohsuke had written some software to automate the process. His motivation for doing so was a desire to contribute to the Maven mission: making it easier to stand on the shoulders of the software that came before you. He saw the synergy between the Maven mission and Sun's mission of bringing the power of network computing to as wide an audience as possible. Like nearly every programmer in this book, Kohsuke views his art first and foremost as a way to make a positive influence on the world.

Kohsuke is certainly not the most famous programmer in this book, but I'm certain you'll find his insights, candor, and wry sense of humor enlightening.

Soft Skills

Ed: What technology was the most useful to you in generating career success, and how did you know that this particular technology was the star to which you wanted to hitch your career wagon?

Kohsuke: Looking back, that must have been eXtensible Markup Language (XML), because without doing any XML work, I [wouldn't be] doing this. I started doing it not because I thought it was a good career move or anything. Specifically, the schema language was what got me into Sun Microsystems, and the only reason I started doing that was [because] my company Swift had been doing some XML work before, and since I was doing it in the business, I thought I'd make it my graduating thesis. So I wrote up a little paper about an XML differential engine. The professor thought that since I wrote the paper, we should go to one of those conferences and talk about it, which we did. (This was "XML Developers Day" in 2000.) That's where I met this guy called Makoto Murata. He was trying to sell his schema language. It just so happened that the conference was held in a remote place from Tokyo [where my University was located]. He was living in Tokyo, too, so we took the return train back together. We were sitting in this train for two hours, and he was very enthusiastic about what he was doing. That somehow got to me. He was trying to encourage me to write a Java implementation of the [XML] validator. Somehow his enthusiasm just convinced me that, all right, "Maybe it's fun to do something to see what's gonna happen from this." You never really know what can happen!

Ed: Would you say it was just as important to meet this individual as well as the attributes of XML itself?

Kohsuke: It's really more about people, in that sense. He was working for IBM then, but now he's doing something else.

Ed: How do you keep current? Do you have a process for keeping up with new developments? Do you narrow your domain so you only stay current on specific things?

Kohsuke: In the grand scheme of things, I'm probably staying in a very narrow part of programming in general. I don't know if I have any enterprise-scale development skills that will span across lots and lots of computers. I just [have] no idea about what people do on these things. I don't [do] any embedded development either. It's still a very small portion. I guess you just need to…

Ed: Focus? What feeds do you read?

Kohsuke: Sun is a reasonably diverse place; it's good in terms of keeping you open to other interesting things that are happening— like JavaOne. Every year it's a really good source of inspiration, 'cause you really get to see this landscape of things. There a few things that just stand out like beacons, and that's the kind of jump you need to make, and once you know the right place, then you can gradually conquer that small region.

> **Observation**
>
> Joe Nuxoll had a similar thing to say about JavaOne. See page 63.

That's how I do it, but it's still very small. Like, I'd love to spend more time on .NET, but I just don't get any chance for exposure there.

Ed: How important is it to be aware of one's own ignorance?

Kohsuke: When I'm designing a solution to a problem that I don't personally have, it's very difficult. For example, JAX-WS (Java API to XML Web Services) is a solution to a problem that I don't have. It seems to me that what we are doing is not necessarily optimal, but then it's not like I know exactly what the users are trying to do, so those [problems] are hard. Lately, most of my projects are when I'm solving a problem that I have, and that becomes a lot easier. The good thing about hobby projects is that I could say, "That's beyond the scope of the project," so it's very easy. I came to trust my sense of finding problems. I guess I never really thought about that. Maybe I'm not humbled about my own ignorance. If you find another problem, you can just solve it in a different way. I've been writing a schema validator, maybe three or four times now. That's a totally different implementation each time, and that was fun for me. I don't mind later finding out that "this just doesn't work." That kind of experience is very nice. You can try something else. Maybe the short answer is that I'm not really coping with ignorance at all.

Ed: How much of your time do you spend in an introspective mode of thought? This is called meta-cognition.

Observation

Though I didn't interview him in this book, I have met Larry Wall, the creator of the Perl language, and he also places a high value on laziness. In fact, he lists laziness as the first of his three "Virtues of a Programmer." His meaning is exactly the same as Kohsuke's here.

Kohsuke: It's related to this notion that I have of laziness. I'm trying to be lazy. What I mean by that is [I] try to see if I'm doing the same thing more than a few times. Then [I] try to solve that problem. In the end, the cost of solving the problem in a general way is not always optimal. For example, [when] writing Hudson, I ended up writing my own Web framework and my own data binding and so on. If you're [writing software] for a business purpose, you don't want to do that. You need to find the shortest way to get the requirements done. But I guess that's a part of the fun in the hobby projects—I can solve those problems a bit more generally, so that when you take the individual pieces that create your whole stack, each piece needs to be optimal and general enough so that any portion could [be used] in your own way. That's probably in some sense what you're calling meta-cognition. When you're doing something, you should always try to solve the problem in a more general way. Although I do waste a lot of time doing things. It's quite often that I start writing something, then, a few days later, I realize it's no use at all.

I stopped driving for commuting; I'm riding on a bike. When I'm doing that, that's a good time where ideas can detach [and grow]. You're not looking at the code, you're having some distance from what you've been working on, but it's still back in your mind, and it seems to me that somehow those are the times where the good ideas occur. Or the realization will occur that this code is a POS. That's what I'm finding.

Initially, I didn't like driving the car. In Japan, everyone commutes by train, so I was mostly reading books. It turns out that [by biking] I'm not totally wasting that time, I suppose.

Ed: What are some character attributes of successful developers?

Kohsuke: I wish I knew. [pause] I really think one of them must be laziness. Because diligent people don't even think about using a computer or programs in an efficient way. Search and replace is one thing. I often find myself doing it, but making certain changes in a text editor, you just keep typing and using cut and replace and...

Ed: Not using global search and replace?

Kohsuke: Yeah, yeah, and that's the danger that the diligent people have. When you're lazy, then you don't want to do those things by yourself, which is the motivation for having programs do some of the things.

Ed: This intolerance of repetition, this desire to automate as much as possible...

Kohsuke: Yeah. To me, that's the thing. It's not just in the context of automation, but...essentially, the computers are designed for taking mundane work from us human beings because we have better things to do. That's what I meant by laziness. Maybe that's a confusing word.

Ed: Would you say the character attribute of constantly having lots of side projects was a success factor for you?

Kohsuke: Yes, looking back, it seems to be that's helping.

Ed: I've talked to many people in the book so far, and many of them have asserted that multitasking kills productivity. You have a ton of different projects going on; however, you are the most productive programmer I know. How are you the exception to the rule?

Kohsuke: It's just that the time slice is larger. If you get constant interruption about random stuff, it does kill you. But the time span of real concentration for me is a few hours, max. If you're switching beyond that scope, say, doing some work stuff in the office and then doing some hobby stuff at home, that's very easy to manage. I didn't have that problem, I suppose. But there is [a] certain truth in that. Because, sometimes, even though you are working on another project, you can't get off these other things that you want to do, and you end up doing something else, so maybe those are things that kill productivity. But generally speaking, I do a longer time slice. But interruption is becoming another problem. In the day job, I now work on too many things, so people keep interrupting me, which is not good.

Implementing something initially is a very small part of it. The harder part is that once you get something done—let's say this Java logging system—there's this ongoing maintenance work that just has to happen, and that is just eating up some of my time right now. I need to find a way to avoid that. That's one of my current challenges.

Ed: What role does luck play in career success?

Kohsuke: In my limited experience, luck certainly seems to play an important role, but at the same time, you also need to be looking around. Be open to doing other things, which I try to do. That might have also helped. It's hard to say. For example, when .NET came out, I wanted to try it. The only way to do that was to do something serious with it, so I guess it's the same idea, but I eventually wrote a game out of it. That was fun on its own. It didn't turn into a career, but it's important to try and keep doing those things. I guess Hudson [Kohsuke's continuous integration tool] might be one of those things. That might be…that might help you find the right moment.

Ed: How do you build developer and user communities for your projects?

Kohsuke: It's hard; I wish I knew the right answer. It's an important question for me, because the way I get myself motivated is by having users.

> **Observation**
>
> This is how he combats the waning interest syndrome. As I mention on page 133, this is a problem where you lose interest in doing something after a while.

The game [FreeTrain for .NET] is great. Every summer, people show up out of nowhere and they play and they contribute. I guess they are students and they don't have anything to do for summer. On more serious projects, like Hudson, my initial users were my colleagues, and I was also a user myself. The initial hard part, when you [are] not getting feedback, [my interest was] sustained by relying on those people using it. But once it gets to the point when it gets picked up, it becomes easier. I have lots and lots of projects that didn't get to that point. I spent some effort, but my interest with that project declined before it was picked up by someone else. I don't know the right answer. It just seems like if you stick to something long enough at least a year or two, then it does get picked up.

Ed: Persistence.

Kohsuke: Yeah, I think so, and also how you keep yourself interested in that [initial] period.

Ed: Can you talk about how you do that?

Character Attribute

Career-savvy altruism.

Kohsuke: In my case, when I have users, it's very easy to keep me motivated. Ultimately, this is like volunteering. You do it because you know that what you're doing makes some other people happier.

If I'm using my own stuff, then it's very easy to keep myself motivated. That's been true with some of my projects. Even though they don't have so many users or I don't hear from them, I'm still committed to keep them updated and so on. That's a factor, I suppose. Some people just seem to move on to another project even if the project is picking up, so I don't know what's going on in their head, but I guess I'm a bit different in that regard. Maybe they're more interested in the part where they implement their idea, but I'm more interested in making people happier.

Ed: It's clear that providing user satisfaction is something that motivates you professionally. What about what motivates you to succeed personally in your life as a father, a husband, other things?

Kohsuke: I guess I have a problem with that [laughs], I wish I could just hack all day. The trick for me is I try to stay away from home if I want to pay attention to my wife or daughter. When I'm at home, I can't keep myself away from the computer. I don't have my own room at home. A part of the kitchen is my desk. I can always see it, and I always have lots of ideas and features that I want to implement in the back of my mind. The only way to completely shut the programming out from my mind is to not to see any of them—that is, to go out.

Ed: I have the same problem, and I battle with this, and so have several of the others in this book (*see Tor's answer on page 86*).

Kohsuke: You need to tell that to my wife!

Ed: Interestingly enough, one of the other developers I interviewed, Dave Thomas (*see Chapter 12*), told me that his OTI labs used to have educational sessions for the spouses of the people working there to let them know about the balance challenges of the programmer's life.

Do you think there is any correlation between how easily one becomes a victim of the waning interest syndrome and their intelligence? Could you make any generalizations, such as intelligent people are less susceptible to become bored or are more susceptible to become bored?

Kohsuke: Some of the smartest people that I know are very persistent, and yet some other smartest people are, how should we say, project hoppers? So I don't see any correlation. I wish I had a bigger sample base to draw the conclusion from.

Ed: Much of the work of enterprise software development involves being able to zoom in to a very fine level of detail and then zoom out to get the big picture—oftentimes, one right after the other. Do you think this requires a special proficiency in keeping things in perspective?

Kohsuke: I don't think I'm necessarily good at that. When you're designing this grand scheme and you have these beautiful pictures and get down into the details, reality always has a way of biting you back, and you have to realize that this just doesn't work this way. If you can contain the ugliness into small portions, that's fine, but sometimes it forces you to rethink some of the other bigger pictures.

I guess it's also true with anything, not just software engineering, but this inherent thing in any problem is how the small, minute details interact with the bigger-picture stuff. It's not a human-cognitive issue; it's just the nature of the thing that we are dealing with. I don't think it's necessarily just the characteristic of software engineering—it's probably true anywhere else. I guess the amount in which you can be good at those things is probably fairly limited. It's just the nature of things to work in that way, so you have to let the reality bite you hard.

Ed: Can you talk a little bit about the importance of collaboration as a skill in the developer's toolbox? Obviously, it's not as important on hobby projects.

Kohsuke: In a business environment, it is very important, because almost any non-trivial project involves more than one person. It's, frankly, one area where I have difficulty. Language is always an issue—especially in the United States—the people always just seem to work remotely, and we don't have enough bandwidth; that's always an issue.

Another thing is—I hope this doesn't come across badly—let's say you come up with this part of the job that needs to be done. You go looking for someone to do it and you think about how much you need to explain.

You need to give them enough justification about the design so that they feel good about doing something, and you need to explain about the various technologies so they can use them, and you need to explain how it relates to other pieces. If you think about the time it takes to do [all] that [preparation], that's *my* time. Then [you include] the time it takes for them to do the work, and then you think about the time it takes for you to do it. Then, at some point, it seems to make less sense to ask some people to do something rather than just do it yourself. That has been my mode of operation for a long time, but that just doesn't scale very well. My current approach is by having better tools, like Hudson, it reduces the amount of communication that you have to do.

> **Observation**
>
> It finally emerges that Hudson has become, for Kohsuke, a real, practical way that he is trying to change the world around him for what he perceives as the better.

It reduces the amount of work they have to do, too. For example, it used to be the case that you had to ask people to run the tests; now it's done automatically. You used to have to interface with the release engineering group for distribution; now we don't have to do that. We can make other people productive by not asking them to do more things, but actually spending more time boosting their bottom line.

Ed: So you're lowering the barrier to entry?

Kohsuke: Yeah, I find that's much easier. That clicks with me better, because I'm fundamentally a lazy person, and everyone should be lazy. That really works well as opposed to trying to be really diligent about communication. That's the angle that I'm trying to pursue a little more.

The other thing…it's quite possible to architect your software around your team. That's my recent finding. The way your team is organized and the boundaries you have between various people is actually one factor you can put into your design. I find that also [to be] helpful. For example, in Hudson, I spent a little extra [time] designing this architecture for extensibility. What that enables is that any random person can deliver this clear boundary between the part that is the core and the part that they can own. When there is a clear boundary that is defined, it seems to reduce the need for communication.

If your development team is small, like most of the projects I've been involved in, you can actually picture some particular person when you're designing part of the system. If he or she is junior, then you need to shrink it a little more, or maybe you need to dumb it down and separate that into two pieces. I find that kind of thing is possible.

Ed: Had you ever had to hand off a large body of code you've written to someone else and then they own it? You don't own it anymore?

Kohsuke: I need to make that happen, but so far, no. Which is a big problem. I guess it's mostly my fault. When you get to work on this stuff for too long, you develop this affection for it, and you can't just stand this idea that someone else is going to mess up with the code. Which is totally unreasonable.

> **Observation**
>
> On page 74, Tor Norbye of the Java Posse tells a story of how he dealt with the mental anguish of giving up his baby to another programmer.

But I guess it's just a kind of obsession, which is being unable to keep some distance with your own work. Again, it just doesn't scale.

If there is anything that I've learned [it's that] there is such a thing as being too clever. You don't want to do something just because you *can* do it.

Hard Skills

Ed: Why did you decide to write Hudson when there were other gratis and/or open-source continuous integration tools?

Kohsuke: In my mind, there was nothing good out there.

Ed: Nothing good?

Kohsuke: Yes.

Ed: There was Cruise Control, right?

Kohsuke: Yes. Okay. If you call that…I guess [I] shouldn't say those challenging things. At some point, I somehow [get] in this mode when I look at something. I first build a mental model of how it "should have been done."

> **Character Attribute**
>
> Always assessing the quality of software.

Then I start looking at this thing, and if it departs from my expectations too much, I stop looking at it.

Ed: Does this extend to everyday objects and things you interact with in life or just software? When you use a bottle opener, do you think, "How should this bottle opener have been made?"

Kohsuke: Not really. I guess I don't have the sense of mastery of most other things in life. For example, when I read books, I just read them, and I can't even always decide whether I liked it or not. I wish I could start reasoning, "Well, I liked this because X, Y, and Z, but the author failed to deliver W." The same goes for movies, too. It's a real problem, because usually, when you go to see movies with friends, you are supposed to make some witty comments, which I can't do at all. This mindset is really just for computer software, in which I think of myself as a professional.

When I looked at Cruise Control, well, that was very different from what I would have done, and that was enough to say "this is not for me."

I'm more impressed with another tool, called Damage Control, which was implemented in either Python or Ruby. That has a much better user interface (UI), better-looking icons. The only thing is [that] it's written a language that I don't hack. If you look at the features, it's very implementable; you just need to implement it in a different language. The implementation is always fun for me. I thought maybe just for the fun of it, I could do that.

Ed: Why don't you hack Ruby?

Kohsuke: Back then (and to some extent, even still) I didn't think of Ruby as a language for implementing a large system. I didn't have any experience in Ruby at all three years ago. The language was not the only reason. Another motivation for doing Hudson was to write a real Web app in Java, since the group at my day job involves defining a Java application programming interface (API) for those. Hacking Ruby didn't work for me.

Ed: Your opinion of Ruby is surprising, considering you came up in the programming culture of Japan, where Ruby was very popular for a long time before the whole Rails phenomenon. It seems you have a general philosophy of when you encounter a new technology, you ask yourself, "How would I have done this?"

Kohsuke: Right.

Ed: You applied that to Cruise Control?

Kohsuke: It's true of anything. For example, the Web framework [in Hudson]. When I decided to write Hudson, I had some ideas of how I wanted to implement it, but I thought, because there were a million Web frameworks out there, there must be something that I can pick up. I looked at a few of them, like Tapestry and Velocity and what not, and none of them seemed to do what I would have done. I'm sure those are good frameworks, and if I spent a bit more time learning [them], maybe in the end I might have been more productive. I find the time I spend learning something not really enjoyable, so I might rather write it by myself, for the purpose of having done it.

> **Character Attribute**
>
> Values learning by doing over learning by reading.

Ed: Can you talk some about the early days in developing Hudson? How did you get started? How long did it take to get to the first usable version?

Kohsuke: If I recall correctly, I started doing it while I was traveling to [and from Sun's Campus in] Burlington [Massachusetts]. Then, at night, I'm alone and I don't have anything else to do and I did have a computer, so maybe I just started hacking that thing. It also depends on how you define usable. In a certain sense, Hudson is still not very usable today for the kinds of things I want it to do. I don't really have this clear notion that when you get to a certain point it becomes useful. The very initial version of

Hudson was not even in Java, but was a shell script! The only thing it did was check out the JAXB RI and if it fails, send out an e-mail. In a certain sense, you can call that usable, and I don't think that took any more than 15 minutes to set that up. Iteratively improving things is also nice. At work, we used to do this release schedule that took a very long time, every one or two years. There were a lot of processes going on before the release, writing docs and so on. I wanted to do something really drastic, which was this model where I release something every three days.

Ed: Were you consciously applying Agile methodologies to do this?

Kohsuke: If you just look at the result, maybe it's part of it. Maybe that's just what seems to be happening. But I was really just trying to do something else, something very different from my work. It's my way of maybe balancing this thing.

> **Character Attribute**
>
> Turn dissatisfaction at work into a career asset by using a hobby project.

The goal [of Hudson] is to have happy customers. When they report a bug, I want to fix it right away. In work, I have this frustration that, even though I have a fix, [someone] has to wait three months just to get it. With [a hobby project], I can release it today, three hours after the bug report. Those things make people happy. I like that aspect, and that's why I keep doing it.

Ed: When is it appropriate to start over from scratch?

Kohsuke: I guess I have this tendency of reimplementing from scratch. There are obviously dumb programs…like sort, and so on, where the specification is so well defined, there is really no chance for your implementation to do anything. Generally speaking, those very trivial, lower-level, small issues are the ones that you don't have to reinvent, obviously. But there are these fundamentally difficult problems. I was looking at this graph layout algorithm. The problem is that you have a lot of nodes and edges, and you want to lay them out in this two-dimensional space so that humans could easily understand it. There's a lot of research into those…and the algorithm is really non-trivial, and [the research on this problem] has a lot of ideas and tricks about how to make things work. I'd rather not implement those algorithms, but I much prefer to use [them]. Even though the interface is very crude and ugly, the cost of reimplementing seems to be so high that I'd rather just use the code with the ugly interface. But most of the programs, it seems to me, are not in those categories. Communication frameworks are one thing where actually implementing something that works for you is often very trivial. But learning some existing stuff is not very trivial, and it's also not so fun. For example, I look at JXTA (a Java communication framework). I looked at some of the other distributed computing frameworks. I tried to convinced myself that JXTA, they have lots of people working on it, they have [Sun co-founder Bill Joy]…it must be good. I tried to convince myself, "Okay, I'm gonna read this whole tutorial," and I was never able to do it. Every slide I click, I keep finding, "Nah, I wouldn't do this." In the case of JXTA, they have this 60-page slide deck for writing my first JXTA service. If I have to go through 60 pages to get my first thing written, I thought, it's hopeless. I guess I'm quick-tempered or something.

There are several kinds like this. Communication frameworks are one thing. Maybe the XML data binding is another, where you might find it easier to just write it on your own, rather than learning all the ins and outs of those technologies. Web framework, I suspect, is another kind of those things, and that's why we see so many different people doing seemingly similar stuff, because the cost of learning is so high, that if you are reasonably productive, it makes more sense to just reinvent your own.

Now if you're in a team environment, the whole equation would be different. But if you're just doing your one-man project, then that often makes more sense. I keep reinventing myself, which is a bit of a problem.

Ed: What does a technology have to have before you consider it worth your time to learn it? Obviously, there are some tools you use rather than writing them yourself. What does a tool need to have before it passes the Kohsuke test?

Kohsuke: Often, the task of reimplementation is so daunting compared to a small gain that I feel compelled to reuse. That applies to stuff like an XML parser or a graph layout algorithm. The other reason for me to reuse is when I need to work in a team, which changes the cost/benefit analysis significantly. Stuff like Ant and Maven fall into this category (even though I'd love to write my own build system if I get to live long enough!).

It also depends on how much I'm planning to build on top of the library in question. If that's a lot, then I feel more comfortable rewriting it. There's also the people aspect. For example, I tend to trust things from James Strachan, Tatu Saloranta, and Dan Diephouse.

It's hard to narrow that down to a few things. There are a lot of factors.

But back to this Web framework thing, it was more like going to a grocery store to get OJ. When you go in, you pretty much have the exact idea of what you want to buy—let's say, a half-gallon of OJ in a cardboard carton, not from concentrate, any brand. Either you find it there or you don't. When you don't find it, you can insist on getting that half-gallon OJ carton from somewhere else, or you can convince yourself that what you really wanted was apple juice.

In this case, I knew what I wanted. I didn't find it in several existing frameworks I looked at (incidentally, I also don't enjoy shopping—I'd rather go in, grab things, pay, and get out as quickly as possible!), so I debated a little about whether I should keep shopping around or write my own, and decided to do the latter.

Ed: How do you attack hard-to-solve bugs?

Kohsuke: To a certain extent, you can design your program to avoid some of the problems. The architecture and design of things in the right way really helps. The second part is to put some probes in the system so that when the user hits the problem, you ask them to activate those probes, which start doing something. One of the things that turned out to be invaluable in Hudson is that I have Groovy [a Java-based scripting language] embedded in it. I can ask them to run any program on their running system. Let's say someone reported that things are hanging. There must be some deadlock going on. I can ask them to get the thread dump by invoking `java.lang.Thread`—something from the Groovy control. So that ability to probe into the running system is unique to Java. Not available in C. It's very useful. That's one weapon in your arsenal.

Ed: Make it extremely diagnosable?

Kohsuke: Yeah.

Ed: Either through logging or through some stack trace mechanism.

Kohsuke: Yes. Error reporting is also good. When throwing an exception, I always try to ask myself, "If this problem happened at the user site, what would they need to know to fix it. Or what do I need to know to fix it?" Then I try to also report the information right there. Spending that little effort in those things that reduce the necessity to have some e-mail communication with the user, which is always expensive. That can always help. But even with all that effort, there are still really hard-to-find bugs. I don't get to own the whole stack anyway. There are certain cases when I suspect it's a wrong thing in the network, but I can't really have any way to prove my hypothesis. Concurrency ones are always different to track. If it's a deadlock, that's easy, but the data corruption in concurrent environment is [difficult]. I just hope that thing doesn't happen. There is one bug in JAXB that some people reported—it's very hard to reproduce. To this day, I [have] not [been] able to reproduce it. You just have to hope that those don't happen to you.

Ed: What about test-driven development? Do you employ it? How do you know how much testing is appropriate?

Kohsuke: I think dogma is always dangerous. Writing tests as a way of defining a contract seems to be way too extreme to me. Of course, not writing tests at all—some people do it—it also seems to be not a good way. But [what] we as software engineering professionals are missing is this scientific approach to this problem. I read this one paper in Japan. A contractor developed this system and shipped [it] out to their user. Then, after the fact, they correlated the kinds of issues they found in the production system and tried to see if there was any correlation between the code coverage they obtained. They were trying to quantify how much code coverage is meaningful and how much would be marginal. That's real empirical, quantifiable data. We don't seem to be doing those things enough. We just say that "writing more tests should be good." But even if we are measuring the code coverage, we don't really know if 60 percent is good enough or if 80 percent is good enough. We need to [see] a bit more of those [kinds of studies] to be able to really say what test coverage is enough or how many tests is enough. In that sense, we are still very immature as an engineering profession. Just doing things because we think it's a good idea.

That's actually one of my long-term goals in Hudson. I also believe in laziness. I don't want people to do those things by themselves. If the tools are always reminding you…and we're getting close to that. We always work with integrated development environments (IDEs), and maybe there's this build that's going on that's also taking code coverage and the tests and so on, then it should be possible for those tools [to be] combined to collect this kind of information: how much time am I wasting fixing bugs? Whether there was any correlation between the amount of test coverage we have against the issues that we are discovering? If you can get [that] data out, without us doing anything, wouldn't that be nice? That's the long-term thing I want Hudson to be. When I do that, I'm not gonna be popular as an engineer!

Ed: Well, we are all trying to put ourselves out of jobs, in some sense. You made a statement that you don't think that test-driven development (TDD) is a good way to define a software contract. Say some more about that. That goes contrary to the conventional wisdom.

Kohsuke: Really? Maybe I'm getting behind in this regard. When I design my problem, especially at the implementation level of design—you design [this] bunch of classes and interfaces and how they interact with each other, and testability is certainly a big part in designing this—but it's just one of the many factors. There are a lot more important factors, like being able to easily extend, or when you just look at the tiny portion, you want each portion to make sense. You want it to be fast, to have a very strong cohesion within the modules and so on. [When] doing design, you need to take all of these factors into account. Somehow picking out one of them and treating that as this absolute measure seems to be counterproductive. When I'm doing a hobby project, or even when I do a business project, my goal is to have this beautiful system that's implemented. I guess my goal is not necessarily about reducing the amount of effort it takes to ship the software out of the door, which should be the real metric, but I don't really do that. Maybe if someone is really professional in the sense that they optimize against the business goals, maybe it makes more sense to put more emphasis on the test.

Ed: How important is it to be a continual optimizer of your work environment? What's the relationship between being a person who writes shell scripts for everything or the person who writes keyboard macros for every repetitive task and being a successful developer?

Kohsuke: It's a good thing to keep investing some of your time to attack your repetitive work. Because when you remove one problem, you see another that you didn't realize, so this laziness is infinite. You see other things that you didn't realize. The keyboard macro might be one example. If you write keyboard macros enough, at a certain point, it occurs to you that writing keyboard macros is a waste of time, and you find another way to meta-automate some of it. That's been true with me, I guess. There is no way to jump to this higher state; you have to explore it step by step.

Ed: What is the correlation between developer proficiency and tools mastery?

Kohsuke: If you tried to keep an eye on what you are doing yourself, then I guess you realize that "this" part needs to be automated. Sometimes you need some help to realize that. But once you know that it's something the machine can do, then you can't imagine how else you would have done it. You don't have to know everything, although occasionally it's good to look at the list of things they provide, because you might pick up a few things that you didn't realize. But it's not so much learning what the tool supports; it's more important to realize what you are doing intuitively. Most of the good tools are meta-morphic. For example, in IDEs, you can write your own tag names, and I find it really productive to write a few tag names to automate the things you do. Those are usually very tiny things, but it makes a lot of difference in keeping your train of thought without being interrupted by small tiny things.

> ◄ **Character Attribute** ►
>
> Self-awareness. Kohsuke here is demonstrating a keen understanding that he needs to maximize his time in the flow state in order to be the most productive.

Ed: You're saying it's better to—rather than just reading the whole manual and understanding everything—just be aware of what you need and know how to use that feature really well?

Kohsuke: Yeah. What's the opposite of humble? Boastful? Part of it must be that. Because

An IDE Tip from Kohsuke

The "tag names" that Kohsuke talks about here are essentially short key sequences that cause a specific thing to happen in the IDE. For example, pressing ALT-F-F to create a new function.

when you are reading a manual, I guess the mindset is to try to see how others make the most out of it, but I don't do that. I guess I'd rather have this blind belief that "I know better." To a certain extent, I'm very arrogant.

That seems to work for me. It's okay to be arrogant against tools, as long as you don't do it against people.

Ed: What are some attributes of the programming language and environment that people will be developing in ten years?

Kohsuke: I'm no expert in predicting the future, but there are several key elements that obviously must be there. Garbage collection and this notion of having a virtual machine that abstracts the real computer that is running on my desktop. Those are clearly useful concepts, and everyone else is picking those things up, too. The other thing I'm hoping to see in ten years is to be more like functional language, like common Lisp. We already see some of those, like the closures. In JavaScript, you see a lot of those. The introduction of languages like Scala, which tries to mix both worlds with its own abstraction. If you look at the .NET in C# 3.0, they introduce these new features that have a lot of trace from functional languages—stuff like continuations. Because that's also originally in functional languages, it's picking up its place in mainstream languages. I hope to use more of those because those are really productive.

Ed: Why are functional languages productive, do you think?

Kohsuke: If you just write some code, it's quite obvious. In the university, I was exposed to some of those functional languages, like Lisp and ML—in particular ML. That really got me thinking. For one thing, it's a very different way of doing it, but you can write a lot of stuff in very terse fashion. To the point where it's really scary. Once you start doing that, you don't really feel like writing Java code because it's so verbose. But there are a lot of good things about Java and being in the mainstream. We have that much more knowledge and people in the market to justify tools, and so on. Functional languages have never been mainstream.

Ed: Until JavaScript.

Kohsuke: Okay, yeah, well, so that's a good start, but it's still not enough. It doesn't have a pattern matching and the abstract data type construction. It doesn't have the nice tail recursion… Those are the things that I want to see, but I don't know if it's ever gonna happen, but that would be really nice.

Ed: Can you describe the difference between a function pointer in C and a functional language?

Kohsuke: Treating a function as something you can manipulate is a good start. In C, you occasionally do these things, like generating a function on the fly, generating assembly code, and that kind of thing. It's really just a tiny, tiny portion of functional languages. There's a lot more to it that's also hard to emulate in C. We need to start preaching to people that writing code in C is evil now. The only people allowed to do that are compiler developers, and everyone else needs to move on to more productive things.

We have a lot more programs that we need to write, and we just don't have enough time to do C anymore.

Business

Ed: How important are business acumen and entrepreneurial instincts in being a career software developer?

> **Character Attribute**
>
> Kohsuke feels so passionately about software, and so acutely feels the mental strain of knowing how much better the world could be if software made people more productive than it currently does, that he actually seemed angry that people still write in C.

Kohsuke: One of the hard things when I was doing my own company was…it takes a lot of courage and optimism to stick with something for a few years at least. Like I said, for something to be picked up by other people, it takes time. If the only thing you're investing is your own time, like I do [with the hobby projects], then that's really easy. Not really that much is at stake. But when you're investing your own time and money and someone else's money, that takes a lot of courage to stay optimistic about what you do. What I've found [is that] I'm not really that optimistic about that, so I'm not good at becoming a chairman of a startup. But I'd rather just go in and hack the stuff. I really can't say much about the business side. The programs that I'm interested in, for example, developer productivity and making other people more effective in writing programs, it's very hard to make money out of. I don't think there are many companies that do this kind of thing. Even if you had wanted to make some business out of it, in the developer tools business, it's very difficult. I find it nice that I'm working for Sun in this instance.

Ed: Are you worried about outsourcing?

Kohsuke: I feel confident that I'm better than most of the people out there, but I don't know if I'm better like, ten times or three times or whatever the salary difference that we have. It's hard to justify. It's certainly true in the United States, because everyone else in the world speaks this language, so it's very easy to move some of the work elsewhere. It's actually not so true in Japan because of the language barrier. They have a reasonably sized economy to sustain development there. Right now, a lot of interesting [things are] happening here [in the U.S.]. But if that changes, then maybe at some point it becomes more attractive to work in Japan, doing business with Japanese people in this small world.

Ed: Simply because they're outsource-proof? Because there is no pool of outsource programmers outside of Japan that speaks Japanese.

Kohsuke: On the grand scheme of things, I guess it's the right thing to happen. [Outsourcing companies] have every right to become more economically successful. Maybe living in India might not be so bad, so maybe I should try that.

Ed: How important is it to let your understanding of the business of software inform where you invest in stewarding your skillset?

Kohsuke: [Let's say that] your way of building your self-esteem is by having money, which is a good thing, because money is a very real way of showing that people value your work. If that's the motivation, then it makes sense to shape your development skill to optimize against that goal. I'm really more interested in making other developers happier. Like I said, it seems like a very difficult market to monetize. I didn't try to shape my skills around this goal of having a successful business.

Ed: Well, how do you decide to shape your skills then?

Kohsuke: The first layer is I try to experiment with new stuff. Like this .NET thing or this other thing with Ruby or Scala and [gauge] how good it looks. Then if it looks promising, and if you meet with the right people, things start to unfold on their own. You just need to try a few things to see if it works and stuff.

Ed: But how do you know what to try?

Kohsuke: Sometimes it's problem-driven. You have this certain problem that you want to solve, and this might be a good fit. Another factor is how popular things are. If enough people are saying good things about it, then maybe it is really a good thing.

Ed: Listening to the buzz and checking it out?

Kohsuke: Yeah, the combination of those things, but I guess it's always a challenge to [know when] to pick up new things and start using them.

Ed: It's been said that the average person in the workforce will now have several different careers between the time they start earning money and the time they retire. Do you agree with that?

Kohsuke: Sometimes it takes a real amount of time to realize that you're not really the best…sometimes I lose confidence in seeing really clever people…I see the distance, and I just don't see how I can ever cross that way. That makes me very low. I imagine if that happens, at some point, you might want to seriously consider switching your profession. Maybe that's what's happening to some of those people. I certainly hope to be hacking for a long time.

> **Character Attribute**
>
> Constructive self-questioning. Kohsuke is clearly a rock star programmer, but he still questions his abilities.

Ed: Do you have a non-IT plan B for earning a living?

Kohsuke: I should really have [one of] those, but I don't [laughs]. This field just seems to be so fun that in comparison, everything else doesn't look as good.

Personal

Ed: Before joining Sun, you were working for your own company in Japan, called Swift. Tell me more about Swift. What was your role there? Did you sell the company or the IP? How did it end?

Kohsuke: That started as my escape from the university entrance exam. In Japan, everyone has to take the exam to get into university, so people study hard for two years before that to make sure that they go to the school they want. So I had been doing that, but when you're working all the time, you have time to think about what you'd rather do. I was doing software at that time, it was called "shareware" in Japan. I don't know if the term exists here?

Ed: Shareware definitely exists.

Kohsuke: That's the thing, and it was very easy to do. All I had to do was have a computer, and then I hack the code, and then I could sell it. That was going reasonably well. I thought maybe I could recruit some of my friends, and it would be better and it would be fun. So that started when I got into college. Eventually from that, we were working [as contractors] because money-wise it was more stable, so we started doing that. In university, I met with more people who had those technical backgrounds. Before that, it wasn't a company; it was just a bunch of people doing the work and distributing money among ourselves. Then this one guy showed up, and his [recently deceased] father had a company, and the guy inherited the company's name, and he also had a technical background, so we thought maybe we should get together and get a real company behind it, so that's what we did. We did the contract work, and that made a lot of money and it was easy to find. We also wrote some software by ourselves, an XML editor [, for example].

> **Career Tip**
>
> This XML editor gained Kohsuke the recognition in the growing world of XML that got him into Sun.

We ran the Extensible Stylesheet Language Transformation (XSLT) to generate HTML. Then when you edit the HTML, we reverse-transform that back to the original XML, so then you can edit them through XSLT. That technology was interesting, but we based that on the Microsoft technology; we didn't have any source code level access, so that limited what we could have done. Then we were also all engineers. There was no one who had any real marketing or sales experience. Business-wise, that didn't go well. We got most of our money from contracting work, and that was enough to sustain a living.

Ed: Even in Tokyo?

Kohsuke: Yeah.

Ed: You must have been doing pretty well then? The cost of living was very high there, right?

Kohsuke: [laughs] Yes, but we were just a bunch of students! It's not like we had any real life or families to support. We mostly just spent money for having fun. We borrowed an office near the university so that we could commute by walking five minutes. We bought all kinds of game consoles and arcade consoles so that we could play games. It was part business, but it wasn't all that serious in that sense. But it was a lot of fun. We practically lived there, for quite some time, and those are real good friends.

Around the same time, I guess, I got an offer from Sun. I was doing some XML work, the schema language… and someone who was reading the XML forum at the time must have said something to Jon Bosak [who led the creation of the XML spec at W3C and was building the XML team at Sun]. That's my guess. They didn't tell me anything, although how else would he have found me? Then I thought, I always wanted to work in the United States, and I had citizenship because I was born there. The offer seemed very attractive. I just said I'd rather take this offer [the Sun offer], and then they said they would rather stop doing this company. So we just stopped doing all the work and distributed the money among ourselves, and I got the monitors we had been using, and the other guys got the computers, and so on, and we were just done, essentially. The other folks moved on to do other things. One of them went to HP; another went to a start-up. Everyone had their own idea of what they wanted to do. That's what Swift was.

Ed: In another interview, you mentioned that your first computer was a laptop that your mom gave you when you were in seventh grade. What year was that?

Kohsuke: 1991.

Ed: What kind of machine was it?

Kohsuke: At that time in Japan, there was this proprietary architecture. They were selling this series of computers, based on Intel.

Ed: But built in Japan, right?

Kohsuke: Yes. All the things were available in Japanese. The manual, the operating system, the whole thing was in Japanese. The IBM PC AT–compatible stuff didn't seem to have broad market penetration in Japan. I guess the other big thing is the word processing. At that time, most of the business users of computers were writing documents. If you can't type Japanese characters, there's no point in doing it. I guess that's why this proprietary architecture had been very popular. I guess my mom was one of those careful people. She wasn't so tech-savvy, but my father was. Even though at the time a computer was pretty expensive, she somehow managed to get one.

Maybe she just didn't use it that much? I was just sitting in my house and doing nothing, and so I just picked it up. I'm very grateful to them.

Ed: A lot of the people in this book have similar experiences. They got their first computer when they were pretty young and they grew up along with the software industry. What do people who are coming into the field today do? They didn't have the benefit of writing shareware and putting it up for sale on bulletin board systems (BBSs). No one does that anymore!

Kohsuke: The barrier of entry to writing a program seems to be very high now. It used to be that the programs you wrote were very trivial. They were written in BASIC or with a little bit of assembly, and so on. You get gradually exposed to the more complex stuff. I don't know how they do this today. Now that I have my own daughter, I guess I'm going to be finding out!

Ed: How old is she?

Kohsuke: Two and a half years old now, so it's gonna be a while…but I don't know… computers have been around for a long time, and even so, somehow I figured out how to write code. Young people always have more than enough time on their hands.

Character Attribute

Childhood curiosity.

But it's a real problem when you try to educate real programmers in your business. The new people out of college, they don't really know anything. If you think about it, the amount of stuff you need to teach them so they could be useful is just too daunting. I guess that gap would only get worse, so it's hard.

Ed: How good are you at keeping your work and personal lives balanced?

Kohsuke: Hmm, it's one of the problems. When I say those hobby projects that I work on, I spend my personal time outside of the office to do those. That means I'm spending a really significant [amount] of my time writing code. It's just the difference is whether I'm doing it for Sun or doing it for something else. So that's not really a personal life then, is it?

I have stopped watching TV for a long time now. I realized that when you stop watching TV, you don't know what kind of movies they are doing, so you also stop going to movies. In certain ways, that's really not a good thing, because I'm more and more becoming a coding machine. But that said, I still try to do a few things with my family. For example, I started growing tomatoes with my daughter. That turned out to be fun. Or I started doing, you might laugh, this cross-stitching? My wife started doing that, and I thought maybe it's good for our marriage that we do something like that. I started it, and it's actually fun. It's very repetitive, because you have to put the needle back and then bring it back and forth. I briefly talked about "is there any way to automate this or design an algorithm to…" but that was just fun. While doing that, both my wife and I are doing nothing but be at the table, and even though we are not looking at each other, we get the time to talk about all kinds of stuff.

Ed: That's great!

Kohsuke: Those are good things, I suppose. But I'm not doing enough of those. The problem is the coding is just so [much] fun. I hear from other people that when you get older it stops becoming fun. If that's the case, then I really need to get the most out of it! I wish I had more time. One thing I'm trying to do is to cut my sleep…

Ed: [laughs]

Kohsuke: That doesn't always work.

Ed: No, no, you gotta regenerate the brain. Do you think there's any role between success as a software developer and success in life in general?

Kohsuke: I really wish I knew what it means to be a success in life. For example, my parents were…they attained a very high position within their organization. Business-wise, professional-life-wise, they were very successful. But I don't know if they would call their lives very [happy]…they seem to be equating success in life and success professionally… I don't know.

Ed: For me, success in personal life would be knowing how to enjoy yourself. Knowing how to have a good time wherever you are. Of course, on top of that, you layer giving to others, but at the core, you have to be happy in your heart before you can really give. Do you think [there is] any relationship between that and being a successful software developer?

Kohsuke: In that sense, I need to get out and remove myself from the computer more. Just getting out and looking at the stars. But you don't get to do that when you are just commuting between your home and office, so maybe I need to do more of those.

I just wish my daughter was a little bigger. It really limits the kinds of things we can do. The other thing is just my obsession with my retirement.

Ed: Retirement?

Kohsuke: Yes. My parents once told me when I was really small, with our house, that they didn't have enough money. Looking back, that's clearly a lie. Like I said, they seemed to be doing reasonably well. But that really got me as a small kid. Probably I was asking for a toy. Very unreasonably asking my parents to buy it. Maybe it was their means of saying no, but that really got to me. I started worrying about having a sustained life. We are getting paid enough to have a reasonably good life now, but I always have this obsession that we need to save more. That makes it hard to enjoy the worldly things.

Ed: What is your planned retirement age?

Kohsuke: That's the problem, because I don't have this plan. If I did, then I wouldn't have to be so obsessed about this. But I can't picture how I go from here to the retirement, and that worries me a lot. Especially because things can change so quickly, and my memory is failing me, and so on. It's not helping at all. There are certainly some factors to worry about. But it's also pointless to worry about things beyond your control. I need to learn to stop worrying about it.

Ed: Do you find this—you used the word "obsessive"—focus on that particular thing, financial security, is that something that you find in other aspects of your life? The inability to stop worrying?

Kohsuke: Not really.

Ed: Like, if you have a new feature that you conceive, is it just like "I gotta get this done, I can't stop thinking about it about it until it's done?"

Kohsuke: Sometimes it happens, but it's actually a great feeling. In the morning, you wake up with this feature that you just have to implement today. When you are that motivated, you really get that done today, because you don't even care to look at e-mail and all the interruptions; you just do it. On the way to the office, you're thinking about this way of designing things in different ways. By the time you get to the office, you're all ready to hack, and you just write the code and it's there. It really makes you feel better when you get back home. But that's actually a great feeling. The kind of thing that gets me to [that] mode is usually small things. That you can do very quickly. If you have this grand plan that takes like a year to do, then that might be difficult to sustain, but that just doesn't happen to me.

Ed: Could that be one of the reasons why it's difficult to do retirement planning, because it's just sooo long-term?

Kohsuke: Yeah, I suppose so! All things considered, it's not that big an issue for me. If that's the biggest thing I'm worrying about right now, than I guess could say I'm reasonably happy.

Ed: What is the relationship between discipline and methodology?

Kohsuke: Discipline is the thing that I really hate because that implies diligence. You have to be very diligent about your discipline. I try to stay away from it. I try to be very lazy. The only reason I do something is because that's the easy thing to do. I try to drive everything so it's the easy thing to do. Writing tests, for example. If you think of it as a discipline, unless you're diligent, then you can't sustain that. You have to make it so that's the easiest thing to do. The only thing you need to be is logical and rational. Let the other good things follow. Just having tests alone is not very convincing. But what I found doing Hudson is that when I automate, the test runs continually, then I find it's very productive for me. Because when I'm making a change, I can take a bigger risk in making changes, knowing that if I break something, it's gonna get picked up right there.

Ed: Of course.

Kohsuke: In that way, I managed to increase the value of my tests. Now, if I'm rational, I see that writing tests is actually helpful, because down the road it gets me [to be] more productive. I would not be able to sustain it if that was a discipline; it's only sustainable because that's the easiest thing to do for me.

PART 2

Software Pedagogy Experts

Herb Schildt

Fact Sheet

Name: Herb Schildt

Home Page: www.herbschildt.com

Rock Star Programmer Credentials: Best-selling author of programming books, such as *Java: The Complete Reference* (2006), *C++: The Complete Reference* (2002), *C#: The Complete Reference* (2002), and a complete line of "Beginner's Guides," among others.

Date of Birth: February 1951

City of Birth: Aurora, IL

Birth Order: First of two

Marital Status: Married

Number of Kids: Four

Degree: Bachelor of Arts in Philosophy (1973) and Master of Computer Science (1981), University of Illinois at Urbana-Champaign

Number of generations in your ancestry (including yourself) that graduated from college: One

Years as an IT Professional: 28

Role: Author of computer programming books

Introduction

Throughout this book, I have tried to explore how successful programmers take advantage of opportunities and capitalize on them to grow their career and, hopefully, grow their personal fulfillment as well. My relationship with Herb Schildt started with just such an opportunity. My particular introduction to the practice of being a technical writer came when Chris Schalk approached me at a conference with the offer to join him in co-authoring a book about JavaServer Faces (JSF). At the time, JSF was my day job and had been for a couple of years. I knew JSF *really* well, so I would have no trouble with the content aspect of authoring the book. The problem was making time. The factor that convinced me that accepting Chris's offer was worth the risk and commitment was Herb Schildt's role as editor of the project. I would get to work, closely, with the world's best-selling programming author on a real project, where the only challenges came not from the subject matter itself, but from the act of writing about it.

During the project, I learned that Herb was a master at writing books that teach people how to program. I learned how to always be the learner's advocate and about the importance of the covenant between author and reader of technology books. I learned how not to talk down to the reader, how to treat the reader as a partner in learning, and, most importantly, I learned about "organization, organization, organization." In Herb's view, there is an optimal way to teach a programming language or programming technology, and Herb knows how to find it.

One other thing I learned about Herb: Before becoming a rock star programmer, Herb was something of an actual rock star himself, playing keys for 1970's progressive rock band Starcastle. Aside from Herb, at least two other rock star programmers in this book have been professional musicians at one time or another: Andy Hunt and Rod Johnson. I'm not sure about the connection between rock star programming skills and musicianship, but, anecdotally, I've seen plenty of examples of exceptional programmers who are also musicians.

Soft Skills

Ed: You are the world's best-selling programming author. You've had a career that's spanned upwards of 25 years. How did you get started?

Herb: Many years ago, in the early stages of the microcomputer revolution, I had a software company. We were creating programs designed to run on the new (at the time) personal computers. This was in the early to mid-1980s. Most of what we were doing was system software, and, among other products, we had a C compiler.

Ed: That you had written?

Herb: My partner did the vast majority of work on the compiler. At that time, we were involved in several projects, including a spreadsheet and, for a while, a word processor. I was president of the company and I "poked around" in just about every project.

Ed: Okay, so it was something your company had written in-house?

Herb: Yes, that's correct.

Ed: And for what processor was it written?

Herb: The Z80. This is an 8-bit processor that could address only 64 (kilobytes) KB of random access memory (RAM). This was the early 1980s, before the advent of Windows, for example. Although limited, the processor could support a full C compiler.

I sold my interest in the company in 1984. It turns out that at the same time, McGraw-Hill was looking for someone to write a book about the C programming language. They contacted my old company about two weeks after I'd left, asking if anyone there would like to write such a book. The call from McGraw-Hill was taken by the head of marketing, and he suggested that they talk to me.

As result, I got a call from McGraw-Hill. As I recall, they asked two questions. First, "Would I like write a book about C programming?" I said, "Yes!" I'd had a long-time interest in writing and book publishing in general—especially as it relates to computing. I had often thought about writing a programming book. The second question was "Do you have any writing experience?" Again, I answered "Yes!", explaining that in the early days of my software company, I had written several of the user manuals for our products. Of course, I naively thought that this made me eminently qualified to write a book. Despite this, McGraw-Hill asked that I submit a writing sample. Since McGraw-Hill has been my publisher for more than two decades, I guess I passed the writing test!

My first book was published in 1985 and it was *C Made Easy* (1985).

Ed: Was it hard writing your first book?

Herb: To be honest, I found it to be a difficult process. I won't sugarcoat it. It was hard. It turned out that books were much more challenging than the user manuals I had previously written. Fortunately, I got through it, and the book got published. More importantly, it actually sold pretty well. And that's when I reached a real pivotal point in my career.

Ed: Can you explain?

Herb: Even though that first book proved to be more difficult than I expected, I realized two things. First, that writing about programming was something that I had a talent for. It was something that I had the ability to do. Second, that despite the challenges, it was something that I really enjoyed doing. Thus, writing combined something that I liked doing with something that I was good at.

This started me thinking. What is it that I really wanted in a career? What were my long-term goals? Where did I want to go? I don't know how to describe this, but there came a moment of realization, when the answers to those questions became obvious. It was at that point that I made the decision to be a writer of programming books. I have never regretted that decision.

Anyway, back to the story. About two weeks after I finished my first book and recovered from the experience, I was back on the phone with McGraw-Hill saying, "Hey, let's do a follow-up book." And that book became *Advanced C* (1988) and to use the cliché, "The rest is history."

Ed: Okay. Now I want to explore the point in time when this opportunity came to your door. Did you have any trepidation about taking on the task? About doing something that you hadn't done before? How much was it a matter of, "This looks like a great opportunity. I should take it, even though I don't know if I can do it or not." Or was it something where you thought, "Oh yeah, I can do this."

Character Attribute

Confidence and persistence.

Herb: I jumped in with both feet with the assumption, "Hey, this is something I can do." As I mentioned, I had some experience writing user manuals for the software that my former company produced. In today's age of high-powered venture capital, it can be hard to understand that back then, when the computer revolution was just getting started, there were a bunch of small companies that didn't have any real funding. Everything was on a shoestring.

Ed: That's how Microsoft started. Sure.

Herb: As a result, I, like everyone in the company, was doing a fair amount of "double duty." For me, it was working on the user manuals. Because of this, I knew that writing about programming came fairly naturally to me. When I got the call from McGraw-Hill, asking me to write a book, it was one of those classic moments in life. I just thought, "Wow, this is great!" I didn't think twice about it.

Ed: Given that you'd sold your interest in the company, when the invitation from McGraw-Hill came, did you have any fiscal concerns such as, "This book has to succeed so I can continue to provide for my family"? What was your situation in regard to that?

Herb: I got a little bit of money for my half of the company. So I was reasonably secure for a period of time.

Here's the key point, though. Back in the mid-1980s, almost no one was getting a lot of money for little startup companies. This predates the dot-com run-up, for example. But I did get *some* money. But to answer your question, I have to admit that I was a little nervous about the financial return. As you know, the publisher gives an author an advance for the book. However, the advance, while important, is not a substantial amount of money. To be a successful writer, your book must earn out its advance and then begin paying residual royalties. Of course, this only happens if your book sells well enough. As a result, I must confess that I was very much relieved when my first royalty check arrived.

Ed: I want to get a feel for how you tell what the next big thing in programming is going to be. You've been in the authoring business for a very long time. During that time, there have been so many technologies that have come up and gone down. How do you tell when "I'd better get a book out there on this topic, because this is going to be a thing everyone wants to learn about"?

Herb: The truthful, but perhaps unsatisfying, answer is this: intuition. Every so often, a light comes on and says, "Hey, this is going to be something that a lot of people are going to be interested in." But that said, I don't always trust my intuition. Let's talk about this problem for a while and I'll try to give you a better answer.

In the last 10 to 15 years, we have seen the emergence of an amazing number of new technologies. I don't believe it's possible for any single person to be in command of them all. I think that the most one can hope for is to be in command of a specific skillset. And skillsets differ. For example, the skillset needed by an embedded systems programmer is obviously very different from that needed by someone who's doing Web development.

Even if you narrow the focus to Web development, there are all sorts of technologies out there. The problem is the investment in time that's necessary to master a new technology. It is very significant. So you don't want to learn technologies that are ultimately going to fail.

Ed: How do you pick the winners?

Herb: There are two things I can suggest. One is this intuitive sense I spoke of. I think we all have it as programmers. We have a sense when some technology is right. We think to ourselves, "Hey, this actually solves a problem for me. And I like the way it solves it." Those are the technologies that are important. Furthermore, if you are thinking that, you're usually not the only person who's thinking it.

Once you've had this feeling, you can confirm it by checking various programmer Web forums. When a technology's about

> **Observation**
>
> Andy Hunt has a similar answer to this question. See page 247.

> **Observation**
>
> Dick Wall recommends a similar approach to test the validity of one's hunch about the promise of a new technology. See page 56.

ready to hit critical mass, you will see it being talked about extensively. And not just by marketing guys, so to speak, but by real programmers. You can tell the difference. When the buzz is there, and it's from real programmers, it usually means that it's a new technology worth the time needed to learn it.

Ed: Looking at what's going on in programming today, can you say anything about what are the hard problems that programmers are facing? What kinds of problems are the things that people are really just scratching their heads about, and they're saying, "Oh, I've got to figure out something, and I've got to go out and buy a book to tell me how to do this"?

Herb: Let me begin with an important assertion. The overarching problem in modern programming can be summed up in one word: complexity. As it relates to your question, programmers are caught in the middle of some very complex situations that weren't even part of the landscape not that long ago. Here are two: deployment and security. Both can put me into "scratch-my-head" mode sometimes! Of these two, security is probably the worst. It is something many programmers are insecure about. Of course, I'm referring not only to buffer overrun–type problems. We all know (or should know) how to avoid those. (Whether everyone always avoids them successfully is a separate issue…) I'm talking about the entire range of security, including managing permissions, aliases, etc.

Ed: Denial of service attacks…

Herb: Yes, and so on. Basically, if you fail at deployment or security, in the best case, you have a large maintenance problem. In the worst case, you may be facing a liability situation. This is why these things make programmers nervous.

But there's another thing that's going on. It's something that I first saw emerge back when C++ became mainstream. It's an effect that is now beginning to show up with Java and C#. It's an effect that relates directly to what you are asking. These languages have gotten so large and so complex that it's almost like each is really two languages, with one being a simplified subset of the other. To illustrate what I mean, let's look specifically at C++.

C++ is arguably the most complex and powerful computer language invented to date. There's essentially nothing you can't do with it. And, of course, that allows you to create great programs or great disasters, depending upon your ability. In essence, C++ gives the ability to use or abuse its power. But despite (or because of) its power, I find that many programmers use only a subset of the language, ignoring many of its more advanced (and powerful) features. Thus, in practice, there are two C++'s: the subset used by most programmers and the full-featured version that only few take advantage of.

You are beginning to see the same situation in Java, especially since the addition of generics. A lot of programmers are still shying away from using generics. Now, there's no reason to avoid generics. It's really pretty straightforward, but it's that extra level up that makes you ask yourself,

"Do I really need to use this? Does it really contribute to a solution? And, most importantly, am I really comfortable with this feature; do I know what I'm doing?"

Ed: Right. And it's wise not to use a new language feature until you fully understand it. Otherwise, you risk destabilizing the system.

Herb: Right. As a result, now (in practical terms) Java has become two languages: the simplified subset and the full language.

Ed: This effect applies to more than just programming languages, right?

Herb: Yes. This effect is being felt throughout programming. A lot of people are using tools to less than their full capabilities, because some of the more advanced features are tricky to use, not easily learned, or hard to apply. Furthermore, sometimes it is hard to understand what problem a feature solves. If you can't understand what benefit is being provided, why use the feature?

Ed: Right. These advanced options are designed to solve problems that I don't have yet or that I don't know that I have.

Herb: Or I'm already solving the problem in other ways. In each case, it translates into a two-tiered tool environment, with some programmers using only a limited subset of what the tool can provide.

Hard Skills

Ed: I want to get back to the personal history a little bit more, but I have this theory I want to talk about: Those of us that are old enough to have grown up with personal computers and have our careers evolve as the technology itself evolves have an edge over the people that are entering the business today, such as new college grads, or even younger people. If *we* wanted to do disk management, back in the early days of the home computer, we had to write our own I/O routines. We had to do assembly language programming. We were right there down on the metal. As new layers of abstraction came along, we learned them as they were being developed.

Do you have any suggestions for people coming in late to the game, compared to us older folks? How do they compensate for not being born before 1975?

Herb: Well, I'm going to answer your question by answering a somewhat different question. You're touching on something I have discovered and find to be truly fascinating: Younger programmers do not see the machine in the same way that older programmers do. Specifically, they see it differently than I do. Let me explain.

I see the machine in terms of bits and bytes, NAND and NOR gates, and the execution of machine code. Although I haven't written a new assembly language program in many years, it's still the way that I think about code. When I see high-level code, such as C++ code, it's as if I intuitively see the assembly code that it translates into. Although I sometimes joke about it, it's true. Even though I am writing high-level code, I'm not de-linked from the CPU's instruction set.

Perhaps my view of the machine goes back to actually building my first computer.

Ed: Wait, what was your first computer?

Herb: The first computer I personally owned was an IMSAI 8080. And you had to toggle in the bootstrap loader using the front panel switches. It only had 8KB of RAM, so each instruction counted! In those days, the programmer was *very close* to the machine's hardware.

At any rate, I tend to see the computer in terms of bits and bytes and logic—in other words, its low-level physical reality. I think younger programmers tend to see the computer in a more abstract way—more as a "resource" rather than a "device." Furthermore, they tend to think of programming more in terms of architecture, rather than CPU instructions.

Of course, this is a generalization, but I have encountered this difference time and time again. I think that it's due to a number of factors, but the most significant seems to be the current dominance of Web development. As all Web developers know, many issues surrounding the creation of a Web application depend upon the architecture of the Web and how you interface to this architecture. Therefore, a lot of younger programmers who grew up during the Internet revolution see the computer in terms of its architecture as it interfaces to this large global environment of the Web. It has been said that "the Web is the computer." Many younger programmers have embraced that philosophy.

Ed: Yep. "The network is the computer" has been the motto of my employer, Sun Microsystems, since their beginning.

Herb: So you have this difference. You have this dichotomy between the programmers who really had this vision of the computer "as a computer" and those programmers that now see the computer as part of a larger architectural unit.

Ed: They inherently think in terms of distributed systems in some level.

Herb: Right. Is one view better than the other? No. They are just different. I expect that at some future time, the view of the computer will change again. We work in an industry that is driven by change or, more precisely, that is driven by revolutionary change.

Ed: You just used the phrase "revolutionary change." Can you give some examples?

Herb: I can give you two. The first is the creation of the personal computer. It had several far-reaching effects. For example, it mainstreamed computing because it made it affordable. It also began the process of making the computer virtually indispensable in everyday life. However, perhaps its greatest effect was felt by programmers. For the first time, each and every programmer had a computer of his or her own over which he or she could exercise full control. This put the programmer front and center. As a result, programmers began to define the computing environment. This led to the creation of truly great applications. I firmly believe that the personal computer was the catalyst for most of the advances in programming that have occurred over the past couple of decades.

Although the PC revolution had profound effects, they are dwarfed by the second revolution: the Web. It's undeniably one of the most important events in modern times. It has globalized the transmission of information, which has linked people around the world. It has enabled communication that transcends borders, that transcends nations. It's transnational. It's revolutionized the whole concept of what it means to be a country or a nation. It's changed the world. This is why so many programmers today are writing code related to the Internet.

But I think there's another revolution coming. It's something that has been brewing on the back burner for some time.

Ed: What is it?

Herb: Robotics. In a sentence, I think that we are at the beginning of the robotics age.

Ed: Can you elaborate a bit?

Herb: We are just beginning to reach critical mass as it relates to robots. Let me be clear, when I use the term robot, I am referring to autonomous robots that interact with us humans in our environment. Here are two early examples. The first is Honda's ASIMO, which is a very sophisticated humanoid robot. The other is the robotic vacuum Roomba by iRobot. Of these, ASIMO is the most exciting.

It is my view that robotics could have been further along already, but its progress was slowed for one primary reason: Other aspects of computing had a higher priority, demanding the attention of most programmers. Let me give you an example. Over the past decade or so, the Internet utilized much of the world's computing talent. This means that many of the best and brightest programmers have been focused on the Internet and have been part of the Web development revolution. Thus, these programmers have not been focused on other things, including robotics.

But there is a new crop of programmers coming, those who grew up on very sophisticated video games and were surrounded by smart devices, such as MP3

> **Observation**
>
> Andy Hunt has a different take on what the new crop of programmers will be doing. See page 255.

players and feature-rich cell phones. It is my guess that they are the ones who will be at the center of the robotics revolution.

As a point of interest, I think that these programmers will combine both the "bits and bytes" view of the machine with the "architecture" view. This will be the synthesis needed to craft robotic software. Why? Because robotic systems will involve distributed resources (separate controllers for arms, legs, vision, etc.), but will also be tied to the hardware (real-time interrupts, A-to-D converters, etc.). Once a mainstream, autonomous robot is widely available, legions of programmers will begin writing code for it.

Ed: I want to explore this more, because I've heard that sentiment expressed before. There was a 2007 article in *Scientific American* that talked about how the advent of DOS and widespread compilers was the thing that enabled the computer revolution to take place, and the problem with robots is that there's no standard platform. There's no standard operating system essentially.

Herb: I think that's probably a major opportunity. For a comparison, look at the Internet when it was in its infancy. One could have said, "Well, until the Web hits critical mass, we can't create something like a browser." It's the classic "cart-before-the-horse" problem. If you don't have the browser, the Web doesn't take off. If you don't have the Web, you don't need the browser. Sometimes, things just kind of move by osmosis, a little at a time, until at some critical point, it all comes together. I can't fully explain this process, but it does seem to be the way technology moves forward.

Along these lines, it is my belief that this critical mass won't occur in robotics until you have a robot that can operate freely throughout our human environment.

Ed: Why?

Herb: Because to be useful, a robot must be able to interact in our world. Our world is designed for humans. So no matter what robots we use, they must be able to do things in more or less the same way that we humans do them. In short, we will not redesign the world to fit our robots. We will design our robots to fit our world.

I expect that the first applications will be relatively simple, but important. Let me give you an example. There's a lot of movement towards robots that assist the elderly or the disabled. They could retrieve simple items or dispense medicine. This would be an incredibly important benefit for people who need that functionality.

We are reaching the point at which the hardware solutions are being worked out. Next, we'll need the software. Of course, the software probably presents the greatest challenge and the greatest opportunities. There's going to be a huge demand.

Ed: There's one thing you said you wanted to go back to, and that's the notion of handling complexity.

Herb: Yes. When we talked about the problems facing programmers, I mentioned that at its core, it was a problem of complexity. It has been the force that has driven the creation and evolution of computer languages and tools. It has been the central theme that has shaped programming since its early days.

Here's the problem. The programs that we create and the environments in which we work are getting increasingly complex. They are complex not only in terms of their size, but also in terms of the level of detail. Furthermore, we programmers are facing increasing constraints. For example, 25 years ago, security was a relatively minor concern. If the computer wasn't networked, then often, keeping the computer in a locked room was sufficient. Today, it's hard to imagine such innocent times. Now, just about every software application has to address at least some aspect of security, even if it's just avoiding the potential for buffer overruns. Of course, security is just one of many factors that are affecting the complexity of software.

If you look back in the history of programming, much of what has shaped the development and evolution of programming languages has been the need to handle greater complexity. On the first computers, you literally had to toggle in a program using the machine's front panel. Of course, those programs had to be very small. Then came assembly language, which let the programmer write longer programs. Next came the first high-level languages, such as FORTRAN.

FORTRAN was a major breakthrough for two reasons. First, it made it easier to write large programs. Second, it pointed in the right direction. It showed us the way forward. Once FORTRAN was created, programmers had a model that demonstrated that complexity could be abstracted, and, therefore, managed, by the use of a computer language. FORTRAN was an imperfect model, but it proved the concept. It was simply a matter of improving the concept.

The next step was structured programming, exemplified by languages like ALGOL, Pascal, and C. (C is kind of a hybrid, but I call it a structured language.) With structured programming languages, programmers can handle even larger, more complex programs. Of course, programs continued to grow, and this led to object-oriented languages, such as C++ and Java. Using an object-oriented approach, programmers can handle even larger, more complex programs. Now, we are starting to see component-oriented architectures and service-oriented architectures. All of this progress, from assembly language to FORTRAN, to Pascal, to C++ and so on, is about giving a programmer the ability to manage increasing complexity.

But here's the problem, Ed. Complexity is like a balloon. If you press on it in one place, it expands in another. And that's what we've been living with. The issue of complexity keeps popping up.

Ed: Can you give me an example of what you mean?

Herb: Yes. Just before the Internet reached critical mass, it almost looked like the complexity problem was solved. Why? Because we had C++, which is a dramatically powerful, object-oriented language. Programmers were really starting to get a handle on being able to abstract logical concepts but still efficiently translate them into executable code.

Ed: Right.

Herb: Then, the Internet basically blew everything apart again! A new architecture, a new paradigm, introduced new complexities. And once again, applications began to become too complex for our tools and languages. This is why programmers started looking at things like component-oriented and service-oriented approaches.

Sometimes, I use the phrase "vector through history" to describe central themes that are manifested throughout history. For example, one vector through history is consolidation of power. As it relates to computing, complexity is a vector through history. It affects and shapes virtually all aspects of computing. We programmers spend much of our time trying to manage it.

Ed: Interesting point. Do you think that integrated development environments help handle this complexity?

Herb: Yes, at least to some extent. One way we attempt to manage complexity is by creating tools to handle it for us. The tools abstract the complexity. Integrated development environments (IDEs) are one example. Integrated development environments didn't exist early on. I can't remember the precise year, but the first IDE that I remember working with was Turbo Pascal.

Ed: Oh, yeah. Turbo Pascal was an IDE.

Herb: Right. At least to an extent. But the point is that they've gotten better and better, and why? Because we've needed them. And I want to emphasize something. Many of the early IDEs were clunky and hard to use.

Ed: Right.

> **Observation**
>
> Adrian Colyer, on page 38, also emphasizes the key role of the IDE in software technology adoption.

Herb: But today, the evolution of tools has evolved to where they really do streamline development. They are virtually indispensable. But again, what is the key point of this? Complexity. The IDEs help the programmer handle increasing complexity. Programmers today don't have one file. In many cases, they have hundreds of files, with complicated dependencies. Then there's deployment, efficiency, security, versioning, and so on. We programmers keep banging up against this complexity barrier, and so far, we have been able to find ways around it.

Ed: So with all the abstraction that has taken place in programming languages and tools over the past several years, are today's programmers seeing only the abstraction or do they still see the machine?

Herb: Good question! Obviously, abstraction has helped manage complexity. But to use that abstraction effectively, you need to think in terms of the abstraction. This by itself is not wrong. But there is something in my gut that is telling me that we're reaching limits on abstraction. That we may be losing touch with what's really going on in a machine. Maybe too much abstraction is a bad thing. Time will tell.

Ed: Can you hazard a guess on what the next evolution in complexity management will be?

Herb: Maybe the next step will be based on an echo from the past. For example, there is currently interest in functional programming. But functional programming isn't something that's new. It goes back to things like Lisp from the 1950s. My intuition, and I wish to emphasize that it's just an intuitive sense—

Ed: Well, that's what I want to hear.

Herb: —is that we're going to need to start reexamining some of the assumptions of the past 40 years. I think this resurgence of interest in functional programming may be a leading indicator of that. To move forward in our ability to handle increasing complexity, it may mean that we need to reexamine and reevaluate things that were previously set aside.

Ed: Right. So how do you deal with that problem as an author? How do you deal with the problem of teaching people what they don't know that they don't know?

Herb: I'm going to say something maybe a little provocative, but it's something I truly believe.

Ed: I like provocative.

Herb: I believe that all systems of knowledge work the same. Once you understand how systems of knowledge work, you can actually learn pretty much anything fairly easily.

Ed: Can you explain?

Herb: All systems of knowledge are hierarchical. They all have entry points, and they all have logical patterns of flow that allow you to move from one concept to another. In other words, systems of knowledge can be thought of as having a tree structure. To learn something, you must simply move from branch to branch, node to node. The trouble is that sometimes it's not easy to see the structure. This is where a good teacher comes in. A good teacher organizes the topic so that it reflects its hierarchical structure.

Ed: Can you describe your process for teaching a programming technology?

Herb: Mostly what I write about is programming languages, so I'm going to focus this answer on programming languages. I like to start at the beginning, by putting the language in a historical context. Where did it come from? What forces drove its creation? What historical trends acted on it to make it what it is? This is important because it explains why certain aspects of the language are as they are.

This is followed by a brief introduction to several core concepts, such as the general form of a program, a few data types, and a couple of control statements. This is where a "hello world" type program is described. It's necessary to explain some basic concepts without going into too many details. The reader needs to understand enough of the language to enable specific elements to be examined in greater detail.

Then comes data. Specifically, the basic data types of the language. Why do I start there? Because the data types define the scope and range of problems to which the language can be applied. They are the foundation of the language. Some may read these words and say, "Yeah, all languages have these built -n types, such as `char`, `int`, and so on. What's the big deal?" The answer is that the data types affect in subtle ways many aspects of the language and influence how that language is applied. Look at C.

The original version of C did not have a `bool` type, for example. Rather, it relied on non-zero being true and zero being false. This approach profoundly affected the way that C code is written. For example, in C, you can write

```
if(x) x--;
```

instead, of

```
if(x != 0) x--;
```

This attribute gave rise to several standard idioms that are easily recognizable by any C/C++ programmer. For example:

```
while(*p) *q++ = *p++;
```

Here, the loop executes until the value pointed to by p equals zero. This same basic type of loop is found throughout C/C++ code. This idiom wouldn't exist in this form if C had defined true and false in some other way.

Here is another example. Consider the difference in the character type between C++ and Java. In C++, the character type occupies 1 byte, and there are good reasons for it. Whereas, in Java, it's a 16-bit type, and there are good reasons for that, too. Another difference is found in how strings are implemented. Both C and C++ support null-terminated strings (which are character arrays terminated by a null character), but Java and C# rely on `String` objects. This changes the way that certain types of string handling are accomplished. The point is that the data types defined by the language both define and reflect the character and personality of that language.

Then I move on to control statements. Why? Because once you understand data, you need to do something with it. You can't begin to write useful programs without understanding how to control the flow of execution. Like data, the control statements define fundamental aspects of the language. No advanced feature of the language can be described until the reader understands `if`, `while`, `switch`, and so on.

Assuming that I am writing about an object-oriented language, the next thing I do is introduce classes, objects, and methods. Of course, in C++, methods are called functions, but I'll just use the term *method* for the sake of this discussion. With an object-oriented programming language, the class is a foundational concept because it defines the nature of an object. It must be introduced as early as one reasonably can.

After the class has been introduced, I start layering on the additional functionality of the language, adding features in logical order, with each new feature building on what came before. For example, in my C# books, I follow up with operator overloading, indexers, properties, inheritance, interfaces, and so on. Of course, I also include a discussion of the I/O subsystem.

But there is another aspect to all programming languages: the library. Thus, I think of a language as being divided into two logical parts. The first I call the core of the language. This is defined by the keywords and syntax. The second part is the library. From a writer's point of view, the library is the more difficult of the two.

Ed: Why?

Herb: The libraries for languages such as C++, Java, or C# are so big! I could easily expend five times as much page count teaching the library as I do the core of the language. But I don't have the freedom of doing that because of constraints on the size of books. (There is a limit to the number of pages that can be bound together.) The problem is that the library is also very important. It helps frame the way that code is written. Let me give you an example.

One of the most important parts of the C++, Java, and C# libraries is their support for the basic data structures. This support is organized into subsystems called the Standard Template Library (STL) in C++, the Collections Framework in Java, and Collections in C#. All implement the same basic concept: data structures and algorithms. The really interesting thing is that these subsystems are revolutionizing programming.

Notice that I said "revolutionizing." I did not say "revolutionized." The process is still ongoing. We're still not doing everything we can with these libraries. Here is an example. In C++, the STL includes something called a stream iterator. Using this iterator, you can write to an output stream.

This is a powerful concept. However, when I think about doing I/O, I normally think first about using the I/O library, not the STL. It's just habit. This is why it's taking time for the full effect of these libraries to be felt. In general, programmers are still discovering new ways to make use of these powerful subsystems. But, again, the process takes time.

Another library-based feature that is really just starting to mainstream is the regular expression. I must admit that I continue to be amazed at the power of regular expressions. Every time I work with them, it seems like I discover something new. Perhaps most importantly, the regular expression is revolutionizing string handling. This, of course, means that it is changing one of the most fundamental aspects of programming.

But, Ed, here's an important point. Programming, as we normally think of it, has been around for about 50 years, plus or minus. We tend to think we know what it means to be a programmer. But the trouble is that programming is changing all the time. People who are learning to program today are going to find they are programming a whole lot differently in 10 or 20 years.

Ed: How do you deal with conceptual interconnections and the linear progression of text and pages in a book?

Herb: There's an old saying in real estate: "Location, location, location." Well, there's a saying in my office: "Organization, organization, organization." From a technical writing point of view, organization is one of the most challenging tasks. It is also one of the most critical. The reason is the high level of interrelatedness present in all modern programming languages. This makes the order in which topics are presented very important.

Unfortunately, when one begins to teach a language, you always encounter what I call the "jump start" problem. How do you explain any single feature when doing so automatically involves other elements? To overcome this problem, I introduce early on, and in a general way, several language features, but without much detail. This gives the reader sufficient knowledge to begin exploring the language in detail. I actually have a paragraph that I use in nearly all of my books that addresses this point. Let me read you the one from *Java: A Beginner's Guide* (2006):

> "The purpose of this chapter is to introduce Java, including its history, its design philosophy, and several of its most important features. By far the hardest thing about learning a programming language is the fact that no element exists in isolation. Instead, the components of the language work in conjunction with each other. This interrelatedness is especially pronounced in Java. In fact, it is difficult to discuss one aspect of Java without involving several others. To help overcome this problem, this chapter provides a brief overview of several Java features, including the general form of a Java program, some basic control structures, and operators. It does

not go into too many details, but rather concentrates on the general concepts common to any Java program."

As this paragraph illustrates, part of the way I deal with the interrelatedness problem is to say to the reader, "Here's some stuff you've got to take on faith right now. The full explanation will follow a little later on." In other words, I give the reader a "jump start" that helps them get going.

After covering the basics, I find that most of the time, the rest of the features in the language can be organized in a logical fashion, with one following naturally after another. Moreover, often, one feature depends on or relates to another. When this is the case, the organization is easy. It's "first things first." For example, in C#, there is the concept of the delegate. A discussion of the delegate must follow a discussion of the method because delegates relate to methods. The same is true of events, because events are built on delegates. Therefore, it wouldn't make sense to explain events before I explain delegates. And it wouldn't make sense to describe delegates before methods. These types of things all seem pretty obvious when I say them like this, but sometimes it takes a bit of thought to get right.

Ed: How do you keep in mind being the learner's advocate? How do you write for the beginner, even though you are an expert?

Herb: I remember what it was like learning to program. I remember finding the book that really got me excited about programming. It was called *Basic BASIC* by James S. Coan (Hayden Book Co., 1978). Although this was many years ago, I still remember how the light came on, and I realized, "Wow, I understand this. This all makes sense." I was actually jumping up and down with joy when I ran my first program. It was that book that really started me down the path of becoming a programmer. Had the book been poorly written, perhaps things might have turned out differently. But, fortunately for me, the book was well written, and I learned from it. I have always been grateful for that. The key is that I still clearly remember the experience of learning to program. I try to make sure that my readers will have the same positive experience that I did.

Actually, my interest in technical books predates my programming career. When I was a kid, I would go to the library in the town where I grew up. I'm talking about being around 12 or 13 years of age. I read all of the "How To" electronics books that the library had. My favorite one was called something like *How to Build a Five-Tube Radio*. And I did! I got a soldering iron, bought the components, and I built one.

What's interesting is that some of those early electronics books were very much like programming books today. They had very much the same kind of approach. Although they discussed things like resistors, capacitors, tubes, transformers, and Ohm's Law, it was still the same basic method of presentation used by a programming book. To this day, I have extremely fond memories of those books.

So on the bottom line, as the learner's advocate, I just write the kinds of books I want to read. It really is that simple. But I also think that there is one other important part of the process. A writer has an implied covenant with the readers: You are going to teach them something in a way that they can understand. You're not going to talk down to them, and you're not going to talk over their heads, either. The ultimate goal of the book is to help the reader succeed in learning the topic. An author who follows this advice will enjoy the thanks of his or her readers. That is the best reward an author can have.

Observation

Nikhil Kothari, on page 113, mentions the importance of being one's own customer when developing software.

Ed: A lot of what makes a language challenging to learn and challenging to teach is not the core language, or even the libraries, but it's how you deal with the runtime. How does one deal with compiler options, or linker options, or Makefiles, or even the IDEs? Do you cover that in your books?

Herb: Yes, I have, but I include less today than in the past. For example, in my Java books, I just use Sun's JDK. With C# books, I use the Express Edition that Microsoft makes available for free on its website. Furthermore, I use them in their default configuration. In essence, I take the attitude that "however the compiler installs is how we're going to use it." This makes it easy for the reader. Just install the compiler and then start compiling code. Furthermore, for the types of relatively simple example programs that are found in most of my books, the default configuration is what you want.

I used to teach "make" back in the old C days. Of course, I still write about C and C++, but I have almost given up on writing about the runtime environment and tools. Not because it's hard, but just because in C and C++, there is such a divergence of development environments. What applies to one may not apply to another.

Of course, when a language is closely tied to a specific development environment, I do take the time to explain its basic operation to the reader. For example, as we speak, I'm revising my book *C#: A Beginner's Guide* for version 3.0 of the language. This is the version that comes with Visual Studio 2008. I have five or six screens that show how to set up Visual Studio to create a new C# program, how to edit the program, and then how to compile the first example. This is designed to walk a beginner through the proper steps so that they can begin compiling code. However, I don't discuss Visual Studio much beyond those basics. It's too big. A full discussion of any IDE requires a book of its own.

As a point of interest, I still tend to use command-line compilers and tools, rather than an IDE. For me, they're faster and easier than an integrated development environment. Of course, there are exceptions.

Ed: What about Java and C#? Do you spend time talking about how the source code is compiled into bytecode and the bytecode is then interpreted?

Herb: Yes, that's important. Actually, it's fundamental, and I explain it as part of the historical context that is always part of Chapter 1 in my books. As many readers will know, neither Java nor C# compiles programs into directly executable code. Instead, they are compiled into what is essentially a portable assembly language. For Java, this is called bytecode. For C#, it's called MSIL (Microsoft Intermediate Language). In both cases, the compiled form of the program is executed by a runtime system. For bytecode, this is the JVM (Java Virtual Machine). For MSIL, it's the CLR (Common Language Runtime).

Both bytecode and MSIL play a crucial role in Java and C# because they solve two really big problems: portability and security. It's hard to make sense of some of the features in Java and C# without understanding the reasons for and implications behind bytecode and MSIL. Let me explain.

The use of bytecode/MSIL helps keep the programmer out of trouble because the runtime system is in control of the program's execution. It's harder to take down the entire system just because your Java program crashes, for example. Of course, because the runtime system is in control, there are limits to what you can do. For example, Java does not allow pointers, because to do so would provide a means of accessing resources, or even executing code that is outside the environment.

Of course, not all programs can be run from within such an environment. This is why we will need languages like C++ for a very long time. C++ is typically compiled to executable machine code. Thus, it is not executed under the control of another program (other than the operating system, of course). The advantage is that a C++ program will typically run faster than an equivalent Java or C# program. Also, within a C++ program, you are not restricted in what actions you can perform. Of course, this extra power comes with a price: A malicious (or poorly written) C++ program can negatively affect the system as a whole. For example, it can impact resources used by other applications, cause memory leaks, or dominate the system by effectively locking out other processes.

Because of the complexity of the modern programming environment, I expect that more and more applications will be written based on bytecode or MSIL. Doing so prevents the types of problems just described. That said, there will always be a need for programs compiled to actual machine code. Of course, programmers working in such an environment will face increasingly tough demands and accountability. But then, I think that all programmers will be facing the same.

CHAPTER 10

Floyd Marinescu

Fact Sheet

Name: Floyd Marinescu

Home Page: http://infoq.com

Rock Star Programmer Credentials: Co-founder of the ServerSide.com Enterprise Java community, author of *EJB Design Patterns* (John Wiley and Sons, 2002), co-author of *Mastering Enterprise JavaBeans* (John Wiley and Sons, 2001), and founder and lead editor of InfoQ.com

Date of Birth: November 1978

City of Birth: Toronto, Canada

Birth Order: First of two

Marital Status: Single

Number of Kids: None

Degree: Bachelors of Math in Computer Science from University of Waterloo

Years as an IT Professional: Nine

Role: CEO of InfoQ.com

Number of generations in ancestry (including yourself) that graduated from college: One

Introduction

Floyd Marinescu's strong work ethic was apparent the first time I met him. It was at the ServerSide Java Symposium 2005 in Las Vegas. This was *his* conference, at the height of its popularity, and Floyd was very busy: he had hustle. Floyd's mentor, Ed Roman, had started TheServerSide.com, but it was Floyd that turned it into the most popular Enterprise Java destination of its time. As I met Floyd again and again over the next few years, he was always hustling, always had something new in the works. After TheServerSide .com was sold to TechTarget in the summer of 2004, he started over again on his current project, InfoQ.com. The vision for InfoQ.com was born of the realization that the software development technical team leaders, the architects, and the senior engineers of the world needed a place with more controlled and targeted information than was available on TheServerSide.com.

The next time I saw Floyd, he was hustling again, this time with a video camera at the 2006 JAOO conference in Århus, Denmark. The presentations at JAOO recorded by Floyd would serve as part of the early infusion of content into InfoQ. In between sessions, as he was hustling the camera from one room to the next, I approached him for this book. I think Floyd's vision on how to stay current has proven itself in the competitive Enterprise Software journalism market, and I think you'll enjoy hearing from him.

Soft Skills

Ed: Your first effort in the print publishing medium was your 2001 collaboration with Ed Roman: *Mastering Enterprise JavaBeans, Second Edition* (John Wiley and Sons, 2001). How did you get into writing the book? Did you always have tech book authoring as a goal, or was it just an opportunity that came up that you seized and made the most of?

Floyd: To be honest, it was more of the latter. I never thought that I would become an author. But it was an area I had expertise in, so when the opportunity presented itself, I jumped on it.

What happened was, Ed Roman had written [the first edition] and he was working on a second edition. Ed Roman and I were colleagues at The Middleware Company, who was the founder of TheServerSide.com. And he asked me to write a chapter in his book on design patterns that are commonly used in Enterprise JavaBeans (EJB). So, I just started scoping out the amount of space that would be required to write this chapter, and it turned out that we could easily have 200 pages just on that alone. And from that the idea of *EJB Design Patterns* (John Wiley and Sons, 2001) was spawned…because there seems to be a lot of common problems that will be solved in common ways by EJB developers.

Ed: So you took advantage of this first opportunity, delivered on your commitment for the first book, and parlayed that into a book of your own. How did you manage to sell the publisher on the idea for the second book?

Floyd: At the time, there were some Java design pattern books, but there was nothing that was really specifically looking at EJB, and also taking more of a practical approach to explaining the patterns, not so high-level. For example, some of the other EJB patterns that I found were a little too high-level and weren't really getting into the meat of some issues with EJB. And now we wanted something practical, that developers could read and understand.

Ed: The essence of the book in which this interview will be included is discovering how successful programmers create opportunities and take advantage of them to make more opportunities. With many of the people I've interviewed, there were "turning-point moments" in their careers that lead them to their current success. These turning points usually accompany the creation of a personal connection with someone or some organization, but they can also be encounters with new technologies. How do you recognize those moments when they happen to you? Was meeting Mr. Roman one such turning-point moment?

Floyd: I think meeting him to begin with was such a turning point, yes, because that's how everything with TheServerSide.com came about. He had just launched a training company that was teaching EJB based upon his book and wanted to have an online community about EJB. And at the time, I was actually still at university, and I was on a work term, going to conferences trying to network. [I] met him at a conference and then [he] hired me. So I became the force behind TheServerSide. In terms of recognizing those

Character Attribute

Not being ruled by fear.

moments, it was clearly an opportunity for me. It was a huge challenge, and much greater than anything I was doing. And, yeah, in terms of how to recognize it, I'm not sure if there are any "patterns" in that area.

It comes down to: You should know in your heart if it's a big break, if it's a big challenge for you, and even if it does sound much more challenging than you think you might be able to do, then just take the opportunity and you'll figure it out later. For example, I certainly didn't have the experience under my belt to try to actually build an enterprise database website. And before this happened, I barely even had Java experience from the university. But I accepted the challenge and took it on, and it all worked out.

Some people say these moments are chance or fortuitous. I'd say maybe there is an element of luck to it. I also think that these moments can be heavily created by you. It was my choice to go to these conferences and network during my lunch hours when I was on my work term, whereas some other students were just staying in the office playing video games.

Character Attribute

Floyd appears to be an avid reader of practical self-help books. Not just a reader, he also has retained the information in those books so well that he can reference them off-the-cuff. This implies that the self-help books have actually helped him, which, I find in my experience, is rarely the case.

It was my choice to read books on large system design and programming on the subway while I was going to school or I was going to some of my first work term jobs. You have to create these kinds of opportunities. And, actually [that] reminds me of a new disc I saw recently called *The Secret* (TS Production 2006), which you may have heard of. In *The Secret*, they talk about just the power of keeping focused on your goals. If you focus on your goals, then you can make these opportunities. And for me, one of the ways of focusing on my goals was by reading the right books and educating myself and also going out to conferences to network.

Ed: Another dimension that you mentioned was having the courage to do it even though you might not know how to do it all the way.

Floyd: Yeah. Knowledge may be a precursor, of course. Also, I focused myself on domains that I knew were emerging, upcoming, and also domains that were important in the enterprise. When I was in the computer science program at the University of Waterloo—this is '97 throughout 2000 or so—what was "in" for most computer science students was game programming and hard-core data structures and development with concurrency… all these challenging aspects of computer science.

Ed: Wait, so you were doing the ServerSide.com while you were still at university?

Floyd: Most people don't know that.

Ed: So game programming didn't interest you?

Floyd: I just knew that game programming is, first of all, extremely challenging. Second of all, it's a niche market and it might not be that everyone who goes into that can do [it] well. Meanwhile, here was this Enterprise Java thing and Windows DNA and, well, that's where the real money is. So I was one of the very few people [among my peers] who were actually reading about EJB back in '99. Everyone else didn't care. They thought, "Oh, that's boring business stuff. Who cares?" But in the end, I ended up actually getting all these great opportunities. When I was doing my call for interviews, I actually got a job working at a startup in Silicon Valley for four months through the university. He told me I was the only one who even knew what EJB was. So it's about choosing the right domains as well.

Character Attribute

Immune to the herd mentality.

Ed: Have you ever had a career mentor? Someone to whom you go for career advice?

Floyd: I don't have one mentor. I always try to suck up all the knowledge I can [from] everybody around me. That's just something I generally do as a matter of principle. I've had quite a few influences—I always borrow a little from everybody. Probably a single significant influence in my life has been Ed Roman, who actually started the Middleware company, and I've learned a lot about business from him. Probably Peter Coad as well. I read his book *Java Design* (Prentice Hall PTR, 1998), and that was a big influence on me.

Ed: Did you know him personally?

Floyd: No, I didn't. Just from his various works. Scott Ambler also. I do know him personally and I've read his books. But, yeah—in general, I try to learn from everyone. That's very important.

Ed: How did you know that game programming, while difficult, challenging, and also popular, was not going to be as lucrative as something not as popular, maybe not as difficult, possibly just as interesting: EJB? How did you know to ride that crest?

Floyd: I'm more of a people person in motivation. And I enjoy solving problems. And the biggest problems tend to also carry the biggest compensation. The biggest problems were those happening in the enterprise, happening in big business. Whereas game programming is a very niche problem to solve, and it's not really changing the world—you're not helping people writing games—whereas if you're running a business application, you are helping people in some way and affecting the users of that application. So I was driven towards an interest in business application development from a wider personality trait of liking to help people. And actually, it's that same trait that is why I'm in the online community business as well. It's what motivates me to do what I do today. So, in the end, business is about solving problems, and they say that if you can solve most people's problems, then you can have the most business success. It came down to that.

> **Character Attribute**
>
> This belief, that game programmers are not helping people, reveals Floyd's work ethic: Games themselves must not be helping people.

Ed: Were you conscious of saying, "Okay, I'm going to go out there and find where the hard problems are, and I'm going to then look at the current state of the art in attempting to solve those problems?" Was there a conscious approach, or was it just that you were drawn to the problem itself?

Floyd: No, it *was* a conscious approach. First of all, wanting to help people doesn't mean I'm going to go and sit in food shelters. I'm going to help them in areas where I'm most capable, which is software development. So, in that realm, I wanted to work with cutting-edge technology. And I was looking at the emerging technologies that could form the new basis for how enterprise applications are being developed in the next few years.

So, I was attracted to Enterprise Java and also to what at the time was called Windows DNA, which later became the .NET framework platform.

And those just seemed to be quite obvious at the time—at least if you believed all the marketing—to be the emerging platforms that mattered. And that's why I wasn't interested in Common Object Request Broker Architecture (CORBA) or anything like that. That seemed to be older or on the downslide. And I was also very interested in object modeling and object design because I perceived those to be challenges on large-scale systems, and those are the kinds of problems I want to solve.

Ed: Speaking of knowing what problems people want to solve, some have said that Model Driven Architecture (MDA) is an answer to a problem that people want to solve. What do you think about MDA—is it going to be the next big thing?

Floyd: Hmm, that's an interesting one, because people have been asking this question for many years. It's not an emerging trend that can make it or break it. It's always been around and [there have] just been different ways of doing it. So I don't see it becoming any more successful than it is today. It's not really a new trend. It seems to be constant: [there are the kinds of] users who enjoy taking a modeling-first approach and the kinds of users who enjoy a code-first approach. And it seems to be quite mutually exclusive. And, if anything, the whole rise of the Agile movement seems to be taking us away from [the] modeling approach. So, no, I don't really see it changing. I just see it staying the same.

However, this is more with [a] one-to-five-year outlook. After five years plus, it could be quite different, because there are some trends, technologies coming out that could raise the abstraction level of software design to the point where we really are actually working with diagrams and lines and bubbles. But I think we'll go through a phase of domain-specific languages first, where the language itself is a rising abstraction, before we eventually get to the point where we're actually using model tools. It could be 10 to 15 years out.

Ed: Ted Neward also seems to have that notion. Ted has a lecture, you may have heard it, "Why the Next Five Years Are Going to Be About Languages." Do you agree with that?

Floyd: Yes. Although it's going to be different from the innovation of language we saw in the '80s and '90s. Domain-specific languages (DSLs) are an important part of this trend. And one of the reasons is because we are finding, as people start working with DSLs for certain contexts, that DSLs just are better. If you're working for a specific domain, it could be quicker, more elegant, more maintainable to use a purpose-built, domain-specific language as opposed to a complex framework [implemented] in a general-purpose language.

So, for example, recently, Amazon launched its flexible payment service. They wrote a DSL that you can use to represent a payment policy. A payment policy can be quite complex: for example, "bill user X every third Thursday but not on leap years and only during good standing," or something like that. There are all kinds of rules you can put in. If you're to take a general-purpose language approach, you'd probably be given an object model in an application programming interface (API). You'd have to pre-configure a bunch of objects, set some properties on them, and then post them to some method. And it would be accepted. But with the DSL approach, you have just a few lines of code that concisely express the policy that you're trying to implement. And it fell down one-tenth the amount of code and it's more readable. Martin Fowler is suggesting that to learn a complex API object model can be the same learning curve or even more of a learning curve than to learn the matrix of the language and if you're using it in a specific context. So why not, in the future, consider DSL for specific context?

It seems to be more thought leadership in the area of using DSL. But for the majority of community, they were not technically reachable until now. Before Java, programmers couldn't really do DSLs, and there's really no way you can embed a custom language in any viable way into a project. However, thanks to all the innovation on dynamic languages, that's now becoming quite easy. That Ruby scripts directly into Java code, or you can even create other languages. And another trend that is leading towards this multi-language approach is, of course, Ruby on Rails, and we've seen that even the domain of Web development could use a purpose-built language or framework. In the Ruby community, they don't think of Rails as a framework; they think of it as a DSL. So, that's caused a lot of innovation in the Java community, in return.

So, we have things like Groovy on Rails—Grails, that is—and it just seems to continue this level of innovation. Java has opened minds to the idea that you can create parts of the application in purpose-built languages and have other parts of the application in Java. But the key point, however, that will make all this feasible today, in a way that wasn't feasible in the late '80s where you had multiple languages that were actually competing platforms, is that today, we have multiple languages that aren't just sharing the same platform. They're sharing the libraries, the class libraries. They're sharing the deployment environments. You can have multiple languages deployed on Java, and the operation staff can still support Java Virtual Machine (JVM) the way they are already used to. You can have multiple languages all sharing the Java Development Kit (JDK) or other languages that are libraries that developed in Java. So that's a very important difference, because in the '80s and '90s, our language space was

> **Observation**
>
> Dave Thomas notices the same thing, but his experience brings out a particular technical difficulty in doing non-Java languages on the Java Virtual Machine. See page 293.

a whole platform in [terms of] data center choice as well. It wasn't just language choice. And that caused a lot of fragmentation and a lot of wheel reinvention, which is not going to be the case for this new era that we might be entering.

Ed: Can you talk a bit about the hard technical problems being faced by software developers today?

Floyd: Well, if you look at the kinds of domains of enterprise applications, there are obviously high-throughput transaction systems. There are client front-ends, be it desktop or Web. These are still challenges, and they're always challenges. I do think that just the plain business of building a transactional [application] is a lot easier because there are mature frameworks out there—whether they're EJBs or not, they're maturing. There's lots of documentation to build stuff that works. There are a lot of patterns out there. But there still continues to be a lot of innovation in frameworks. There continues to be innovation—or evolution, rather—not just in the technologies, but also in the underlying business trends that are increasing what is expected of the developers and the technical teams. Yeah, it's easy to do Web apps now. Everyone knows how to use Struts and Spring and EJB. But, unfortunately, you're not being asked to build the same kinds of apps as you were three years ago. Now we have this whole trend, with Web 2.0, and now we have users who are elucidated by [Google's] gmail. And they now want us to build them systems with Ajax that are as rich as desktop applications.

So, it's all the same kinds of problems—there are still the same challenges now as in 1990. It's that new trends in technology and new needs of business are requiring us to build those applications in newer ways. And it's always a challenge when something's new. The next year of innovation—at least in Web, in client front-end—seems to be this merger between the Web and the desktop. How do you do that?

Observation

I talked with Nikhil Kothari, lead architect for Microsoft Silverlight, in Chapter 5.

So, now you have tools like Silverlight from Microsoft and the consumer Java Runtime Environment (JRE) from Sun, and you have Adobe Air [that] allows you to build Flash apps which run on desktop apps.

Everything is always changing, so it's all the usual answers in terms of what is still challenging for developers today.

Ed: The stated goal of your current venture, InfoQ.com, is "tracking change and innovation in the enterprise software development community." Given the time demands of high-level software professionals today, an individual may only have time to read one site. How important is it to you that that site be InfoQ?

Floyd: It's quite important, but in a certain domain. We want to be a one-stop shop for certain kinds of readers and for certain topics. We don't want to be one-stop shop for people interested in Python or [GNU/]Linux—Slashdot is for that. We want to choose the domains that are not being very well served today and be the best at serving those domains and hope that anyone who's in those domains would always be at InfoQ. For example, there aren't any sites that are covering Agile with the daily rigor of a news organization, with news and online video presentations, interviews, and books. There's no one covering service-oriented architecture (SOA) like that. We're a unique community. We're probably one of the only places that is covering Ruby with such rich content. Ruby is quite heavily covered in the blog space now.

We want to be the best in the domains that we're choosing to serve, and in those domains, it's quite important. Not that we want to replace any other sites, but I would argue that the majority of technical people, developers, are not RSS (Really Simple Syndication) addicts and don't even use feed readers. They're just really busy, and for that class of person, I would definitely want us to be a one-stop shop.

> **Observation**
>
> Floyd's argument is confirmed by Max and Libor, on page 300. Both of them expressed something approaching disdain for those who spend lots of time on RSS feeds.

Ed: Given that the intent of the site is to cover change and innovation in software, how do you get your scoops? Do you have investigative reporters out there looking for new things? How do you do it?

Floyd: Well, we have a whole lot of part-time domain experts who work with us as writers. So, they write news and do interviews and such. All of them are asked to surf their networks, surf their blog rolls, just keep an eye open on a regular basis for things that are new and important. And we also have a lot of vigorous discussions internally about trends that matter. A lot of companies will come to us if they want to get exposure and they want to be seen, but I would say that a lot of it, probably a lot of our news is driven by blogs. Reading discussion forums, seeing what matters to technical people, and that will trigger us to go into more depth and read more and write a summary for all the other readers out there who don't have time to read blogs and discussion forums. All of the news is community-driven.

> **Character Attribute**
>
> Ability to build and maintain a team composed of individuals with diverse interests and skills.

It's technical people trying to distinguish important changes or important innovations that are occurring and then writing them out in one place on InfoQ. We're trying to create an essential resource for technical team leads and architects to come and find out what matters, what are the trends that matter. And what are things that they should keep their eye on.

Ed: But you also have a fair amount of exclusive content. How do you go about getting that?

Floyd: A lot of dedication and passion. In terms of exclusive content, we should probably change that word, but really, what it means is that it's good content, but not news. It consists of streaming video interviews, with transcripts, video presentations with synchronized slides. We'll go out and see if someone knows what's a good topic. We'll ask them to write an article. Often, we can find people by seeing who's blogging about what, or maybe it's people in our networks on the [lecture circuit]. We keep an eye out on whatever conference is coming up, and we'll go there and actually film a session, often with permission of the conference or speakers. We invest a fair amount of money in them, in going out and doing this, and we want InfoQ to be a place where all the best sessions from various worldwide conferences can be found. A lot of people out there don't go to conferences; they can't afford to. So now we have access to those same presentations. And we do interviews in quite the same way. We usually will go to a conference, and we'll invite various experts to come meet us and do a video interview. And then we have a whole lengthy process by which we do post-production and editing and transcripts and stuff, and then put [it] online.

Ultimately, it comes from a motivation of just really enjoying helping others, helping the community. All of our editors are domain experts. They're not journalists. They're doing this mostly out of passion, not out of competition. When we launched InfoQ, I was running around like a madman with a camera on my shoulder to get sponsors and I actually personally filmed probably about 60 hours of video that you can see there.

Ed: How has your training in computer science helped you with InfoQ?

Floyd: I've found that understanding the principles of object-oriented design and encapsulation has made me a better writer. When I write news on InfoQ, I actually treat each paragraph almost like an object. I think about it being self-contained. I think about when the reader reads this piece of text, is this text dependent on the knowledge that is encapsulated here? So I try to minimize dependencies. For example, not making passing reference to something the reader probably doesn't know [about]. That dependency will cause the mental stress when they read it. I think it's cool to apply programming best practices to other areas in life, and you'd be surprised how well they do apply.

In fact, another favorite metaphor I have is looking at the lessons learned from optimistic concurrency strategies and applying them to other parts of life. For example, in optimistic concurrency, you're setting things up so that your data operations and your requests will be faster 'cause there's no locking, and because you're taking the optimistic case that there's not gonna be a collision between requests missing data. Because you're

> **Observation**
>
> Dave Thomas, on page 295, strongly advises *against* doing this, which only goes to show that one's mileage may vary with this sort of advice.

taking the optimistic case, your application runs more smoothly, and in the unlikely case [that] a collision does happen, then it will be a little slower. Now if you take that strategy and apply it to life, it's actually quite useful. So, for example, some people say that I give trust too much. I say it is a strategy, because by trusting right off the bat, 90 percent of the time, things'll happen more efficiently. I don't need to waste time checking or taking extra precautions in case someone is malicious. So applying this notion of optimistic concurrency strategy to other areas of life, you can yield the same results: you can be more efficient and more productive. But then, obviously, with the awareness that in the bad case it'll cost you more, at least you're doing it on purpose and it's with reason.

> **Character Attribute**
>
> Doesn't compartmentalize knowledge, but seeks to apply it wherever it fits.

> **Character Attribute**
>
> Floyd clearly has a well-defined value system that is consistently applied in his life.

Ed: You're not the first person I've heard that from. Andy Hunt mentioned that. He put it this way, "You want to look at life from a position or assumption of abundance rather than an assumption of scarcity, and more often than not, things will prove to be more abundant." If you look at things from a viewpoint of scarcity, you'll be self-limiting and miss out on some things you otherwise would see.

Given the wealth of information about software development out there, on your site and others like it, in bookstores and magazines, do you think the actual state of the quality of software has improved over the past decade? Consider the self-help section of the bookstore. There are a ton of great books in there, but are there actually fewer people who are depressed, compulsive, lonely, overweight—whatever the self-help section is doing?

Floyd: I hang out with a very expert lot: the kind of people who speak at events, the kind of people who write articles. That's my job: I talk to these guys all the time. So I tend to hang out with artists of sorts. [I get] a skewed view of the [practice of] software development. What I do hear, however, is that a lot of real-world software development is really bad. I would argue from a macro trend perspective that software development has improved because the underlying platforms have improved. They've become more abstract. It's harder to make mistakes. Java innovates so much because we're not worrying about pointers now. That's improved the quality of software without developers needing to learn anything. We also have new methodologies, such as Agile software development, test-driven development (TDD), and all these are obviously increasing quality. I do think that software development has gotten better due to the increasing level of abstractions, of the way we plan software, and also in terms of the application of lessons learned along the way. Those lessons learned come in the form of improvements to software development process, for example,

Agile; in the form of design patterns; and also in the form of frameworks that are continuing to provide better solutions to problems. These frameworks are now readily accessible and, more importantly, free, which was not the case, not even five years ago. So, I think open source and Agile and just the overall trend of increasing abstractions has essentially improved software development.

These things have not necessarily improved people's commitment to delivering quality, but it does that anyway.

Ed: When you encounter a new technology, how do you assess its quality?

Floyd: A lot of what I do with InfoQ is at the level of analysis. I would look at the business and social factors, because on one hand, yes, you want something to be of high quality. And on the other hand, you want to pick the winner and make sure you invest your time in technology that should be important ten years from now and not on fringe cool stuff that'll never make it.

Ed: Well, how do you do that? How do you pick a winner?

Floyd: There are so many things. I look at the strength of the community. Does it have a user following now, even if it is just grass-roots? What is the strength of that community? I look at the application. Is a problem being solved here? I look at how much [of an] improvement it is over what we have now. Is that improvement worth a massive migration or massive investment on the part of developers in businesses to learn this? Is the return on investment (ROI) good enough to warrant learning this? So, that's one axis. Another axis is just politics: Who's behind it? Every Smalltalk lover says that Smalltalk is better, but Java had the support of IBM and Sun and various coalitions of companies. So it was quite clear in the second half of the 1990s that if you looked from that respect of who's supporting it, who's putting the muscle behind it, Java would be a winner over other various technologies that were out at the time.

> **Observation**
>
> For more insight on Java vs. Smalltalk, see page 293, in the interview with Dave Thomas.

You have to look at that, and you have to look at the political and the business angle. Who are the people behind it? Are they themselves winners and do they matter? Does it offer enough value to the problem space? So, the biggest choice of technology that we can look back in hindsight in the last ten years is probably Enterprise Java. And if you put yourself back in 1997 looking forward, there were a lot of indicators to suggest that Enterprise Java could become a mainstay [rather than] some multi-language development using CORBA as an abstraction. There were a lot of indicators, and I think one of them was, again, who is behind Java? What value does it add? Is it huge value? Obviously, the abstractions it provided were very important for Enterprise projects, where there are lots of developers. It lowered the number of possible errors that could come up. It was huge. It was solving a huge problem, and all the right companies were behind it.

The indicator of ROI and the indicator of who's supporting it were both there and both supportive of Java. You can look today at some technologies that are getting headlines. Ruby Rails probably does have the ROI indicator. It doesn't have the backing indicator. It remains to be seen whether that will become a mainstay in software development for Web applications. Those are some indicators I look at.

Ed: You just answered the question of how you assess the quality of a software technology. How about the quality of software technologists? What makes a smart developer?

Floyd: A developer who's constantly upgrading his skills and has good awareness of what's going on in the industry. I look for a developer who has very strong problem-solving skills. Preferably somebody interested in understanding the business so they can understand and directly see and feel good about their work as being connected to the success of the business and not just see it in terms of a code master. A good team player and someone who cares about integrity. Won't make commitments they're not serious about and will keep the commitments they make. I think those core items would make someone good to work with and a good developer.

Hard Skills

Ed: When you write a piece of code that you just *know* has been written before, do you search for reuse or do you just proceed and go ahead and rewrite it?

Floyd: I almost always search to see—if it's not reusing, at least so I can see how someone else did it so I can get some ideas and make sure that my solution is good enough or better.

In fact, when I first started programming for the very first time back when I had no experience, I remember I was actually browsing the JDK source base 'cause at the time, it was the only large amount of Java code that was available. And I used to read it to see what code and conventions they used and just generally how they worked. I was trying to mimic that when I was fresh out of school.

Of course now, with open source, you can do that with a large number of other projects.

Ed: So let's say the method you need to write is doing a really well-defined task, and you're sitting down to write it and you just have this feeling, "God, I *know* that this code has been written before, but I don't know where to go to find it." For example, you've got a list of things and you want to do something to them.

Floyd: So I'll go see what's there and see if I can reuse it. In general, I think it's also a good strategy for maintainability to use external libraries wherever possible that have been reused by multiple projects, 'cause they're generally more bug-free and have been looked at by more people. I think companies that have a culture of "build it here" have a problem, because that just means it's gonna be more expensive for them to maintain in the long term.

Ed: What is the correlation between developer proficiency and tools mastery: knowing your way around your integrated development environment (IDE), knowing every possible keyboard shortcut, knowing how to do everything with the tool? What's the relationship between being a really great developer and having great mastery of your tools?

Floyd: Hmm. I don't think I'm the right person to answer that question 'cause I haven't coded in a while. But one opinion I do have on that is the true master should be able to get things done with nothing more than a text editor. A true software master should understand enough of the underlying plumbing that they could actually go in and hack it with simple tools. Now I'm not saying that's a good idea. I'm not even saying that you'll be productive—you'll certainly be unproductive and you shouldn't have to do that, but you also shouldn't have to rely on your tools and not really understand what's going on under the hood either. And if you are relying on your tools and don't know what's going on, it's great that it's a black box. But when things go wrong, you're gonna be stuck not knowing what to do. You need to understand what's going on.

Ed: How important is it to be a continual optimizer of the way you work? For example, personal processes, such as how you read e-mail and on down to the level of using scripts and macros to automate repetitive tasks.

Floyd: I see continually optimizing as another way of being committed to quality and productivity. It's quite important to do that; it'll just make you more efficient and productive and make you more valuable to the company and possibly speed up a lot of your time. If your manager asks you to do something and thinks it'll take three hours, but you automated it last time he asked and it takes you ten minutes, then you have almost three hours break, or you can tell him that you can do it ten minutes and be a superstar. So I think it's quite important to automate. In some ways, it's an extension of the core philosophy and best practice of reuse and encapsulation. If you're gonna solve a problem, find a way to automate it in a reusable fashion and then you don't need to reinvent the wheel every time. You can think of your actual time as something that can be reused or not, and you should try to aim not to reinvent it and have the output of your time be maintainable and reusable just as much as your code. A lot of people don't apply the same kinds of thought processes towards non-programming functions as they do to programming, and I think that's a mistake. I think you should really think about encapsulation and reuse and productivity in other aspects of life as well.

Ed: How do you cope with schedule pressure and long hours and high expectations from clients—in general, that kind of stress?

Floyd: I make sure I do first things first. When the day starts, I'll first resolve anything that's related to projects that have to do with money coming in to the company. And then, after getting those things done, then I'll look at everything else, the software issues in the company. I find that the best strategy is just to have a very high amount of integrity, meaning don't make promises that you can't keep. Communicate whenever there's anything that might change or impact a promise you've made—make sure you communicate those changes before so the person knows. Be extremely explicit and extremely careful with your communications and expectation setting when it comes to any form of commitment. If you can manage expectations properly, that'll lead you to have enough time and to do well. I think the stresses of all that kind of work—it all comes down to expectation setting and integrity.

Ed: How would you categorize the skills of a successful software developer?

Floyd: It's understanding what business guys need and then having the people skills to actually deliver what they're asking for and to interact with them midway, especially now, especially with Agile development technologies. Ultimately, we're solving business problems—I think a lot of developers need to remember that the purpose of the job is to build applications [that are] useful to users. The software is only as good as how it serves the functional and non-functional requirements of the application. I think that's the most important. And second, I think, would just be an appreciation for delivering quality and maintainability. I'd say one of the indicators of maintainability is how readable is it by other people who are not involved in the project and also how will it stand the test of time.

Ed: What are some character attributes of successful developers?

Floyd: A passion for learning and a passion for solving problems, but I'd say people problems, not just odd, boutique, algorithmic problems. What's the third one: commitment to constantly be improving oneself. Making sure that the work you're doing is as good as it could be

Ed: As a software developer and in life in general, how important is it to be aware of your own ignorance?

Floyd: I think it's very important. For me, personally, I think one of the reasons why I've been able to get to where I have is 'cause I've always kept tabs on being aware of what I don't know. It's very important, because if you're aware of what you don't know, you're more likely to invest time to strategically plan what you spend your time learning and finding out when you do have time to do it. And also you'll be able to take on work

Character Attribute

Floyd is good at operating in the meta-cognitive mode.

Character Attribute

Floyd is comfortable taking on projects where he has large amounts of first order ignorance. For an explanation of the "Orders of Ignorance" see Appendix B from Phillip Armour.

and contracts that you maybe otherwise would have been uncomfortable taking on. For example, when I was first asked to write TheServerSide when I was still in university, I had just basic Java programming experience and only a couple weeks' experience with the database and no experience building Web apps. But when I was asked to do it, I already had it in my mind that I *kinda* understood what the various technologies were, so I knew what I didn't know. I just knew what I would need to learn to be able to do the project, so I said, "Yeah. I'll do it." Then I went out and found the right books and taught myself, and the rest is history. So it's very important to always be aware of what you don't know.

Knowing your own ignorance is always important, especially in the industry of software where things are so competitive. There's so much pressure to save money in software development, that you need to know what you don't know and invest time to learn that. If you don't, you have no job security. Job security in our space comes from continually increasing your skills, continually doing things better. If your job is something that can

Career Tip

Understand how you add value to the organization, and make sure your management understands it as well.

easily be done in some other place, then you should just assume that you can lose your job to emerging economies. If there is a spec sheet and it can be handed off to India, then that's where it's going to go. Why would it come to you? You need to make yourself invaluable. To make yourself invaluable, you need to be aware of what you don't know and every technology you need to continue learning in your part time. And unfortunately, that's the nature of the job. People have gone into software either in entry or from previous fields, [work hard], and do pretty good work. People who come in here expecting to have just regular routine lives like construction workers will probably soon be unemployed. You should always keep evolving.

Ed: When you look at the history of innovation, there are many examples of individuals who were able to lift their heads up from the march around the proverbial grindstone to question conventional wisdom. Sometimes, such individuals end up discovering a much better way to do things as a result. How does one improve one's skill at being able to get one's head above the problem and see the forest for the trees, as it were?

Floyd: In general, I think it's good for someone to always question their beliefs or question their assumptions. Always believe in your beliefs, but always consider that they could be incorrect.

Ed: Know why you believe in them.

Floyd: Yeah. Know why you believe it and always be ready to challenge those assumptions and also be able to put those assumptions in the context of what you're doing right now. It's important to note that any wisdom that we have about software development is very contextual. For example, at the last QCon conference in London, it came out that eBay and Amazon and a lot of really high-volume sites were not even using programmatic transactions or transactions managed at the server layer. They weren't doing that at all. They were actually avoiding any code-level transactions and managing stuff at the database level for performance. So here we have pretty much unquestioned best practices that work well for 95 percent of software applications, but then, when you get to special circumstances, for example, super, super, super high-volume applications, then those same assumptions don't hold.

> **Observation**
>
> Dave Thomas concluded the same thing. It all comes down to the database. See page 280.

So you have to consider the context and whether what you're doing applies to it. Another thing is trust your gut. I find very often when I'm having this gut feeling that something's wrong or something doesn't feel quite right about what I'm doing, it almost always has to do with something with me…that something maybe I'm doing wrong or believe wrong or something about the current process is wrong. And, for example, look at running a startup. I have certain tasks that I do and then I get so busy and eventually I experience the stress and dissatisfaction of being too busy to get everything done long enough to probably realize, "Wait a second. There's more stuff I should be delegating here and probably there's a mismatch of my role." That [realization] only happens when you feel that something's wrong and you start to mistrust it and try and investigate what actually is wrong. I'd say those two, and in general I think you should always be looking at the bigger picture. Whenever you're doing anything, you should know why you're doing it. In fact, in the book *Getting Things Done* by David Allen (Penguin, 2002), which is actually a book I highly recommend, he talks about how before we start any project or even a subset of a project, you should always understand—you and the people you're working with—why you're doing it. What's the value of this? 'Cause if why you're doing it [is that] it's easier to motivate yourself and you can actually better understand how your work fits into the overall bigger picture, that's very important.

Ed: I'm trying to uncover the relationship between developer success and one's ability to break out of the intense, laser-focused concentration required when working at the code or algorithmic level and see things at a higher level. Do you find that you just get so focused that you don't want to get out of that mode?

Floyd: Yeah. That happens. Happens to everybody. Yeah, sometimes it's a good thing; sometimes it's not. I think it's a good thing when you want to get something done no matter what and you're gonna stay up late to finish it 'cause then the next day you can relax and focus on other things. So there are pluses and minuses. But it's a minus when you're doing this at the expense of other things that have a greater priority.

Ed: Right!

Floyd: In that book *Getting Things Done*, he advises many times a day stepping back and looking at all the outstanding tasks that you have to do and choosing the ones that are the most important. And if you don't know what's most important, then you should step back to an even higher level of abstraction and look at, well, "What are your job responsibilities? What is your role?" And then try and choose something. And if, even at that level of abstraction you're having trouble choosing what's the next thing to work on, then step out even further higher up. I find this works for me. If you're feeling obsessive about one thing and you're not sure if this is actually the most important thing to be doing, try and step back and look at all the things you have to do and just look at many positions. Try and step back further and examine what's your actual role and job function, and that might help you make a choice of what you should do.

Ed: This ties in to something we talked about earlier, the idea of reuse and the pros and cons of reinventing the wheel. How much do you care about reinventing the wheel? Is that something you try to avoid, or is it ever appropriate in your opinion to reinvent the wheel?

Floyd: If you can do it much better and have much cleaner code—and based on newer design, newer APIs and much of the code is much smaller and better done—I think it makes sense. There are many other reasons why that might make sense [to rewrite]. For example, when we started writing InfoQ, we implemented our own application framework as opposed to just fitting our solution to work on existing Content Management System (CMS). We knew CMSs were generic solutions that could be applied for many of the different places, but our requirements were a bit more specialized. We would have to "shoehorn" it into their data model and framework if we wanted to use them. It was just actually quicker to develop. Our productivity increased by building it ourselves, and we figured, long term, it just looked better if we have it so we're not too constrained by another tool that might have different design paradigms or might change in the future. I think it depends on your requirements, right? How specialized are the requirements and just what are the projected maintainability [goals] if you do or do not use a third-party tool?

Business

Ed: How important is it to let your understanding of the software business and the specific domain in which you are working inform where you invest in stewarding your skillset?

Floyd: I think people should constantly be upgrading their skills, constantly be reading sites like InfoQ and such to know what's going on. You need to have an understanding of what's going on in the space. What frameworks are being used? What are various experts saying about various technologies and what's coming down the horizon so you can make the right choices later [and] not be stuck making wrong choices.

So in terms of your own business domain, I don't think it's necessarily as important as keeping up-to-date generally with technology. But it is important if you want to be important to the business. Any developer who is noticed by upper management of actually taking the effort of being aware of what's going on in the business and [considering] how IT can be prepared for it is quite likely to be promoted eventually and one day find himself/herself the CTO. A lot of the others just don't do that. And those who do, I think, will get noticed and promoted 'cause the higher you go up in the development organization, the more you're expected to be business-minded and make sure IT aligns its business. If you're looking for an upward career growth strategy, perhaps even out of pure development, then it's something that you should be doing.

Ed: Are you worried about outsourcing?

Floyd: I'm not worried.

Ed: How do you recognize when it's time to change jobs?

Floyd: When you're just not happy. When you just feel deep down that it doesn't feel right and you're just not happy with it anymore. No matter what you try and change about what you're doing, you're not getting happy, you're not getting motivated. Your heart's just not in it. If your heart's not in it, then it's time for a change. I've been in situations where I was making more money than I knew what to do with, but I just wasn't happy there. I couldn't motivate myself. Once I switched my job, I was quite the happiest and it was worth making less money to have a better life.

Ed: It's often said that the average person in the workforce will have several different careers between the time they enter the workforce and the time they retire. Do you agree with that?

Floyd: I think so, yes. Because even if you start your career as a developer and you stay in the realm of technology, over the course of 40, 50 years, you're likely to not be doing the same kind of development. You could eventually become a manager. You could eventually become consulting presales. You could eventually go into executive. I don't know. It's probably a minority of people who might be doing just pure programming all their lives. So yeah. I would agree with that.

I don't know if people would change careers out of a certain domain. I can't see someone technical then going to become a plumber or a doctor. Although it does happen, but I think [the] majority of people will change careers within their domain and where they have a lot of knowledge they can reuse and stuff.

Ed: Do you have any career plan B, a contingency plan? Let's say the bottom drops out of the IT industry. Look at airline pilots. That was a very, very, very good employment option for a long time, and then the airlines had a lot of financial trouble and there were layoffs. As a result, a lot of airline pilots had to take enormous pay cuts and even to this day, they're not back to where they were. They've seen their retirement plans decimated by the corporations that were struggling to stay in business. That's a specific instance of where the bottom fell out of an industry and people had to rethink their strategies. Let's assume that does happen in the IT industry at some point. Do you have a plan B to handle that case?

Floyd: Yeah. I'm always generally thinking about and concerned with financial security…probably coming from having been raised in North America by an immigrant family that came here and had to make ends meet. So I have backup plan, and there are a lot of layers to it…a lot of layers of backup plans. On one layer I very much believe in the principles from the *Rich Dad, Poor Dad* books by Robert Kiyosaki (Time Warner Paperbacks, 2002), and in particular, the book *The Cash Flow Quadrant* by Robert Kiyosaki (Business Plus, 2000), where they talk about wealth not being net worth and wealth being passive income. I'm constantly looking to invest part of my salary into cash flow–building investments. Not mutual funds, not stocks, not things that might increase in value to sell one day; but things that actually have a cash payout. So my favorite is actually real estate. So I think cash flow properties are the best, because you actually see a cash flow coming out of it from day one and over the years, as you buy more and more, eventually, the cash from real estate might even replace your actual income and then you can just choose to retire whenever you feel like it.

Ed: Rental properties?

Floyd: Yeah, that kind of stuff. Not buying and flipping, but just buying and holding and renting.

But there are other ways to get cash flow. There are financial instruments that do the same thing. So I would say that at the most concrete level, I look at alternate income strategies as a backup plan. At the software level, I'm always looking at networking. "Are your skills transferable within your field? Do you understand your business domain well enough?" Maybe you can do other work in that domain. So I'm always trying to cultivate more of a general view—trying to cultivate software skills that could be reapplied in other ways.

Ed: What is your planned retirement age?

Floyd: Well, depends on what you mean by retirement. 'Cause, I don't see myself doing nothing. To me, retirement means no longer having to work out of necessity—

Ed: Financial independence.

Floyd: Right—but working on things that I want to because I want to. I hope to be there in my 30s. And I think it's perfectly possible, especially with the incomes people make in software development. If you start early with a strategy of building passive income, don't worry about all these silly retirement plans and stuff. Just keep your money and buy income properties, and you'll see how quickly you'll have an alternate income stream you can rely on. And then, eventually, once you're big enough to cover your standard of living, then you're home free.

Personal

Ed: What were some useful classes you took in college?

Floyd: Not much [of] what I learned in computer science was readily transferable to what I'm doing now. Concurrency was probably useful. Even though we dealt with concurrency at a much lower level, it helped me understand what the applications were actually doing. Also data structures. Those are very important in order to actually be a proper designer, not just a code man. But university overall, the intention is to teach you how to learn. And give you the historical foundation to understand modern technologies, which you wouldn't get through university or through some other approach.

Ed: What are some computer books that you found helpful over the years?

Floyd: The best book I ever read was a book that inspired me to have a real love of object modeling and the love of patterns and the love of actually just wanting to build quality software. It was a book called *Java Design* by Peter Coad (Prentice Hall PTR, 1998).

Ed: Do you keep a journal?

Floyd: I wish. I'd like to if I had the time.

Ed: Do you use a day planner? What is the system that you trust?

Floyd: It's all inside Microsoft Outlook. I use a combination of the calendar and a folder structure to store actions that I need to accomplish and track projects, and I also make heavy use of notes in Outlook. You can actually post a note to a folder. I have a folder, for example, called "Next Actions." It'll contain e-mails that I need to follow up on. But if I think of something I have to do, I just make a note and post it to that folder, for example, "Feed Cat" or "Go To Bank" or something. So it stores all my next actions in one place and it's easy to find and I know that they're there. And I use the calendar for things I need to be reminded of—things I need to worry about on a particular day that I don't need to think about now, I'll push it to a day further out and then forget about it. That structure helps.

Ed: What would you say is the relationship between success as a software developer and success in one's personal life?

Floyd: Unfortunately, there's no correlation between your skills with women and your skills with software.

Ed: Or skills as a parent or—so yeah, you think there's a different set of skills entirely?

Floyd: Well, I think that the skills we enumerated for being a good software developer can also help you succeed in life, in general. But I don't know if the reverse is true. And probably girls will just distract you, so that wouldn't be good.

Ed: How good are you at keeping your work and personal lives balanced?

Floyd: I wasn't that good before, but I read the book *Getting Things Done*, and that really helped me. The book promises "stress-free productivity," and the basic way you achieve that is by making sure that all the things you have to do—all your tasks, all the things you want to be reminded of—are stored in a system that you trust and then you can get it out of your head and you can stop thinking about it. So as a result, I no longer have to worry about work when I'm actually out on my personal time. I don't have that stressed-out feeling worrying about what I'm gonna do or if it'll get done in time, and that was really important to me. So I highly recommend that book for everybody.

PART 3

Software Development Experts

CHAPTER 11

Andy Hunt

Fact Sheet

Name: Andy Hunt

Home Page: http://toolshed.com

Rock Star Programmer Credentials: Co-founder of the Pragmatic Programmers, founder of the Agile Alliance, sought-after consultant and lecturer

Time of Birth: Mid-1960s

Region of Birth: Eastern United States

Marital Status: Married

Degree: Bachelor of Science in Information and Computer Sciences, Georgia Institute of Technology

Years as an IT Professional: 30

Role: Entrepreneur and co-founder of the Pragmatic Programmers LLC

Introduction

The speakers who frequent the IT lecture circuit are a gold mine of rock star programmer talent. The premiere series on that circuit is Jay Zimmerman's "No Fluff, Just Stuff" (www.nofluffjuststuff.com), at which I had the pleasure of speaking in Reston, Virginia, in the fall of 2006. The keynote speaker at this particular conference was Andy Hunt, who presented his engaging "Refactoring Your Wetware" talk. Just ten minutes into Andy's presentation, I knew I wanted to share his insights in an interview for this book. He puts out the vibe of a true Renaissance man, and he is—right down to toting his well-worn Moleskine notebook and fronting his own rock-jazz-swing band, the Independent Memes (www.independentmemes.com).

Andy's career arc has brought him through most of the roles one can have in the IT industry, from rank-and-file programmer at a Fortune 100 company, to senior architect, to independent consultant, to his current role as the co-founder of the Pragmatic Programmers LLC. The Pragmatic Programmers are widely recognized in the IT business for high-quality content (no fluff, you might say). They are also seen as a programmer-friendly publisher for IT authors. This is probably because it is run by two programming pioneers who "get it" when it comes to managing the process of authoring a technology book because they've read, used, and written them themselves. He and fellow Pragmatic Programmers founder Dave Thomas are seen as true thought leaders in today's global programming community.

Soft Skills

Ed: Andy, I like to start out with some soft-skills questions to warm things up. From your vantage point at the helm of Pragmatic Programmers, I bet you get to see a lot of new technology just as it's taking shape. How do you tell when something new is going to also be something big?

Andy: Well, that's an interesting question because—and this isn't just true of me or Dave or anyone else in particular in the industry, but just in general—when you've been in the industry a long time, people start to watch you and watch what you're interested in, so past some particular tipping point, it becomes a bit of a self-fulfilling process.

Ed: You mean, you create the trends?

Andy: You start getting interested in, say, Erlang for concurrent programming, and now people start thinking, "Ooh, these guys are interested in Erlang. That must mean something."

Ed: That's a nice place to be.

Andy: You can cause your own industry swings, and I think it's far too early to say that about Erlang yet, but certainly I think that was the case with Ruby.

Dave and I wrote the first English-language Ruby book (*Programming Ruby*, Addison Wesley 2001) and really brought that to the attention of the Western world. Dave, in particular, has been instrumental in beating the drum and getting people interested in it, using the language, bringing it to people's attention.

Ruby was something that we were particularly looking for…that kind of technology.

I had just done a large data mining project in something like 50,000 lines of object-oriented Perl, and for various reasons, that was the environment I needed at that point. It was frustrating, but it was also really quite promising because it was *so* close to being a really nice environment, except for the fact that in Perl you had to do all the object orientation by hand. But the promise of having a scripted object-oriented language that had regular expressions, as well as good access to the operating system internals, and ran as an interpreted scripting language was a powerful thing.

At the conclusion of that project, both Dave and I started looking explicitly for that technology. We said to ourselves, "Okay, here's a need. This is something I want to see. What's out there?" And we looked and we scoured around, and Dave actually stumbled on Ruby in Japan. He found this website and said, "Hey, well, what about this? Take a look at this. This looks pretty cool."

We started looking at it, and that started the ball rolling. In that case, it wasn't really a question of looking at emerging technologies and picking the winner. It was a question of "I have this need. What is out there that could possibly fulfill this now or in development?" It was very much need-driven.

In general, I think that's a better way to look at the question. New technologies pop up all the time. We get book proposals for new frameworks, new libraries, new languages, some stuff I've never even heard of, and it comes flying across [my desk] and [I] say, "Well, what's this? Is this interesting? Does this have promise?"

You look at it, and the question I always try to ask is, "Okay, what's the problem they're trying to solve?" Concurrency is a big, hairy problem and trying to do it properly in a more traditional language like Java or C++ or C is problematic at best. You can do it, but it's like the object-oriented Perl. You can do it, but there's a certain amount of pain involved.

Then you'd look at something like Erlang that says, "Okay, well, here's this problem and we're gonna solve this in a completely different way and rather elegantly, so that a lot of the problems that you were facing just simply disappear by virtue of how the technology is created."

Ed: Let me characterize what I've heard you say regarding the process here. After you were done with that project with the 50,000 lines of Perl, you had an idea of the attributes of a solution and then you went out looking for a technology that filled those attributes, right?

Andy: Yeah.

Ed: In essence, it's almost like you had a requirements document and you were looking for something that filled those requirements.

Andy: I wouldn't use the phrase "requirements document." It's a genuine requirement. This is something that I can see a need for, or clients or friends have had a need for, so there is a definite requirement.

Ed: There's a tension between always moving on to the next new thing and sticking with it long enough to achieve true mastery. I want to find out if you think there's any relationship between personal intelligence and one's susceptibility to losing interest in something before achieving mastery.

Andy: I think there's definitely a correlation there because, again, one of the facets of the programmer's personality that I think is very important is curiosity. If you have mined the territory pretty thoroughly and there's nothing left to be interested in, then, yeah, you're gonna be in a world of hurt on a two-year long project. One of the challenges for a project manager or sponsor is to somehow keep some level of interest going for your smartest developers because the less skilled, less curious developers really won't run into that problem.

> **Career Tip**
>
> Andy is giving insight here into the mind of the manager. He closely associates curiosity with "smart developer." Do what you can to cultivate curiosity and let others know what you've discovered.

They'll be perfectly happy still discovering the rudiments of it two years later. They'll be fine. The best and brightest expert is gonna be bored in a week—it's no longer a novelty. Once the novelties run out, [boredom] becomes an issue; there are a couple of ways around this.

Some of the folks who advocate pair programming say rotating team members around all the aspects of a project helps ameliorate [boredom] because you don't get so completely inured to one aspect of the project. You may work on that for a while, but then you're in a totally different area, so that it becomes a little bit more novel. I think that's probably a pretty good way of going about it. Maybe not necessarily pair programming, but certainly having different roles to play in a project.

If it's a very large project, I've seen a lot of teams that will rotate out programmers to work in quality assurance (QA) for a while and see the other end of the spectrum or be more closely allied with the end user's requirements, elicitation, or whatever, but something just to literally break up the monotony of sitting there and writing the same bit of the same report module for two years in a row or whatever it may be. Variety and novelty is really the key there.

If you've got *real* experts that get bored very quickly, it might be profitable to actually swap them out between entire projects on some periodic basis. If you've got some hotshot you just can't keep ahead of and he's churning out code so well and so fast and you can't keep him engaged, give him a day [or] a week to go work on some open-source project and donate the results to the Web. It'll keep him engaged and interested and [he won't] leave your company and you're not actually losing any real productivity 'cause they're such hotshots to begin with. In extreme cases, you can look to doing something like that.

Ed: The attributes you're describing seem like desirable character attributes. But there is a flip side to it. How do you tell when someone is actually like that or they just get distracted real easily? They don't necessarily achieve true mastery. They just get tired of working on it.

Andy: Well, that's a good question. That's more towards burnout than boredom, really, and there's a distinction, because if you do have someone who's fairly well skilled, they can be subject to burnout just as well. They've been looking at the same thing over and over again and they're just tired of it, and that's where just rotating people among different roles, even within the team, is probably useful. Nobody wants to work on the report module for a year straight. If anyone did, would you want them to? That sorta would be a danger sign. If somebody says, "No, I'll just stay over here in the corner and work on this little piece all the rest of my life," that's probably an issue.

Ed: Say you're hiring someone. Is there ever a case where it's a desirable attribute to have someone just stick with one thing for a long time, or is it always a danger sign if someone is like that?

Andy: I think it would almost always be a danger sign. I'm sure there's probably a counterexample somewhere, but, in general, I want developers working for me that have an insatiable curiosity.

Ed: I think it's important that this insatiable curiosity be focused inward as well, increasing self-awareness. How important is it as a software developer to be aware of one's own ignorance?

Andy: It is absolutely vital. That's a real, real important thing. You know, understanding our own limitations, understanding the constraints that we're operating against, whether it's our ignorance or the situation, that's a real—that's a real, real

> **Observation**
>
> This one hit close to home for me. When Andy and I talked, I had been leading the development of JavaServer Faces at Sun for nearly six years. I feel I've been growing and learning that whole time; however, Andy's perspective is likely common among hiring managers. Perhaps when they see six years of JSF on my resume, they may question the insatiability of my curiosity.

big thing. It is absolutely vital to know what you don't know and to be okay with it.

It's just that people have a lot of difficulty answering a question with "I don't know." That's a perfectly valid answer, yet it shouldn't be your final answer on the subject by any means. All too often, I'll see folks in a corporate environment where the culture is such that they can't say, "I don't know." So they make something up or they do some waffle words around it or the famous politician thing of [saying], "Oh, we're having a blue ribbon committee look into that." That's just nonsense. That doesn't really help anyone. I'm a big fan of saying, "I have no idea. I don't know how that works, but I'll try and find out."

Ed: How much time do you spend in a meta-cognitive mode, being aware of your own thought processes and how you are interacting with the world around you?

Andy: Not as much as I should. For me personally, that's one of those things that just varies as life moves on. When I can [go meta-cognitive], things work out better, and when I get crushed under time pressures and scheduling pressures and I don't [go meta-cognitive], things tend to go a little bit worse.

One of the things that we've always advocated in our books and seminars is to set something akin to an alarm clock to interrupt you periodically. Every couple of hours, stop what you're doing, get out of the mud for a minute and take a deep breath and re-evaluate: "Does what I'm doing even still make sense? Am I still on the right track with this or do I need to adapt and adjust a little bit?"

Ed: Forced meta-cognition.

Andy: Yeah, exactly. And it really needs to be interrupt-driven, because if it's a sure thing, where if you said, "Okay, tomorrow at eight, I'm gonna take stock and take a deep breath and evaluate stuff," that doesn't seem to ever work. It's one of the few things that's better interrupt-driven.

Ed: Yes, that's true. But I've heard you say in your "Refactoring Your Wetware" talk that "multitasking kills." So this is not multitasking, it's putting everything else aside and doing the meta-cognition stuff.

Andy: Yeah, and it's being deliberate. That's another consistent focus through a lot of the stuff I talk about—the idea of being deliberate about something, not letting it just happen accidentally or as a by-product. But taking deliberate steps to say, "Yes, this is what I'm doing right now and here's why."

Ed: Being deliberate is certainly an attribute of a successful developer. What are some other attributes of successful developers?

Andy: My stock answer may be different from what most people think. The biggest thing I look for is language arts skills. I would rather have an English major learn to program than a math major or an engineer learn to program.

I think that's a somewhat contrarian stance, but when you look at it, the two things that we as developers do the most are communication and learning. And by communication, it doesn't necessarily mean sending e-mails or writing white papers or that sort of stuff. Programming is an act of communicating to the computer, getting requirements—we're communicating with the end user, with other people. Working in a team to develop the software, we're communicating with the other members of the team, with the team as a whole, all these sorts of things.

But we [software developers] are really the communication hub between various other humans and various business technologies, and that's a big thing of what we do. I would much rather have someone who was more trained in the communication arts. Writing a program, to me, is much more like writing an essay or a novel than, say, a mathematical theorem. [A program's] logical flow, progression of ideas, all these sorts of things that come over from the language side are much more important than being a hard math geek.

Ed: Well, this fits very well into the next question. How would you break down the technical skills one needs to possess as a software developer? The first one on that list would be communication skills?

Andy: Communication would be big. I think curiosity is [also] a huge one. Curiosity is probably the biggest thing. That's really what drives us. You know, as you said before, you're getting to know the project, and all of a sudden you realize you don't know about something. You know, for most developers, it's not the schedule, it's not the attributes of the project itself that drives them; it's the curiosity.

Persistence is a key trait that goes along with that. You can't give up on the first "page not found" or if the first article you find, you don't understand.

Most of the best developers I know are both very curious and very persistent. So they track it down. Now, all of that has to be over a bed of a deep understanding of the fundamentals. You know, I don't particularly care if somebody knows Java or Lisp or C# or Ruby. These things, you can pick up once you learn more than a few languages. The big deal is to learn how the operating system works internally.

Ed: Looking into the future a bit, new layers of abstraction are constantly being added on top of what has come before. How will future programmers deal with the necessity to understand the whole stack, all the way down to the metal?

Andy: I suspect what will happen is [that] the lower levels will begin to fall off. Even now, thinking in assembly language or working at that level is becoming more and more rare. I remember there was a time when even just endian-ness and differences between processors was a huge issue. This was a *big* deal. People spent a lot of ink, a lot of network protocols, and this and that to try and get around it, and now it's like, "Well, hell, everyone uses an Intel." It hasn't gone away, but it's certainly lessened.

There'll always be a need to go down to the MOSFET [hardware] level and the gates and the K-maps and whatnot and chip design and lower levels, but fewer and fewer folks will do that and, unfortunately, I suspect fewer and fewer folks will even be aware of it.

> **Observation**
>
> On page 90, the Java Posse expresses a similar regret at the loss of appreciation and awareness of the complexity in computing technology.

Ed: Regarding [the] skills one needs to have, did you have any courses in college that you continue to use today?

Andy: Yeah, it's kind of tough. Thinking back, I remember a couple of courses on finite automata, where it was bits of theory that would make you think, "Okay, this really is foundational." You know, "This is stuff you can leverage on."

That was much more valuable than learning the OSI protocol stack, which ended up being [something] nobody used. You know, TCP won the day. Technical education tends to overemphasize transient technologies. Whether that's the current programming language or even the current programming style. You know, procedural versus object-oriented, versus functional, versus declarative, versus whatever. You should learn one of each of those kinds of languages in school so that you've got a good basis going forward.

A lot of people coming up don't know what functional languages are, like Erlang or Haskell; they never tried declarative programming in PROLOG or something like that. Their idea of object-oriented is Java, which is unfortunate because that's really not an object-oriented language. I really want to see the real solid base-level fundamentals. When you get out of school, four or five years after your freshman year, the technology is all gonna change anyway. We're not doing what we did five years ago. We're not gonna be doing this five years from now. In that time span, it really doesn't make sense to get too hot and heavy into the flavor of the day.

Ed: Well, there's an unfortunate tension between what you and I know is a sound approach to longevity and what hiring managers who are faced with thousands of resumes are dealing with.

Andy: Oh, absolutely. My recommendation would be spend the first three, three and a half years of your college career mastering the fundamentals and basics and putting [yourself] in the position so that you can learn the technology du jour very quickly.

Then you spend the last semester saying, "Okay, this is what you guys are gonna be doing when you get out there."

Ed: Can you say anything else about fundamental skills?

Andy: First, learn the fundamentals of assembly language, real basic stuff. Meeting most developers—I can tell whether they grew up hacking inside of a operating system and writing assembly code or if they went to college and were taught Java and don't really know anything lower than that. It really shows. The folks who have the grasp of the fundamentals are different without doubt. When something weird happens or something crashes or something new comes along, it's less of a big deal. They can roll with it more. And for the folks who came in somewhat late to the game and have been, I think, robbed of a proper education—to them, how it all works is kind of magic.

> **Observation**
>
> Dave Thomas says *exactly* the same thing in his answer to this question on page 283.

Ed: But to you, it's not magic. Is that because you are old enough to have grown up along with the computing and software industry itself?

Andy: My first computer was an Ohio Scientific [OSI Model C4P], and I was 12 years old [when I got it]. It did make a difference, because in those early days…my first several computers really didn't have an operating system. They had a firmware monitor and everything else was do-it-yourself.

I remember when the first TRS-80s came out with their TRS DOS. I was leery of the fact that when you saved a file, it would pick what sectors on disk to put it on. You didn't specify that by hand. I was, like, "What the hell is this nonsense? I don't want this thing guessing for me and fragmenting my file and jamming it up all over!" I was perfectly happy with do-it-yourself file system maintenance and allocating sectors and dealing with the fragmentation by hand.

And, similarly, in the days of CP/M, where you had to do your own memory management, you had to use overlays to swap out portions of your program because there wasn't enough main memory to fit. That's a really interesting exercise in architecture and design. I hate to sound like an old fart, but kids today really have no awareness of that.

Ed: That's the thing. It's not their fault; it's just a product of the time. We had this benefit that this was the only way you could do it. There was no other choice. We had to go up through the bootstraps.

Andy: I agree wholeheartedly. I think that the folks who came out of that era where you started really close to bare metal are better suited to understanding the larger order of things.

Ed: So then maybe the takeaway would be [that] if you were a curious person, it wouldn't sit well with you to *not* know how it worked all the way down to the bottom. Even if you have no interest in learning an assembly language, you have to know there is a benefit to doing so. So maybe the moral is study computer history?

Andy: No. There's no future in history, somebody once told me. What you want to do is play. I do see the curious young developers now, they're running [GNU/]Linux in several flavors at home, and they're building their own media centers and screwing around with very low-level protocols and cables and soldering stuff together and writing device drivers. That's really what you want to do. That gives you the most modern equivalent to the sorts of experiences that the rest of us [older folk] had growing up, just getting in there and hacking, because that teaches you a fair bit, and you start getting an appreciation for—by the time you end up in a high-level language and ability on top of an operating system, you've got a good understanding of all the bits and pieces and how this all hangs together.

Ed: From the past to the future. What are some attributes of the language and environment that people will be using to develop software ten years from now?

Andy: Oh, I love this question. Okay, so here's my thought on that, and I have no idea if this is actually going to work this way or not, but it strikes me that there is a real aspect of the cobbler's children having no shoes here.

If you look at any of our popular computer languages today, with very few exceptions, you could render any popular program today onto paper tape or punch card. It's a limited character set. It's a limited line length for the most part. It's black and white. It's two-dimensional. It's text. Gutenberg could print virtually any computer program in use. Any computer language program in use today could be printed on a Gutenberg press. It's that basic, that simple, and it occurs to me in a lot of environments, given the richness of what we're trying to express, that that's a pretty poor model. You look at where, say, the gaming community is at, even simple things—the use of color, but even going into three dimensions, use of spatial cueing, any kind of a richer environment, it strikes me that there's an awful lot of opportunity there for a far richer expression of programming constructs.

And I'm not talking necessarily just about graphical programming or boxes and lines and that kinda stuff, but something more along the lines of interacting in, say, Second Life or some very rich virtual environment like that for a couple of reasons. Writing programs in black and white text seems pretty limiting, bandwidth-wise. That's a waste of bandwidth.

Peter Coad had a book out a few years back on UML modeling in color (*Java Modeling in Color with UML*, Prentice Hall PTR, 1999), which I thought had quite a lot of merit to it. He basically had a color-code scheme for different archetypes of classes. I thought that was an interesting approach.

Looking at a model real quickly, you could easily discern yet another facet of things that wasn't shown by the class diagram box style or the font. For the most part, that really didn't seem to take off very well. It didn't really capture the imagination of the population. I think that's a shame. We're back to syntax highlighting for convenience in IDEs (Integrated Development Environments), but it's not part of the language proper. You can't make a variable static by making it red or what have you, and it occurs to me that we're really missing an opportunity for much richer expression there.

So you couple that with the idea that the folks just entering the workplace now are much more imbued with this idea of gaming and first-person shooters and virtual reality and all these sorts of things that us fuddy-duddies are far less comfortable with. Even if we do it, it's not bred into our DNA. And the groups that are growing up with that now, I think they will end up making a large impact on the very notion of what we consider a computer program to be.

So I would say—I don't know about 10 years from now but maybe 20 years from now, they'll look back on these syntax-colored IDEs with curly braces in them and snicker the same way we look back at paper tape rolls and say, "My goodness. How primitive! Those poor people. How on earth did they survive?"

Ed: Ha!

Andy: I don't know the exact form it would take, but I can well see it looking more like Second Life and less like the Gutenberg print.

Ed: One pragmatic approach that has emerged recently, in part due to new ideas entering the workforce, but also due to advances in processor hardware, is the use of desktop virtualization products such as VMware and Parallels. Do you see virtualization playing a larger role in future software development practice?

Andy: Yeah, I can definitely see that. I've seen that in an embryonic sense already, and I can just see that as systems get more and more powerful and memory gets cheaper and cheaper and more dense, I could see having—on a small, modest computer—having 20, 50, 100 different setups, a couple of different QA ones with different configurations, testing the networking in between them in the box but pretending it's a large grid cluster, whatever. Yeah, I could see that really becoming much more prevalent. I especially like the idea of extending version control to the operating system image level. This is a very powerful idea at Internet service providers (ISPs): You roll out some new bit of the stack or upgrade the operating system, and if it doesn't work out, you just roll back to the previous image, and in a matter of minutes, you're back to where you were and then you can go straighten it out again.

Look at some of these massive outages—airline reservation systems or air traffic control or customs, most recently, I think was a big problem out in L.A.—any of these kinds of headline-making outages because some software update failed somewhere and took the system down…it could certainly help ameliorate that sort of thing. And even on the developer's desk, just having the freedom to say, "Well, let's try it with all 14 different versions of this." Yes, I think would help a great deal.

Ed: Can you give me an example of one of the really hard problems in computing today?

Andy: I think this is a two-fold thing. One problem is a cross between a cultural issue and a computing issue. The hard problem in computing, I don't think, is stuff like facial recognition, voice recognition, trying to emulate these aspects of human senses. Yeah, they were a real pain, and a lot of researchers have spent a lot of time and a lot of energy trying to work it out, and they'll figure it out someday, somehow. They've made great strides. These aren't areas that I'm expert in, [and] they're very hard, but they're not the real hard ones.

The real hard one, to me, is getting any kind of a computer system to exhibit situational awareness and actual judgment. Getting some sort of a system that has any kind of situational awareness, I think, is the really hard part, because the danger you run into now as the computer becomes ubiquitous is you end up with an entire class of computer workers, not programmers, but the folks who work in fast food or banking or a call center, where they are genuinely slaves to the machine.

How many times have you called up your credit card company or a utility or ISP or phone service and there's some problem with your account and the person on the other end of the phone says, "I'm sorry. The computer won't let me" or "I can't do this 'cause the computer won't let me" or "It's not showing on the computer." "It's all the computer's fault." Whatever the problem is, something has gone wrong and the person has no capability of correcting it and the computer has no capability of correcting it. This is the stuff of science fiction fear-mongering: you get to the point where nobody knows how to fix it. Your civilization is some thousand years in the future and you're all slave to some computer that can't fix itself until Kirk and Spock come along and make it blow itself up.

Ed: Right, kinda like the Nomad machine in that episode of *Star Trek the Original Series: The Changeling.*

Andy: It's a legitimate gripe: When something out of the ordinary happens, software in general is not designed to deal well with that. It's designed to deal with the average case and the normal situation, and as soon as something happens outside the norm, our software is not sophisticated enough to learn from that, to realize that there are other venues, other possibilities.

Ed: Okay. Now to me that is essentially a complexity problem. As an analogy, consider the goal of software quality. One proven solution to achieving that goal is to use a fine-grain level of unit testing. So you keep doing this unit testing and you break it down small enough that you can achieve quality by having enough unit testing throughout the breadth of the system.

Now is there some analogous thing here to address the notion of exceptional cases and the permutations and combinations of these exceptional cases that lead to the computer operator being unable to take any effective action?

Andy: I don't think so because I think the combinatory explosion of everything that's possible would just simply be overwhelming even for the fastest quantum-based computer. I think that's kinda the wrong way to go.

The hard problem basically comes down to having a system in the largest sense of the word that can actually be aware and learn, because you cannot necessarily teach it what to do when something happens a priori. We don't do that with human education and human training. You can't prepare your children for every single eventuality that'll hit them in life. You hit the high points to give them the tools to make their judgment calls when the time comes. I think that's the big chasm that we have to cross from the very literal, almost naïve, approach of, "teach the computer these 12 steps and it will do them forever" to having a system that can actually learn and apply the basics, the principles you've given it to novel situations.

Hard Skills

Ed: Jumping from a really hard problem…You might find my next question easy, but I'm quite certain our readers would still like to hear your answer. When you're working on an existing system as a maintenance programmer and you make performance optimizations to the code to make it go faster, for example, what are some effective ways to avoid introducing bugs and fostering maintainability?

Andy: That's a simple answer compared to the *Star Trek* computer thing. That's the combination of what we've always called a safety net. [It consists of] having the basic technical practices in place of version control so that you've got an ability to roll back changes to be able to compare and contrast and test the system at any point in time from before your changes, after your changes, months and months before any of that even started, when it was peak load, whatever, to be able to just dial the old time machine to any point in time and work with the system as it existed then.

And that's a little bit beyond what most people can do with version control. You roll the system back a certain amount. Suddenly, you don't have the right libraries to work with that version. You don't have that same compiler anymore, so there are some potential issues there, but, ideally, what you want is to be able to re-create the system as it existed at any point in time. That's on the one hand.

[On] the second hand, you need the fairly comprehensive unit tests so that you can prove this is exactly how it functioned then. For example, you can say, "I've made these changes, and guess what, it still functions exactly the same or these things have changed but we can migrate that and have a plan for that." So you have to have version control, you have to have unit testing, and you have to have automatic artifact creation.

If you're in compiled language, building object files, linking, installing, slamming a WAR [Java web archive] file somewhere or a JAR [Java archive] file somewhere else or whatever your particular platform demands—however you actually construct and deploy the software needs to be completely automated and those instructions for that automation need to likewise be under version control so that there's really nothing left to chance.

The production process is ironclad and subject to version control. The unit tests are fairly complete so you can test anything that you've introduced for good or for bad, and it may be acceptable. You may decide to change things as a result of it, but at least you know if you've introduced anything that makes a material change to the functioning of the software.

With these three low-level technical practices in place, it's pretty safe to do almost anything to the code base. You can optimize it for speed. You can add functionality, remove outdated functionality, change things depending on changing business needs, refactor the design, because now you've got to hand it over to maintenance programmers who aren't as up-to-date on the techniques you used originally.

Ed: Speaking of maintenance programmers, how do you hone your sense of smell for where a bug might be?

Andy: The best place to look for where a bug might be is quite near the last one you found. That's my number one tip. You can look this up in the ACM papers—there are studies that show bugs tend to clump. [They're] not uniformly distributed at all. They come in clumps. So when you're doing code review of other people's code or you find something you did horribly wrong, the odds are pretty high it's not sitting there by itself and it's gonna have something else real nearby. So that's always a good starting point.

Ed: Assuming they've already tried that and it didn't work, do you have any advice to help people track down hard-to-find bugs?

Andy: The number one thing to do when you're stuck on a problem [such as finding a bug] is to step away from the keyboard. Take a break. Go walk around the parking lot. Go get a soda. Go get a beer if you're so inclined. Whatever your environment is, it's to remove yourself from that immediate L brain track. And this is one of the interesting things I discovered from the research [I did for the "Refactoring Your Wetware" talk]. You know, when you're stuck on a hard problem, sitting at the computer is literally the worst place to be. I've given talks—many dozens of times now—and I've had so many people come up to me to corroborate the anecdote that you're sitting there and you're debugging or it's a design problem that you just, you can't get the ends to meet, and how are you gonna work this out.... And they'll sit there and sweat bullets for some arbitrary amount of time and then, in disgust, go walk off to the bathroom, the parking lot, go home, whatnot, and halfway through the parking lot, bang, the answer hits them. You know? Or, worst case, it will be in the shower the next morning or on the commute or whatever it is, and it just asynchronously pops into their head.

That brilliant idea popping into your head will not do it most of the time when you're sitting there pounding on the keyboard in frustration. You know, it just blocks you from doing that. So the number one advice I have when stuck is stop. You know, take a deep breath, literally take a deep breath, 'cause that actually does help re-oxygenate you and get things kicking along a little bit better. Mom was right when she said, "Stop, take a deep breath, and count to 10." There are actual real physiological reasons you should do that.

Ed: Okay. Well, what about reproducing the bug or writing a test case, an automated test case, adding a test case to the test suite?

Andy: Oh, yeah, yeah. Yeah, you do all that stuff. That's the currently approved way to do a bug: have a test case that will demonstrate it conclusively first. Before you touch it in code, make sure you can reproduce the bug via a test case. Then go in, fix the code, and then re-run the test case to make sure that it's fixed. But those are the easy ones. That's Agile canon and certainly the best way to go about it. But what do you do when the bug is more elusive than that? You know, it's non-deterministic. You can't reproduce it well. There is a race condition somewhere, some area deep down somewhere, and you really don't know all the constraints that apply to it. That's where it gets a lot more interesting, and that's where you need to try what you can and then when you're just not figuring it out, walk away from it for a little while.

Because then, when you step away from it, you'll find, "Well now. I did never consider that this would be something in the cookie on the user's machine" or this or that or some other factor that comes into play that you might not have thought of.

Ed: Since you are one of the pioneers and leading proponents of Agile software development practices, let's talk a bit about test-driven development. Specifically, how do you deal with bugs in the tests and the time it takes to debug the bugs in the tests? Some of the Agile detractors will point that out and say the test code is just as likely to be buggy as the production code.

Andy: Yeah, there are folks [who] say that. I don't really buy that as an argument. Certainly from a philosophical point of view, that's true.

You know, code is code, and you can write bugs in test code just as easily as you can write bugs in normal code. However, test code by nature tends to be pretty simple stuff. You're setting up some parameters and you're calling something, and it's not rocket science. I can make a typo in "hello world." I'm not throwing stones here. I can certainly introduce bugs in the simplest of circumstances, as can everyone. But on the whole, properly written test code is not some big monstrous morass that's hard to figure out. It's very simple, small methods, four or five lines of code each. Pretty easy to take a look at and say, "Yes, this is reasonable," or, "Yeah, it's a little bit suspicious." On the one hand, I don't buy [their argument], but on the other hand, you've got a nice validation mechanism. If you are suspicious of your test code, it's pretty easy to go in and deliberately introduce bugs into the real code and make sure that the test code catches them.

I don't really buy their argument. The parallel argument is, "It takes a lot of time to write the test code." [Is equally specious.] No [it doesn't]. It's like an investment strategy. You're spending an incremental amount of time to write test code, but if you get nailed with a hard bug, it may be exponential time to solve it.

It's really kind of a false argument. They only say that because it's easier to measure the amount of time that you're spending on test code.

Ed: Is it ever appropriate to not write tests?

Andy: It depends. There have been lots of times where I've done test-driven design, test-first design, and it's saved my bacon. I've had some times where that's been less appropriate, where it's something more exploratory and I'll go more bottom-up. You know, develop something first, kind of play with it, and then quantify the unit test and work from there. As with most things, the real danger is dogmatism where "this is my hammer and everything looks like a nail."

That's what you want to avoid. You always want to use the right tool for the job in the right context. So I'm a fan of test-first development. I don't always do it. It's not always appropriate.

It's the same with anything else. You know, pair programming or even big up-front design. There are some cases where that's actually the best way to go. There are more cases where it's not, but every technique has its place somewhere in the world in some context.

Ed: Several of the people I've interviewed had some things to say about the intrinsic value of the tests in a software system. Do you have anything to say about that?

Andy: Some venture capitalist type once asked me where the real value was in a software system, and he was thinking it was in the source code and we were trying to convince him that, no, that's actually not the case.

If you think about it, the most valuable part of a well-constructed software system is not the code itself. It's the unit tests. That actually defines the behavior of the system. It is a functional working specification. In terms of intellectual property, that's actually far more valuable, 'cause given that you could re-create the source code in any number of ways, the source code becomes far more disposable when you think of it that way.

Ed: Right. Isn't it the case that the unit tests represent a very, very specific and strongly constrained set of requirements?

Andy: Yes, absolutely, and whatever you choose to do that happens to fulfill them, that's a much larger set. There's the system that happened to be written, but that doesn't preclude writing a completely different one that would fulfill the same requirements and provably so.

Ed: Yes, it's proven that automated testing is a bulwark against human nature. But here's a situation often faced by human programmers. Let's say it's late at night, you're up against a deadline, and you're desperate to get a piece of code working and checked in. You come to a situation where you're faced with the choice between doing the right thing and doing the quick thing. How do you motivate yourself to do the right thing?

Andy: I think Douglas Adams' advice is real key there: "Don't panic." This is the number one place where we get into trouble as developers. We feel the crushing pressure of the deadline and we do something stupid because it's expedient. It's like gambling or Powerball. Every so often you win the $5 prize and go, "Woo-hoo. There's some success to this." Every so often you will take that cheap shortcut and it works out. You don't get caught, you get away with it. You think, "Hey, this is great." And then, of course, you take the next shortcut and the whole thing goes tits up and you're just totally blown.

So the first thing I suggest is, don't panic. If you feel like you're compelled to do the wrong thing because it's quicker, step away from the keyboard.

Ed: Switching to an easy subject, when you get a new machine, what do you have to do to it so it's useful for development?

Andy: Typically what I do is I set up the connection to my CVS archive and I [do a] checkout, and then I've got 99 percent of what I need.

I actually had to do this the other day. One of my machines blew up, and I took it into the Mac store and they replaced it. And here comes this working machine, and I have things set so that I was back in business literally in under a half an hour.

Ed: Wow. That's great.

Andy: So, again, people: Use version control, but use it for *everything* that's important to you—you know, not just the source code of your project, but also the important stuff, config files and that sort of thing. So that's real big with me.

Ed: That's an excellent use of version control. I hadn't seen that before. Version control systems are one example of the tools used by software professionals to achieve great results. How important is mastery of tools?

Andy: The key there isn't so much [mastery of tools]—it's always good to have real facility with your tools. I can fly through vi and do stuff in a very short amount of time, and it doesn't matter whether I'm local or SSH'd (connected via a secure terminal protocol, from another machine) in somewhere. I've seen people who do things in Emacs that I don't know how the hell they manage it, but they're expert at that tool.

And that's all very helpful, but I think the real underlying thing isn't so much proficiency with a given tool. The real expert isn't necessarily the one who flies through Emacs, but the one who knows that "when this situation comes up, oh, I can go use this and knock this problem out in no time flat."

So it's more being aware of the whole catalog of what's possible, what's available—be it algorithms, tools, languages, products, whatever—just knowing that something's out there and being able to apply it. I think that's probably more key to productivity than anything else.

Ed: Who is the most productive programmer you've ever worked with, and why were they so productive?

Andy: I think the key to the most productive programmer doesn't necessarily have to do with cranking out lots of code or doing it faster or that sort of stuff. I think the key is—and this is gonna sound contradictory to what I said before and I'll just warn you up front—the key is not to be distracted. Take [this] scenario: A user says they want the program to do X and Y and Z, and you start looking at that and it's very easy to get distracted by, "Ooh, there's this neat algorithm I could put in here" or "Hey, I haven't used the last five of the Gang of Four patterns lately. I can put that in." And there are all these sorts of—for lack of a better word—"distractions" coming up. You harp on one thing that the customer said and miss their main point or miss what's most important to them, or you seize on the first solution that comes to you and doggedly go down that road even if it really doesn't make much sense.

So there are the usual consultant tricks you can do: Any time you come up with a solution, make sure you come up with at least three so you have two that you can throw out.

A lot of times, in the interest of speed and trying to impress each other, we blurt out the first architecture or design or idea that comes to mind and roll with it, and that's usually not a very good idea. It's a distraction, if you will.

So when I say "not distracted," I'm saying the best programmers actually look at the genuine problem and work on a real solution to it without being distracted by dead ends, obvious false starts, that kinda thing. Everybody runs into trouble eventually, but the best programmers I've seen run into that kinda thing a lot less. They may get [a slower start] outta the gate. They may [get a faster start] outta the gate, but they take fewer wrong turns.

Ed: How important is it to be a continual optimizer of your workstation and work environment?

Andy: I'll admit I'm not particularly diligent about that. I'm the sort who will let small annoyances build up to the point where it's like, "What the hell is going on here?" And then I'll take a day and clean up six things, write a couple of shell scripts, do whatever needs to be done and get back on track again, and it's like that story of the boiled frogs that was back in Pragmatic Programmer that we tell all the time: If you put a frog in boiling water, [it will] jump right out.

Ed: Right. Yeah, yeah.

Andy: If you put [it] in cold water and turn the heat up very slowly, [it doesn't] notice and you cook the frog, and, as I like telling people, that is actually how we all end up in hot water. It gets turned up slowly and you don't notice, and then you do notice and you say to yourself, "Whoa! This is a problem." This is very true in terms of personal productivity. Small delays add up fast. Waiting for your e-mail client to load, clicking a message and waiting for the next message to show up. I cut my e-mail handling down by a half when I read this technique of how to optimize its internal database.

And the world is full of stuff like that—your browser cache, things on your disk, things related to the operating system, whichever one you happen to use. There's a myriad of small things all over the place that can make that application run faster or smoother, or there's a shortcut key that you could use that you haven't been using—all that kinda stuff.

The irony of it is because this is what we do all day and for so long, learning one keystroke combination instead of a mouse sequence could end up saving you days at the end of a year 'cause it's such a repeated activity, so I'm a big fan of keystrokes instead of mouse moves, key macros, anything like that.

Ed: You mentioned earlier that being aware of what's out there in terms of algorithms, tools, patterns, etc. was hugely important for a successful developer. One aspect of that is reuse. Let's say you find yourself writing a small piece of code that you *know* has been written before. How do you decide when to reuse or not?

Andy: There's a real tension there. We like to invent and reinvent wheels over and over again, and we've got piles of industry-reinvented wheels. So you could argue pretty successfully that we actually haven't invented anything new in computer science since about 1968.

Ed: Yeah.

Andy: Everything is in some flavor a retread. Java is a retread of C++, which was an enhancement to C.

The other side of it is you go to look for something else to repurpose or reuse off the Net, programming by Google [for example], and you'll find 15 implementations that are close to what you want. Then you run the danger of [using] Google [as an] IDE and you end up with Frankencode. You get this patched-together monster [that] is all stitched together and never quite works right, because each piece they drag in has a couple of pieces they didn't really need, but it came along for the ride. And that's where you run into real danger. What will happen is I'll look at five implementations on the Net of something, get the best idea of how I want to proceed, and use one of those as a starting point, or just do it from scratch.

Are you really reinventing the wheel there? And in that case, I'd say no, because every project is different, every situation is different. You know, you have to make local adaptations. But on the grander scale of things, why is it something you have to go out and look for anyway? Why isn't this a feature of the service or framework you're using or the language you're using? There's a successful argument that says the design patterns as expressed in the Gang of Four book (*Design Patterns*, Addison-Wesley 1994) really shouldn't exist. There are, what, 23, 26 patterns in the GoF book? And many of them are there due to limitations in C++.

You know, it's very much limitations of one particular language at one particular point in time that doesn't have a certain regular expression that forces you into these things. And I think that it was Paul Graham who made this argument in that particular case. But I think there's a general case to be made: we do that [kind of reinvention] a lot of the times. It's not strictly reinventing the wheel, but what we're doing is inventing patches to a crappy wheel, when, instead of a wheel, we ought to be making a jet ski or whatever it may be. And I think you can really see a lot of this in the historical things that came out of the C++ community, CORBA (Common Object Request Broker Architecture) being a big example. CORBA, despite its language neutrality, was extremely influenced by C++, similarly with Unified Modeling Language (UML). There's a lot in UML that you can look back and go, "Oh, my God, that is C++." If you had started simply off looking at Smalltalk or Lisp or Self or PROLOG or something weirder, Erlang, you'd get entirely different results. And that tells me, well, that's not such a general-purpose wonderful thing. That's really got a big old giant Band-Aid for something that wasn't what it should have been in the first place.

Ed: On the flip side of reuse is the idea of starting over from scratch. When is it appropriate to do that?

Andy: The philosophical note I'll throw in here is [that] a number of philosophies suggest looking at life from the point of view of abundance, not scarcity. So rather than bitching and moaning that something is scarce, be grateful and [appreciate] the abundance you actually do have. I think that is particularly true in the coder's world, and I think a lot of the danger we get into from deploying things that are too buggy, too early, writing it too quickly, any of these sorts of issues all come from the basic idea that "That code was so hard to write the first time, I could never possibly write it again" or "The code that we have took so long to develop, we have to keep it and Band-Aid it because we couldn't do it again," and that's taking a viewpoint of scarcity, which is the wrong one. And, in fact, even going back to [Fred] Brooks, there's this idea that, hey, guess what? The second time you write it, it's gonna go 100 times faster and end up better because you had the experience of writing it the first time. Now you actually *know* what to do.

So you're better off doing it the second time and not hanging on to this fundamental idea of scarcity and hanging on to the first version, which really wasn't that good to begin with.

Ed: And the act of making software is the act of learning. So the second time you try to learn something, you're gonna learn it better and faster.

Andy: Absolutely. You've already prepared the bed, as it were. And jokingly, a lot of people say, "What's the best thing I can do to enhance my code?" and I say, "Take a big magnet to the hard drive." That's the number one issue for code cleanliness 'cause you will tend to do it much more straightforward.

Ed: Yeah, but like anything else, though, there's—there's the flip side of that, because if you're developing something really complex, over the years, you get the bug fixes in there and a lot of other people are working on it, but sometimes it's very attractive and seductive to just say, "Let's just throw everything out and start again from scratch."

Andy: That's another tension where developers love to do that. The reason they love to do that is because they *know* they can do it better this time. Certainly on large systems, where you've had a lot of different people's input, you need to weigh, okay, "Are they all in that same position to contribute again?" or "Do we not have that opportunity anymore?" It's different if you're talking one or two people versus a 10- or a 50-person team.

You know, that introduces a new dynamic there. If you got the same 50 people together and they all have learned and know better than what they did the first time, then, yeah, you might be better off scrapping that first two-year effort and replacing it with a new six-month effort. But if 45 of the people have moved on, then that doesn't work out so well.

Business

Ed: How important is it to let your understanding of the business of software and the perceived demand for specific skills inform where you invest in stewarding your skillset?

Andy: Well, that's all a question of managing what we call your "knowledge portfolio," and this is a concept that was put forth in the original Pragmatic Programmer book—that everything that you know is part of your knowledge portfolio and, like a regular portfolio, this is something [where] you want to play with the balance of risk and reward, return on investment ratios.

Something that's new and hot, if everyone's doing it, then it's actually fairly low-risk. You could be assured that we will get some kind of a gig out of it 'cause everyone's doing it, but it's also fairly low-reward. You're not gonna get handsomely rewarded, because everyone else is doing it. Something like Java in the very early days or Ruby perhaps or Erlang now—there's a lot of risk associated with it.

You could invest heavily in it and it might turn out that no one ends up using it. It could be a flash in the pan or it could be the next hot thing, so you've got a high risk but a commensurate high return on investment if that's the thing that pans out.

If you got involved in Java back when it was Oak and in the very early days and positioned yourself there, you'd have done very well for yourself. You could get involved in whatever the latest hot thing is this week and who knows?

Observation

Rod Johnson had the same experience when he started out. See page 6.

Ed: Right.

Andy: That might turn out to be the next hot thing; it might not. So like anything else, it's a mixture of trying to balance that—the risk to the reward ratio.

Ed: Sure.

Andy: What Dave [Thomas] and I have long suggested in our seminars and our writings is you want to balance yourself out, learn a couple of each. Learn some high-risk, high-reward things in case it pans out, but pad the stable out with some fairly sure bets of, "well, there will always be a need for XYZ," and balance it out that way.

Ed: How does that relate to outsourcing?

Andy: As long as you're problem-solving, making decisions, helping the business grow as more of a business consultant, you're probably going to be much more tied into the business and have greater longevity than if you're just a replaceable code monkey, one of a hundred that's not thinking, not doing anything particularly valuable.

Those are the jobs at the very bottom. They're the first to get outsourced to whatever the next country is on the outsourcing list. An interesting side note there—one of the most interesting books that we came out with on career development is entitled *My Job Went to India and All I Got Was This Lousy Book* by Chad Fowler (Pragmatic Bookshelf, 2005). And the title was meant to be somewhat tongue-in-cheek because, obviously, there's a lot of concern about jobs being outsourced to India, to other low-priced countries, and the whole book really takes the tack of "Here's what you need to do in terms of career development so that yours is not the job that gets outsourced. Here's how to market yourself internally. Here's how to make sure that your boss and the powers-that-be understand what it is you do that adds value to the organization, where do you add value that others don't"— all this sort of approach, and I think that's really quite valuable, because at the end of the day, you have to add some proven value to the organization or it's their responsibility to replace you.

Everyone harped on India because they were the first out of the gate to attract outsourcing, but the irony is I've got a few friends who run outsourced operations in India and they're quite concerned because they're losing business to the next set of countries down the rung—Eastern Europe, Vietnam, Southeast Asia. Other places are filling in. They're fighting the cheapness war and winning, and so it goes. Those will get comfortable for a while. Then they'll lose out to the next rung down the ladder, and on it goes.

Ed: It's clear, then, that the organizational structure of a company has an impact on job security. How about developer productivity? Can you give me an example of where it has a negative impact?

Andy: This is a popular dysfunction in some companies, where the maintenance folks are on a different budget than the developer folks. There's no incentive for the developers to write bug-free code. There's incentive for them to write code fast and get it the hell off their plate. So that is not an optimal way to structure your organization.

There are actually a lot of oddball things like that, that have nothing to do with software development. Instead it has to do with some accounting rule somewhere and how it affects the dynamics of what the team can do and what they're paid for that ultimately affects the code. There are whole classes of organizational dysfunctions that just stem from accounting rules, oddly enough.

Personal

Ed: Speaking of accounting, how organized are you in your personal life?

Andy: My desk is neither spotless nor [a] pigsty. What I tend to do is organize by piles, very much pile management, so I'll have a hot and important pile and maybe several stages of archived piles or different topics. But I find trying to sort it to any real finer grain ends up being a waste of time, and not sorting at all becomes a problem where you can't find stuff. So I take a predictably pragmatic approach and sort it in fairly large-grained piles—enough so that if I need to find something, I may not be able to put my finger right on it, but it's kinda like "bucket sort." I can go to the right bucket and within a quick linear search be able to locate it fairly rapidly.

Ed: Do you keep a journal?

Andy: Not in the diary sense, but I do keep a Moleskine notebook with me at all times. So you always want to have something with you to jot down on. I've got mind maps in it, bullet lists, thoughts, designs, archive stuff. It's more like an engineering journal, but really more like a notebook. Not like a diary. It's useful for me to reload context.

> **Character Attribute**
>
> Pragmatic fashion awareness. According to www.moleskine.com, "Moleskine is the legendary notebook used by European artists and thinkers for the past two centuries. It accompanies the creative professions and has become a symbol of contemporary nomadism."

You know, "I figured this out once… I don't remember what conclusions I came to. What were the constraints, what were the issues? Oh, yes, that's right." So it's like a quick memory reload for important thoughts that you had.

Ed: How about a day planner? Do you use one of those?

Andy: I do not.

Ed: Okay.

Andy: I use the calendar app on the Mac, which synchronizes with my cell phone, and it beeps at me when I have to do something.

Ed: What are some things you can say about how to successfully do schedule negotiation with a client, and how do you ensure that you and your client agree on a schedule that's realistic?

Andy: I think—in general terms, I think the best way to manage that is to take small bites. I had a very demanding client some few years back where it was a very difficult sell. They wanted to know two years from now what I'd be doing on a Tuesday… and clearly that was going to become a problem. We had a couple of heart-to-heart talks and I said, "Listen. Let's just try it this way." And I gave them the Agile song and dance and ended up just trying to say, "Okay, let's just do this—let's take this one step at a time," and really ended up doing what looked more like scrum than anything else.

I'd start off with a backlog, just a private list on my Wiki of "here's the things I'm gonna do next and you tell me what's most [important]"—it's really a matter of relationship building more than anything else. That's how people get to trust you. That's how they know that you're not trying to pull the wool over their eyes. So we ended up developing a relationship where they came to know that if it was something that they deemed important and of high relevance to them, something they needed fast, they knew that they would tend to get it pretty quickly, within a week, within two weeks.

It's as much a matter of training the customer to know what your speed is as anything else. Once they get a flavor for it, then you say, "Oh, that's gonna take us a long time. Can we do something else in the meantime or can we break that apart? What are our choices here?"

What you need to do by whatever means is train the customer. When the Agile folks say "work closely with the customer," that's really what it means. It means "gain their trust." Let them see how you work, how fast you work, how fast your team works. Get them to have a reasonable set of expectations of your capabilities.

With that kind of relationship, negotiation is not adversarial. It's "Hey, we both want your company to make a lot of money and succeed. Otherwise, we're all out of a job, so what can we do to make this happen?"

Ed: Right. It's kind of just realizing that we're all on the same team.

Andy: Yeah, exactly. Exactly, and that's a hard road for some folks to go down. Especially in a larger, more bureaucratic organization, there is very much the idea that it's not all the same team.

Ed: Small teams, big teams—in every team, collaboration is vital to success. How does one increase one's proficiency at collaboration?

Andy: I think it's the same answer as how to increase your proficiency in anything, and that's do it.

Ed: Practice. Okay.

Andy: Practice. Practice. Practice. You know, "How do you get to Carnegie Hall?" "Practice, man, practice." That's the joke, but that's really it. This is something I harp on in my talks: "go with experience." You know, experience really is the best teacher, so you want to set yourself up to be able to play with stuff, be able to work with it, be able to do it, 'cause, otherwise, even just reading about it, it's not the same.

Ed: Right. Okay, well, what do you when you're on a team that is having trouble with collaboration? How would you approach improving the collaboration when it's determined that the collaboration is the problem?

Andy: I get them to talking. Anytime I've gone and consulted [with] a team where they've had those sorts of communication issues in between themselves, the number one thing that seems to help is something like a scrum standup meeting. It's a daily meeting. It's very focused on the agenda. You answer your three questions and you get the hell out of there. It's not some lengthy meeting or discussion or diatribe. You don't problem-solve; you don't discuss. You answer the scrum three questions: here's what

I'm doing today, this is what I was doing yesterday, here's what I plan to do tomorrow, here's what's in my way.

The idea is [that] whatever is in your way the manager takes as his to-do list, and you just go bop, bop, bop, bop around the room, and now everyone knows what everyone else is working on [and] if there's an issue with that, but they don't need to be working on it 'cause you did something similar last week, or you decided with somebody else that that's not the way this project is gonna go or whatever. Now you're aware of it. You know what everyone else is doing. You know what they were working on yesterday; you know what they're blocked on. This person needs a QA machine. This person needs you to finish what you're working on. You know, whatever it is, you get a sense of everyone's pace, everyone's velocity, because you hear day after day, "I'm doing this, now I'm doing that, now I'm doing this other thing." You can tell if somebody's falling behind.

It's a really, really effective way just to get everybody playing on the same page. And then from there, can do the little spur-off meetings, say, "Okay, well, let's—let's work this out. Let's solve this problem," you know, whatever it takes. So that is the number one way to kick-start getting a team to communicate with each other.

Ed: Let's close up with some personal questions. What sort of student were you in college?

Andy: Curious. I was a curious student.

Ed: All right. How much stock do you place in GPA and other traditional academic measures of success as a predictor of real-world success?

Andy: I actually don't place a lot of stock in GPAs. I had a very high GPA within my major and so-so overall, but I didn't place much stock in it then or since. I knew quite a few folks who dropped out and were very successful. They made a lot of money. I knew quite a few folks who had 4.0 averages who I wouldn't trust to clean my garage because they didn't have any real-world experience or abilities. I don't find it to be a particularly well-correlated indicator of practical expertise.

Ed: What was the most useful class you took in college?

Andy: This is actually quite an interesting question, and I'm gonna expand it to cover grade and high school as well as college, but I would say for the entire educational process, the most valuable class that I took anywhere was Latin in high school.

Ed: Cool.

Andy: And that, I think, is just supremely ironic, because if you had asked me at the time, that would surely not have been my answer. At the time, I thought it was the most useless waste of space to study a dead language that no one actually speaks anymore. You know, what was the point? That just absolutely didn't make it for me, but in retrospect, that gives you the basis for the language skills that's really unparalleled. It really expands your vocabulary. It expands your ability to understand vocabulary or even foreign languages, at least Latin-based languages, that you may not know how you say this in French or Spanish or what have you, but you'll see something that's close and you'll be able to figure it out enough to get by. And, again, I said before that I favored language skills far and above mathematical skills for the most part, so I think that was something that was quite, quite useful, far above and beyond any of the other classes of that sort.

Ed: How good are you at keeping your professional and personal lives balanced?

Andy: It's very difficult for me to think of myself as separate people. You know, a "work me" versus a "home me" versus the "research me" versus the whatever. It's really all one thing. And my situation is a little bit unusual. I've very much gone the career arc from in-the-trench programmer at a Fortune 100 company, through to working at really boutique, interesting, high-tech software companies, to being a consultant for all of the above and then some, to being an author, to being a publisher.

I'm firmly in the entrepreneur seat at the moment. It's the same challenges with a different twist. So with the entrepreneurship hat on, work, home, play is really all one thing, or it's a continuum. It's not discrete, different elements.

Ed: Are you married? Are you a parent?

Andy: Yes, we have children and they are very much a part of the business as well.

Ed: Talk more about that, because that's really interesting to me, how that works.

Andy: It's a fascinating thing. My kids are young. They help me pack or prepare when I go off and give lectures and speaking gigs. They help with some of the aspects of the business.

> **Character Attribute**
>
> Inclusive with kids.

It's not like the old days, where dad would come home at 5:00 after commuting on the train and knock back a few martinis and then make that transition from work life to personal life. You know, we don't have that sharp distinction. You know, I could be sitting at the pool with them, with my laptop, working on an article for a magazine, or working on sales figures for our publishing business, or writing code, or doing something for them. It's all one continuum.

Ed: Interesting. Now, obviously, you have to be on the same page with your wife if you're gonna mix the two so closely together. How does she feel about it?

Andy: She's a great contributor to our business. She also does consulting for companies in her field and, of course, managing the house and the kids. But really, the family knows we're all in this together. We're really all in the same boat.

Ed: Let's say you're working on a really engrossing problem, perhaps a creative coding problem, perhaps an article that you have to really think about deeply. How do you context switch and put that aside when it's time to spend quality time with your kids and do the dad thing in a real concrete way?

Andy: It depends. It's really a matter of prioritization. If the kids have something that is high priority—they've got a performance or a show or some event that's at a particular scheduled time we know that's coming up, then you make allowances for that. Okay. Now, I can't work on this then, whenever that may be, because this is what we have to go do. But they're also very aware that if it's at night time or on the weekend and I'm hunched over a laptop and deep into something, they pretty much will respect that, too, and they know, oh, "dad's in the middle of something." It's a give and take both ways, and it's certainly something I try not to overuse.

Ed: Do you have a non-IT Plan B to earn a living?

Andy: [immediately] Yes, I do.

Ed: Okay, what's that?

Andy: I'm not sharing it with you.

Ed: That's fine.

Andy: [laughs] Yes, I do and it's classified.

Ed: Okay.

Andy: Quote me on that.

Ed: What's your personal life goal?

Andy: I can make that short and sweet. I'll just say, "To understand."

Dave Thomas

Fact Sheet

Name: Dave Thomas

Home Page: www.davethomas.net

Rock Star Programmer Credentials: Object-oriented software pioneer

Date of Birth: July 1946

City of Birth: Ottawa, Ontario, Canada

Birth Order: First of one

Marital Status: Married

Number of Kids: Four and four grandchildren

Degree: Bachelor of Electrical Engineering – Carleton University (1969), Master of Systems and Computer Engineering – Carleton University (1976)

Number of generations in ancestry (including yourself) that graduated from college: One

Years as an IT Professional: 37

Role: Many roles, most recently chairman and founder of Bedarra Research Labs

Introduction

Dave Thomas has the distinction of being the most senior programmer I've interviewed in this book. As a self-professed "Old Country Programmer," Dave has experienced all of the major revolutions in computing since 1970. Rather than enumerate his many distinctions, about which you can read on his website, I'll relate a little story about a dinner I shared with Dave during the JAOO 2006 conference at which I made his acquaintance. The occasion was the speaker's dinner, and also at our table was Len Bass, a senior technical staff member at Carnegie Mellon's Software Engineering Institute (SEI). Len is intimately familiar with SEI's Capability Maturity Model Integration (CMMI), a process model based on software best practices. The effectiveness of CMMI as a means to increase and ensure the development of high-quality software has long been questioned, most recently by practitioners of Agile development. Incidentally, Dave is at the vanguard of the Agile development movement, as you can also learn from his website. Sensing an opportunity to observe some fireworks, I posed a question along the lines of "where does CMMI fit with respect to Agile?" and sat back to watch these two veterans of software engineering converse.

I saw two men very passionate about the practice of software development. I saw excellent listening and communication skills. I saw a professional camaraderie born of both men having spent so many years in the industry and having enjoyed so much success in those years. But most importantly, what I saw was that Dave walks what he talks. I feel the interview that follows will provide a good insight into what Dave's "talk" is all about. By the way, the conclusion of the conversation between Dave and Len was that CMMI and Agile can be complementary and that both have their place in the world. Dave and Len respectfully disagreed on the exact specifications of those places, however.

Background

Ed: You've had a long and illustrious computer science career. How did you get started?

Dave: I started out [in the late 1960s] in the computer center at Carleton University in Ottawa, Canada. In those days, computer centers were where all the interesting work in programming languages was being done. This was prior to mainstream computer science.

[At that time,] Simula 67 [was] coming out of the Norwegian Computer Center and so on, and computer centers did the language development. So we [at Carleton University] did Pascal and other language work for Xerox and Honeywell, and as a result, we got known in that community [as being] reasonably good at programming languages. This resulted in the Canadian Defense Department calling on us to say, "There's this new language coming out. We don't know whether it's yellow, red, or whatever." And so we got involved in Ada, in reviewing language designs. I also did a lot of work on end-user programming, programming by example, using actors to model office processes, which are much better than trying to use BPEL (Business Process Execution Language) and things like that.

> **Character Attribute**
>
> Dave's vast personal historical perspective allows him to see beyond the current fads and discover the core value of technologies.

Ed: I read on your curriculum vitae (CV) that you went on to become associate director of computing services and professor in the School of Business at Carleton. Why did you choose to go to the School of Business from the computer side?

Dave: I didn't know anything about business, so this was a chance to learn. And I was at the top of my area of [computing] expertise, and I'd done a lot of work for people in business, including modeling and contract work for business professors or companies that these business professors worked with. The dean and the head of the business school approached me and said, "Look, I'd like you to put together a modern IT program in the business school. Would you mind doing that?"

> **Character Attribute**
>
> No fear of jumping right in to an area in which he has no experience.

I had also just completed my Master's in Systems and Computer Engineering. There was a battle between the Systems and Computer Engineering and Math departments about where computer science would be, and I have a wide-spectrum view, so I just said, "Well, I don't really think I want to stay in this department." The business school was going to set up a new Information Systems department, so I got a green field and got to learn very quickly, from a fire hose, about business. I started doing work on business semantics, and it was interesting because it was also new.

Ed: Right, I mean, this was 1978, so it was very new. It must have been exciting.

Dave: To me, computing is this window you can take around and put in a new area and look in and see what all these people are doing and learn about it. The concept of office automation (OA) started around those days. My original work on office automation and workflow was all dataflow-driven, and I realized the problem is that dataflow isn't general enough, so I needed a better model. I was inspired by the work on Actors and the work on "Office by Example," and this lead quickly to objects, Lisp, and Smalltalk. We built our first Smalltalk system in APL from an article in *Byte Magazine* and felt this was the direction we should go for our research.

Ed: So that was your first encounter with object-oriented programming. Then you left the university and went to Dy-4 Systems, a hardware startup company. What did you do there?

Dave: We built a distributed network operating system that was object-oriented, and everything compiled down to Forth. Basically, it was what you would call today a network appliance. It was really fun, but I learned that building one's own object language and maintaining it and everything else was really, really hard. Dy-4 decided to focus on embedded hardware and I returned to the School of Computer Science to form the Object-Oriented research group. Determined that we need to understand objects more thoroughly, we made the decision to base our research on Smalltalk because it offered the benefit of being a pure object-oriented (OO) system with a comprehensive language and programming environment. If you want to do interesting things, you have to do them at the edge. Ask yourself, "What's the best, cleanest way to do this and forget that it's too slow. It isn't standard or anything else." That's what research should do. We were fortunate to obtain industrial funding from the DREO [Canadian Defense Lab] to explore multithreaded, multiprocessing (MP) embedded systems using Actors. We leveraged customized MP virtual machine hardware from Dy-4 and developed a multiprocessor Smalltalk system called Actra. In order to convince the Department of National Defense (DND) that Smalltalk could be scaled to multiple developers, we developed a fine-grained team configuration management system called Orwell, which eventually became our very successful Envy/Developer product at OTI (Object Technology International Inc.) [Dave's most commercially successful and widely known venture]. Our success in research was such that our DND sponsor wanted us to go further and provide a commercial-grade version. I was fortunate to have all these great students, and they wanted to keep doing this stuff, and it's not fair to pay them graduate wages and have them do real work, so I formed OTI in the spring of 1987. Tektronix was our first commercial customer for embedded Smalltalk, and this led to other commercial Smalltalk developments, including IBM Smalltalk.

Ed: Right, and later, OTI was acquired by IBM in 1996, but you stayed on as president and CEO of OTI, now IBM Ottawa Labs. Towards the end of your time at the helm of IBM OTI, you started Bedarra. How did that happen, and what is your present role at Bedarra?

Dave: OTI was operated as a separate company owned by IBM for seven years. I stayed until 1998, when I started Bedarra, and then consulted for IBM for another three years. I started Bedarra to work on new things and explore new directions, primarily working with startups. In 2003, I started Bedarra Research Labs as chairman with my partner Brian Barry (who was CTO, the CEO of IBM OTI). Bedarra Research Labs builds virtual teams to conduct applied research.

Soft Skills

Ed: How important is it to be aware of one's own ignorance?

Dave: Very aware—the biggest problem is believing your own bullshit. I used to use the line "only the paranoid survive," but there's a book out by the former CEO of Intel, Andy Grove [the book is *Only the Paranoid Survive: How to Exploit the Crisis Points That Challenge Every Company* (Currency 1999)]—but I really believe that.

For us at OTI, knowing that there are always smart people at Sun and Microsoft and other places doing things was really good, because fear is a big motivator. (*Hani Suleiman, page 139, also stated that fear is a motivator, but for a different reason.*)

If you believe that you're the only ones who have the idea and the only ones who can do this, you quickly become vulnerable. So it's important to listen to people from outside your own company! OTI ran an annual five-day technical conference, and at least 50 percent of those talks were outside people who had very different ideas.

When we [at Bedarra] do technical reviews or I work with companies as a virtual CTO, one of the first things we say is, "Why don't we get these other outside experts in here so that your guys can hear their views?" because the internal spin tends to block out information. This is particularly a problem with new product managers, who want to build their own little product kingdom. They start hoarding all the information and block out any light from coming in. So ignorance removal—admitting you don't know something—saying, "Can we get somebody in here to talk about this?" These are the signs of a healthy culture.

Ed: You mentioned fear as a motivator. What else motivates you to succeed professionally, and is it different from what motivates you to succeed personally?

Dave: I like the problem. To me, it's all about problem-solving. I love to be able to get into an area where someone has a problem, and they say, "This is important and hard." It's the challenge of the problem.

Ed: What about the payback you get when the solution is delivered? How important is it that you get the love from the user?

Dave: I think it's in the problem-solving itself. Clearly, you have to solve the problem—you have to produce an acceptable solution. It's good that people can say, "Oh yeah. I did that." Well, so what? I should also say all the things I did wrong too, right? The applause isn't really important. The quiet acknowledgment from the users: "This helps. Thanks." That's enough.

> **Character Attribute**
>
> Dave's motivation derives from factual and objective evidence, not something as ephemeral and subjective as customer praise. Such praise may derive from political and other nontechnical reasons as much as from objective, results-based reasons—and, therefore, would only be of limited use as a real motivator.

Ed: I was at the doctor's office this morning filling in some new patient paperwork, and I've heard a lot of press recently about the increase in the drive towards personal health records online, electronic personal health records (PHR), and you've certainly heard a lot of things about the inefficiency of the healthcare industry in America, right? I know you're in Canada, so you don't have this problem as much as we do—

Dave: Yes, we have that, too.

Ed: While doing the paperwork, I just had this strong feeling that the age of doing all this copious paperwork and all of this inefficiency is starting to come to an end because more and more of the offices are getting online with better software and such.

In the long scope of your career, you must have been through several of these circumstances where there was a palpable feeling that something is going to change, and then it did or it didn't. Can you talk about things you sense that tell you when a big change is going to happen in technology?

Dave: I think the problem you're talking about with healthcare is really just a big enterprise application integration (EAI) problem. The problem is that vendors control both ends of the cloud, so it's really like the old IBM system network architecture (SNA) or the Nortel switch that you couldn't open up or connect to because the current vendor had lock-in and controlled everything inside the cloud.

The people who have control want to maintain control, so they're very, very reluctant to open up the format or data and protocols. It's just a giant version of that old game of control.

In the end, government is going to force it. If the governments say, "It's [an individual's] right to get [one's] health records electronically; I can demand them from any source," then that gives me the ability to place those health records somewhere they can be shared and communicated (including my own highly encrypted personal media).

I probably can get benefits from doing that, like reduced costs and so on, because I can walk in [to a new healthcare provider] and nobody has to reenter my information: It's already available. With respect to the healthcare industry, I think you need an event like deregulation or open healthcare. So it's not the technology, per se; it's someone perceiving that things need to change based on the economic imperatives with healthcare.

Perhaps if healthcare providers were paying the fees … if Humana or their competitors said, "Wow, we actually forced this on the world, and we were the leaders, and we agreed to say, 'Look, if you manage your records electronically in this common format, we will give you a discount for doing this.'"

Ed: Wouldn't that be nice? Speaking of ideal situations, what is your ideal programming language and environment?

Dave: Very simply, I want a language and a runtime that allows a person who is knowledgeable in their domain to write software that can be implemented quickly and efficiently. I'm looking for something that allows one to build an interesting and quite complex application, solve the problem that's relevant by pair-programming—where one of the pair is a domain expert and the other of the pair is a very, very good programmer—and I'm interested in technologies that empower those individuals such that they can sit down and write their application or build their product without having to get involved in dealing with the plethora of complexities associated with the kinds of things one finds in middlewares and old operating systems and so on.

From a language point of view, that will require a synthesis of ideas from Scheme, Spatial Extract Transform and Load (SETL), and APL, and some objects from Smalltalk or Ruby. Each of these allows the user to see the world as higher-order collections. But I think objects will be much less important than they are presently. Objects will be a modeling construct. They may not be an execution construct.

Ed: How important is having a customer focus when crafting a software system?

Dave: My whole life in computing has been: if there isn't someone who wants a problem solved, I don't know what to do. I don't do recreational programming [said with stern finality]. There has to be a customer. I started developing software at university to make money from business students to do their assignments. So I've always naturally been, "Oh, okay. What do you need? What's the problem? Who can give me some examples?"

I think you have to look at what the customer wants to do. Most applications just work with collections of data and put it on the glass. My opinion is that everything from high-performance financial processing to computer games can actually be expressed fairly elegantly as CRUD programming.

> **Observation**
>
> CRUD stands for Create Read Update and Delete, the standard operations one does on a relational database. CRUD programming is programming that mostly just does CRUD operations on a database.

Ed: Really? That's quite an assertion.

Dave: Yes. Please see my rant in the *Journal of Object Technology* (vol. 2, no. 5, September-October 2003), "The Impedance Imperative – Tuples+Objects+Infosets=Too Much Stuff!" (www.jot.fm/issues/issue_2003_09/column1).

Ed: So that would explain why Rails is really a great idea because Rails does CRUD really well, right?

> **Character Attribute**
>
> Dave keeps very organized records of talks he has given over the years—144 since 1900, as of this writing. These talks are an externalized and highly refined representation of the knowledge and experience he has amassed. You can check out his talk index at www.davethomas.net/talks_index.html.

Dave: Yes. Well, it does it not badly. It targets a specific and currently popular point in this space: doing websites.

Ed: Right.

Dave: So it's good for doing websites. I'm not sure it's good for doing applications in general.

Ed: Right. So can you expand on this? For example, how would you do an immersive first-person shooter game with CRUD as the basis?

Dave: If you actually look a game, it consists of some objects that model the players in the game—the actors and so on—so you need some object programming for that, and clearly, you need the rendering engine for the graphics. Then, most of the stuff that goes on, particularly in multiperson games, is actually just updates of the position. Most of the time, all you're doing is reading the state from the system—dare I say, database, because it has to persist—and writing updates—moving your position or you're shooting or whatever, but in the end, all those things are really updates. It has to be persistent. I claim that one could model those with a dialect of extended Structured Query Language (SQL). I wouldn't want to use SQL because it's an upside-down programming language, but essentially, you could. If you did that in a language with collections and higher-order functions, it would be much simpler. Plus, there are a lot of things you don't want to worry about, such as backing out various actions and undoing state. That's the case where you can handle a lot of stuff with lazy evaluation.

I really do believe that by using the compute power of today's systems, that one can empower people who understand their problem to express their ideas in their conceptual domain-specific language (DSL), whether it's a real DSL or not, and that they can basically write down at a high level, "Here's what I'm doing. These are the things that I need. Here's the state. Here's when I need to update it." Of course, you need some graphics guys to make it look good [and] make it fast. But the actual core guts of the system is really CRUD, and of course a really great story line.

The problem is that it must deal with heterogeneous CRUD because it's on multiple platforms, applications, and databases. There are lots of technical issues with the infrastructure, but there's probably only part of the system that's really objects. For example, you need to model the actual players with objects.

Objects have been oversold. There are lots of things that are just data. The whole object relational and serialization thing is madness. Bringing dates into memory, turning them into objects, and racing the garbage collector … all that stuff is really a big and expensive waste of time as well as additional complexity.

> **Observation**
>
> Dave's statement about objects being oversold is particularly striking coming from him. After all, Dave's claim to fame and fortune was Object Technology International Inc. Therefore, I take Dave's statement as an indicator of his true engineer and scientist nature.

Ed: So would you assert then that the whole object database thing is a waste of time?

Dave: That's always been a waste of time. I have argued that from the beginning.

There are certain niches, like CAD (Computer Aided Drafting) where, due to performance, object databases [are useful], but with today's technology, you do not need an object database to do that, even in CAD applications.

Ed: Well, there's a tie-in here to one of the questions I have. Do you think we'll ever have something like an operating system that, instead of running on one machine, functions on a large number of distributed computers and presents a programming model as if all those computers were one big computer?

Dave: You've got it today!

Ed: Where?

Dave: Go to Amazon S3, Salesforce, Second Life, and Google. They may not providing general-purpose capabilities, but that model's already been proved successful. Not generically, but the proof that it works is there. It will take some time for the mainstream—your nearby bank is not going be running on a Googleplex any time soon—but it's a proven architecture.

Ed: The specific example, in today's world, would be writing an application to one of Amazon's application programming interfaces (APIs)?

Dave: Right, you've got a simple set of APIs that you can write any application you want, and that lets an application team deploy an application independently. They don't need to go ask the database guys, transaction processing monitor guys, etc., for permission. They don't have to go into the "glass house" [physical datacenter with big machines, raised floors, Halon fire suppression, and lots of air conditioning] and say, "Please, Mother, may I?" They just write it and deploy it, and they own it. My understanding is at Amazon, if you write an application, you own everything—you even answer the beeper if your servers are out.

Google has many high-performance teams. They just go do their "application," and they don't need to go through many gates with regard to databases and middleware and infrastructure. There's no stupid object middleware. There's no mainframe. None of those barriers are there.

Ed: So how long will it be before this paradigm has a general influence on the way—

Dave: Max, ten years [again, with stern finality].

Ed: Okay. If you're a computer science student training right now, what are some things you can do to prepare yourself for this?

Dave: There's an article I wrote called "Computational Diversity" [www .oopsla.org/2005/ShowEvent.do?id=77]. I think you need to understand what computation is about. You need to focus on first principles and not some particular programming language. So when we interviewed students at OTI, we would ask them questions like, "What's a higher-order function? When would you use them? Have you ever written an interpreter? What's a binding? What's the difference between functional programming and object-oriented programming?"

You want people that have read Abelson and Sussman's *Structured Interpretation of Computer Programs (SICP)* (MIT Press, 1996), Donald Knuth's *The Art of Computer Programming* (Addison-Wesley Professional, 1998), and probably *Mythical Man Month* by Fred Brooks (Addison-Wesley, 1995). Essentially that's the core. Know the first principles, know about environments and bindings, and understand how a computer works (meaning you can program in assembly language). Those who have this foundation are never fazed when a new language or processor comes out. Within minutes, if not hours, they analyzed and categorized it. Hence, they're never bothered by a new language because they know the key concepts. Inside the community who share these core concepts new languages and platforms are disseminated very quickly.

> **Observation**
>
> Adrian Colyer, page 37, also cited these books as fundamental.

> **Observation**
>
> Andy Hunt, on page 253 gives a very similar answer, but adds the color that such individuals are less disturbed and set back when the system behaves unexpectedly, because they are confident they understand the whole system from the hardware on up.

Ed: If I had asked you this question 10–15 years ago, I would think you'd have given the same answer, right?

Dave: Absolutely! [stern finality]

Ed: All right, so what's different—is there anything different now than—

Dave: Oh, no. I think the big thing is not being sideswiped by all the noise in the market. There is so much accidental complexity that it is overwhelming. In some cases, it is more valuable to know the bizarre behavior of a poorly defined API than it is to know how to design one yourself.

> **Observation**
>
> Max and Libor, on page 303, said exactly the same thing in answer to this question.

Consider research in software today, for example. Students are forced to do something like, "You need to take your really good idea, and it's really breakthrough, which you've done in Scheme or Haskell or whatever, but in order to actually get any research funding or have your professor sponsor you, you have to make it work with Eclipse or NetBeans or Visual Studio, and you have to program it in some arcane static OO language." So you spend two years of what's supposed to be a fantastic research experience trying to manufacture this in a technology that's guaranteed to be obsolete.

The problem is that industrial funding, whether it's Defense Advanced Research Projects Agency (DARPA) [U.S. Defense Department] or otherwise, basically drives people to take really good new ideas and implement them with a previous generation's bad technology.

Ed: Let's call this the "new idea/old technology" problem. Do you see any of those environmental factors that cause this problem going away? Is there more of a general openness to doing things differently, or is it still the same thing: It's gotta fit into the existing paradigms?

Dave: I think you always have cycles, when you go through an economic downturn, with the associated consolidation, one returns to, "If IBM and Microsoft and Sun or Oracle don't like it," then people are afraid, so there's gonna be a resistance. On the other hand, there are some problems for which the good news is computers are getting a lot faster, and the bad news is that the current technology doesn't really help. So there are people with problems that current technologies really don't help with, and they say, "I'm business-driven, and I'm doing a new venture; hence, I'm prepared to bet on this new thing, because I know if I build it in Java, it costs X, and if I build it in something else, it costs a tenth of X." Basically, it becomes an economic cost or productivity decision. Innovators challenge the conventional approach and all it takes is a couple of successful reference customers [for something to start catching on].

> **Observation**
>
> Max and Libor, on page 308, came to this same conclusion: Today's dynamic languages, such as Python and Ruby, have hugely amplified the competent programmer's productivity.

I mean, Google, for example, is proving that an architecture that many people argued could be built has been.

And the whole Asynchronous JavaScript and XmlHttpRequest (AJAX) thing is proving that dynamic languages are something that everybody's going to be using, and they're using JavaScript, perhaps leaving Java as the legacy language.

Ed: All right, so the knack is being attuned to these cycles of things that make an idea catch fire again.

Dave: The major challenge for an innovation in platforms or languages is to keep the idea alive until the opportunity becomes available. One of the problems with injecting venture capital (VC) funding or rushing to market where there's no customer is that no amount of money can force this idea into the wider market. You can't bet an emerging technology with easy money, because you can't bet that it's going to [have an] initial public offering in three years or five years or even eight.

So the key thing for a new technology is to find a niche where it can grow and where people will pay for it. Then it can be a healthy, stable business. Most successful things need to be incubated in a safer, more stable environment than VC funding or research funding.

Ed: Well, what environment is that?

Dave: It's having customers. There are some really exciting technologies and lots of really cool proprietary stuff that's being funded by customers, who use it for competitive advantage.

I know three or four companies that have private niche markets, and they don't really care that anybody else knows that they're there, and they're running nice profitable businesses. They're not huge. They have a small team constantly improving their technology, and that's the way you're going to get a new great language or a new engine.

That's done by a small team. Wrapping a sales force and the executives around it and pounding it out—I think those days are gone. One must have customer pull.

Ed: As far back as 1980, you were giving talks with titles like "The Way Ahead." Looking back on those sorts of talks, what did you say and did it turn out you were right?

Dave: Well, I don't think anyone can predict the future with 100 percent accuracy. My friends and associates, including a few of my favorite critics, will give me a 75 percent or better success rate, which I think is really 50 percent plus luck.

I think it was pretty clear that in 1980, we basically started predicting that object technology would be very successful, and it was. When I first gave the dinner talks—they were dinner talks then because people thought it was funny—I talked about things like Radio Frequency Identification (RFID), every object being self-identified, being able to send a message, etc. People would come up and they'd all laugh and say, "Thanks, it is really good to have a pointy-headed guy come and give a spacey talk [like] you just did!"

The thing that makes predicting technology challenging isn't the technology per se; rather, it is the accidents of the market like Java and Netscape, for example. Hence, most of my errant predictions occurred because of a discontinuity, since you can't really predict a discontinuity in the market, which happens for business rather than technical reasons.

I've been a big follower of [Douglas] Englebart and hypertext, and one of our big plays at OTI was an environment that is called the "Unibrowser," which was essentially a universal browser. Lots of people followed on Doug's work, so it certainly wasn't unique, but I was really surprised how long it took for the Web and the Internet to take off. I really thought that was going to happen in the '80s.

I remember giving a talk at Honeywell, having seen the Xerox Alto at the Palo Alto Research Center (PARC), about multiple windows on the screen, and Honeywell was just horrified that you wouldn't be able to get 132 characters on the screen. You wouldn't be able to see a print page if you had windows and things like that. It's always pretty shocking that mainstream companies just can't see things that are pretty much known to be doable within five years.

On the other hand, I certainly didn't anticipate the kind of wild cowboy days of the Internet era and the sort of wild abandonment that would be applied to software. The whole notion of "just put your source code repository on the Web" was really a shock. It was a big shock for us at OTI.

Ed: You mean open source?

Dave: "Web time" development and later open source. We were used to a beta program where you had 10 or 20 really talented people who participated in your secret beta program. The whole idea of putting all your code out there before it's ready was a real shock.

Ed: The Web 2.0 idea of the perpetual beta? I want to take a tangent here. I want to understand how [you got] to the point in your career where you could get paid to predict the future. Was this something where you said, "I want to be a guy who gets paid to predict the future?" How did it get to there?

Dave: I don't think I ever made predicting the future a goal. I've always been very interested in how a small group of people who know what they're doing can build software quickly that has high performance and productivity. Hence, I tend to be an early adopter of new techniques.

The real core of computing is about how languages evaluate. All of these, from my point of view, are just different expressions of language.

When we heard Java was coming out, I had a team working for me in France that prototyped a universal virtual machine (UVM) that ran Java and BASIC and some other languages. The UVM capability was part of what IBM bought when they bought OTI, because we actually had a technology—visualized for Java, of course—that was completely written in Smalltalk and ran both Smalltalk and Java byte codes. Unfortunately, the Java lobby beat on IBM to drink from the cup, saying, "You're not doing everything in Java." Therefore, Eclipse had to be in Java and everything else, so IBM stopped the UVM project, and that's when I left because I don't believe in mono-culture. It was only when Microsoft introduced .NET that IBM realized the magnitude of the bet they [had] placed on Java.

IBM has a team that could do this, but I don't think either IBM or Sun has the energy because they've got so much vested in Java, which, to me, provides a great opportunity for everybody else. Even when IBM and Sun want to change, they're going to have a hard time getting out of that hole because they have all their legacy customers.

Ed: Okay. But getting back to the meta-issue of turning points in your career—you've taken me through this whirlwind tour of how you got to where you are—but we glossed over several things that seemed like they would be turning points. Can you call them out more explicitly and talk about how you recognized, either maybe before or after the thing was happening, that this was a turning-point moment for you?

Dave: I think using interactive computing through APL was one of the first turning points. Even though it was so horrible to write, it was so incredibly powerful. So at some point in the '70s, that was just a "Wow!" to me.

Ed: Okay, okay—and you knew it at the time. You thought, "Damn, this is going to be great!"

Dave: Yes, or "I don't understand how you can get so much done with so little."

Ed: Any other turning points?

Dave: There's a set of papers at MIT that is likely the most significant unpublished work in our field called the Lambda Papers.

Ed: I've heard of them.

Dave: The Lambda Papers, for most of the people I know who have read them, are mind transforming, and after reading them, you can only talk to people who have read them or understand the ideas.

Ed: You're kidding me?

Dave: No.

Ed: This almost sounds like a mythical, Holy Grail–type thing?

Dave: For me, it was—and still is—the papers, which are really the notes of Guy Steele and Gerry Sussman trying to understand Hewitt's Actors and which resulted in Scheme. *Structure and Interpretation of Computer Programs* (MIT Press, 1996) is substantially derived from the Lambda Papers.

There was a wonderful conference—the APL conference, around 1980—where Alan Perlis, Gerry Sussman, Charles Moore, and Guy Steele all gave amazing talks. What you saw in one conference was thought leaders in languages who enjoyed talking to each other about the issues, even though they're from what many people considered to be very different language cultures.

Character Attribute

Ability to communicate flawlessly in spite of deeply held differences.

Ed: So you observed this meeting of the minds?

Dave: Yes. Another "Wow!" occurred while I was working with Xerox: seeing Smalltalk in the late '70s, and seeing multiple windows on the screen—a complete system with objects all the way down, and something better than Scheme or APL for interactive programming. When you see these things, touch them, and talk to the people, you see that they think differently about how computers and people should interact.

I've been fortunate to cross disciplines a lot, so often I see opportunities to apply ideas from one domain in another. For instance, someone in business who is working on the very challenging problem of consolidation and merger typically isn't exposed to data structures and recursion. They are delighted when you observe, "Well, really, the problem here is that you need [to] write a recursive function that converts a graph to a tree by applying the percent ownership of the different subsidiary businesses." But that's not the kind of thinking you typically find in a business school, so you get rewarded by other people who give you similar "aha's" because they think about your problem differently. Hence, I always like to be in some kind of interdisciplinary environment. In general, I prefer to talk to people who actually *have* these problems because that's where you get the "aha's."

Ed: Can you tell me about a time when you were presented with an opportunity and you seized it and what happened?

Dave: When the research that I had done with the Defense Department was going commercial, they basically said, "Look, we either have to have this in the Ada programming language or we have to find a commercial Smalltalk vendor that can provide us with this technology."

Ed: Right, and so you became that commercial Smalltalk vendor.

Dave: Yes. At that point, I went to my wife and said, "I'm going to start a business that focuses on doing embedded Smalltalk." And she said, "Is there anyone who believes that this is possible?" and I said, "Probably not." And so she said, "Well, then I own 50 percent."

Ed: But it sure did turn out right. You ended up shipping the world's first embedded Smalltalk runtime, in Tektronics oscilloscopes.

Hard Skills

Ed: What do you think is the correlation between developer proficiency and mastery of tools?

Dave: I believe developer proficiency is really related to mastery of concepts and discipline. Definitely, being competent with the tools helps. For instance, when you watch Robert C. Martin (founder and CEO of Object Mentor) refactor with IntelliJ or Eclipse, it's like watching someone play a musical instrument. He can just fly. But many people who use these tools can't find the refactor button.

So I think there's definitely a need to train people on how to use these complicated tools. On the other hand, I think that begs another issue. If you need complicated tools, then perhaps the technologies you're using are the wrong ones.

Ed: Who is the most productive programmer you ever worked with and why were they that way?

Dave: Oh boy! I have worked with lots of really productive people.

Ed: Can you share some of the characteristics they had that made them productive?

Dave: The most important thing is they knew it was more important to get things done, keeping it simple and making constant progress. You need the focus and discipline to make things to work one bit at a time, but always having a good sense of the whole. What does the customer really need? But in terms of their development skills, the ability to essentially say, "Okay, I *have to* get this done. I'm going to focus and do this." (*Max Levchin states the same thing in his answer on page 311.*)

On the other hand, any time something was difficult, or they weren't sure that something was working, or they were trying to debug something, or trying to patch or fix something, they would find another talented person and they would pair with them.

Ed: Okay, so "execution wins." Would you say that's an ingredient of success as a programmer to know that execution wins and to focus and study on that?

Dave: Absolutely! Focus and execution win, right. At OTI, I used to say, "Shut up and ship, and those who ship get to speak."

Just ignore the noise. Forget that there are all these really smart guys at Sun doing Java, and we don't even know Java. We are going to get there. If they're really that smart, we'll lose, and we'll have to go get new jobs as truck drivers. So ignore the noise. Just focus and just keep shipping.

One of the pleasures I have today [at this point in my career] is that I don't have to focus, because it's really demanding. It takes great discipline to just focus and get your stuff done and get work done. It's really hard, because there are all sorts of exciting things, and then you get behind, and everything else piles on top of you.

> **Observation**
>
> A real rock star programmer is someone who has found a sustainable balance between getting lots of things done *and* keeping up with all those "exciting things" as Dave mentions.

Ed: Right. I mean, you can't do the stuff that brings you to the place where you're paid to talk about the future if you're just focusing on execution all the time. But what you just said is "execution wins," so there seems to be a tension here, no?

Dave: Well, again, it depends on what hat you're wearing. For product development, it's the focus on the business and the execution. At OTI, the focus was "objects everywhere." We built this ten-year research agenda for object utopia and turned it into a business, and we got objects to mainframes.

We didn't get Smalltalk into a watch, but we did make it to cell phones and pagers. We had a big enough research agenda and a big enough vision, but we also had to focus on the execution. In the case of tracking future trends, one needs to be on top of the major companies, the start-ups and industrial and university research. This takes effort, but is much broader in nature than the narrow focus required to build working software that ships.

Ed: You bring up two levels of detail there. Much of the work of software development involves being able to zoom in to a very fine level of detail and then zoom out again to get the big picture. Do you agree with that?

Dave: Absolutely!

Ed: So do you think that this requires special proficiency in keeping things in perspective and if so, does that proficiency carry over to your personal life as well?

Dave: You'd probably have to ask my wife on the personal side. I always approach a problem with a big picture [view], which I think is essential, and this lets one zoom in on specific aspects. Without a global view, you get lost in the details and lose the whole.

I see lots of people who are so focused on their particular idea that they don't see the other things happening around them. So I think you need both. I think this is one of the strengths of an engineering style of education. Basically—you're thrown into a world where things are very complex, and you can't possibly know everything, and so you have to live in a world of approximations and so on. You learn quickly that you can't possibly know everything. This teaches you that one has to live in a world of simplifications and approximations to make progress. In math or science or business, there's often a "right answer," such as a proof, whereas in engineering, you're always working with models and other abstractions of reality.

One of the reasons objects don't work well in IT, for example, is the [relative] lack of engineering genes [among the IT practitioners].

Ed: You mean IT as opposed to pure computer science or software engineering?

Dave: Many IT professionals don't have the concept of "component" or "system." It's just not how they think about the world. This is one reason why enterprise business objects and business architectures often run into difficulty. These organizations are frequently driven by a *project* culture versus a *product* culture; hence, components, reuse, and other long-term investments have little value. Trying to do component engineering in a project culture is very, very difficult because the driver is "How does this help me get my application done faster?" This is always in conflict with any kind of object architecture, business objects, etc.

Ed: Yeah, but that project-think, that's the same thing that drives the notion of "execution wins," which you just said was really important. So there's that tension again.

Observation

This distinction between *project* culture and *product* culture is also covered on page 24 in my interview with Rod Johnson.

Dave: I think the way it happens in an IT organization is "execution wins and ignore the component architecture." One may argue that the business would be better if it actually adopted objects and things like that, but my position is it's probably the wrong technology for a project culture. Objects work really well if you have a product culture. In that case, it's a great technology. If you're building apps, it's not clear to me that you are not better off with a modern 4GL or a generator such as Rails.

Business

Ed: What role did luck play in bringing you to where you are now?

Dave: Luck is essential, and followed closely by focus and timing, especially with language or platform technologies. I think with regards to technology, you have to be a wildly optimistic downside planner.

Ed: What does that mean?

Dave: It means you can't bet [on] when a new technology is going take off, when it is going to be small enough or fast enough to cross the chasm. This means that you have to tack towards your end goal. You can't just get a big injection of VC money and say, "Okay, we're going hit the market in three years." Many people will point to the most recent set of IPOs or large buyouts, but inevitably, you will see that the core technical work for a technical innovation was done over a period of 5 to 15 years or more.

Today's market is much like the '70s—dominated by major players. In niche markets, you really have to dominate your niche and you have to grow in your niche. Owning a narrow niche allows you self-sustainability. You can constantly improve your technology and be in a position to move into a broader market when the time or luck arrives. When I was a professor, my research grant got cut to zero when logic programming became the "in" thing. So we had to go out and look for dollars from industry to keep the object research going. Fortunately, we had a very modest lab, which used PCs and Macs rather than expensive workstations. The secret to sustained innovation is being creative within a budget. While it isn't always the case, necessity is the mother of innovation and sometimes less is more. Just being in a niche constrains you to work on a smaller set of problems and really address them. For example, in our case, it was embedded Smalltalk, which in the mid '80s was a niche market of about five customers.

Ed: Your operating costs were small?

Dave: Right. The ideas we were working on really didn't need a lot of people. We accepted things were slower, and we couldn't do some of the real examples we wanted, but we understood that it really wasn't important that we used high-performance workstations, for example. The real trick to building successful products is to build them three times. You need to throw at least two or three away. For example, the virtual machines (VMs) that IBM runs today are the fifth- or sixth-generation VMs. They've been completely tossed and rewritten in many cases.

Ed: You've had some experience in the telecommunications industry. Do you have anything to say about the "new" AT&T being basically a merger of the baby Bells that were split off from the "old" AT&T when deregulation happened in the first place?

Dave: There is a strong tendency for organizations and industry that have many of the same people to return to the same shape they had before. That's why organizational change is so hard. This is a larger version of the inventor's dilemma (see Clayton M. Christiansen's 2006 book *The Innovator's Dilemma* [published by Collins]) and with respect to organizations and industry, many *don't* change. In the case of [the baby] Bells, of course there was an artificial forcing function in terms of the government. The change did, however, allow many new enterprises, such as Cisco, to thrive as well as improving the overall infrastructure, so there have been clear benefits.

You might think, if you really want to do something new, you should be able do it inside an existing successful organization, right? Well, just forget it. Most organizations cannot possibly deal with an emerging technology that threatens one of their established businesses. You have to start a new business. If you have a good idea in your business, and your business really doesn't believe in it, if you really believe there's potential in it, then what you need to do is get it out as quickly as possible. The best practice is for the large company to invest in the start-up, retaining sufficient equity to reap the benefits should it be really disruptive.

This is upsetting advice for my friends who work in large, successful companies, because they naturally assume that their company's a technology leader. I mean, you do get accidents of history like Java, but there's no way Sun would have made that as a rational business decision process.

> **Observation**
>
> Anecdotally, Dave mentioned IBM and Transarc as an example of this. IBM owned a majority share in Transarc at the time they bought it, back in August of 1994. Back then, the technology was called *transaction processing monitor software*. Eventually, its objects were added to the mix and the result became Common Object Request Broker Architecture (CORBA), which became a mainstay of IBM's middleware for many years.

Ed: Would you say being privately held is an essential ingredient for the success of a new technology?

Dave: I believe if you're a technology company, you have to be in control of the company until the period where the technology is really ready to enter the market. I think most really successful technologies probably were in small businesses or tiny business units in large companies.

Ed: Are you a licensed engineer?

Dave: I didn't sign the professional paperwork, because in Canada, where I am qualified, the only benefit for a software or even electrical engineer is portable insurance. Here, engineers wear an iron ring, which often gives the appearance that you're special, and I don't like people who are "special."

Ed: What is your opinion of the movement to introduce formal licensing for professional software engineers?

Dave: I understand the concerns; however, I'm not impressed by anything that Institute of Electrical & Electronics Engineers (IEEE) or anyone else has done to date. I really do believe the best way is to work on the educational system, which, to be fair, is something that IEEE and the Association for Computing Machinery (ACM) are actively engaged in through Accreditation Board for Engineering and Technology (ABET) certification. The important thing for professional engineers, professional accountants, is the core body of knowledge that is offered in good educational programs, most of which are accredited. This is followed by mentored practice, but it isn't clear that the accounting exams following the practice really make a difference to the quality of the accountants.

If you don't understand computation, it won't matter, right? I'm not a supporter of any of the professional certification efforts that I've seen to date.

Ed: From your vantage point of being a longtime supporter of Smalltalk and other dynamic object and functional languages, can you say anything about how Java has succeeded or failed with respect to other languages in the years since your team in France developed the Universal Virtual Machine, which ran Java as well as Smalltalk and other languages?

Dave: Java, more correctly the Java Virtual Machine (JVM), deep-sixed most interesting languages, including functional (Scheme, Lisp, ML) and dynamic object languages (Smalltalk, Self, Clos, Effiel, Beta), because most of these languages require features such as higher-order functions, tagged integers, dynamic dispatch, full runtime reflection, and runtime modification. Although some of these features have made it back into the JVM, it is still far from an ideal target for building a dynamic language. Corporations moving to Java have given the vendors a push, making the JVM the only runtime available in the browser or the server. The situation was further compounded by Java Native Interface (JNI), which provided an impoverished way to leverage existing C or C++ libraries, deep-sixing many products implemented in C.

Java became a weed language, which, because of the JVM, choked out other languages, including Smalltalk. This was compounded by the economic impact of almost-free Java from Sun, IBM, and Microsoft (Microsoft Visual J++ for Java sold at $9.99 at one point), followed soon after with free open-source software tools, making it virtually impossible for independent software vendors to survive. At IBM OTI, we were acutely aware of these JVM constraints. When we developed VisualAge for Java, we ran Smalltalk, Java, and some other languages on an extended byte code called the UVM. Unfortunately, IBM decided not to take that research to market. Finally, the Smalltalk community and vendors decided to fight Java rather than try to embrace and extend it. I am pleased and encouraged by Ruby and the effort in JRuby and IronRuby to finally implement dynamic languages on the JVM and to see JavaScript emerging as a dynamic language for Web development.

Personal

Ed: What about ego—how does ego fit in as a successful developer character attribute?

Dave: I think it's very important that people have personal pride in their software. Pride is different than its sometimes ugly brother, ego, when pride spills over and starts pushing into other people's space.

I've always felt that you can print whatever you wanted on your business card when you took it outside, but inside, you were just Ed or Dave. I think it's very important to manage strong egos because they can really disrupt teams. It is important that people understand that they're team players and they need the other people on their team. Clearly, they should have pride in what they do and write clean, efficient code. Trying to take care of a bunch of prima donnas is very difficult, no different than hiring a star on a sports team. The whole team becomes hostage to that individual ego. I don't believe in being hostage to egos. Unfortunately, there are some people you just can't afford to have in your team, even though they're amazingly talented.

Ed: We talked earlier about the importance of being skilled at keeping things in perspective. Do you think that would make one a good parent?

I'm trying to bridge these gaps because I'm struggling with this myself. I've got two small kids and I'm trying to see how these two skillsets interact—being a parent—

Dave: I think that's a fatal mistake to assume that one can take one's personal life experiences in software and apply them in parenting. I've seen too many people who try analyzing their children and figuring out what they're doing, and I really think that's a rat hole. I think you have to step out of software and talk to people who are parents, often your own, for a start. If you find analogies that are useful, they are often by accident because you are looking at them through your software glasses.

I think it's really important to see parenting as potentially a complete unknown and hence engage and explore it: "Okay, I'm going to read, go to talks, whatever about children and parenting from people who actually have seen the movie and not try and talk to my friends who are analyzing everything from the perspective of 'the world is just software.'"

I never, ever, think of the human system and software in the same conversation. I think the principles of "focus" and "encapsulation" are universally useful, but I don't think they were invented by software. So I wouldn't attribute those successful things that I've found to be software. They were just probably other things that existed in life, which happen to be adapted to software. The entire lean and agile approach we used for talking about software processes was taken from product design and manufacturing where "just in time" changed the way in which people worked together. Many of the successful practices, even with their weaknesses, such as systems and components, were not invented for software.

Ed: How good are you at keeping your work and personal lives balanced then?

Dave: When I was running a business, terrible. I would always go on vacation when it was planned, and I seldom got interrupted. So I have never had a problem with that. But in terms of working very late, taking calls, doing e-mails, stuff like that—certainly. I think when you're a founder, running a business, you do get consumed by your work. One simple thing I did was schedule family events [as if they were] critical business events. My business calendar contains family events, which have priority above all others. My wife and my children have traveled with me on conferences and business trips, and this has been very positive. We have a gained a perspective on the world that we think is really important. So I think there have also been lots of benefits for our family.

However, it is far too easy to lose one's balance. I've been fortunate to have the support of my family. If there's anything in the family that's really important, everything else gets dropped. In any business that I've been in, that's always been the rule. If someone's sick or somebody's got a personal problem, it doesn't matter how critical they are to the team; the right thing for the business and team to do is to support the individual. But it's a constant battle. For me, computing is a passion, not just a job. I admire people whose hobby is completely different from their work. I've found boating and swimming great in this regard. That said, it's been a great ride for us. But when you work on crunch projects, such as when OTI did IBM Visual Age for Java and then Eclipse, we had to accept that this [project] was so hard that people needed to be able to opt out. For a period at least, this is more or less the way the OTI team worked. I was very proud at OTI that we gave every employee four weeks of vacation as well as closing through the Christmas and New Year holidays, but I just don't think it was enough time for people to mentally relax and enjoy their personal time. If I were to do another OTI, I would give people three months off each year.

Ed: After the crunch time project was done?

Dave: For the most part, yes, that is when people would take the time, and I don't care when they take the three months, as long as they can schedule it with their team. The work is so intense on a crunch project that you really just have to tell people, "Okay, look, you're going be working like crazy for six to nine months, but you're going to have three months off."

Ed: Just the nature of the work is so consuming and—

Dave: It's bursty, and there are just times when 38 hours per week doesn't work, even when you have great focus and discipline. I think in any creative field there are days when you get "writer's block" or, at the very least, the words just don't come easily.

Ed: Right.

Dave: We tried to educate spouses, explaining to them, "This is the way it works, and when your Johnny or your Sue tells her team that they must have this done by that date, it's really not THE BOSS telling him they have to have it done by that date. Johnny or Sue actually told their team and so they're counting on them. Now, did your Johnny or Sue cram in school? Guess what? If you want to help your Johnny or Sue, what you have to do is talk to him or her about the estimates that they're doing, so you don't have the kind of stresses at home that are associated with this, because in the end, at least in our organization, people are responsible and accountable for their own estimates."

Ed: So you're saying you undertook a developer education initiative where you told them, "You've gotta tell your family what it—

Dave: Yes. We would actually have spouses come in for testing parties and events like that. Sometimes it would help people's relationships by actually exposing [the spouse] to the culture of development. When our admins were frustrated, we would just say, "Look, don't do anything, just serve pizza.

They have to get this stuff shipped. They're going be complete jerks at that point." I think teaching people a lot more about the animal helps.

Clearly, some people can't live that life, and I respect that. I've worked with amazing people who just couldn't handle the stress for some projects. They were smart enough to know that their personal health or their relationship just could not handle the stress. Developers also learn that having someone who's got great insight or great experience, even if they are only available part-time, is still way better than not having them [at all].

I spent a lot of time in social engineering inside of some of our client companies [through Bedarra]. It is a challenge because often the senior management has no life experiences like those of the developer. So you really have to spend a lot of time explaining it to people. Most human resource (HR) experts don't appreciate the intensity and stress associated with software development. They would say to me, "You know, this is what these people are really like, isn't it?" and I said, "Yes." And they said, "Wow!" That's why I think books like *Mythical Man Month* by Fred Brooks (Addison-Wesley Professional, 1995), *Psychology of Computer Programming* by Gerald M. Weinberg (Van Nostrand Reinhold Company, 1971), and *Soul of a New Machine* by Tracy Kidder (Back Bay Books, 1981) are so important for non-developers to get a glimpse of what it is like fighting in a software trench.

CHAPTER 13

Max Levchin and Libor Michalek

Fact Sheet

Name: Max Levchin

Home Page: www.levchin.com

Rock Star Programmer Credentials: Co-founder of PayPal, Inc.

Year of Birth: 1975

City of Birth: Kiev, U.S.S.R. (now Ukraine)

Marital Status: Single

Number of Kids: None

Degree: Bachelor of Science in Computer Science, College of Engineering, University of Illinois at Urbana-Champaign, 1997

Years as an IT Professional: Ten

Role: Founder, CEO, and chairman of Slide

Name: Libor Michalek

Rock Star Programmer Credentials: Co-founder of Slide

Year of Birth: 1973

City of Birth: Brno, Czechoslovakia (now Czech Republic)

Birth Order: Second of two

Marital Status: Married

Number of Kids: One

Degree: Bachelor of Science in Computer Science, College of Engineering, University of Illinois at Urbana-Champaign, 1995

Number of generations in your ancestry that graduated from college (including yourself): One

Years as an IT Professional: Ten

Role: Senior engineer at Slide

Introduction

Everyone interviewed in this book has ridden the career crest to one place or another, but of all of them, no one has ridden a bigger wave than Max Levchin. His wave was the dot-com boom itself, and Max managed to gracefully surf ashore after his time on its crest. Max's claim to fame: He's the guy who made the Internet safe for mass personal commerce. As co-founder of PayPal and lead architect behind their fraud prevention measures, Max helped grow PayPal to their rocket-ride initial public offering (IPO), and later that same year, to their acquisition by eBay in 2002. Even after these two major liquidity events, Max is still driven by a desire to create successful startups that bring value to the world and make lots of people lots of money.

Libor's renown is much less than Max's, and I think that's how he wants it. Libor is all about getting it done and getting it done right. The first few hits when Web searching for "libor michalek" are CVS commit logs for his work on the Linux kernel. Libor had a hand in several successful startups, including being an early participant in eGroups, which was acquired by Yahoo! in August 2000.

Max and Libor started working on their current venture, Slide, in late 2001. I remember Libor showing it off at a social gathering of University of Illinois Association for Computing Machinery (ACM) alumni in San Francisco. At the time, slide.com really was just that: a JavaScript/DHTML–powered slide show that people could easily include on their webpages. Like any successful technology, it existed at the intersection of several emerging trends and was well suited to capitalize on them. In this case, the trends included online photo sharing, social software, and other attributes of the so-called "MySpace generation." According to their website, slide.com is now the "largest personal media network in the world, reaching more than 134 million unique global viewers each month and 30 percent of the U.S. Internet audience."

But more than all that, Slide is also very well positioned as the most popular provider of applications that build on top of social platforms. They're the leading application developer on Facebook and have a strong presence on every major global social portal. With the recent buzz around Web 2.0 and social software, Max and Libor are riding the crest again.

Soft Skills

Ed: Has it become more difficult to stay current on IT developments since we graduated from college 12 or so years ago? Does that make it harder for someone entering the IT workforce today versus when we came out—the fact that there's so much more to learn?

Libor: There might be this issue. It's a fact of life in general that's different from 15 years ago. There are a lot more things calling for your attention. One thing [all three of us here] have learned, working through that, which [might be] more difficult for someone to learn just coming out of school, is how to be extremely frugal and selective with your attention.

Ed: That's the core of this book. Can we talk about that? How do you know what technologies to follow? How do you stay current? How much to pay attention—

Libor: Well that's it: Don't stay current.

Ed: *Don't* stay current?

Libor: Don't stay *too* current is probably the point.

Max: There's no point in staying current at all. Remember the WROX series? Eventually, when I looked at them, I thought, "I'll find some of these books that I want to read." Then I realized that every book that was published, at least when I looked at it last time, had a version number on it that had to do with the substance being described, such as, "JavaScript 1.2." I thought, "Well, that has to be the world's most worthless book, because if there's a JavaScript 2.0 I have to use for work or JavaScript 3.0 that comes out a year later, this book isn't going to be good enough. That's a 1,000-page book. I'm not going to read that."

Libor: That's another thing. Anything that requires 1,000 pages, don't bother reading it.

Max: A good rule of thumb is the books have to be really thin to read.

Libor: When I used to go to Computer Literacy [a legendary Silicon Valley bookstore dedicated entirely to technology books], any topic, I'd just say, "Okay, what's the smallest book on it?" There's no need for 1,000 pages on anything—

Max: Unless it's a reference. But if it's a reference manual, it should be online. There's no reason for it to be printed. I think the [trick] is primarily the filtering, and filtering is primarily—

Libor: It's a huge bullshit detector.

Max: Yeah, exactly. I was going to say that. There are lots of rules of thumb. If it's a book written by more than three people: not worth reading. If it's a book that has more than 1,000 pages: not worth reading. If it's a book that has a specific operating system name on it: think twice. If it has a specific language on it: it's probably worth it if the language hasn't been around more than ten years.

Libor: That's another one. The more specific, the less likely it is to be something that you need to know.

Max: Given the cheap bandwidth [for] the really specific stuff, you should just find the answer online. There's no value these days to going to a Barnes and Noble and picking up the book on Perl to answer the question about—

Libor: Perl for Windows! [Note: Perl is an interpreted language and, therefore, is no different to learn on Windows, Unix, Mac OS X. The runtime does the platform-specific work. Libor is pointing out the inanity of such a book.]

Max: Yeah, Perl for Windows. But on the other hand, a good thin book on [Microsoft] COM (Common Object Model) or DCOM (Distributed Common Object Model)—whatever the current thing is—I actually have one of those books even though I never touched Windows and probably never will. I thought, "This whole binary compatibility, late binding stuff," I read about it in Lisp, but it would be fun to see how it's been applied in the real world. So I actually bought a book on .NET—just enough to know that I'm not going to like the stuff.

Libor: That's a huge thing, just learning how to wade through all that BS and ignore most of it.

Ed: We talked about books, but what about online forums or RSS feeds or blogs or any of that stuff?

Max: I don't read any blogs. That's a waste of time.

Ed: Do you have people you trust to read them, and you listen to what they say, and the *people* are the filter and you get things that are passed around?

Max: There are generally one or two developers who I think are really awesome that I know personally. When I have a very specific question about how to do something, I try to rephrase it as the most general question and then I ask them, and they generally have an answer that's really powerful. More than likely, I am one of those people for someone else because I get those questions relatively frequently. I think it's just enough of a filtering process. The guy who's the CTO at Yelp was my chief architect at PayPal and a super awesome programmer. [He] knows his stuff really well. I don't know if he reads up on a lot of stuff, but he definitely keeps tabs on stuff more than I do. So when I say, "How do you do this?" he's says, "Well, here's how Ruby does it." Okay, well, that's not really about Ruby. It's about how to do a good pattern for a Web process.

Libor: It's like a distributed bullshit detector, because you've got all these people that you trust and everyone is an expert in some area or is more interested in [other] areas. There are areas in which you're generally interested and

> **Observation**
>
> See page 56 for a similar observation. Though the Java Posse camp is clearly all about staying current in the Java world and they don't focus on fundamentals as much, it still exemplifies Libor's "distributed bullshit detector."

you keep up on, but it doesn't have to be all of computing and then there's all the other stuff.

Max: It's impossible to keep tabs on all of computing. There's a famous quote from [computer science pioneer] John von Neumann. Right before his death, he said, "Back when I was young, it was actually possible to know about *half* of known math," implying, of course, that he was one of the people who knew about half of known math. "At this point, I don't even know if anyone understands 10 percent." Even that [very thing] indicates [the impact of the] increase of bandwidth, because people used to write each other *letters* to exchange math knowledge, and by the time John von Neumann was old, electronic communication was possible. So I think just the overload of research and collaboration indicates or precipitates the impossibility of knowing everything. Therefore, one is probably better suited to be an expert in a few fundamental things than just trying to keep tabs on everything.

Libor: The other thing is there's really not much new on a year-to-year basis. The better your bullshit filter or your distributed bullshit filter is, the less you're really going to have to go out of your way.

Max: I don't think I've learned anything since school.

Libor: What I've done is do different startups. I enjoy startups. Before [Slide], I was at a hardware networking company and also did enterprise software for aerospace and financial markets. I just learned different things by doing it and [being] exposed to people with domain knowledge. There's no substitute for just building up knowledge over time.

> **Observation**
>
> Dave Thomas, on page 288, accords similar importance to staying close to people with domain knowledge.

Max: That's true. Building stuff is the best experience.

Ed: And then the building of the relationships and your distributed bullshit detector.

Max: Most of the relationships that you build in your bullshit detector are people [with whom] you sweat out some late-night hours hacking, and then you trust them because you have seen how their brain works and it's efficient, easy for you to model what they would think is good. A lot of the time, actually, my friend will tell me, "Well, you should use this," and I say, "Well, no. Actually, the way your brain works, you think this is good. But this, in fact, tells me that this is bad or bad for me." But, nonetheless, they're great developers.

Hard Skills

Ed: When you think about the way software is done today, with so many layers upon layers upon layers away from the hardware, do you find that having a hardware foundation in your training is something that is really valuable? Even though you're doing scripting or Python or whatever, there's a virtual machine (VM) there.

Libor: I actually find it helpful, especially when you get into things like debugging a complex system. You've got lots of machines doing lots of different things, all talking to each other. I saw one of your questions was: "Where do you start with debugging?"

Ed: Do you want to talk about that one?

Libor: There are a lot of different places to start, but I think you have to have a good understanding from top to bottom to have a good sense of where to jump in.

Max: `printf` debugging.

Libor: Yeah.

Max: My preferred debugging method is still `printf` debugging. The way I start is I basically do a binary search to figure out where the crash is and split the code in half and see what prints before the crash or what doesn't print after. So it must be a—

Libor: You're in good company. That's Linus' [Torvalds] preferred method as well. [Linus is the creator of the Linux kernel, the heart of the GNU/Linux open-source operating system.]

Max: Right before college, and in college, I was really very hung up on assembly language, so I spent a ton of time freshman year and as a senior in high school doing a lot of 386 assembly, and I really got into step-by-step debugging. Then once I got to a UNIX command prompt, I thought, "This is so much better than [interactive] debugging." All these people were saying, "Oh, `printf` debugging is such a joke. You should try step-by-step." I said, "I know step-by-step debugging better than you do, but I despise it compared to `printf` debugging." It's such a higher logical level, and you can always get more data because you can have them do lots of useful printouts for you. Step-by-step was just boring and mind-numbing a lot of times.

Libor: You should know the code well enough anyway to be able to know what's going and not need to step through [it]. At some point, you get to where you can look at code [and] you know what it's going to do. You don't need to step through it, and especially when you get into different concurrency techniques, step-by-step debugging, it's pretty—

Max: —It's not very fun.

Libor: In those [hardware] classes [in college], they give you a good understanding of all the different levels of a system, and it helps you to move from level to level in a complex system and have an idea of what's going on at different levels, but [it] helps you in that sort of traversal of—

Max: I think all three of us are lucky to have gone through a foundations education that was very practical. [Max, Libor, and I all went to University of Illinois at Urbana-Champaign (UIUC), as did Herb Schildt.]. A lot of other schools—I know a lot of people who went through Stanford [for whom] the fundamentals classes were the single most useless thing they've ever done because they say [to me], "What the hell do I need red/black trees for?" I agree. They're not that useful, unless you're designing a database. Red/black trees are more or less as efficient as B trees, except the B trees are used [in the real world] and red/black trees aren't, but you *do* [use] tree rebalancing algorithms in the real world. I still have that burnt into my memory, but I've never used it since school.

Libor: I've done it once.

Max: I've never done it, but I think we actually have the benefit of having school that wasn't all that hung up on [having us] memorize every single one of these. Hash tables are going to be really important. Just try to remember that. Hash tables, I think, are the single most important data structure there is. It's only O(1), so everything you can, try to fit it into a hash table, and if it doesn't work, you have to figure out something else that's not O(1) and [that] attaches itself to hash table cells.

Pretty much any high-level language is based on very large numbers of hash tables that make everything happen faster because that's the only way to make it happen fast. [But] I think it really depends a lot on schooling, though. It's not a lot to say, "Fundamentals are the thing that makes it work." It's more like, "Fundamentals *that are grounded in reality.*" Somebody who's written a compiler can teach you that compilers are basically just a bunch of hash tables plus some lexing.

Libor: There must be a breadth of fundamentals.

> **Observation**
>
> Though I can see Max's point of view, my personal preference is to use source-level debugging (what Max is calling "step-by-step" debugging). I think the choice of debugging method depends on what kind of programming you are doing. If you are doing systems or exploratory programming, source-level debugging may be more efficient. Perhaps for Web service or transaction-based programming `printf` debugging is better.
>
> Also, Libor's statement, "you should know the code well enough to know what's going on and not need to step through it," is classic rock star programmer. Unfortunately, most of the time the person working on the code does *not*, for one reason or another, know the code well enough to obviate the need for source-level debugging. The code in question could be someone else's code, it could have a dependency on other code for which the source code is unavailable, or many other reasons. Clearly, the choice of debugging method is very context dependent.

Max: Sure.

Ed: Right. Computer Science at UIUC definitely did focus on having a broad curriculum.

Libor: Yeah. The broad curriculum is one of the things that helps when you get into working with complex systems. [It helps you] be able to traverse them. That's a huge thing in the industry. I feel like I left school and within a year or two was able to look at the source code for fairly complicated systems and be able to navigate it fairly well.

Ed: What are some things you consider when deciding to use an existing framework versus writing your own? How do you assess the quality of a framework?

Max: Some of my friends are really into package libraries. There are all these blocks, and you can just combine them together and it's really great. Yeah, the libraries may be a little overweight, but who cares? I actually prefer building my own libraries from scratch so I can go all the way down to the hardware and find out which bits are being pushed where. Neither one is necessarily a great or a bad way, but if one of these guys who loves packaged libraries tells me—the people who work on Apple love the idea of libraries.

Ed: The `-framework` gcc compiler option on Mac OS X.

Max: They're swimming in frameworks. Right. I can't stand frameworks in Apple because they're always overweight. [They say], "Oh yeah, it'll also send and receive e-mail for you." Every framework they have will send and receive e-mail.

Observation

Kohsuke Kawaguchi said something similar on page 183.

Libor: I only like frameworks where I've written an analogous framework at some point. Then you actually have a good sense of, "Okay, the framework I'm looking at is somewhat sane because I've done something similar."

Max: Yeah, but usually when you've done that, you think, "Well, clearly this framework is actually crappy because the one I was building was one-tenth the size and did pretty much everything I needed it to."

Libor: Yep.

Max: Most of the time, when you build your own framework, you don't have time to do it, so you say, "Well, this was done by ten people in some corporate environment or, worse yet, in an open-source mailing list, and they've built in all the kitchen sinks they could and it's"—

Libor: You don't need them.

Max: Yeah, most of the time.

Max: The best thing about Python is it's really geared towards not giving you more than one way to do any specific task. So if you've got—

Libor: It's the anti-Perl.

Max: Yeah, it's the anti-Perl.

Ed: There's only one way to do it.

Max: Yeah, exactly. Python is all about "one way to do it," and if you can't find it, "That's okay. We'll help you." If you try to find another way, you're wasting your time.

Ed: I met Larry Wall (the creator of Perl) a long time ago when he gave a talk at Silicon Graphics. I had him sign my camel book [the authoritative book on Perl had a camel on the cover] (*Programming Perl*, O'Reilly, 1991). He wrote his name and underneath he wrote, "There's more than one way to do it!" If I was to get Guido van Rossom [creator of Python] to sign a Python book, he'd write, "There's only one way to do it."

Max: Actually, I've seen Larry Wall and Guido have a verbal fight. That was really fun.

Ed: I bet.

Max: That was really, really fun, actually. They respect each other, but they're just so different in every way. Larry's this bouncy, random, angry, almost psychotic guy and Guido's measured, really cerebral. He'll say, "Yeah, I know. I understand your argument, but I think it's completely wrong." He just rolls it off, and Larry says, "But no, see, there's more than one way to do it."

Ed: So would you say that you can see those personalities reflected in the language design?

Max: Certainly. The only stuff that I read actually is the notes from the language creators. Whatever language I'm using, I will read up on what the guy who's really running the show thinks.

Libor: Well, reading source code or just talking to or reading anything from developers is a great way to actually figure out if these people not only know what they're talking about, but also: are they good? Looking at code or listening to people speak, you're looking for a consistency and clarity of thought. It doesn't even have to be the same as yours or the same as someone else's. There just has to be a self-contained consistency.

Max: But mostly the texture needs to be ringing: "This guy's probably smarter than me," [as an indicator of a] good product to use.

Libor: Yeah.

Max: "This guy's probably smarter than me. Okay, that's probably good." You have to gear for: "He's probably smarter than me and he's not insane," because a lot of people are smarter than me, [but] they're completely nuts.

> **Character Attribute**
>
> Libor is demonstrating some non-judgmental behavior that served him well. He gave the guy in the example the benefit of the doubt, assuming he knew what he was talking about. I think this is another manifestation of the usefulness of Andy Hunt's way of looking at the world from a place of abundance rather than scarcity (see page 265). This probably served Libor well as a means to grow in the organization.

Libor: The last place I worked at was primarily a hardware company. I had not done hardware before, and we had this guy, and every time I talked to him, I just got this barrage of terms that I did not understand. I thought, "Oh, man, I have got so much uphill to do." After six months, I realized that this guy had no idea what the hell he was talking about.

Max: It's easy to throw in terminology to confuse people.

Business

Ed: It seems to me that we're living in a time of platform explosion. In addition to the traditional C, C++, Java, .NET choices, now you have all these Web platforms: Facebook, Ning, PayPal, all these different Amazon Web services… where do you see this platform explosion going? Is it going to continue to just get more and more diffuse or will there be some consolidation?

> **Observation**
>
> At the time this interview was being conducted, unbeknownst to me, Max and Libor were already deep into talks with Google to have Slide offer applications on top of Google's OpenSocial meta-platform. The main idea behind OpenSocial is to address the problem of platform explosion by providing some level of standardization across social software such as Ning, MySpace, LinkedIn, Friendster, etc.

Max: Economic fundamentals drive all this stuff very clearly, and there will be short-term messiness, but long-term—fortunately, economics is not really a science, but it's definitely a well-understood phenomenon. Platforms are only useful if developers are there to make things to run those platforms. Platforms aren't really fun for their own sake. They're useful to someone who maintains the platform because they can stop developing everything themselves and shift the labor cost onto a third-party developer, who then has to be financially incented to do so. There are only so many people that will hack open-source stuff for the glory of being mentioned in Linus' annual letter or something like that. Most of the time, people are feeding their families, they're running companies. So they need some kind of incentive to do so. Long term, what's going to happen is: there's some amount of money that is the required modicum of how much you have to earn from a platform as a developer before you decide it's just not worth it.

For example, we [slide.com] could be building on the Facebook platform or we could be hacking on OS/2. [There are] still probably a bunch of people writing for OS/2, and those apps sell for some amount of money, but they're not very popular. It's actually primarily driven by not so much the number of platforms but by the number of platforms with a sufficient user base. Because most of the platforms these days exist in a browser, [the economic viability of the platform] can pretty much correlate nearly perfectly to two things: the size of the platform's audience and the people that the platform controls. You have high-growth platforms and phased growth [platforms]. You have a reasonably high-growth platform on Hi5 and Friendster. Xanga, on the other hand, lost 55 percent of its user base in the last year.

If a new platform comes out tomorrow morning, no one's going to give a shit because it's a small platform. That's one [part]. The other part is [that] platform owners intrinsically control the revenue model for developers. There are explicit and implicit choices they make or implicit and explicit messages they hint to developers. The explicit ones are, for example, if you sell ads.

Let's say you monetize ads; you get to keep 100 percent of the revenue. [On] Facebook, that's a very powerful message to developers. "Do whatever you like, make money. We just want the users to be happy. You can make some money," or, for example, the platform decides to announce, "You can't sell ads because it competes with our own advertising process, *but* you can monetize through e-commerce sales." It's a much harder bar for someone to scale, because if you're a good app developer it doesn't mean you're a good e-commerce developer. Moreover, most apps aren't e-commerce. So you'll immediately reduce the value of that platform.

At a certain point, the platform will cease to be meaningful, much like there are lots of users who use OS/2. OS/2 has a very powerful installed base, but no one builds any new apps for it, really, because it's just not an economic incentive for developers. So in that sense, OS/2 as a platform is dead. The other [part] that's really important [is] the implicit things that platforms do [to work] with the developers. For example, they either compete or they don't compete with [their] developers.

Microsoft as a monopoly had enjoyed effectively unlimited competition opportunities. So they could go and attack or perfect and destroy [competition], and no one thought, "Well, I'm going to stop developing for Microsoft because they might go after my business now." What everybody did say was, "Well, we'd better learn our lesson, dig in deeper, figure out more complex, engaging applications so there's less chance they can look at us and say, 'We're going to go invest $100 million to go take you out.'" Microsoft has never really put in a full-on effort against Adobe because Adobe is such a complex product. There's no chance that they'll really compete with them successfully in less than a ten-year course and that's just too long a horizon. On the other hand, they looked at Intuit and thought, "Well, I know this is probably a worthy attack." They attacked Intuit; they failed. [The product called Microsoft] Money was discontinued; Quicken won. But that was actually a pretty hard battle that lasted three years and hurt public [opinion] and stock prices.

Most platforms in the Web [are] fortunate [that Microsoft] can't do that at all, because there are just plenty of opportunities for the developers to say, "You know what? I can't really be here. I've got to go somewhere else. These guys are trying to beat me up in their own backyard." So the combination of explicit and implicit messaging side of the platform and revenue opportunities for the developer will shape the number of platforms.

One interesting side effect will happen. Assuming there's an equilibrium where there's some competition, lots of advertising or revenue opportunities, a sufficient user base, and five or six of these [platforms] standing in the end that will actually automatically generate a downward action, where every platform will say, "Well, we're going to keep 1 percent for ourselves and you guys [the developers] keep 99 percent." The only way the other platforms can get the best developers to shift away from that platform and onto their own is to say, "Well, 99 percent for you, 1 percent for them? Screw this. 100 percent for you, none for us. Just come to work for us. [That is, develop on our platform.]" So that's a very good reason for companies like Slide to exist, ultimately, because there's a natural economic incentive for platforms to start sharing more and more revenue [with developers].

Libor: The other thing is that it's gotten just so much simpler from a developer point of view to get distribution. You need far fewer people, far less capital investment to get big distribution. For example, Yahoo!, ten years ago, it didn't make sense for them to be a platform, because who's going to come to the party [and develop apps for Yahoo!]? Now, Facebook can open up and know that they're going to have thousands of one- and two-person teams—

Max: [Facebook touts] eighty thousand developers.

Libor: Yeah. I think that's one of the big unwritten stories of the last ten years is in writing software: what took a [whole] team [of developers] ten years ago now can be cranked out by a person or two. Rather remarkable.

Ed: To what do you attribute this big boost?

Libor: I think it's open source and also the new languages. Python, Ruby, to some extent, and some of the other ones. Obviously, there's the whole list of [factors], but just high-level languages and open-source software to run it on and, to some extent, cheap hardware.

> **Observation**
>
> This fits very well with Dave Thomas' experience. Cheap hardware and powerful languages enabled his team's innovation with Smalltalk. See page 291.

Cheap hardware has been around, I think. Not quite as cheap, but ten years ago, you would have gotten hardware to run stuff on.

Max: I think the fundamental root development of it all is cheap bandwidth. Bandwidth actually drives the whole thing where all these people could get their hands on information very inexpensively. When I was growing up in Ukraine, I was dying to learn assembly language. I couldn't get enough of assembly language. It seemed like, "Well, there is absolutely no way for me to learn it."

I would go to my crude bookstore every day and scour through the computer section, and I'd read every single computing book there was, and there were lots of computing books. I knew IBM System/370 structure, IBM System/360. Even though I had no access, never had it in my life, [never] touched one of those computers even since, but they were the only books I had. I actually went back there [recently]. I was back in Kiev a year ago, and I went back to the same store just to see how it changed, and it had the same poor selection of books. It was a primarily academic bookstore, so you get a lot of good books in Russian and English and all these sorts of interesting classics, but not so much on engineering. There are still books on IBM System/360. They had the "For Dummies" series, but they didn't really have any good assembly books.

I thought, "Well, this sucks," and it hasn't changed. I realized the reason they don't have it now is different from the last time. The last time, actually, there was just no way to get them. They wouldn't get translated, it was difficult to ship stuff, the Soviet block was against the United States. Now, none of that really exists.

You can get anything you want, but there's no need. It's online, instantly available in any language you like, and there's huge opportunity for you to go discuss with like-minded people any question you have. Back in the day, you posed a question—"How do you do this?"—in some [programming] language and check up in a week, and some newsgroup dude would answer and give you a big flame war. Nowadays, you say, "I'm sure somebody already answered this question," and sure enough, there it is. Most of the time, when you're asking a question and there's no answer on the Web today, it's not worth asking. Someone just already decided it was a bad idea. Cheap bandwidth makes the whole thing go

Personal and History

Ed: What technology was the most useful to you in generating career success, and how did you know that this particular technology was worth learning about and spending time to master?

Max: Hash tables.

Ed: Hash tables, all right. Fundamentals.

Libor: Yeah, I'd say fundamentals, algorithms, compilers. Compilers was a great one, just the same with operating system (OS) basics, but the compiler is even more so.

Ed: Would you say that your compiler course in college was useful?

Libor: Yeah. I'd say in terms of practical or pseudo-practical knowledge that I would then take with me and hope to become a better programmer. That was probably number one. What about you, Max?

Max: I didn't take the compilers class. I read the compilers book, but I didn't take the class.

Ed: What about any other classes that you found were really great, useful in life?

Max: It's all a big blur [facetiously]. No. I really enjoyed most of the fundamentals classes. For some reason, I actually really enjoyed the hardware lineup. So I went 231, 232 (Computer Architecture I and II), 331 (Embedded Systems), 333 (Computer System Organization). I took every single hardware class available, and they were all pretty useful.

Libor: I remember those. The 333 especially was—

Max: Yeah. 333 was basically as close as you could get to compilers without essentially figuring out efficient use of pipeline processors and all the crazy tricks like shooting instructions below the jump because you wanted to make sure that the pipeline had the available slots, just a lot of really good "get down to a cycle level," but [with a] logical [approach]. In 331, we actually built a fake processor in Mentor [Graphics].

Max: Plus, it was [a notoriously demanding professor] Andrew Chien, so everything had to be A+ or you were fired.

Ed: Much of the work of enterprise and large-scale software development involves being able to zoom into a very fine level of detail and then quickly zoom out and get the big picture. Does this require a special proficiency at keeping things in perspective? If so, does that carry over into your life in general?

Max: The skill that makes me a good developer, and good at what I do, is easily the worst thing that happens to me in my personal life. I'm very good at chopping off anything that matters even slightly less than 100 percent. If there is a crisis in the company, I can easily identify what it is and I am very capable of putting 110 percent of my capacity to solve that crisis *right now*. That has happened many times, and most of the time, I appear to emerge victoriously. However, the world doesn't work like that at all. In a company, you can say, "Well, the most important thing right now is, the server doesn't scale. I'm going to drop everything [stop being CEO], log on that server, and help [the engineer working on it] if he needs my help, or look over his shoulder and bother him." What are the influences that I think I can build the most on to get things done? If you have a girlfriend or a wife, it's not like there is one thing that you need to do for them and then you're done and you can move on to the next problem. It's usually four or five things you need to be planning at any one time, and it's actually—well, it helps to be slightly defocused. You want awareness of the world around you while you're running software or you're running a company, [but] you actually want blinders on [when] focused on the one thing that you're solving right this second. So it does carry over to a personal life, but I don't think it's doing anything. It's actually the exact opposite.

Libor: Yeah. I think it's a negative on human interaction and personal interactions with other people, but it is important in writing software.

Max: Yeah. Laser-sharp focus, I think, is the single best quality you can have.

Libor: Being able to abstract, being able to focus, and anything that's distracting you is taking away brain capacity from the task.

Max: Exactly. I usually listen to music, but if I have to think really hard, I turn off the music because I think it just takes away the extra bits available in your brain.

PART 4

Actual Rock Star

CHAPTER 14

Weird Al Yankovic

Fact Sheet

Name: Al Yankovic

Home Page: www.weirdal.com

Rock Star Programmer Credentials: The programmer's rock star

Date of Birth: October 1959

City of Birth: Lynwood, California, U.S.A.

Birth Order: Only child

Marital Status: Married

Number of Kids: One

Degree: Bachelor of Science in Architecture, California Polytechnic Institute, 1980

Number of generations in ancestry (including yourself) that graduated from college: One

Years as an IT Professional: Zero

Role: Satirist, band leader, parodist, accordionist

Introduction

By Ed Burns

In October 2006, I had the pleasure of giving a presentation at the Ajax Experience Conference in Boston, Massachusetts. The second day of the conference, I think, midway through the day, I was reading some e-mail on my laptop out in the hall between sessions. Howard Lewis Ship, a rock star programmer in his own right due to his creation and promotion of the Tapestry Web framework, approached me and said, "You gotta see this." Weird Al's video for "White and Nerdy" had just hit YouTube. Along with many other hilarious images well known to members of the programmer culture, the video included a snapshot of David Flanagan's book *JavaScript: The Definitive Guide* (O'Reilly and Associates, 2006). The corresponding lyric is, "I'm fluent in JavaScript as well as Klingon." Since JavaScript is the J in Ajax, it didn't take long for the video to spread all across the venue, and it could be seen on laptops everywhere for the rest of the conference. I had been a Weird Al fan since "Buy Me a Condo" in 1984, and I felt all along that Al spoke to my inner geek as an aspiring rock star programmer. When I saw the viral spread of "White and Nerdy" at the Ajax Experience, I knew that Al was the programmer's rock star and I had to have him in this book.

I contacted my friend Joe McCabe, whose book of interviews titled *Hanging Out with the Dream King: Interviews with Neil Gaiman and His Collaborators* (Fantagraphics, 2005) gave me the idea to write this book. Joe's current gig as associate editor of horror portal www.fearnet.com is all about entertainment industry interviews, so I contacted him and asked him to try to interview Weird Al Yankovic for me. While this interview is sadly shorter than the others in this book, I'm sure you'll find it enjoyable.

Soft Skills

Interview by Joseph R. McCabe

Joe: So many of the artists you've parodied have fallen out of the public eye, while you've stayed in it. What accounts for this longevity you've enjoyed?

Observation

The observation on page 55 lists a similar thing. The importance of keeping yourself associated with a core group of talented people whose skills you esteem.

Al: I can't give you a good answer for that. I guess I'm just very lucky, for one thing. I've managed to surround myself with a lot of very talented people. My band has stayed with me from the very beginning; they're all incredible musicians. I've got a core group of people I've surrounded myself with. I think we make a pretty good team. And a lot of my fans have stuck with me over the years as well. I tend to pick up new fans every time I put out an album. But I've still got a lot of the same fans that I got with my first few albums back in the '80s. My concert tours are bigger every year. For whatever reason, people continue to like what I do. As for why the other acts have not managed to sustain that, I can't tell you.

Joe: Do you consider Frank Zappa to be an influence?

Al: Oh absolutely. Yeah, he's a huge hero of mine.

Joe: Would you consider him your biggest influence among songwriters?

Al: I don't know if I'd say anybody's the single most influential songwriter. But, by all means, he's in my top ten—I'd probably say in the same breath as Spike Jones and Allan Sherman and Tom Lehrer and Stan Freiberg and Shel Silverstein, people like that. But, yeah, Frank was always a huge influence and an inspiration to me.

Joe: For the most part, you've stayed away from controversial material in your work. Has that been a deliberate choice? To what extent do you feel the non-controversial nature of your work has helped your success?

Al: Well, what would you consider controversial? I tend to stay away from politics for a number of reasons—one of which is that most of the subject matter is very topical, and it would not have much of a shelf life. And also, if I were to take sides, as it were, I would probably be putting off half of my audience. I don't say that I stay away from controversial material, but there are a lot of things that I probably wouldn't use, just because I don't think it would be appropriate for my fan base or [would] work with the context of my material.

> **Character Attribute**
>
> Puts the customer first.

Joe: Is there a particular case where you had an urge to take on a political topic but didn't feel it would work right?

Al: I can't say of any off the top of my head. I certainly don't have a vault of songs that were too hot for TV or something like that. It's just in general something that I've stayed away from.

Hard Skills

Joe: How do you choose which songs to adapt? Does the choice of song influence the theme and the lyrics, or vice versa?

Al: It can work either way. Basically, it all boils down to me finding a popular song that I can come up with enough funny ideas for. I keep a master list of songs that are candidates for parodies based on airplay, video play, chart action, things like that. I go down the list and I try to see if my

Character Attribute

Patience and organization.

brain can warp a few of them into something that I think would be amusing. Sometimes, a song seems like it's a good candidate for parody that I can't think of a good enough idea for. Sometimes I think of a good enough idea for a song, but it's not even that popular. And then I just have to wait until all the right parameters are in place before I think it's a decent enough idea to pursue.

Joe: Once you do pursue it, is there a time of day that you set aside to write? Or when an idea strikes you at a random time, do you just run with it then and there?

Al: Yeah, I don't keep any office hours or a certain time of the day that I write my material. But I tend to think of my best ideas and I'm most productive in the middle of the night, after everybody else is asleep and the phone's not ringing and there's nothing good on TV. So between midnight and six in the morning, usually.

Joe: Do you see your albums as having any kinds of themes, and if so, what would you consider the latest?

Al: The newest one is pretty much all about global warming. No, I don't know. There's nothing really. It's pretty random. In fact, I try to make each song as different from the other songs on the album as possible. I like the whole train-wreck segue concept...having a gangster rap song followed by a polka song, followed by a reggae song...I just try to take people's heads off with the incongruity.

Joe: How many revisions do you tend to go through when recording?

Al: Fourteen [laughs]. I don't know. I'm a bit of a perfectionist, so I might go over lyrics for weeks before I go into the studio. Then I'll think about whether to put a comma in a line or a semicolon, and that'll take up an afternoon. I don't know. It takes me a while. In fact, in the old days, I'd just dash off the first lyrics that came to my mind, and I thought that was good enough, because I was just [trying] to get airplay on the Doctor Demento radio show. But now that I have a fan base that actually cares what I'm trying to do, I tend to put a lot more time and effort into things.

Joe: A lot of your work is targeted at a specific pop subculture. Do you have a specific process for assimilating the spirit of a subculture or community (such as USENET culture with your song "All About the Pentiums") to make yourself sound like an insider and then integrating that spirit into a song?

Al: I suppose, although I am pretty computer literate. I am a bit of a nerd, and it's not like I'm taking on that character quite so much, especially for a song like that and "White and Nerdy"— that *is* my subculture. Certainly there are some songs where I'm taking on a character and speaking with another person's voice. But it's not like I had to read up on computers and USENET and figure out what the kids were doing, because I was right there with them.

Joe: Were you surprised by the success of "White and Nerdy"? It really took the Net by storm.

Al: Yeah, I was. I liked it. I thought it was clever and I thought it was fun. And I was very happy with the video. But I never expected it to be my biggest hit ever, which ostensibly it was. It's my first top-ten hit. It sold more copies than "Eat It", so, to date, I guess it's my biggest hit. And who knew? I had no idea. I was hoping for the best, and I was very pleasantly surprised when it took off the way that it did.

Joe: I noticed that you used both a reference to the "Star Wars Kid" and the cover of David Flanagan's book *JavaScript: The Definitive Guide* in your "White and Nerdy" video. How did you know about these two?

Al: Well, the "Star Wars Kid" is a viral video that I think pretty much anybody who's been online in the last two years has seen. And the JavaScript? I have to admit I hadn't read the book, but I was looking for a logo for JavaScript, and as I was going through the Internet, that particular logo for the book seemed like it was the most closely associated with JavaScript. So I decided to go with that one.

Joe: Ed spoke with David Flanagan about it, and he was very honored.

Business

Joe: Do the critical accolades influence you at all? Your latest album is among Amazon.com's "Best Music of 2006."

Al: Well, I love accolades. I like it when anybody says nice things about me. What the critics say about me means as much to me as what anybody else says. I try not to believe the hype, but I also try not to get too upset when I hear somebody denigrating my work. But, I can't help but feel good when somebody says nice things [laughs].

Character Attribute

Pride tempered by humility.

Joe: Your film *UHF* touches upon the halcyon days when local broadcasters produced lots of their own content. With the rise of YouTube, the local broadcaster is again able to reach large audiences. Where do you see the future of participatory media going?

Al: It's hard to say. Certainly we're in the middle of a major paradigm shift at the moment. The record industry and the movie industry, they're all trying to catch up and adapt to this new medium. I'm not sure where it's all gonna wind up. Right now, it's an exciting time because it does level the playing field. If you have a song or a video or a short film, you don't have to get the blessing of an executive or a suit. You don't have to go through any channels or red tape or jump through hoops. All you have to do is upload your stuff to the Internet, and, if it's good, people will see it.

Joe: Will the Internet finally bring us to the point when artists like you can produce content and market it directly to consumers without a middleman?

Al: Well, there's certainly the potential for that. I don't know what the future will bring, but certainly I've heard from other artists [who] are wondering why they need their record label at this point. Certainly, I like my record label [laughs]. I want to stay with them. But if you're an established artist… It's just a very difficult question to answer, because it's hard to say what the future's gonna bring. But it opens up a lot of opportunities for people [who], in the past, didn't have access to that kind of exposure.

Personal

Joe: In your song "This Is the Life," the main character claims such excesses as eating filet mignon seven times a day and buying a dozen cars when he's in the mood. Now that you have reached a level of success on par with that character, do you feel compelled to similar excesses?

Al: No, no. I don't really eat filet mignon seven times a day because I'm a vegetarian. So it wouldn't work with my lifestyle, really. And I only drive one car at a time, so that seems a little excessive to me, too. I live in a nice house, but I'm not ostentatious. I've always been very conservative. I just don't like to be in debt, so I try to live well within my means.

> **Character Attribute**
>
> Awareness of the fleeting nature of fame and success.

Joe: With your live shows, do you like to satirize the rock-and-roll tour experience, as your recorded songs satirize other songs?

Al: Maybe in subtle ways, I don't know [laughs]. When I'm talking in my rock concert voice, sometimes it's hard to know if I'm sort of mocking that whole mannerism or whether I'm being sincere. And when, at the end of show, when I tell the city that I love them, it is a little bit tongue-in-cheek, because that's what everybody does, but…I really *do* love them [laughs]. So it is sincere as well.

Joe: Equally? Do you have a favorite city?

Al: Oh, I can't really pick and choose. Any city that comes out to see me, I'm thankful for it [laughs].

Joe: Do you see a point where you'll tire of touring? Do have the same enthusiasm for it you always did?

Al: Well, I still enjoy performing live as much as I ever did, but the whole touring thing isn't as alluring as it used to be because I've got a family now. I've got a wife and I've got a four-year-old daughter at home. So I want to come home as often as I can, but that's difficult when you're doing five or six cities a week. So we're trying to work out a balance that seems like a good compromise to everybody. But that's the only thing. I love performing as much as I ever did. It's just hard to be away from home at this point.

Joe: I guess that's why so many acts take up residence in Las Vegas: performing without touring. What continues to motivate you professionally, either on a long tour such as the one you're on now or in creating an album?

Al: Well, on the tour, I'm working off the energy of the fans pretty much, even though it's [basically] the same show every night. It's a different audience, or at least most of them are different. Sometimes [laughs] we'll have tour-chasers that follow me from city to city, and the front row will be the same for several nights in a row. Any time the audience is into a show and excited and laughing and having a great time, I have a great time, too, and so does the band. So we definitely feed off of that.

As far as the albums, music and comedy are my biggest passions, and I just am thrilled that I get to make a living doing that. I'm definitely a bit of a perfectionist, so I can spend as much time in the studio as I like. I just go over there and try to have a good time.

Joe: Thank you very much, Al.

Al: Oh, my pleasure! Thank you, Joe.

Index of Common Questions Asked of Interviewees

I intentionally avoided including an "analysis of my findings" chapter in this book for several reasons. Most importantly, I did not want to give the impression that this book included any kind of rigorous psychological, sociological, or scientific study of the responses of the interviewees. Of secondary importance is my personal belief that readers of this book should follow Hani Suleiman's advice on page 129 of Chapter 6: to "be skeptical" about what you read and how you take it in. To that end, I present an index that allows the reader to quickly discover the thoughts and opinions of the rock star programmers in this book on any topic that happened to come up in the interviews with two or more different rock stars. Note that some of the rock stars have more entries in this table than others. This is because I favored spontaneity over sticking to the scripted questions, and some interviews just went their own way, while others allowed me to stick more to the scripted questions. Finally, this is not intended to be an exhaustive index (there is a real index for that). This index is intended to give you an easy way to look across the software development industry, as represented by this collection of rock star programmers, and see how some common important questions were answered.

		Software Technology Experts								Software Pedagogy Experts		Software Development Experts		
	Topic	Rod Johnson	Adrian Colyer	The Java Posse	Chris Wilson	Nikhil Kothari	Hani Suleiman	James Gosling	Kohsuke Kawaguchi	Herb Schildt	Floyd Marinescu	Andrew Hunt	Dave Thomas	Max Levchin and Libor Michalek
Awareness	Being aware of your own ignorance	8		64	93	117	130–132	165	177		235	249	277	
	Spending time in a meta-cognitive mode	8	36	77	94	118		165	177			250		
	Attributes of successful developers	14		61	92, 93			167	178		233, 235	250	293	
	Questioning the value of something that is generally accepted practice	7				117			183		236, 237			
	Becoming aware of problems you don't know you have	7									236	263		
Innovation	Getting a new idea adopted							164	180				283	
	Reinventing the wheel?	9, 10	34				154	170	183		233, 238	263, 264		304
Business	Importance of business acumen and entrepreneurial instincts	20	48	64	103				191					
	Fostering innovation	23						171						
	Project culture vs. product culture	12											289	
	Categorize the software industry	20	32	61			147	171						
	Business and stewarding your skillset		33	62	103		148, 151		192			266		
	Outsourcing		50		103		152		191		239	266		
	Working at a startup			80, 81, 87		124			193					

Topic	Software Technology Experts								Software Pedagogy Experts		Software Development Experts		
	Fod Johnson	Adrian Colyer	The Java Posse	Chris Wilson	Nikhil Kothari	Hani Suleiman	James Gosling	Kohsuke Kawaguchi	Herb Schildt	Floyd Marinescu	Andrew Hunt	Dave Thomas	Max Levchin and Libor Michalek
Attributes of the language and environment developers will be using in ten years	19	35		97				190			254	281	
Hard problems in software today							169		206	228	256		
Most useful technology for advancing your career								176					309
Ideal programming language and environment							164					278	
Platforms					122, 123								306, 307
Collaboration			60	93, 95			167	181			251, 268, 269		
Avoiding introducing bugs		45		100		144					257		
Dealing with hard-to-diagnose and hard-to-fix bugs	16	43	77	100		129, 139, 141		187			258		
Doing the "right thing"	4	47	88	95		138, 142	169				261		
Preparing a new computer		42	69			145					261		
Organization				108			173				267		
Relinquishing ownership of your code			73					182					

Technology and Hard Skills

		Software Technology Experts								Software Pedagogy Experts		Software Development Experts		
Category	Topic	Rod Johnson	Adrian Colyer	The Java Posse	Chris Wilson	Nikhil Kothari	Hani Suleiman	James Gosling	Kohsuke Kawaguchi	Herb Schildt	Floyd Marinescu	Andrew Hunt	Dave Thomas	Max Levchin and Libor Michalek
History	Your first computer				109				194	208				
History	Academic success	25		67								270		
History	Luck	13	39					166	179				290	
History	Great texts on computing	18	37, 39, 40, 45		109			174			241		282	300
History	Useful courses				109			173			241	252, 270		310
History	A substitute for experience: how to make up for not being involved in software development since the early 1980s							166	195	207		251, 253		302
Career Maintenance	Motivation to succeed	26		83	107		139		180				277	
Career Maintenance	When is it time to change jobs?	21		71	93						239			
Career Maintenance	A non-IT plan for making a living	22, 23	49	82	104	126	151		192		240	272		
Career Maintenance	Retirement								197		241			
Career Maintenance	Job choices and technology trends			63					192	205				
Career Maintenance	Seizing opportunities					115			176		222, 223	246	287	
Career Maintenance	Turning points				96			172		203	222, 223, 224		285	
Work/Life Balance	Work/personal balance	27	51, 52	85		120, 126	155		180, 195		242	271, 272	294	
Work/Life Balance	Professional and personal success	26	52				158		196		242			
Work/Life Balance	Getting your kids into IT	26	52	90	109									

Phillip G. Armour's
The Five Orders of Ignorance

Summarized by Ed Burns with permission of Phillip G. Armour, from his book *The Laws of Software Process* (Auerbach, 2003).

I've been a long-time member of the Association for Computing Machinery (ACM), ever since my formative days in the student chapter at the University of Illinois at Urbana-Champaign (where I met rock stars Chris Wilson, Max Levchin, and Libor Michalek). The flagship magazine of the ACM is called *Communications of the ACM*, and I've also been a long-time subscriber. In the October 2000 issue, I came across a column that has profoundly influenced how I think about knowledge acquisition in general and software development in particular. The column was Phillip G. Armour's "Business of Software," and the title was "The Five Orders of Ignorance." I immediately made copies of the article and shared them with everyone in my work group at the time. I think the main reason the article resonated with me so well was the simplicity of the ideas it presented and the conclusion I drew from them: Questions are more important than answers.

Character Attribute

Sharing useful knowledge with work group as quickly as possible after acquiring it.

In spite of what Søren Kierkegaard, James Gosling, and "Wayne's World" say about classification schemes (see page 171 of Chapter 7), I find them very useful in dealing with the world. The Orders of Ignorance is one such scheme that breaks down knowledge into five different levels.

0th Order Ignorance: Lack of Ignorance

"I have 0OI when I *provably* know something."

Having 0OI means having the question and the answer. For example, Question: "What programming environment is well suited to building maintainable enterprise software?" Answer: "Java." There are many other answers to this particular question, of course, but the point is you have the question and the answer. In this case, you can demonstrate your lack of ignorance by writing some maintainable enterprise software in Java. When you get to 0OI, it's only a matter of time and execution before you have a working solution.

1st Order Ignorance: Lack of Knowledge

"I have 1OI when I don't know something."

Having 1OI means having a *well-formed* question that includes enough context about the question domain to constrain the answer. For example, "What can I use to quickly build a Web user interface to my database that supports create, read, update, and delete operations?" In this case, one answer would be Ruby on Rails. With 1OI, the question itself contains a wealth of concrete knowledge. A counter-example that does *not* illustrate 1OI is: "What are the requirements of the system?" This question is too vague to be called 1OI, and is really an indicator of 2OI.

2nd Order Ignorance: Lack of Awareness

"I have 2OI when I don't know that I don't know something."

Having 2OI means I don't even know what questions to ask, *but* (and this is important) I have some way of finding out what questions to ask. I'll give a personal example from my authoring process for this book. When transcribing the audio for an interview, I found I was wasting a lot of time switching between working the playback controls on the audio player and typing into the word processor. I thought, "Wouldn't it be nice if I could control the audio player with foot pedals as I typed?" Phillip Armour calls such "wouldn't it be nice if…" statements "meta-questions," and they are one indicator of 2OI. I quickly reduced this to 1OI by asking, "Is there a product out there that allows me to control audio playback with foot pedals?" And sure enough, there is a whole raft of such products on the market. I went out and bought one, reducing the problem to 0OI. In this case, the problem itself: "I need a way to do transcriptions more quickly" was my key to reducing the 2OI to 1OI. In many cases, having domain knowledge is an important key to reducing 2OI to 1OI.

3rd Order Ignorance: Lack of a Suitably Efficient Process

"I have 3OI when I don't have a *suitably efficient* way to find out that I don't know that I don't know something."

Having 3OI means I don't know what questions to ask and I don't even have a good way of knowing what questions to ask. The emphasis on "suitably efficient" is very important. In software development, a great way to discover 3OI in your system is to put it into production. Depending on your software development philosophy, this may or may not be a "suitably efficient" way to discover 3OI. If you come from the Internet school of the perpetual beta, it may be. If you prefer a less cowboy-like approach, it may not be.

For example, let's say I'm writing software to analyze Web logs in order to produce a report about people visiting my website. Such a problem falls under the domain of "Web analytics." Being faced with the problem of writing web log analysis software, but not knowing about the problem domain of "Web analytics," is an example of having 3OI. Another example: I need to write some software to process many terabytes of data. Not knowing about Google's MapReduce framework (http://labs.google.com/papers/mapreduce.html) would be an example of having 3OI.

4th Order Ignorance: Meta Ignorance

"I have 4OI when I don't know about the Five Orders of Ignorance."

In Mr. Armour's scheme, this one is a bit tongue-in-cheek: 4OI is ignorance of the Orders of Ignorance.

Phillip Armour expands on the underlying philosophy of the Five Orders of Ignorance in his book, *The Laws of Software Process* (Auerbach, 2003). I highly recommend that book to anyone who enjoys this one.

If you read through the interviews in the book you're holding now, you'll find that the most oft-cited key developer skill is knowing what questions to ask. In other words, have a large store of 2OI and have a great process for reducing 3OI to 2OI. This is why Max and Libor, on page 304 of Chapter 13, cited the importance of a broad curriculum in a university education. If you get exposed to lots of different things, you will be better able to come up with questions, which lead to answers. It is often said that there is no substitute for experience. I think having a great store of 2OI is the very definition of experience, and what the quote is really saying is the only way to get this great store of 2OI is by doing something for a long time.

Index